Democracy, Strategy, and Vietnam

Democracy, Strategy, and Vietnam

Implications for American Policymaking

Edited by

George K. Osborn
Asa A. Clark IV
Daniel J. Kaufman
Douglas E. Lute
U.S. Military Academy

Lexington Books
D.C. Heath and Company/Lexington, Massachusetts/Toronto

Library of Congress Cataloging-in-Publication Data

Democracy, strategy, and Vietnam.

   Papers from a conference sponsored by the Dept. of
Social Sciences, U.S. Military Academy, and held at
West Point in June 1985.
   Includes index.
   1.   United States—Foreign relations—1981–   —
Congresses.   2.   United States—National security—
Congresses.   3.   Vietnamese Conflict, 1961–1975—
United States—Congresses.   4.   Vietnamese Conflict,
1961–1975—Influence—Congresses.   5.   United States—
Foreign relations administration—Congresses.
I.   Osborn, George K.   II.   United States Military
Academy. Dept. of Social Sciences.
E876.D46   1987   327.73   87–3632
ISBN 0–669–16340–6 (alk. paper)
ISBN 0–669–16341–4 (pbk. : alk. paper)

Published simultaneously in Canada
Printed in the United States of America
Casebound International Standard Book Number: 0–669–16340–6
Paperbound International Standard Book Number: 0–669–16341–4
Library of Congress Catalog Card Number: 87–3632

The paper used in this publication meets the minimum requirements of
American National Standard for Information Sciences—Permanence of
Paper for Printed Library Materials, ANSI Z39.48–1984. ∞™

87 88 89 90 8 7 6 5 4 3 2 1

In commemoration of Robert E. Osgood, whose wise counsel inspired and guided so many

Contents

Foreword

T he duke of Wellington, we are told, once said of his own troops, "They may not frighten the enemy, but they surely frighten me." The same may be said of the U.S. experience of losing the Vietnam War. It is we Americans ourselves, and not our allies or adversaries, whose view of the role of the United States in the world was profoundly shaken. It was Richard Nixon, not Helmut Schmidt or Leonid Brezhnev or Fidel Castro, who expressed the conviction that failure to prevail in Vietnam would lead other peoples to feel that the United States—now a "pitiful, helpless giant"—would not meet its commitments.

Defeat in Vietnam did indeed mark the end of the era of what had seemed to be U.S. omnipotence, but to a large extent that omnipotence had been the creation of Americans' own imaginations. By the mid-1960s the special circumstances that had made possible the post-1945 predominance of the United States had substantially changed, and the world was much less tractable than U.S. diplomats and publicists and, most of all, ordinary citizens had become accustomed to thinking of it as being. Omnipotence had not given way to impotence, however. Despite failure to stay the course in Vietnam, the United States remained a superpower with widespread interests and the means to defend them. During the war and afterward, core allies such as West Germany and Israel came to doubt not the strength of U.S. commitment to their security and well-being but the wisdom of placing so much blood and treasure at the service of a cause—the maintenance of a non-Communist regime in South Vietnam—that seemed so far from a vital interest.

This book is about the long-term consequences of U.S. involvement in the war. It does not focus on the human toll: the nearly 60,000 Americans and the many hundreds of thousands of Vietnamese who lost their lives as a consequence of the escalation of violence brought on by U.S. intervention in the ongoing Vietnamese civil conflict. That toll this book takes as a given, the tragic backdrop against which the drama was played. Moreover, wounds heal and populations reknit. Even memories numb, especially when the pain of recollection is too great. Rather, this book is about policies, organizations, and institutions. How has U.S. national security policy changed as a result of the searing Vietnam experience? What lessons have been learned by the organizations that fought the war—the military services and the intelligence agencies—and how (if at all) does their present behavior, and present U.S. foreign policy, reflect the assimilation of those lessons? How have U.S. institutions, both governmental and societal, changed?

Policies, organizations, and institutions are intimately related. Have presidents, as it is often alleged, been less prone since 1975 to use force on behalf of what they have defined as vital national interests? Indeed, have they defined what is vital differently than their pre-Vietnam predecessors might have done? The tides of war left their high-water mark on the Congress in the form of the War Powers Act and a number of other measures that enlarge congressional powers of oversight and control and in important ways shift the balance between the legislative and executive branches. How has this history affected congressional behavior and congressional-executive relations now that the flood tides of congressional activism have receded? Did Vietnam dissolve the partnership between the two branches and bring about the end, as well, of bipartisan foreign policy? Readers will find answers to these questions in this book.

Underlying all these questions is the one that gives this book its focus: did Vietnam make a difference? The answer seems to depend on the sharpness of the analyst's focus. It is undeniable that policies, organizations, and institutions changed in significant ways under the impact of the war. Moreover, they changed in ways that were far more significant than mere short-run adjustments. Many such changes are duly noted in this book.

Yet the editors (and most of the authors of the individual chapters) answer this key question in the negative. Much has changed, they argue, but much more remains the same. Containment of the Soviet Union continues to be the core strategy of U.S. foreign policy. Presidents have not been notably more reluctant to employ military force; when they have chosen not to do so, it has not been because of any debilitating Vietnam syndrome but because the interests at stake have not been judged as vital. Congress has used its new (and rediscovered) powers with relative caution. Its assertiveness has led administrations to define their objectives and their methods more precisely. Except for a legislative proscription against covert action in Angola—now repealed—it has not in any fundamental sense posed a roadblock.

The roots of this book lay in a conference of scholars, journalists, political figures, and present and former government officials and military officers convened by the Department of Social Sciences of the U.S. Military Academy at West Point in June 1985. That the army should have sponsored such a retrospective analysis is scarcely surprising. Of all the uniformed services, its involvement in the Vietnam conflict was deepest and of longest duration. The first U.S. Military Assistance Advisory Group, led by an army lieutenant general, reached Saigon on the heels of the withdrawing French Expeditionary Force shortly after the creation of the South Vietnamese state in 1955. The army not only bore the brunt of the U.S. effort to train South Vietnamese forces, but hundreds of its majors, lieutenant colonels, and colonels served as advisers to the Vietnamese officers who were the governing authorities in the districts and provinces. From 1965 on, when the war increasingly became a U.S. effort, the bulk of the U.S. fighting men—and the bulk of those who lost their lives—wore army uniforms. As several of the chapters in this book make clear, for an organization that had defined its essential mission in terms of set-piece defensive battles against massed Soviet forces on the North German plain, the war it was called to fight in Indochina was a traumatic experience. If organizations can be said to feel pain, Vietnam was acutely painful for the U.S. Army. That pain was a primary impetus behind the pages that follow.

Another impetus was the predilection for far-ranging and careful analysis that characterizes West Point's Department of Social Sciences. Among military institutions of higher learning, not only in the United States but worldwide, the department has played a unique role. Since World War II, the courses its members teach have comprised a major part of a West Point education. Conversely, tours of duty teaching in the department have figured importantly in the careers of a large number of senior army officers. A common experience for civilians serving in the upper reaches of the U.S. defense and foreign policy establishment is to discover that army officers are, on average, much more knowledgeable and nuanced in their thinking about national and international problems than are their colleagues from the other uniformed services. More than any other factor, the Department of Social Sciences deserves credit for that sophistication.

A final point: this book is about the U.S. experience in Vietnam. The policies, organizations, and institutions examined here are all those of the United States. Readers will find little about the impact of the Vietnam War on other nations, even on the nations of Indochina themselves. The organizers of the West Point conference were well aware that their focus was limited. They felt that limitation to be unavoidable, given the magnitude of their primary task: the systematic exploration of the long-term impact of the war on the way the United States approaches the problem of national security.

After all, only in (and of) the United States can one hear talk of the Vietnam syndrome. We have often been told that the war's outcome severely damaged U.S. credibility in the rest of the world. Indeed, as an aspirant for the presidency, Ronald Reagan made that contention a central part of his indictment of his predecessors' policies. Yet in Reagan's hands and in others', the contention is nearly always general, not specific. Thus it would clearly be worthwhile for analysts to attempt to show exactly how U.S. embroilment and eventual defeat in Vietnam affected the policies and practices—short run and long term—of other members of the international system. The authors of the chapters that follow would for the most part agree that the long-term effects, at least, have not been great. For practical reasons those issues could not be explored at length in this book. They are, however, eminently a focus for another.

Richard H. Ullman

Preface

For two decades and more, the U.S. Military Academy has sponsored the annual West Point Senior Conference as an informal seminar to facilitate an open exchange of ideas on important issues in U.S. national security affairs. Those conferences have focused on such diverse topics as arms transfers, NATO, military education, U.S. trade policy, defense reform, the Pacific Basin, industrial planning, nuclear force posture, and defense technology. The twenty-third conference had a potboiler of a theme: "Vietnam: Did It Make a Difference?" The responses to that question form the genesis for this book.

The 1985 meeting was organized around three topics setting the parameters for discussion: "The Legacy of Vietnam: Change or Continuity in American Foreign Policy?" "Policymaking," and "The Use of Force." Many of the arguments made in the ensuing chapters of this book were first presented at that conference to an audience composed of prominent scholars, government officials, and representatives of the armed forces. The electricity generated has been captured in this book in an effort to provide interested citizens and serious students of U.S. national security affairs a balanced range of incisive thoughts on the long-term impact and implications of the Vietnam experience of the United States.

Although the academy's central mission is to educate, train, and inspire cadets for their future role as leaders in the U.S. Army, events such as the Senior Conference have long added depth and lustre to the quality of the West Point experience. Such events display an academic involvement with institutions and issues outside its own gates and at the same time demonstrate a little-known aspect of West Point's contributions to country. Blessed with an intellectually gifted and energetic faculty of soldier-scholars and enjoying both a direct linking to and an academic distance from the pressures of the Pentagon, it bears a special responsibility to contribute to and participate in the examination of issues significant to the army, the military, and U.S. national security. This book is yet one more product of that special responsibility.

Although the contents of this book in no way represent an official policy position of the U.S. Military Academy or any other agency of the U.S. government, it is my hope that the book itself will make a contribution to strengthening the security of the United States.

Lieutenant General Dave R. Palmer
Superintendent, U.S. Military Academy

Acknowledgments

Vietnam traumatized the United States. In particular, it traumatized the U.S. Army and its relationship with U.S. society. What are the long-term consequences of this trauma? What do these consequences suggest about the ability of U.S. policymaking to adapt to a complex and rapidly changing world? There are two reasons for pride that this anthology has been conceived by army officers at West Point. First, this book testifies to the military's commitment to understanding the Vietnam experience. Second, this research reflects the academic and professional focus of the U.S. Military Academy at West Point: "I must study politics and war, that my sons may have the liberty to study mathematics and philosophy, in order to give their children a right to study painting, poetry, and music," (John Adams).

We owe much to the members of the Department of Social Sciences and to its head, Colonel Lee Donne Olvey, for their support, encouragement, and assistance. Without the professional competence of our outstanding office staff, led so ably by Barbara Thomas, this project would have taken far longer and would have been much less enjoyable. In particular, we thank Justine Monken for her patience, dedication, and skill in typing the manuscript. Finally, we thank Jaime Welch-Donahue and the rest of the fine staff at Lexington Books for all their help.

All royalties from this book will be deposited in a fund for faculty research and development at West Point. This special arrangement was made possible only by the generous willingness of the contributors to donate their time and considerable talents.

Finally, the editors dedicate this book to our wives and children for their patience; and to the soldiers, sailors, airmen, and the nation they serve for whom understanding of America's Vietnam experience is so critical.

Part I
Vietnam in the Context of U.S. Security Policy Since World War II

Prologue:
Assessing the Impact of Vietnam:
Dangerous and Necessary

George K. Osborn

> What's past is prologue.
> —William Shakespeare, *The Tempest*

The origins of this book lie in the attempt to look into the future and the past. If one believes there are no final solutions in international politics and that the international system fundamentally remains an anarchic, self-help system, then one tends to see the future as replete with conflict, both intranational and international. In such a world, the United States as a power with global interests, some real and some imagined, will be faced with shaping strategy and security policy to enable it to intervene when and where those politically responsible for U.S. policy decide it is necessary to do so.

The United States will use military force again to intervene in foreign conflicts. As a recent and major instance of U.S. military intervention, Vietnam stands as a case rich in evidence about the use of force and the conduct of U.S. policy. Despite the failure of the United States to achieve its national objectives through intervention in Southeast Asia, there is value in assessing the long-term consequences of Vietnam for U.S. national security policy, foreign policy, and U.S. politics and for the organizations and institutions that must act and interact in the shaping and implementation of policy.

The value of assessing the experiences of the United States in Vietnam between 1945 and 1975 suggests two questions: (1) was intervention in Vietnam a great event in the U.S. historical experience, comparable to the Civil War, World Wars I and II, and the Great Depression? and (2) what is the lasting impact of such events on internal processes and institutions? Put another way, if the past is prologue to the future, did Vietnam make a difference for the United States?

In chapter 1, Ernest May argues that although it may be too soon to judge, the judgment may be important. This contention especially is so if one posits the proposition that either the French intervention in Mexico in the

4 • *Vietnam in the Context of U.S. Security Policy*

1860s or the Crimean War of 1853–1856 could be analogs or even metaphors for U.S. intervention in Vietnam. Professor May would have us wait another decade to let the dust (or mud) settle, let the data accumulate, let the analysis be postponed before making a final judgment. His is an appealing argument, particularly if one contemplates the potential dangers of mistaken judgment that might become the basis for consensus. As George Kennan put it, "Only the diplomatic historian, working from the leisure and detachment of a later day, will be able to unravel this incredible tangle and to reveal the true aspect of the various factors and issues involved."[1]

The press of events and the imperatives of statesmanship, however, deny the luxury of patient, meticulous assessments; the Grenadas, El Salvadors, Angolas, South Africas, Lebanons, Libyas, and others cannot be placed on hold. Occasionally, it is true, some conflicts can be frozen—for example, the cease-fire line in Kashmir, where an internationally supervised status quo has obtained, for the most part, for many years. Interesting as such cases may be for practitioners and students of international politics, they are the exception. Further, the dynamics of domestic politics may force policymakers to make national security decisions and bring into play all of the actors in the policy implementation process, as well as their critics and overseers. Critical allocations of resources also have to be made well in advance, and rarely can they be delayed until the cool and enlightened judgments might be better made by historians and others.

Statesmen and strategists always live in the future conditional tense; their judgments must be made on the basis of the past and present, and their information on which to base judgment is incomplete. The central problem is to attempt to reduce uncertainty to the maximum extent feasible and make a decision in full awareness that to delay is a decision and has an impact on one's own state, one's allies, and one's opponents. With respect to Vietnam, U.S. policymakers and those who advise them must make judgments about the impact of the involvement of the United States in that set of events leading to and ending in the ignominious departure from Saigon in April 1975.

It is only prudent to accept Professor May's conclusion that it is too soon to assess fully the impact of Vietnam on U.S. policy. The same might be said of the effects of the Spanish-American War, if one views current issues involving the United States and Cuba, the Philippines, and Puerto Rico. At the same time, policymakers must make decisions. Dedicated to the goal of promoting wise decisions, this book presents the conclusions of interim assessments of experts for the benefit of current and future U.S. policymakers. At the very least, such a process should raise major questions and advance tentative, if conditional, answers. Further, it should suggest the location and magnitude of the lacunae needing further study. Finally, it may provide policymakers with alternatives to "gut feeling" or "seat of the pants" bases for assessments.

The organization of this interim assessment is straightforward. First, we consider the U.S. intervention in Vietnam in the broad context of U.S. security policy since World War II. The intent is to set the stage for detailed analysis of the impact of the Vietnam War on U.S. security policy. Second, we examine the effect of Vietnam on policymaking by focusing on a number of key institutional actors. The focus here is to determine if the interrelationships among these actors changed as a result of Vietnam. In part III, we consider the impact of Vietnam on U.S. attitudes about the use of force as an instrument of national policy. How, if at all, have U.S. perceptions of the role of force changed since the United States failed to attain its policy objectives in Vietnam? In part IV, we examine the consequences of Vietnam for U.S. foreign policy. What are the broad, long-term implications of the Vietnam experience? Will the experience influence future foreign policy? Will there be a Vietnam syndrome similar to the Munich syndrome that so influenced U.S. policymakers after World War II? Finally, in the Conclusion, we provide our response to the question, Did Vietnam make a difference? It is important to note at the outset that the contributing authors do not always agree in their assessments of the influence of the Vietnam War on U.S. security policymaking. Attempts to ascertain the effects of the war may be as contentious as U.S. involvement in the war.

Although no definitive answers are forthcoming, we hope that this assessment of the influences of the Vietnam War on U.S. national security policy and policymaking will contribute to the necessary (if dangerous) self-examination that so costly and contentious an episode requires. Shibboleths of the "no more Vietnams" or "we were not allowed to win" variety contribute little to the process of determining how the United States should define its interests in the world and what means it may have to employ to protect those interests. It is toward a reasoned appraisal of the lasting consequences of the U.S. involvement in Vietnam that this book is aimed. All those who gave so much deserve no less.

Note

1. George F. Kennan, *Memoirs, 1925–1950* (Boston: Little, Brown, 1967), p. 500.

1
Great Events and U.S. Politics

Ernest R. May

The topic of this book presents four closely connected questions:

1. What is a great event? What distinguishes one event from another making it great?
2. What are the common patterns or characteristics of great events?
3. If one has a working definition of a great event, does the Vietnam War fit that definition?
4. What are the chances that, if there are patterns common to great events, they are still playing out in consequence of the Vietnam War?

To define a great event is difficult. *Great* is, in many circumstances, a subjective term. Its use brings to mind an apocryphal but utterly true story told of Lyndon Johnson in the mid-1960s. Allegedly he was visited by a delegation of schoolchildren, one of whom asked him, "Mr. President, is it true that you were born in a log cabin?" Placing his huge hand on the child's head, he said, "No, son, that was another great president. That was Abraham Lincoln. I was born in a manger." Judgments of great events depend on angle of vision. For a business historian, for example, one of the greatest of all events is the invention of the double-entry bookkeeping.

Since the focus here is on wars and rumors of wars, one can start the process of definition by thinking about the events in that category that everyone would designate great. The wars of the French Revolution and World Wars I and II are clearly great events for the Atlantic world. In U.S. history, the War for American Independence and the Civil War equally clearly qualify. One can move toward definition by agreeing that some events are not great. One nonstarter is the War of 1812. Not long ago I looked at some periodicals of 1825 to see if there had been anything like the current orgy of ten-years-after retrospection. I found nothing of the sort. There seemed little recollection that any event in the war had taken place other than Andrew Jackson's victory in the post-peace battle of New Orleans. The war as a whole appeared to be regarded as a losing enterprise best forgotten.

The Korean War is a borderline case. One can make an argument that the Korean War was a great event. Certainly some important developments in U.S. history and the history of the rest of the world are associated with that war. On the other hand, most people would not classify the war itself as a great event. In an undergraduate-graduate course on the international relations of the United States during World War II and the cold war, I sometimes give a map quiz as part of the final examination. One of the entries to be identified this year was "scene of war, 1950–1953." It happened that a fair number of students in the course were Europeans, and they all marked Indochina, not Korea. So did some Americans.

If these examples help to define what is and what is not a great event, one can go to the closely related question: What are the key characteristics of a great event? What are the common elements present in the first set and absent in the second? One characteristic of a great event is that many people think, then and later, that the event makes a difference. Things are not the same after. In significant respects, the world is changed by the event.

The best example, perhaps the ideal typical case of the great event, is the rise of Islam in the seventh century:

> In the whole history of the world there has been nothing comparable, in the universal and immediate nature of its consequences, with the expansion of Islam in the 7th century.
>
> The overwhelming rapidity of its propagation was no less surprising than the immensity of its conquests. It took only seventy years from the death of Mohammed (632) to spread from the Indian Ocean to the Atlantic. Nothing could stand before it.
>
> . . . Henceforth, all these regions were subject in religion and political obedience, to the most powerful potentate who had ever existed, the Caliph of Baghdad.[1]

Modern wars have brought about political changes. They changed the landscape. They changed the world physically so that the map was different— the real map, not just the boundaries drawn by cartographers. They also changed the maps in people's heads: sets of beliefs. World War I changed the ways in which people thought about nations, political systems, and the meaning of war itself. World War II changed not only the physical map but the ways in which people thought about power and about the distribution of power around the world. It liberated hundreds of nationalisms. In other cases, one does not see that kind of change. An event not great is one that leaves the landscape, both physical and mental, more or less similar to what existed before.

Clearly the question central to this book is whether, or to what extent, the Vietnam War produced significant changes. Was it a great event in that sense? One can make an argument that it is. One also can make an argument that it is not. I shall do no more than sketch the two answers because several chapters elaborate each side of the case.

On the one hand, it can be contended that in the world, including the United States, and in the minds of humans everywhere, things are very much what they were before the Vietnam War. The map has not changed much except in a small area of Southeast Asia. It is arguable that there really has not been much change in American thinking. There has been a lot of writing about a lost consensus. As a historian, I find much of this writing short-sighted. When one tries to think when that great consensus existed, one can recall a great debate about European policy. There developed a consensus against isolationism and in favor of a proposition that the security of the United States and the security of Europe were intertwined. That consensus has persisted. With regard to Asia, the earlier period was marked by the purge of the "China hands" and the fierce debates over whether to unleash Chiang Kai-shek. I am not sure that consensus ever existed. Thus one can make an argument that there has not been much change.

On the other hand, one also can argue that the Vietnam War is a great event. There may have been little change in the map, but the global presence of the United States—military, cultural, and other—may be vastly different from what it was before that war. The behavior of the United States can be said to be different, and the world's expectations with regard to the United States are also different. Compare the U.S. role in Lebanon in 1958 with that in 1983. One can argue—as some chapters will—that the ways in which Americans think have changed and that American institutions are not what they were earlier.

My own verdict is that it is too soon to judge. In part this is because the war clearly was not in its own right a great event. If it has that character, it is because it has catalyzed changes. Whether it has done that or not, we probably shall not know for another decade at least.

One question on which to focus is that of whether other changes are in progress of which the Vietnam War may be merely one indicator. Regardless of how one feels at this moment, we may look back later on the Vietnam War as one of the series of events cumulatively producing the effects associated with great events. Two troublesome analogies occur to me. One is with the French experience in Mexico in the 1860s. I do not mean to press the partic-ular parallel. There are many points of dissimilarity as, for example, between U.S. intentions and French intentions. There are points of similarity that are at most superficial. The French fought valiantly and skillfully. But people at home concluded that the war was not worth its cost. The possible similarity in longer-run significance is arresting, however. The withdrawal from Mex-ico was part of a series of events that eroded the faith of the French in their country's power and, not altogether coincidentally, eroded respect for France in the minds of other people in Europe. It was part of a chain of events that changed the face of Europe in that period.

The other possible analogy, which worries me even more, is that of the Crimean War. After the Napoleonic Wars, there developed a system in Europe that bore some faint similarity to the system that has existed in the world since World War II. There was a prevalent assumption that the Russian Army was the most powerful military force in the world and that it was dedicated to the preservation of order of a certain kind in Europe. The other powerful military force in the world was the British Navy, and there was an assumption that if the Russian Army should be used for purposes other than the restoration of order in Europe, the British would be able to mobilize again a coalition such as the one they had organized against France. These assumptions about Russia and Britain underpinned the peace and kept some restraints on movements for national unity and for political change that were bubbling under the surface. Much happened in the course of the 1840s and 1850s to change that system, but the Crimean War was a very important one. It exposed to everyone, the participants included, the weakness of the Russian Army. It was not the instrument it had been supposed to be. It also exposed certain weaknesses on the British side, certainly in the political and diplomatic skill and imagination of the British. It was one of the series of events that changed the ways in which people thought about international order. It liberated forces of nationalism and liberalism, which then raced through Europe in the middle of the century.

This analogy is disturbing because today's international order depends on two beliefs that may be myths: that nuclear weapons matter and that the Soviet Union and the United States are superpowers. Both may be products of illusion. There is at most what Denis Healey termed a microscopic likelihood that nuclear weapons will be used. It is not impossible that we will some day decide that there is no likelihood at all. And the Soviet Union is not a superpower in many respects other than nuclear might, ready military forces, and world-class athletes. It is a country with pathetic income per capita, great difficulty feeding its own population, and a labor force composed of people who are drunk most of the time. It not only cannot meet the quality control standards for high technology goods; it cannot even make a nut fit a bolt. Its huge military establishment may be chiefly a constabulary force for policing subject peoples. At any rate, it would not be hard for the world suddenly to look at the Soviet Union and say, "That's no superpower." Nor is it out of the question for the world suddenly to reach the same conclusion about the United States. The United States is a rich country. It accounts for a quarter of the world's product, but it used to account for a larger fraction. The United States may be approaching bankruptcy. It certainly seems unable to manage its own purse. The United States presents the curious spectacle of a nation saying that it has an absolutely vital interest in El Salvador but that it will commit only fifty-five men there and they may not fire a shot. It would be easy for Americans and for people elsewhere in the world to come to think of the United States again as it was thought of earlier: a country immensely rich but unable to organize itself for effective action.

If the twin underpinning beliefs—the reality of nuclear weapons and the superness of the superpowers—were to be eroded, the world would certainly be different and, I think, much more dangerous. Along with Afghanistan and developments yet to be seen, the Vietnam War may form part of a pattern of change such as that of the early nineteenth century.

One has to think about the question of whether the Vietnam War really leaves things significantly different from what they were before. Is it a great event in that sense? One also has to consider whether, if it is not, it might nevertheless be a catalytic event in a series leading to changes, some of which Americans might welcome but others of which they might bitterly rue.

Note

1. Henri Pirenne, *History of Europe,* Vol. I (New York: Doubleday, 1958), pp. 25–26.

2
Containment in Asia: The Road to Vietnam

Norman A. Graebner

The military involvement of the United States in Vietnam rested on foundations carefully constructed through a dozen years of global strategic planning. Still, the path to Vietnam was not inherent in the country's postwar security policies. Washington's initial postwar planning emanated from World War II itself. Pearl Harbor had demonstrated that an unwanted and unanticipated war could come to the United States from afar, leaving the nation defenseless.[1] During subsequent months the country, protected by the oceans, managed to keep the fighting distant from its own shores, but the new weapons of war convinced the nation's military leaders, as well as some members of Congress, that the United States would not escape destruction in another major war. Senator Arthur H. Vandenberg of Michigan, a leading prewar isolationist, warned the Senate on January 10, 1945: "I do not believe that any nation hereafter can immunize itself by its own exclusive action. . . . Our oceans have ceased to be moats which automatically protect our ramparts. Flesh and blood now compete unequally with winged steel. War has become an all-consuming juggernaut."[2]

To protect its cities and its economy—the basic structure of its civilization—the United States of necessity would assign its predominant power to the prevention of another general war. Should that mission fail, it would, as a secondary objective, seek to guard its own territory from the predictable ravages of such a catastrophe. If such strategic purposes demanded a global reach, they did not presage a U.S. war in Southeast Asia. The specific notions that transformed the struggle for Indochina into a threat to world peace and U.S. security came only with the success of the Chinese Communists, the outbreak of the Korean War, and the globalization of containment. The gap between an infinite declaratory policy of containment and finite capabilities to implement containment opened the door to U.S. involvement in Vietnam.

In June 1943, the U.S. Army, on General George C. Marshall's advice, organized the Project Planning Division to plan the postwar U.S. military structure, one sufficiently awesome to preserve world stability after the conclusion of the war. The assignment was difficult because no one could name the enemy. Nevertheless, for military planners the issue was not that of designating the next opponent but of anticipating the nature of the war that the enemy would unleash. In that war, it seemed clear, the safety of all countries would be precarious. James V. Forrestal, secretary of the navy, phrased the danger in May 1943: "There is no such thing as security, and the word should be stricken from our dictionary. We should put in every school book the maxim that power like wealth must be either used or lost."[3] All service chiefs agreed by 1944 that the next enemy would be, like Germany and Japan, a military colossus, probably totalitarian, prepared to unleash a lightning attack over great distances. War, ran the general prediction, would be total. To avoid destruction, the country would require a military structure capable of meeting aggression before it could reach the United States.

The need to counter aggression far from U.S. shores rendered the entire globe an area of potential strategic concern. "It no longer appears practical," observed Marshall, "to continue what we once conceived a hemisphere defense as a satisfactory base for our security. We are now concerned with the peace of the entire world." U.S. security would require no less than a system of bases that would command the Atlantic and Pacific oceans. Air Force General H.H. Arnold argued in February 1945 that the "potentialities for production of weapons capable of sudden and overpowering attack are such . . . that the air power on which we must rely for protection against them must have available to it and under our control a system of air bases extending far beyond our domestic shores and not limited to our present insular possessions."[4] Naval planners emphasized the need for a ring of bases around the Western Hemisphere that might permit the United States, in time of crisis, to concentrate force effectively in outlying regions. Should aggression actually occur, the United States could launch strikes at the enemy's offensive power and thereby limit further damage.

To preserve its strategic hegemony in the western Pacific, the United States pressed the allies for permanent rights to the captured Japanese mandated islands. In 1944 the Joint Chiefs of Staff advocated outright annexation, arguing that the islands properly belonged to the United States as the victor in the Pacific. Secretary of War Henry L. Stimson, on February 20, 1945, requested the president to prevent countries without legitimate security interests in the Pacific from interfering with the disposition of the mandated islands; it was unthinkable, he said, that the United States would give up any of its bases in the Pacific. In April, Forrestal urged the president to negotiate for permanent bases in the Philippines as well. At the San Francisco Conference in June, the United States secured control of the Japanese bases through a trusteeship arrangement.[5] Following the defeat of Japan in August, Washington quickly converted Okinawa into a powerful military base off the Asian coast.

If Soviet behavior toward Eastern Europe already was casting shadows over the future of East-West relations in postwar Europe, U.S. military dominance from Japan to the Dutch East Indies seemed to ensure the peace of the western Pacific. For half a century, Japan had been the major, if not the exclusive, threat to a stable, peaceful Orient. By the summer of 1945, the United States had destroyed Japan's army and navy, burned out its cities and factories, and reduced its possessions to the four islands that comprised its territories before imperial days. During September Japan came under the direct control of U.S. postsurrender policies, designed to ensure a peaceful nation. Nowhere in the ruins of the Far East could most Americans detect any dangers to U.S. security. Still, for some observers, the Soviet Union's late entry into the Pacific war raised the phantom of Soviet maneuvering in the north Pacific and presaged Moscow's claims to a sizable stake in the creation of Asia's postwar order. Such a Soviet role, they warned, could affect U.S. interests adversely. "In Asia as in Europe," noted *Time* in May 1945, "Moscow seems to be organizing a cordon sanitaire in reverse, an immense chain of pro-Russian buffer states about her heartland."[6] Erwin Lessner wrote that it "would be surprising indeed, if Russia does not do her best to create a . . . protective chain along her Asian frontier." The *New Republic* added that in Asia "the rising shadow of Russia . . . grows increasingly ominous."[7]

Soviet armies in Manchuria and northern Korea were a reminder that the Soviet Union was a Pacific power with interests in East Asia spanning more than a century. That country's emergence in 1945 not only as the dominant power in Europe but also as a principal arbiter in Asiatic affairs blurred the historic division between Europe and Asia. Harold Isaacs observed in late May: "Straddling the vast distances between the Baltic and the Sea of Japan, the new Russia will symbolize the greatest geopolitical fact of our times: not Europe and Asia as separate entities, but Eurasia, the greatest single land mass on the face of the earth."[8] The *New Republic* observed that the Soviet Union was the only member of the Big Three with a geographic presence in East Asia. If Soviet power confronted the United States across a divided Europe in 1945, it endangered U.S. postwar hegemony in the Far East as well. The country's overwhelming victory in the Pacific had removed the Japanese danger only to resurrect the specter of Soviet expansion in East Asia, largely at China's expense. The triumphant war against Japan had, in effect, destroyed the old balance of power in the Far East, which had held Soviet ambitions in check. The new bipolarization of power in the world not only shifted the problem of the Far East from Japan to the Soviet Union but magnified it. John Fischer wrote in August 1945: "It is clear . . . that there are now only two nations—America and Russia—of really predominant power. They alone possess the resources to wage war on a global scale. If there is another world war, it must be between them."[9] Even as the United States embarked on its successful occupation of Japan, signaling the beginning of a promising new order in the Far East, the bipolarization of power, added to the Soviet Union's presumed ambitions in the Far East, predicted a bitter, debilitating Soviet-U.S. confrontation along the eastern as well as the western rim of the Eurasian continent.

By the summer of 1945, the notion that the Soviet Union already threatened the creation of a stable postwar order had become commonplace among State Department officials. Military leaders in general did not share such fears of Soviet expansionism in either Europe or the Far East. Until the autumn of 1945 defense planners had little interest in contemplating a future war against the Soviet Union. U.S. Air Force officers foresaw an enemy with high technological competence; that could be only Germany or Japan. The navy discounted the Soviet danger because the Kremlin displayed little interest in naval power. Although the Soviet Union possessed great land forces, U.S. Army leaders could visualize no future conflict with it across Europe.[10] Military officers, with some notable exceptions, were not prepared emotionally to view the nation that had carried the major burden of the war as a potential enemy. General Marshall continued to discredit the reports of Soviet duplicity and argued that the Soviet Union had good reasons for maintaining tight security. But even then such views were receding before the pressure of events. An intelligence staff paper of July 6 insisted that the Soviets were bent on world domination. "The limit has been reached," the writer warned, "to which the United States can subscribe to Soviet expansion."[11] Stimson observed at Potsdam in late July, "I believe that we must not accept the present situation, for the result will then almost inevitably be a new war and the destruction of our civilization." General Arnold recalled that by the time of Potsdam, he had believed that "our next enemy would be Russia."[12] By 1946 U.S. military leaders had adopted views of the Soviet Union that varied little from those of the State Department.

For military planners, the surest defense against the Soviet Union lay in the capacity of the United States to deter aggression. The prevention of war, Forrestal assured members of Congress, required a military structure that no nation could defeat and the willingness to employ that power against aggression anywhere. Service chiefs then and later would not agree on the shape of the ideal military structure. Still, during the war, air power had gained a major role in the country's strategy. For air force spokesmen, the airplane was not merely another weapon; it was the ultimate weapon for global peacekeeping. Even Marshall agreed that air power would be the country's first line of defense and the major source of its deterrent power. Air force officers anticipated the perpetuation of the amazing wartime triumphs in technology and production. Ultimately the atomic bomb, in its capacity to ensure the success of the nation's quest for an effective deterrent, would enable the United States to manage the peace. Yet some wondered how the United States could render even an atomic strategy effective against aggressive behavior that threatened the peace but not U.S. security.

U.S. power, resting on an amazingly productive economy, untouched by war, as well as an atomic monopoly, appeared capable of controlling the international environment. U.S. economic and strategic decisions after 1945 succeeded in stabilizing the periphery of Soviet occupation from northern Germany through Greece to Turkey and Iran. Europe was so reliant on the United States for both the means of rehabilitation and its postwar security that Western leaders scarcely questioned the policies that emanated from Washington. Still, the purpose of stabilizing the postwar order, so reasonable in itself, faced the need of containing the power and influence of the Soviet Union as well. From the beginning, the critical task of U.S. leaders—one far more taxing politically and intellectually than maintaining an adequate military structure—was that of defining the Soviet danger and designing a proper defense against it. In Europe the formation of the North Atlantic Treaty Organization (NATO) in 1948 and 1949 assumed that the Soviet Union confronted Western Europe with a traditional military threat.

The Soviet challenge outside Europe was complicated by the simultaneous tendency to attribute the Kremlin's expansionary power less to Soviet armies than to the Marxist-Leninist advocacy of world revolution. Thus the immediate threat to Eurasia lay not in Soviet military capabilities but in the chaotic economic and political conditions that prevailed through much of Europe and Asia. The political and social turmoil in India, China, Indochina, and the Dutch East Indies, the economic paralysis of Germany and Japan, the Communist movements in France and Italy, and the collapse of most traditional sources of international stability seemed to offer limitless opportunities for Soviet ideological exploitation. The doubtful viability of liberal ideas and capitalistic institutions in a revolutionary world suggested that much of Eurasia and its resources might well escape the West and fall into the clutches of the Kremlin. President Harry Truman furthered the tendency to view the Soviet challenge as one of ideology when he refused to distinguish between Soviet policy and the Communist-led assault on the Greek government. His central cold war assumption attributed to the Soviet Union the unprecedented capacity to expand without direct armed aggression and advance its power and influence in regions far beyond the reach of Soviet armies. It mattered little whether Soviet forces or even Soviet officials were present at all.

By 1948 some U.S. officials could detect no visible limit to Soviet power and ambition. The National Security Council's (NSC) study, NSC 7, dated March 30, 1948, emphasized the Soviet challenge's global dimensions:

> The ultimate objective of Soviet-directed world communism is the domination of the world. To this end, Soviet-directed world communism employs against its victims in opportunistic coordination the complementary instruments of Soviet aggressive pressure from without and militant revolutionary subversion from within. . . . The Soviet Union is the source of power from which international communism chiefly derives its capability to threaten the

existence of free nations. The United States is the only source of power capable of mobilizing successful opposition to the communist goal of world conquest.

With its control of international communism, the Soviet Union had engaged the United States in a global struggle for power "in which our national security is at stake and from which we cannot withdraw short of national suicide."[13] Succeeding NSC documents refined this theme. NSC 68 in April 1950 comprised the final and most elaborate attempt of the Truman leadership to arrive at a definition of national security policy. This document, like its predecessors, described the danger of Soviet expansionism in global, limitless terms. It concluded that the Soviet Union, "unlike previous aspirants to hegemony, is animated by a new fanatic faith, antithetical to our own, and seeks to impose its absolute authority over the rest of the world. Conflict has, therefore, become endemic and is waged, on the part of the Soviet Union, by violent and non-violent methods in accordance with the dictates of expediency."[14] Clearly the Kremlin design called for subversion of the non-Soviet world. "To that end," the document continued, "Soviet efforts are now directed toward the domination of the Eurasian land mass. The United States, as the principal center of power in the non-Soviet world and the bulwark of opposition to Soviet expansion, is the principal enemy."[15]

In 1945 the realization that the Soviet Union was a Pacific power with historic, if limited, ambitions in East Asia was sufficient to challenge the easy assumption that the United States, with its redesign of Japan's political structure, could ensure a stable Orient. After 1948, the NSC's strategic documents broadened Soviet political and territorial objectives to include vast portions of Asia, including China, and also assigned to the Soviet Union the power to expand across Asia through revolution alone, however limited the Soviet involvement in any revolutionary assault on Asia's pro-Western governments might be. Japan's wartime successes in the Far East had unleashed a nationalist upheaval of such magnitude that the colonial powers receded before the new demands for self-determination. By 1947 Great Britain had granted independence to India, Pakistan, Ceylon, and Burma; the Netherlands, with greater reluctance, granted independence to Indonesia in 1948. France alone emerged from the war determined to maintain its Southeast Asian possessions, whatever the cost.

Most Asian revolutionaries found their intellectual encouragement and guidance in Western political philosophy. Some, such as China's Mao Tse-tung and Indochina's Ho Chi Minh, turned to the anti-imperialist writings of Marx and Lenin for inspiration. After 1946, Mao and Ho led powerful and determined revolutionary movements to gain control of their countries and, in the process, rid them of their traditional European domination. As indigenous movements of long standing, the Chinese and Indochinese revolutions were scarcely examples of any alleged Soviet maneuvers to expand through Moscow's command of international communism. Already George F. Kennan and other Washington officials had observed that the Kremlin was concerned far more with its power to control other Communist governments, such as those of Eastern Europe, than with the ideological purity of such regimes. Yugoslavia's successful break from the Soviet Union in 1948 demonstrated as well that Soviet control of even Communist-led governments extended only as far as the reach of Soviet armies. There were no Soviet armies in non-Soviet Asia.

Such distinctions between indigenous Communist movements, whether in Europe or Asia, and Soviet imperialism the leading NSC documents between 1948 and 1950 scarcely recognized, nor did they separate the task of containing Soviet military power from that of limiting the spread of communism, largely a political challenge. By failing to make such fundamental distinctions, Washington ran the risk of placing regions peripheral to U.S. economic and security interests on a par with areas such as Europe that were fundamental to the security and well-being, economic and political, of the United States itself. Any effort to oppose communism everywhere in the name of containing the Soviet Union would compel the United States to seek allies and extend its military resources around the world, and to defend regimes that would reject any Kremlin efforts to control them and thus were potentially enemies rather than allies of the Soviet Union. As early as 1947 Walter Lippmann predicted that global containment would compel the United States to stake its policies

> upon satellites, puppets, clients, agents about whom we know very little. Frequently they will act . . . on their own judgments, presenting us with accomplished facts that we did not intend, and with crises for which we are unready. The "unassailable barriers" will present us with an unending series of insoluble dilemmas. We shall have either to disown our puppets, which would be tantamount to appeasement and defeat and loss of face, or must support them at an incalculable cost on an unintended, unforeseen and perhaps undesirable issue.[16]

Rejecting other conceptual choices before it, the Truman administration assumed the existence of a monolithic communism, centered in Moscow, and proceeded to build its defenses in the western Pacific on that assumption. As early as February 1947, Secretary of State Marshall explained the administration's critical decision to support the French war against Ho Chi Minh with the assertion that "we do not lose sight of the fact that Ho Chi Minh has direct Communist connections and it should be obvious that we are not interested in seeing colonial administrations supplanted by philosophy and political organizations emanating from and controlled by the Kremlin."[17] For the Truman leadership, the French struggle in Indochina was the initial phase of a burgeoning effort to prevent Soviet expansion in Asia. Marshall's rationale for the pro-French policy of the United States in Indochina defied the warnings of the State Department's Division of Southeast Asian Affairs that Ho was a nationalist fighting for the independence of his country and thus did not endanger U.S. or Asian security; moreover, it predicted, the French would never win.[18]

Behind the growing fear of Communist expansion in Asia was the larger issue of China, where Mao's Communist-led revolution threatened to topple the Nationalist regime of Chiang Kai-shek. As the Nationalist armies continued to lose ground to the Chinese Communists in 1947, Chiang pressed Washington for greater support, arguing, as did the French in Indochina, that he was protecting China from Communist aggression. To counter such demands and determine a feasible course of action, Marshall, in July 1947, dispatched General Albert C. Wedemeyer on another special mission to China. In his report of September 19, 1947, Wedemeyer declared that most Chinese opposed a Communist regime, whatever the failures of the Kuomintang. He doubted that any policy would save Chiang. Still he concluded: "A China dominated by Chinese Communists would be inimical to the interests of the United States, in view of their openly expressed hostility and active opposition to those principles which the United States regards as vital to the peace of the world."[19] During 1948, State Department officials warned the administration that Communist advances were bringing China under Kremlin control. "In the struggle for world domination," declared the State Department's report of October 13 to the NSC (NSC 34), ". . . the allegiance of China's millions is worth striving for . . . if only to deny it to the free world. In positive terms, China is worth having because capture of it would represent an impressive political victory and, more practically, acquisition of a broad human glacis from which to mount a political offensive against the rest of East Asia."[20] Except for Soviet imperialism in China, the report concluded, the Chinese Communists would comprise no threat to Asia.

During subsequent months, Washington could not ignore the fact that shortly 900 million in the Eurasian land mass would be living under Communist-led governments. Indeed, the fall of Chiang in 1949 sent the United States into a deep intellectual crisis. What mattered during the critical months of decision was the role that U.S. officials, editors, and political leaders—the creators of policy and public opinion—chose to assign to the Soviet Union in the triumph of Communist power in China. What had appeared indigenous suddenly appeared to some in Washington and elsewhere as possibly the initial triumph of Soviet aggression as it moved into the Asian sphere. Throughout autumn 1949, the administration continued to search for a definition of the Asian problem, troubled by a lack of evidence. In November foreign service officer Karl Lott Rankin warned from Hong Kong that Communist China would, through subversion, attempt to extend its influence throughout South and Southeast Asia. "Now that communist control of China proper is all but assured," he wrote, "it may be taken for granted that efforts will be redoubled to place communist regimes in power elsewhere in Asia. . . . China may be considered weak and backward by Western standards, but . . . in Eastern terms, communist China is a great power, economically, militarily, and politically. Supported by communist dynamism, China might well be able to dominate not only Indochina, Siam, and Burma, but eventually the Philippines, Indonesia, Pakistan, and India itself."[21] Such perceptions of danger, emanating from the executive branch, quickly drifted into Congress.

Mao's eventual triumph on the Asian mainland compelled the Truman administration to formulate an overall strategic defense for the western Pacific. As early as February 1948, Kennan, head of the State Department's Policy Planning Staff, advised the department "to see what parts of the Pacific and Far Eastern world are absolutely vital to our security, and . . . concentrate our policy on seeing to it that those areas remain in hands which we can control or rely on."[22] In Tokyo shortly after, General Douglas MacArthur agreed with Kennan on the need for a defense perimeter that would include the Philippines, Australia, New Zealand, and former European-held islands in the southwest Pacific. In March 1949, MacArthur argued for an island defense perimeter, with specific strategic commitments to the Philippines, the Ryukyus, Japan, and the Aleutians. That month Kennan suggested a defense perimeter in which Okinawa would become the most advanced base of a U-shaped security zone that embraced the Aleutians, the Ryukyus, the former Japanese mandated islands, and Guam, excluding Japan and the Philippines as long as they remained militarily neutral. In June 1949, the Joint Chiefs of Staff agreed that "the ultimate minimum United States position in the Far East vis-à-vis the U.S.S.R., one to which we are rapidly being forced, requires at least our present degree of control of the Asian offshore island chain."[23] The Joint Chiefs agreed with MacArthur that U.S. access to Japanese bases was essential for the defense of the western Pacific.

Meanwhile, the administration made the fundamental decision to avoid any extension of the containment doctrine to the Asian mainland. In June 1949, as the last U.S. troops left South Korea, the Joint Chiefs concluded that a U.S. police action in Korea would overcommit the country's manpower and resources in the Far East.[24] Similarly, the administration rejected any commitment to the defense of Formosa. When it became clear in 1949 that the Chinese Nationalists would take possession of the island, the State Department dispatched Livingston T. Merchant to analyze Formosa's political future. He advised Washington to disassociate itself from the exiled Chinese. But late in December 1949, Senator William F. Knowland of California, returning from a trip to Formosa, urged the administration to send a military mission to the island. Early in January, Knowland released a letter from former President Herbert Hoover that declared that the United States should continue to support the Kuomintang and, if necessary, extend naval protection to Formosa and the Pescadores. Truman replied on January 5 that the United States had no intention of becoming involved in China's civil war by committing U.S. forces to protect the Nationalist government. Economic aid would continue, but "no military aid or advice."[25] That day Secretary of State Dean Acheson informed Knowland that U.S. resistance to the Chinese Communists had ended.

By early 1950 the Joint Chiefs, the NSC, and President Truman had adopted the concept of a perimeter defense of the western Pacific. Acheson acknowledged that decision publicly when, in his National Press Club speech of January 1950, he proclaimed a defense perimeter that ran "along the Aleutians to Japan and then . . . to the Ryukyus . . . [and] from the Ryukyus to the Philippine Islands."[26] When Acheson excluded Formosa and Korea from the perimeter, he was merely reflecting established policy. Supported by MacArthur and the Joint Chiefs, the secretary was puzzled that anyone would accuse him of innovation. The concept of a perimeter defense assumed that bases on the Asian mainland were both unnecessary for U.S. security and an overcommitment of U.S. power in the Pacific.[27]

During the spring of 1950, U.S. leaders completed their conceptualization of a Soviet-based Communist monolith that extended the Kremlin's authority across Asia. When revolutionary China appeared to be achieving true national independence, Acheson told the Commonwealth Club of California, its leaders were forcing it into the Soviet orbit. "We now face the prospect," he acknowledged, "that the Communists may attempt to apply another familiar tactic and use China as a base for probing for other weak spots which they can move into and exploit." He warned Asians that they must "face the fact that today the major threat to their freedom and to their social and economic progress is the attempted penetration of Asia by Soviet-Communist imperialism and by the colonialism which it contains."[28]

U.S. officials in Asia took up the new theme. Ambassador Loy Henderson agreed before the Indian Council of World Affairs at New Delhi in late March that the United States, with its long tradition of involvement in the Atlantic nations, understood better the culture of Europe than that of Asia. Recent events in the Far East, however, had given the American people a new and enlarging interest in that region. "It should be borne in mind, in considering various policies of the United States in respect to Asia," he said, "that the United States does not pursue one set of policies with regard to the Americas and Europe and another with regard to Asia. The foreign policies of the United States by force of circumstances have become global in character."[29]

Much of this expanding fear of Soviet aggression centered on Indochina, where the French continued to fight their losing war for empire against the Communist-led revolution of Ho Chi Minh . Official Washington now viewed

Ho as the mortal enemy of the independence of Indochina. In early February 1950, the United States recognized Bao Dai as the new ruler of Vietnam; thereafter the notion that this Paris-chosen native aristocrat had better claims to Vietnamese leadership than Ho and eventually would triumph became official U.S. doctrine. Assistant Secretary of State Dean Rusk denied before the Senate Foreign Relations Committee that the struggle for Indochina was a civil war: "It is part of an international war, . . . and because Ho Chi Minh is tied in with the [Moscow] Politburo our policy is to support Bao Dai and the French in Indochina until we have time to help them establish a going concern."[30]

The French now carried the heavy burden of Communist containment in Southeast Asia. In March 1950, State Department officer Livingston T. Merchant reminded the administration that another Communist triumph on the Asian mainland "could be expected adversely to affect our interests in India, Pakistan, and even the Philippines." In April the Joint Chiefs defined Indochina's importance in similar terms: "Southeast Asia is a vital segment in the line of containment of communism stretching from Japan southward and around the Indian Peninsula. The security of . . . Japan, India, and Australia . . . depends in large measure on the denial of Southeast Asia to the Communists."[31]

For U.S. officials, the North Korean invasion of South Korea on June 25 was the final demonstration of the Kremlin's control of the Communist forces of Asia. The president explained his decision to order U.S. air and sea forces to Korea: "The attack upon Korea makes it plain beyond all doubt that Communism has passed beyond the use of subversion to conquer independent nations and will now use armed invasion and war."[32] U.S. officials, in attributing the Korean War to Soviet imperialism, placed enormous faith in China's refusal to become involved. To Washington observers, China's decision would be a measure of its independence from Kremlin domination. This view explains why the Chinese advance across the Yalu in November 1950 produced a traumatic reaction by Washington. China's intervention seemed to demonstrate not only Peking's irrationality but also the absolute control that Moscow had gained over China and its external policies. "Those who control the Soviet Union and the international Communist movement," Acheson warned on November 29, "have made clear their fundamental design." Truman declared the next day, "We hope that the Chinese people will not continue to be forced or deceived into serving the ends of Russian colonial policy in Asia."

President Truman repeated the charge of Chinese subservience in his State of the Union message of January 8, 1951: "Our men are fighting . . . because they know, as we do, that the aggression in Korea is part of the attempt of the Russian communist dictatorship to take over the world, step by step."[33] John Foster Dulles, in his capacity as State Department adviser, brought the notion of China's subjugation to its ultimate rationale in May 1951: "By the test of conception, birth, nurture, and obedience, the Mao Tse-tung regime [of China] is a creature of the Moscow Politburo, and it is in behalf of Moscow, not of China, that it is destroying the friendship of the Chinese people toward the United States."[34]

For Washington the U.S. interest in opposing Asian communism, in Korea, China, or Indochina, had become a given, rarely explicated, rarely questioned by those charged with the conduct of national security policy. Early in 1952 the NSC issued a statement, "United States Objectives and Courses of Action with Respect to Southeast Asia," that presented the following proposition: "Communist domination, by whatever means, of all Southeast Asia would seriously endanger short term, and critically endanger in the longer run, United States security interests." What those security interests were neither that document nor any other that followed defined. The document went on to warn: "In the absence of effective and timely counteraction, the loss of any single country would probably lead to relatively swift submission to or an alignment with communism by the remaining countries of [Southeast Asia]. Furthermore, an alignment with communism of the rest of Southeast Asia and India, and in the longer term, the Middle East . . . would in all probability progressively follow. Such widespread alignment would endanger the stability and security of Europe."[35]

President Dwight D. Eisenhower accepted without question such suppositions of global danger emanating from the expansion of Soviet communism across Asia. The new president warned the nation early in 1953 that it stood in greater peril than at any other time in its history. On January 27, six days after he assumed his new office as secretary of state, John Foster Dulles informed a national radio and television audience: "Already our proclaimed enemies control one-third of all the people of the world. . . . At the end of the Second World War, only a little over seven years ago, [the Soviets] only controlled about 200 million people. Today, they control 800 million people and they're hard at work to get control of other parts of the world." Soon that Soviet grip would include sixteen nations and 900 million people.[36] Their alleged membership in the Kremlin-dominated Communist monolith continued to render Peking and Hanoi dangerous to Asian and world stability.

Ambassador Karl Lott Rankin in Taipei acknowledged the extent to which the presumed Communist monolith governed U.S.-Chinese relations. He reminded Ambassador George V. Allen in India in July 1953 that the United States could maintain its anti-Peking posture only by denying that Mao Tse-tung enjoyed any independence from Moscow. Whether or not this was true, wrote Rankin, the Chinese Nationalists feared that Washington might accept it as true and thereafter follow the course of Britain and India in recognizing the new Chinese government. "Only so long as they are persuaded that Americans continue to regard Mao simply as a Soviet tool," ran Rankin's warning, "will they feel reasonably assured as to our China policy."[37] For Eisenhower's Washington, the Soviet control of China, unless countered by a successful policy of liberation, eventually would undermine all national entities in Asia and create one vast community under Communist domination. Nationalism was the Asiatic agent for the new universalism. "The Soviet leaders, in mapping their strategy for world conquest," Dulles warned in November 1953, "hit upon nationalism as a device for absorbing the colonial peoples." The danger, continued Dulles, rested in the ability of Communist agitators to aggravate the nationalist aspirations of people so that they would rebel violently against the existing order. Before a new stability could appear the Communists would gain control of the nation and convey it into the Soviet orbit.[38]

China's internal stability, well established by 1953, rendered Indochina the immediate Asian challenge to the new administration. Dulles turned to the Indochinese danger as early as January 1953: "The Soviet Russians are making a drive to get Japan, not only through what they are doing in Korea but also through what they are doing in Indochina. If they could get this peninsula of Indochina, Siam, Burma, and Malaya, they would have what is called the rice bowl of Asia. . . . [I]f the Soviet Union had control of the rice bowl of Asia, that would be another weapon which would tend to expand their control into Japan and into India."[39] Vice-President Richard Nixon elaborated on the danger in December: "If Indochina falls, Thailand is put in an almost impossible position. The same is true of Malaya with its rubber and tin. The same is true for Indonesia. . . . That indicates . . . why it is vitally important that Indochina not go behind the Iron Curtain."[40]

By early 1954 the French position in Indochina had become critical as Ho Chi Minh's forces closed in on the French fortress of Dienbienphu. When a program to save the French proved to be elusive, the perceptions of danger remained acute. On March 29, Dulles informed the Overseas Press Club of New York that if the Communist forces gained control over Indochina or any substantial part of it, "they would surely resume the same pattern of aggression against other free peoples in the area. . . . Communist control of Southeast Asia would carry a grave threat to the Philippines, Australia, and New Zealand, with whom we have treaties of mutual assistance. The entire Western Pacific area, including the so-called 'offshore island chain,' would be strategically endangered."[41] On April 7 President Eisenhower explained to reporters Indochina's strategic importance: "You have broader considerations that might follow what you would call the falling Domino Principle. You have a row of dominoes set up, you knock over the first one, and what will happen to the last one is the certainty that it will go over very quickly." The dangerous and predictable sequence of events could include "the loss of Indochina, of Burma, of Thailand, of the Peninsula, and Indonesia . . . the so-called island defensive chain of Japan, Formosa, of the Philippines and to the southward . . . Australia and New Zealand."[42]

However grave the danger emanating from Indochina, the Eisenhower administration had no intention of meeting it on the ground. Despite the doubtful applicability of nuclear power to limited-war conflicts, the Eisenhower administration assigned its formulations of massive retaliation to Asia no less than to Europe. The fact that Dulles made his formal announcement of the new strategic doctrine in January 1954 suggests that the administration had Indochina in mind.[43] That spring the president hesitated to commit U.S. ground forces to prevent the French collapse. "The jungles of Indochina," he explained later, ". . . would have swallowed up division after division of United States troops, who unaccustomed to this kind of warfare, would have sustained heavy casualties until they had learned to live in a new environment."[44] Even as Eisenhower sought to avoid a war in Indochina, he warned Winston Churchill of the dangers of further Communist advances in Southeast Asia: "We failed to halt Hirohito, Mussolini and Hitler by not acting in unity and in time. This marked the beginning of many years of stark tragedy and desperate peril. May it not be that our nations have learned something from that lesson?"[45]

Massive retaliation provided the necessary and fundamentally risk-free program for preventing further unwanted aggression in Asia. The formula assumed that the United States could manage the future of East and Southeast Asia simply by threatening to use the nuclear power at its command. The added assumption that the dangers emanated from the Kremlin added to the credibility of the deterrent; a major force would take the threat of nuclear retaliation more seriously than would a minor one. That major force allegedly had driven Chiang Kai-shek into exile and had brought aggression to Korea; by 1953 it threatened to overrun Indochina as well. Vice-President Nixon described the ongoing struggle in Southeast Asia as a simple matter of Communist imperialism on French soil. Dulles attributed the threat to the "mighty land power of the Communist world."[46] Unwilling to resist such power in another conventional war on Asian soil, the administration had no choice but to accept the expansion of Communist influence in Asia or seek to prevent it with the deterrent of massive retaliatory power. At the organizational meeting of the Southeast Asia Treaty Organization (SEATO) in Manila in September 1954, Dulles warned the new Asian allies that the United States, because of its global commitments, would not engage in another conventional war on the Asian mainland. The United States would grant logistical, naval, and air support; beyond that it would resort to weapons of massive destruction. To create a U.S. conventional force in Asia, the secretary informed the Congress, would be "an injudicious overextension of our military power."[47]

After 1954 Ngo Dinh Diem shouldered the chief responsibility for defending his own and U.S. interests in the stability of Southeast Asia. Diem's political and military success remained the only barrier to an uncertain future of chaos and war, which in some measure would involve the United States. Still, until the end of the decade, Washington predicted disaster if containment at the seventeenth parallel, the line separating North from South Vietnam, should falter. Eisenhower repeated his fears to a Gettysburg College audience in April 1959: "Strategically, South Vietnam's capture by the Communists would bring their power several hundred miles into a hitherto free region. The remaining countries of Southeast Asia would be menaced by a great flanking movement. . . . The loss of South Vietnam would set in motion a crumbling process that could, as it progressed, have grave consequences for us and for freedom."[48] As Eisenhower left office, his commitment to the future of the regime in Saigon remained firm. At the same time, spokesmen of his administration could recall years of U.S. success in containing Communist expansion in Asia without war.

The Eisenhower-Dulles formula for containing Communist power in Asia left the United States with the choice of accepting what its Asian allies could achieve or resorting to nuclear weapons. But Ho Chi Minh long had demonstrated that the strategy based on SEATO and threats of massive retaliation offered no defense at all. After eliminating the French from Southeast Asia in 1954, Ho never permitted the Geneva settlement of 1954 to weaken his determination to unite all Indochina under his leadership. His subsequent guerrilla war against the Saigon regime exposed the hollowness of the nuclear deterrent as a controlling element in the politics of Asia, especially when any revolutionary movement had an interest in defying it. By 1960, long before South Vietnam had experienced the full impact of either Communist-led subversion or North Vietnamese infiltration, the Saigon government controlled only half of South Vietnam.[49] Hanoi had demonstrated its capacity to counter whatever force Saigon or other Asian allies could mount against it. Still, the Eisenhower administration had anticipated no conventional war against Hanoi, much less against Moscow or Peking, to underwrite its pervading commitment to South Vietnam. Nor had it designated any avenue of retreat from the country's inescapable dilemma.

By 1960, U.S. containment policies in Asia embraced goals that far transcended Washington's attention to means. In Asia, containment had been marginal, with limited strategies to confine limited threats. But official reactions to events in Asia had permitted the perceived dangers to outrun the strategies of containment, both nuclear and conventional. Unprepared to commit conventional forces, especially the U.S. Army and Marines, the U.S. government was left with little choice but to explain away its accumulated rhetoric of falling dominoes and abandon containment beyond the island chain, or to escalate its commitment to the ongoing struggle for Indochina in the face of its lack of preparedness and its proclaimed intention to avoid another Asian war. Supposedly rendered effective and inexpensive by declarations of massive reprisal, U.S. support for Saigon had failed to thwart Ho Chi Minh's dedication and determination to unify his homeland under Hanoi's control. That Ho endangered peace in Indochina was clear, but his threat to U.S. security, hardly demonstrable, lay in a vast body of official U.S. rhetoric that many Americans believed but that ever-larger numbers would reject. Even for those who took the rhetoric seriously, policies at the margin threatened to be far costlier than they had contemplated.

Notes

1. Marquis Childs expressed this reaction forcefully in *Time,* December 15, 1941, p. 18.

2. Vandenberg's speech of January 10, 1945, in Arthur H. Vandenberg, Jr., and Joe Alex Morris, eds., *The Private Papers of Senator Vandenberg* (Boston: Houghton Mifflin, 1952), p. 135.

3. Forrestal quoted in Michael S. Sherry, *Preparing for the Next War: American Plans for Postwar Defense, 1941–1945* (New Haven: Yale University Press, 1977), p. 57.

4. Arnold quoted in ibid., p. 112.

5. Thomas M. Campbell, *Masquerade Peace: America's UN Policy, 1944–1945* (Tallahassee, Fla.: Florida State University Press, 1973), pp. 139, 170; Thomas M. Campbell and George C. Herring, eds., *The Diaries of Edward R. Stettinius, Jr., 1943–1946* (New York: New Viewpoints, 1975), pp. 210–211. For a lengthy report on international trusteeships in the Pacific, see Stettinius to Roosevelt, n.d., Map Room, box 23, Franklin D. Roosevelt Library, Hyde Park, N.Y.

6. *Time,* May 28, 1945, p. 40; ibid., June 4, 1945, p. 45.

7. Lessner quoted from *Harper's Magazine* 191 (July 1945): 37, 44; *New Republic,* May 28, 1945, p. 736.

8. Isaacs quoted in *Newsweek,* May 28, 1945, p. 50.

9. John Fischer, "Odds against Another War," *Harper's Magazine* 191 (August 1945): 97.

10. Sherry discusses the views of the military planners toward the Soviet Union in *Preparing for the Next War,* p. 168.

11. See ibid., p. 182.

12. H.H. Arnold, *Global Mission* (New York: Harper, 1949), p. 586; *Foreign Relations of the United States, 1946* (Washington, D.C., 1972), 1: 1165, 1166.

13. For NSC 7, see Thomas H. Etzold and John Lewis Gaddis, eds., *Containment: Documents on American Policy and Strategy, 1945–1950* (New York: Columbia University Press, 1978), pp. 166–167.

14. NSC 68 quoted in ibid., pp. 385–386.

15. Ibid., pp. 386, 387.

16. Walter Lippmann, *The Cold War* (New York: Harper and Row, 1972), p. 16.

17. Marshall to Caffrey, February 3, 1947, in *Foreign Relations, 1947* (Washington, D.C., 1972), 6: 67–68.

18. O'Sullivan to Marshall, July 21, 1947, in ibid., pp. 121–123. See also Department of State, policy statement on Indochina, September 27, 1948, in Gareth Porter, ed., *Vietnam: The Definitive Documentation of Human Decisions* (Stanfordville, N.Y.: E.M. Coleman, 1979), 1: 180.

19. Department of State, *United States Relations with China* (Washington, D.C., 1949), p. 773.

20. Policy Planning Staff, memo (NSC-34), September 7, 1948, in *Foreign Relations, 1948* (Washington, D.C., 1973), 8: 147.

21. Rankin to Department of State, November 16, 1949, in Karl Lott Rankin, *China Assignment* (Seattle: University of Washington Press, 1964), p. 35.

22. Kennan's review of current trends, February 24, 1948, in *Foreign Relations, 1948* (Washington, D.C., 1976), 1, pt. 2: 525.

23. For MacArthur's views, see John Lewis Gaddis, "The Strategic Perspective: The Rise and Fall of the 'Defensive Perimeter' Concept, 1947–1951," in Dorothy Borg and Waldo Heinrichs, eds., *Uncertain Years: Chinese-American Relations, 1947–1950* (New York: Columbia University Press, 1980), p. 64; Dean Acheson, *Present at the Creation: My Years in the State Department* (New York: Norton, 1969), p. 357. For the views of the Joint Chiefs, see "Strategic Evaluation of United States Security Needs in Japan," June 9, 1949, in *Foreign Relations, 1949* (Washington, D.C., 1976), 7: 774–775.

24. Memorandum for the Chief of Staff, U.S. Army, June 23, 1949, in *Foreign Relations, 1949,* 7: 1056–1057.

25. For Merchant's views, see *Foreign Relations, 1949* (Washington, D.C., 1974), 9: 324–326, 337–341, 463–467. On Knowland see *Foreign Relations, 1950* (Washington, D.C., 1976), 6: 258–263. For Truman's statement of January 5, 1950, see ibid., p. 264.

26. Acheson's speech before the National Press Club, January 12, 1950, in Department of State, *Bulletin,* January 23, 1950, p. 116.

27. For Acheson, the defense of East Asia, contrasted to that of Europe, was marginal. See his statement in John Lewis Gaddis, *Strategies of Containment* (New York: Oxford University Press, 1982), p. 114.

28. Department of State, *Bulletin,* March 27, 1950, pp. 469–472.

29. Henderson's New Delhi address, March 27, 1950, in ibid., April 10, 1950, p. 562.

30. Rusk quoted in Porter, *Vietnam,* 1: 266.

31. Merchant to Butterworth, March 7, 1950, in *Foreign Relations, 1950* (Washington, D.C., 1976), 6: 750; Johnson to Acheson, April 14, 1950, in ibid., p. 781.

32. *Foreign Relations, 1950* (Washington, D.C., 1976), 7: 200, 202.

33. Department of State, *Bulletin,* January 22, 1951, p. 123.

34. "Sustaining Friendship with China," in ibid., May 28, 1951, p. 844.

35. Ibid., March 26, 1951, p. 484; "Policy Statement on United States Goals in Southeast Asia, 1952," in Neil Sheehan, ed., *The Pentagon Papers as Published by the New York Times* (New York: Quadrangle Books, 1971), p. 28.

36. Dulles's address to the nation, January 27, 1953, in Department of State, *Bulletin,* February 9, 1953, pp. 212–213; Walter S. Robertson, "America's Responsibilities in the Far East," June 3, 1957, in ibid., June 24, 1957, p. 997.

37. Rankin, *China Assignment,* p. 173.

38. "The Moral Initiative," speech before the CIO, Cleveland, November 18, 1953, in Department of State, *Bulletin,* November 30, 1953, p. 742.

39. Dulles's survey of foreign policy problems, January 27, 1953, in ibid., February 9, 1953, p. 213.

40. Radio and television address, December 23, 1953, in ibid., January 4, 1954, p. 12.

41. Dulles's speech before the Overseas Press Club, March 29, 1954, in ibid., April 12, 1954, p. 539.

42. Department of Defense, *United States–Vietnam Relations* (Pentagon Papers), House Committee on Armed Services, 92d Cong., 1st sess., 1971, 7: B-11.

43. Dulles's speech before the Council on Foreign Relations, New York, January 12, 1954, in Department of State, *Bulletin,* January 25, 1954, pp. 107–108.

44. William Bragg Ewald, Jr., *Eisenhower the President: Crucial Days, 1951–1960* (Englewood Cliffs, N.J.: Prentice-Hall, 1981), p. 119.

45. Dwight D. Eisenhower, *Mandate for Change, 1953–1956: The White House Years* (Garden City, N.Y.: Doubleday, 1963), p. 347.

46. Norman A. Graebner, *The New Isolationism* (New York: Ronald Press, 1956), pp. 162–163.

47. Department of State, *Bulletin,* May 14, 1956, p. 788; Department of State, *American Foreign Policy: Current Documents, 1956* (Washington, D.C., 1959), p. 779.

48. Speech at Gettysburg College, April 4, 1959, in Department of State, *Bulletin,* April 27, 1959, pp. 580–581.

49. See, for example, Robert Shaplen, *The Lost Revolution: The U.S. in Vietnam, 1946–1966* (New York: Harper and Row, 1966), pp. 140–143; George McTurnan Kahin and John W. Lewis, *The United States in Vietnam* (New York: Dial Press, 1969), pp. 99–120.

3

The United States and the Use of Force: A Historical Summary

Philip D. Zelikow

At a press conference on February 23, 1977, President Jimmy Carter was asked to comment on reports of atrocities committed at the behest of the president of Uganda, Idi Amin Dada. President Carter responded in part, "In Uganda the actions there have disgusted the entire civilized world."[1] Offended, Amin announced on February 25 that all Americans in Uganda, about 300 people, were to gather in the capital, Kampala, for a meeting with him by the following Monday. They were forbidden to leave the country meanwhile. He also sent a long message to Carter voicing his discontent with U.S. condemnations of his government. Radio Uganda pointed out that friendly Americans were welcome in the country, but disseminators of anti-Uganda, Zionist, and imperialist propaganda would have "to take the consequences."[2] Americans familiar with Uganda were concerned. The last U.S. ambassador there, Thomas Melady, warned that from Amin, "we may get bombast, he may sing songs and so forth, or it could be something rather unpleasant."[3]

Reaction was swift. A State Department working group monitored the situation, and public indignation was coupled with tough private warnings conveyed to Amin through foreign intermediaries.[4] To reinforce these warnings, an aircraft carrier task group dispatched on a routine Indian Ocean cruise was ordered to move to a position about 275 miles off the coast of Kenya.[5]

The movement of this task group, which included the nuclear-powered aircraft carrier *Enterprise,* along with two nuclear-powered guided missile cruisers and a nuclear attack submarine, did not escape the notice of the Ugandans. Their armed forces were alerted, and Radio Uganda broadcasted that "the presence of American naval vessels off the East African coast should

I gratefully acknowledge the assistance received in the preparation of this chapter from the International Security Studies Program at the Fletcher School of Law and Diplomacy, the Operational Archives and Ships' Histories Branches of the Naval Historical Center of the U.S. Department of the Navy, Barry Blechman, Edward Bullard, and Robert Pfaltzgraff. They are, of course, not responsible for any opinions expressed here. This chapter is an updated and substantially revised version of an article that originally appeared in *Journal of Strategic Studies* 7 (March 1984).

be taken seriously."[6] Acknowledging the presence of the carrier task group, Amin announced that Uganda was ready to repel an attack, but he declared that his meeting with the Americans would be postponed for two days and added reassurances about their safety.[7] Rapidly losing interest in the whole matter, Amin subsequently postponed the meeting indefinitely and lifted the ban on American departures from Uganda, leaving the Carter administration quite satisfied with the handling of its first crisis.[8]

In late December 1979, the Carter administration, already beleaguered by the somewhat less satisfactory developments in Iran, was confronted with the need for a response to the Soviet invasion of Afghanistan. Politically, it met the invasion with a grain embargo, a resumption of draft registration, a boycott of the Olympic games, and the announcement of the Carter doctrine, which declared that any attempt by any outside force to gain control of the Persian Gulf region will be regarded as an assault on the vital interests of the United States of America, and such an assault will be repelled by all means necessary, including military force."[9]

Militarily, these declarations were underscored by a series of demonstrations meant to deter further Soviet aggression and reinforce ties with U.S. allies. In January 1980, the U.S. Air Force conducted joint exercises with Egypt using U.S. SR-71 and airborne warning and control system (AWACS) reconnaissance aircraft.[10] In February, an amphibious ready group with 1,800 marines joined U.S. naval forces on station in the Arabian Sea.[11] In July an air force squadron of F-4E Phantom fighter aircraft, along with support aircraft and personnel, arrived in Egypt for three months of training.[12] In November the U.S. Army and Air Force joined with the Egyptians in an exercise called Bright Star, in which a battalion of paratroopers flew directly from its U.S. base to conduct a mass parachute drop into Egypt, accompanied by A-7 tactical support aircraft and a number of helicopters.[13]

Clearly force can be applied without war. The principle is certainly not new. It has long been recognized that military power is used most successfully when soldiers do not fight. The ancient Chinese theorist Sun Tzu considered battle the worst of all strategic options: "For to win one hundred victories in one hundred battles is not the acme of skill. To subdue the enemy without fighting is the acme of skill."[14] Writing of the Roman Empire, Edward Luttwak explained:

> In the imperial period at least, military force was clearly recognized for what it is, an essentially limited instrument of power, costly and brittle. Much better to conserve force and use military power indirectly, as the instrument of political warfare. . . . Above all, the Romans clearly realized that the dominant dimension of power was not physical but psychological—the product of others' perceptions of Roman strength rather than the use of this strength. And this realization alone can explain the sophistication of Roman strategy at its best.[15]

U.S. strategy in the postwar period has similarly relied and continues to rely on the psychological dimension of power, the use of force without war.

This chapter will catalog the political uses of U.S. armed forces in the post-Vietnam era, from 1975 to the end of 1984.[16] Such a record serves two purposes: it compiles the available data for others interested in this subject, and it allows a comparative analysis between the trends and patterns of the 1946–1975 period, already documented by Blechman and Kaplan, and those from 1975 to the end of 1984, helping to sharpen analysis of the concrete impact of Vietnam on U.S. political-military policy.[17]

The methodology for this chapter will follow generally that used by Blechman and Kaplan. The incidents selected for examination do not include all routine military actions, such as regular exercises and port visits, that may have some general political meaning. The focus is on "discrete military moves to influence a particular situation,"[18] defined as follows:

A political use of the armed forces occurs when physical actions are taken by one or more components of the uniformed military services as part of a deliberate attempt by the national authorities to influence, or to be prepared to influence, specific behavior of individuals in another nation without engaging in a continuing contest of violence.[19]

This definition excludes certain kinds of activities. The military forces involved had to change their disposition physically; plans to deploy forces in a particular region are not an incident until the deployment actually occurs. There also had to be a conscious political purpose behind the action; for example, the compelled withdrawal of U.S. soldiers and airmen from Thailand during 1975 and 1976 did not serve a deliberate political purpose of U.S. design and is not counted as an incident. The decision maker also must have used force to influence conduct, not just to seize an objective physically. Although U.S. deployments during the Iranian hostage crisis were designed to influence Iranian conduct, the April 1980 rescue mission itself was not meant to influence the Iranians to release the hostages; it was aimed only at taking the hostages by force. Similarly, military assistance and advisory groups are not considered here. This study focuses instead on the use of combat and combat support elements. The factors involved in analyzing the political effects of military assistance to other countries are quite different and those effects are stretched over long periods of time.

There is a problem in categorizing naval cruises aimed at asserting U.S. rights of innocent passage in what the United States considers to be international waters. These cruises are designed to influence state action on a specific international issue. On the other hand, such cruises have become so frequent since the late 1970s, due to increasingly broad maritime claims by states, that inclusion of all of these cruises as incidents would badly distort the overall picture of U.S. military activity.[20] This chapter therefore includes for study only those cruises that in my subjective judgment are related to very active international disputes. Such disputes often are characterized by attacks on or severe harassment of U.S. naval units. The U.S. action asserting rights of passage in such instances often displays the U.S. valuation of the significance of the dispute in the assignment of, say, one or more aircraft carriers to support the deployment.

Using the definition explained, seventy-one incidents were identified where the United States used military force to achieve political objectives between May 1975 and December 1984. Only declassified sources were used to compile this list, but past comparisons reveal that the incidents available from declassified sources correlate substantially to those that can be discovered in classified materials.[21]

The Historical Record

The following seventy-one incidents were identified of U.S. uses of armed forces as a political instrument between 1975 and 1984 (for the sources of this list, see appendix 3A):

Incident	*Beginning of Relevant Change*	
1. Security of South Korea	May	1975
2. Improved relations with China	May	1975
3. Soviet and Algerian support for insurgents against Morocco	January	1976
4. Civil war in Lebanon	March	1976
5. Dispute between Kenya and Uganda	July	1976
6. Security of Tunisia	July	1976
7. U.S. soldiers killed in Korea tree cutting incident	August	1976
8. Safety of Americans in Uganda	February	1977
9. War between Ethiopia and Somalia	February	1978
10. Invasion of Shaba province, Zaire	May	1978
11. Concern over rights of passage in sea of Okhotsk	June	1978
12. Civil strife in Nicaragua	September	1978
13. Soviet request for joint maneuvers with Finland and concern over rights of passage in Baltic Sea	September	1978
14. MiG-23 aircraft stationed in Cuba	November	1978
15. Political crisis in Iran	December	1978
16. War between North and South Yemen	March	1979

Incident	*Beginning of Relevant Change*	
17. Soviet troops in Cuba	October	1979
18. Park Chung Hee assassinated in South Korea	October	1979
19. Hostage crisis in Iran	November	1979
20. Peace treaty in Rhodesia	December	1979
21. Soviet invasion of Afghanistan: Carter doctrine	January	1980
22. Civil strife in South Korea	May	1980
23. Vietnamese incursion into Thailand	July	1980
24. Security of Persian Gulf: Iran-Iraq War	September	1980
25. Political crisis in Poland	December	1980
26. Improved relations with Morocco	January	1981
27. Insurgents in El Salvador	January	1981
28. Border dispute between Ecuador and Peru	February	1981
29. Improved relations with Liberia	April	1981
30. Syrian missiles in Lebanon	May	1981
31. Dispute over rights of passage in gulf of Sidra	August	1981
32. Security of Central America	October	1981
33. Sadat assassinated in Egypt and security of Sudan	October	1981
34. Security of Middle East and Persian Gulf	November	1981
35. Nicaraguan support for insurgency in El Salvador	January	1982
36. Egypt-Israel treaty: Sinai peacekeeping force	March	1982
37. Falkland Islands war between Britain and Argentina	May	1982
38. Israeli invasion of Lebanon	June	1982
39. Ethiopian attacks on Somalia	July	1982
40. Security of Honduras	July	1982
41. Cease-fire in Lebanon: Beirut peacekeeping force	August	1982
42. Massacre of Palestinians: Beirut peacekeeping force	September	1982
43. Dispute over rights of passage off coast of Vietnam	November	1982
44. Improved relations with Morocco	November	1982
45. Relations with Oman and security of Persian Gulf	November	1982
46. Security of Honduras	February	1983
47. Tension between Libya and Sudan	February	1983
48. Nicaraguan support for insurgency in El Salvador	March	1983

Incident	*Beginning of Relevant Change*	
49. Security of Caribbean states	March	1983
50. Thai forces clash with Vietnamese troops in Thailand	April	1983
51. Insurgency in Central America	June	1983
52. Syrian involvement in civil strife in Lebanon	June	1983
53. Security of Central America	July	1983
54. Libyan intervention in civil war in Chad	July	1983
55. Civil war in Lebanon	August	1983
56. Bomb attack on government officials of South Korea	October	1983
57. Security of Persian Gulf	October	1983
58. Disorder in Grenada	October	1983
59. Security of Western Europe	November	1983
60. Attacks on U.S. forces in Lebanon	December	1983
61. Nicaraguan support for insurgency in El Salvador	February	1984
62. Elections in El Salvador	March	1984
63. Libyan air attack against Sudan	March	1984
64. Security of Central America	April	1984
65. Security of Caribbean Sea	April	1984
66. Iranian threat to shipping in Persian Gulf	May	1984
67. Cut in U.S. aid to Nicaraguan insurgents	July	1984
68. Concern over rights of passage in gulf of Sidra	July	1984
69. Mines in gulf of Suez	August	1984
70. Bomb attack on U.S. Embassy in Lebanon	September	1984
71. Security of Central America	November	1984

Several patterns can be discerned in the political use of force in recent years. It is clear that most of the incidents are associated with only a few types of situations in each region of the world (table 3–1). In South Asia, there was no activity at all, although throughout this period the United States and the Soviet Union were increasing the size of their naval forces in the Indian Ocean area. In the 1946–1975 period, there were only three incidents in South Asia, all related to conflicts involving India. In the absence of such a conflict in the more recent period, there were no political actions by U.S. forces.

In sub-Saharan Africa, there were five incidents: two related to the Amin regime in Uganda, one related to instability in Zaire,[22] one to support for the Rhodesian peace process, and one demonstrating ties to the government of Liberia. South America also remains an area of relative inaction, with only one minor incident actually occurring on that continent.[23]

Table 3–1
Percentage Distribution of Incidents

Time Period	Western Hemisphere	Europe	Middle East and North Africa	South Asia and Sub-Saharan Africa	Southeast and East Asia
1946–1975	28	20	18	6	28
1975–1984	30	4	45	7	14

Note: The incidents for 1946–1975 are from Barry M. Blechman and Stephen S. Kaplan, *Force without War* (Washington, D.C.: Brookings, 1977), p. 33.

In East and Southeast Asia, there were ten incidents. Five of these involved Korea. Activity in East Asia in recent years has dropped well below the postwar historical level. While the Vietnam conflict continued, between 1966 and 1975, over 36 percent of U.S. military actions throughout the world occurred in this area.[24]

Another area of reduced activity is Europe. This continent was the scene of only four incidents during the period under study. Although the use of U.S. forces to influence policy had been declining in Europe since the very active 1946–1948 period, the present level of activity is the lowest in the entire postwar period.

In the Western Hemisphere, almost all U.S. military actions were focused, as in past periods, on the Caribbean and Central America. The Reagan administration has shown a willingness to get involved in the region, and the use of force to influence local governments in the area has begun to rival the attention given to such efforts between 1956 and 1965.[25]

The most dramatic redirection of U.S. military involvement has been toward the Middle East and North Africa. Between 1966 and 1975, U.S. actions in this region had risen to 32 percent of the worldwide total, with continued activity expected.[26] Yet with instability in the Persian Gulf and the Horn of Africa adding to the omnipresent Arab-Israeli turmoil, the level of involvement has increased even further, to comprise nearly half of all worldwide U.S. uses of armed forces in the 1975–1984 period.

Static or routine deployments of U.S. forces should broadly reflect inherent security interests along with the persistent needs for the political use of force depicted in this study. For years, the gradual increase of conflict incidents in the Middle East failed to prompt a change in the overseas deployment pattern of U.S. naval, air, or ground forces. The cumulative effects of events such as the oil crises of the late 1970s and the Soviet invasion of Afghanistan, however, finally provoked corresponding shifts in military force deployments. One and occasionally two carrier task groups now operate regularly in the Indian Ocean area, limited basing rights have been obtained in the Middle East, and substantial air and ground units now routinely exercise in the region.

The identities of the participants in the incidents of the political use of force illustrate another interesting trend. To be considered a participant in an incident, a country's behavior had to have been a target of the U.S. military action or a country had to play a special role in determining the outcome of the incident.[27] The rapprochement with China clearly has had an effect. Yet involvement of the Soviet Union in U.S. military action is consistent with historical levels (table 3–2).[28]

Other trends can be observed in the nature of the military forces used in the incidents being studied. One trend that remains constant is in the use of naval forces (table 3–3). Throughout the postwar period, the United States turned most frequently to naval units as an instrument of crisis management and political influence. Aircraft carriers were a frequent component of naval action, involved in 35 (64 percent) of the recent incidents where naval forces were used. The common use of naval forces should come as no surprise. Ships are more easily moved; they are less intrusive; and such activity is a traditional function of the navy.

Ground combat forces have been used less often than naval forces, though there has been an increase in recent years. As in the past, when ground combat forces are used, they are usually used in strength. In the majority of deployments or changes in the disposition of ground forces, over a battalion of troops was involved.

Table 3–2
Percentage of Incidents in Which the Soviet Union and China
Were Participants

Time Period	Soviet Union	China
1946–1975	34	14
1975–1984	32	1

Note: For the time period 1946–1975, see Blechman and Kaplan, *Force without War*, p. 36.

Table 3–3
Percentage Use of Armed Forces in Incidents

Time Period	Naval	Army	Marine	Land-based Air Forces
1946–1975	82	18	36	48
1975–1984	77	32	27	56

Note: For the time period 1946–1975, see Blechman and Kaplan, *Force without War*, p. 36.

The use of land-based air forces generally has been more frequent. This use does not necessarily equate to the use of combat aircraft. On numerous occasions transport aircraft alone provided the support that demonstrated U.S. interest, and transport aircraft almost invariably accompany any deployment of army ground combat units. A noteworthy feature of more recent uses of land-based aircraft is the increasing use of AWACS aircraft for political ends. While reconnaissance aircraft were used in the 1946–1975 era, most often they were maritime patrol aircraft looking for Cuban-supported guerrillas in the Caribbean.[29] The AWACS planes, with their modern dimension of long-range detection and communications, command, and control (C[3]) capability, are a new element of air power that has become a significant tool of crisis management. In ten incidents (25 percent of those involving land-based air forces), AWACS aircraft were used, often on their own, to defuse a situation by illustrating the U.S. power to monitor events.

Different levels of force were used by the United States in the various incidents. To aid analysis, Blechman and Kaplan adopted the following scale to reflect the varying levels of military effort (see table 3–4 for definitions):

Level 1. Use of strategic or theater nuclear unit plus at least one major force component (naval, ground or air).[30]

Level 2. Two or three major force components used but not strategic nuclear units.

Level 3. Either one major force component or strategic nuclear unit used.

Level 4. At least one standard component used, no major components and no strategic nuclear units.

Level 5. Minor components of force used only.

This scale is related to ordinary usage of such forces in past experiences; for example, combatant naval forces used in an incident usually include one carrier task group, and combatant land-based air forces used in an incident typically consist of a squadron of aircraft.

Table 3–4
Levels of Force

Level of Force	Naval	Ground	Land-based Air
Major	Two or more aircraft carrier task groups	Over a battalion	One or more combat wings
Standard	One carrier task group	Up to a battalion, over one company	One or more combat squadrons
Minor	No carriers included	Not over one company	Less than a squadron

Table 3–5
Levels of Effort, in Descending Order of Magnitude

Level of Effort	Percentage of Incidents, 1946–1975[a]	Percentage of Incidents, 1975–1984[b]
1	7.0	1.4
2	8.4	11.3
3	21.4	32.3
4	29.8	25.4
5	33.5	29.6

[a]From Blechman and Kaplan, *Force without War*, p. 52.
[b]During the August 1976 incident arising from the killing of two U.S. soldiers in Korea, F-111 aircraft were sent to Korea from the United States, and B-52 bombers based in Guam flew demonstrative missions as part of a display of U.S. power. See Bernard Gwertzman, "U.S. Carries Out a Show of Force at Korean DMZ," *New York Times*, August 22, 1976, p. 1. Although variants of both of these types of aircraft are employed by the Strategic Air Command in a nuclear delivery role, there is no evidence that the aircraft used in this incident were operating in such a role at the time of their deployment.

Using the scale in table 3–4, one can assess the levels of force used for political purposes in recent years and compare the conclusions with those of the remainder of the postwar period (table 3–5). As might be expected, the most significant uses of force have been less frequent in the post-Vietnam era.[31] Such a decline, however, is not a new development. The majority of all level 1 efforts in the postwar period occurred between 1956 and 1965. The same atypical concentration was true for level 2 and level 3 efforts. Indeed, since World War II, the absolute majority of all U.S. uses of force for political ends, at all levels, is found within this same period of 1956–1965.[32]

To test the post-Vietnam contraction hypothesis, it may be revealing to compare the nine and a half-year period under study here (May 1975–December 1984) with the nine and a half-year period immediately preceding it (January 1966–May 1975) (table 3–6). The earlier period shows more incidents at the highest force level, yet the recent period has many more incidents at the three highest force levels. Table 3–6 does not show that the post-Vietnam era has been less active but instead suggests that more recent policymakers have been equally willing to use standard and even major force components, being more reluctant only in the use of nuclear forces to deal with the political situations that they have confronted. The Reagan administration has contributed dramatically to this conclusion, with 63 percent of the incidents in the 1975–1984 period occurring during President Reagan's first term.

The data also help to provide an answer to the question of whether different types of forces are more likely to be used as the overall level of force increases or declines. Policymakers seldom resort to using major (two or more aircraft carrier task groups) components of naval forces on the frequent

Table 3–6
Comparison of Levels of Force

Time Period	Military Level of Effort					Total Number of Incidents
	1	*2*	*3*	*4*	*5*	
1966–1975[a]	2	6	6	13	20	47
1975–1984	1	8	23	18	21	71

[a]Data from Blechman and Kaplan, *Force without War*, p. 52.

occasions when such forces are used for political purposes. This fact is probably a reflection of the delicate balance in the assignment of carriers to their respective fleets around the world. The prolonged assignment of two carriers to any particular location is bound to create weaknesses elsewhere in a fleet's area of responsibility (with the current number of available carriers). One aircraft carrier task group is more likely to be used and, since each carrier usually has a complement of nearly a hundred aircraft, it can provide significant power projection capability.

In contrast, on the more infrequent occasions when ground combat forces are used, they generally tend to be used or prepared for use in strengths of more than a battalion. This fact continues to verify the Blechman and Kaplan statement that ground forces are likely to be used only in the more significant actions where such substantial deployments are most appropriate.[33]

Patterns in the use of land-based air forces probably are indicative of three facts. First, land-based air forces—usually home based in the United States or Europe—are more difficult to use on a large scale for temporary overseas deployments because they require substantial support elements. Second, many of the uses of such air units in this study involved the use of AWACS aircraft, which are deployed in small numbers (usually two or four). Third, the common availability of substantial air support from nearby aircraft carriers has obviated some of the need for use of land-based air forces.

The Question of Utility

Decision makers continue to rely on the armed forces to support foreign policy. It is difficult, however, to ascertain whether the armed forces have been useful in achieving the goals expected of them. There are infinite sources of human behavior, and it always will be difficult to pinpoint why people acted the way they did in a given situation. An honest recognition of the limits of the data, however, does not foreclose all possibilities for analysis.

Blechman and Kaplan have devised a methodology that this study employs, with one exception. Deeming it impractical to discuss the utility of 215 (actually 218) separate incidents, Blechman and Kaplan limited their analysis to a carefully selected cross-section of 33 of the 215 incidents. Since the sample for this study is somewhat more manageable, all 71 of the incidents are included in the examination of utility.

There are three important features of this methodology. In order to analyze what U.S. policymakers hoped to achieve in a particular instance, Blechman and Kaplan focused only on tangible operational objectives. It is difficult to know in retrospect what goals or motives may impel a policy-maker to act in a particular way, but it is easier to recognize the immediate objective. For example, in looking at the Iranian hostage crisis, some observers felt that certain U.S. military moves were motivated, at least in part, by President Carter's domestic political concerns or his self-image as a decisive leader. This perception may or may not be true, yet it is clear that Carter's decisions had the immediate tangible objective of securing the safe release of the hostages.

Another feature of this methodology is that tangible objectives usually have tangible outcomes. We cannot know with confidence whether a U.S. military presence caused the hostages to be released unharmed and without having been put on trial, but we do know that the hostages were released. Rather than asking problematic questions of causation, this method focuses on outcomes. The persuasive value of the conclusions lies only in the persuasive force of the correlations.

A final aspect of this methodology is the distinctions drawn between different modes and styles of using force. In coercive diplomacy, force can be used in one of two ways to threaten an antagonist: to deter the target states from doing something undesirable and to compel the target state to take some action (to do or stop doing something). In cooperative diplomacy, military force can support a friend by serving one of two functions: it can assure a friendly target state that the user of the force will continue to do or not do something, or it can induce a friendly target state to do or not do something itself.[34]

During the May 1978 invasion of the Shaba (formerly Katanga) province in Zaire, for example, the United States airlifted Belgian and French paratroopers to the scene and alerted a brigade of the 82nd Airborne Division for possible use in the area. In addition to the humanitarian goal of rescuing Europeans trapped in the mining town of Kolwezi, the United States sought to compel the insurgents in Shaba to terminate their invasion and to compel Angola to curtail its support for the insurgents. The United States also sought to deter the Soviet Union and Cuba from giving indirect support to such adventures. At the same time, the United States hoped to induce Belgium and France to provide troops to restore order in Zaire, and it sought to assure the government of Zaire of U.S. support in the maintenance of the central government's authority.[35]

Regardless of the mode of use, armed forces also can be used in a variety of styles. A direct use of force occurs when military action is aimed explicitly at a target without any intermediaries. An indirect use acts on the target either through an intermediary or by an implication unrelated to the action itself. In the Zaire example, the United States acted directly against the Shaba insurgents in order to act indirectly against the insurgents' backers in Angola, Cuba, and the Soviet Union.

Force is sometimes used neither to deter, compel, induce, nor assure a target. A military unit might be alerted or deployed without any concrete intention as to how it will be used but simply to have force available to indicate U.S. concern and readiness. In such a situation, the substantive action desired from the target is not tied explicitly to the military movement, and the movements may not be known even to the target. In such instances force is used only as a latent instrument.[36] During the 1981 confrontation between Syria and Israel over Syrian activity and missile emplacements in Lebanon, the United States kept two aircraft carrier task groups off the Lebanese coast. Although the United States was deeply involved in trying to resolve the crisis and deter Soviet intervention, there was no clear connection between these diplomatic efforts and the military movements.[37] Yet, "when used as a latent instrument, military activity will often serve to remind the actor that the United States can and might act."[38]

Appendix 3B presents, for each incident examined for the study reported in this chapter, the actors and the primary action (if any) that the United States desired from the actor in the incident, along with a description of the mode and style of the force used to achieve the desired outcome. The appendix also contains a judgment, many of them subjective, as to whether this outcome was achieved in the short term (6 months or less) or in the longer term (three years).

Several general patterns emerge from the data in appendix 3B. A cursory review shows that U.S. armed forces recently usually have had the political objectives of either affecting the use of force by others or reinforcing relationships with friends and allies. When U.S. policymakers sought to influence the use of force by others, they almost always sought to contain or terminate the use of force. When U.S. policymakers concerned themselves with the maintenance of authority in other governments, they invariably sought to preserve and maintain existing governments (with the possible exception of Nicaragua). In contrast, the Soviet Union, which has a rather more dynamic conception of the way non-Communist countries ought to evolve, often has used its military forces to upset the authority of existing regimes.[39] Even in dealing with fraternal Communist regimes, Soviet military forces have been used five times more often in a coercive role than in a cooperative one.[40]

Table 3–7
Modes of Using Armed Forces
(in percentages)

	Modes				
Time Period	*Compel*	*Deter*	*Induce*	*Assure*	*Latent*
1946–1975[a]	29	19	8	18	26
1975–1984	14	19	18	31	19

[a]From Blechman and Kaplan, *Force without War,* p. 83.

Of 199 operational objectives sought in the 71 incidents, U.S. armed forces were used to compel, deter, induce, or assure with respect to specific conduct about four-fifths of the time. The remaining fifth of the targets were influenced by latent uses of force. Armed forces were used most frequently to assure friends and least frequently to compel enemies. This pattern differs greatly from the general pattern of the postwar years (table 3–7).

Compelling an opponent to modify behavior to perform some concrete action is the most difficult task that the military can be called upon to achieve. Whether from experience or from a sense of diminished power, policymakers now apparently have taken this lesson to heart. Yet in this period of changing perceptions of power, much more attention is being paid to cooperative uses of force, inducing U.S. allies to assist it and reassuring them about U.S. commitments.

As in the 1946–1975 period, force is used most often to support directly or coerce a particular actor. Indirect efforts to support or coerce an actor by supporting or coercing another actor have remained infrequent.[41]

Findings

The decision to use military force for political ends is bound to be the product of a mix of perceived interests and capabilities. The information presented in this study suggests how, in the short term, the mix of U.S. interests and U.S. capabilities has been perceived by policymakers in the aftermath of U.S. failure in Vietnam. Tentative inferences can be made from the data presented, demonstrating areas of both continuity and change.

In the area of continuity, U.S. policymakers did not withdraw to the neo-isolationism that some observers predicted. They continued to perceive U.S. interests with a broad sense of global responsibility and acted frequently to support those interests. U.S. military deployments to support U.S. policy, despite some variation among administrations, have continued to occur at a rate consistent with the pattern since 1946 and with the level of the preceding decade. During the 1960s, policymakers indicated that U.S. troops were in Vietnam not just to protect the people and resources of Vietnam but also to defend the credibility of U.S. commitments all over the world. The concern with credibility has not diminished. The most common rationale for U.S. military action has been and remains the desire to underscore the credibility of U.S. commitments around the world to both enemies and friends.

There have been changes. The geographic focus and targets of U.S. action have shifted to new areas of concern, particularly the Middle East. The focus on the Soviet Union has not changed, though, and there has been a revival of historic interest in the Central America–Caribbean area. The most important changes are probably in the perception of U.S. capabilities. The style of U.S. military deployments has shifted somewhat to lower levels of force employed in a less intrusive way. The key question, then, is whether a growing asymmetry has developed between interests and capabilities, leading to increasing frustration and inadequate half-measures, or whether a less direct military style has served U.S. interests just as well or better than in the past. This chapter does not try to offer an answer to this question, which I suspect has a mixed answer, yet some superficial evidence to be used in formulating an answer can be found in reviewing the outcomes of recent uses of forces.

To determine overall outcomes from the use of force, this study again follows Blechman and Kaplan; an outcome of an incident is considered to be favorable if at least two-thirds of the operational objectives were achieved. By this criterion, about 86 percent of the incidents in the 1975–1984 period had favorable outcomes in relation to the objectives of the decision makers. Where calculable, this high correlation of successes remained relatively constant in both the short and long term. This level of favorable outcomes compares well with the 73 percent short-term and 45 percent long-term rates of positive correlation in the 1946–1975 period.[42]

Most of the explanation for recent improvements in the rate of favorable outcomes is linked to changes in the objectives being sought and the way in which force was used. Policymakers recently have been more reluctant to use force to compel behavior by an antagonist. This choice has improved the likelihood of a positive outcome from military action; between 1946 and 1975, force used to compel action by another tended to be successful 68 percent of the time in the short term and only 18 percent of the time over the longer term. Between 1975 and 1984, the rate of positive outcomes associated with efforts to compel conduct remained relatively low, at only 52 percent; in the recent period, this mode of force was used for only 14 percent of the operational objectives as opposed to 29 percent in the 1946–1975 period.[43]

Additionally, past efforts to use force often (20 percent of the objectives) were aimed, without great success, at influencing third parties to curtail or withhold support from nations or groups hostile to U.S. interests.[44] Policymakers recently have used the armed forces less frequently to achieve such elusive goals; occasional efforts in this area, as in Central America, have not been notably successful. This point is consistent with another: both currently and in the past, direct actions are more likely to be effective than those aimed indirectly at another target.

It also may be useful and informative to examine the nature and level of force used in the incidents. This information is compiled in appendix 3C. In the 1946–1975 period, the evidence tended to show that outcomes were less favorable when higher levels of force were used. Blechman and Kaplan speculated that this lack of success was because greater levels of force were used in situations of greater difficulty and risk.[45] Yet in the 1975–1984 period, probabilities of success were consistently high at all levels of force, and although the rates of positive outcomes were slightly lower at force levels 2 and 3, they are still quite high. (Refer to appendixes 3B and 3C.)

This evidence suggests that regardless of the general level of force being used, positive outcomes will remain likely if the force is used in a realistic mode and aimed at immediately achievable objectives. As in the past, recent favorable results "occurred far more frequently when the objective was to reinforce behavior than when it was to modify behavior."[46] This conclusion may best explain the generally higher success rates for the political uses of force in recent years.

What conclusion can one infer from these data about the post-Vietnam isolationist hypothesis—that the United States became reluctant to use military force in the wake of its Vietnam experience? Viewed in terms of the incidence of the use of force, U.S. military employments since 1975 have continued at a rate consistent with that of the 1946–1975 period. This is an important conclusion, one that refutes much conventional wisdom. As illustrated by the Nixon doctrine and the 1973 War Powers Act, U.S. declaratory policy and official rhetoric have avowed a greater disinclination to use military force since Vietnam. In fact, however, the incidence of military employments has continued at a consistent rate; the Vietnam experience has not changed the frequency with which the United States resorts to the use of force short of war.

Qualitatively, however, the U.S. use of military force has changed since Vietnam in important ways: locus (increasingly concentrated in the Middle East), level of force used (a shift away from the use of substantial force), and, most important, objectives served by the use of force (a shift away from efforts to compel or constrain behavior; a shift toward efforts to assure allies or reinforce behavior). Apparently motivated, in large part, by concerns for buttressing the credibility of U.S. commitments, the United States increasingly has used military force since Vietnam to reassure—rather than to coerce—other countries. As a result of these changes, the United States has been more successful in its use of military force since Vietnam.

Notes

1. Bernard Gwertzman, "Carter Voices Concern of U.S. at Uganda Move," *New York Times,* February 26, 1977, p. 6.

2. Michael T. Kaufman, "Amin Prohibits Exit by 200 Americans," *New York Times,* February 26, 1977, p. 1. Most of the Americans then in Uganda were missionaries.

3. Robert D. McFadden, "Ex-U.S. Envoy to Uganda Fears for Safety of Americans There," *New York Times,* February 27, 1977, p. 10.

4. Gwertzman, "Carter Voices Concern," p. 1.

5. Barbara A. Gilmore, "Chronology of U.S. Naval Events 1977," unpublished document prepared for Operational Archives Branch, Naval Historical Center, Department of the Navy, April 25, 1978. This task group, number 77.6, had been in the Indian Ocean since the beginning of February 1977; it was due to return to the Seventh Fleet toward the end of that month.

6. "Uganda Invites U.S. to Send Observers for Amin's Meeting," *New York Times,* February 28, 1977, p. 1.

7. Michael T. Kaufman, "Uganda's Radio Says U.S. Need Not Worry over Citizens' Fate," *New York Times,* February 28, 1977, p. 1.

8. Graham Hovey, "Washington Pleased as Amin Lifts Ban on Americans' Exit," *New York Times,* March 2, 1977, p. 1. For a discussion of U.S. policy toward the Amin regime, see Richard H. Ullman, "Human Rights and Economic Power: The U.S. versus Idi Amin," *Foreign Affairs* 56 (Summer 1978): 529. For a discussion of U.S. naval power in the Indian Ocean and its strategic role with regard to Africa, see Chester Crocker, "The African Dimension of Indian Ocean Policy," *Orbis* 20 (1976): 3.

9. This announcement was in the State of the Union address delivered on January 23, 1980. Jimmy Carter, *Keeping Faith: Memoirs of a President* (New York: Bantam Books, 1982), p. 483.

10. Bernard Gwertzman, "U.S. and Egypt Hold Joint Air Exercises as a Crisis Reaction," *New York Times,* January 9, 1980, p. 1; see also Richard Burt, "Carter, under Pressure of Crises, Tests New Foreign Policy Goals," *New York Times,* January 9, 1980, p. 1.

11. Brent Baker, "Naval and Maritime Events 1980," *United States Naval Institute Proceedings* 107 (May 1981): 50–52; Barbara A. Gilmore, "Chronology of U.S. Naval Events 1980," unpublished document prepared for Operational Archives Branch, U.S. Naval History Division, Department of the Navy, January 25, 1981.

12. Christopher S. Wren, "U.S. Phantoms Arrive at Egyptian Base for Operations," *New York Times,* July 11, 1980, p. A3. In connection with this exercise, code named Proud Phantom, over 400 U.S. Air Force personnel were stationed in Egypt.

13. R. Lopez, "Exercise Bright Star," *International Defense Review* 14, no. 2 (1981): 140; see also Richard Halloran, "U.S. Troops Taking Off for Egypt, Get

Some Advice on Camel Drivers," *New York Times,* November 12, 1980, p. A6; Henry Tanner, "Egyptians Welcome Troop Ties with U.S.," *New York Times,* November 12, 1980, p. A7; see generally Hermann Eilts, "Security Considerations in the Persian Gulf," *International Security 5* (Fall 1980): 79.

14. Sun Tzu, *The Art of War,* trans. Samuel B. Griffith (New York: Oxford University Press, 1963), p. 77.

15. Edward N. Luttwak, *The Grand Strategy of the Roman Empire: From the First Century A.D. to the Third* (Baltimore: Johns Hopkins University Press, 1976), pp. 2–3.

16. Barry M. Blechman and Stephen S. Kaplan, *Force without War: U.S. Armed Forces as a Political Instrument* (Washington, D.C.: Brookings Institution, 1977). The use of U.S. armed forces to influence events short of war was the subject of a major Brookings Institution study authored in 1977 by Barry Blechman, Stephen Kaplan, and several contributors. Covering the period between 1946 and the *Mayaguez* incident in 1975, the study systematically cataloged all declassified incidents in which U.S. armed forces were used for political objectives, documenting 218 such incidents. Ibid., pp. 547–553. This work was well received, and a companion volume was subsequently published on the political use of Soviet armed forces. Stephen S. Kaplan, *Diplomacy of Power: Soviet Armed Forces as a Political Instrument* (Washington, D.C.: Brookings Institution, 1981). The figure usually referred to is 215 incidents, but the authors noted that they omitted 3 incidents from the list cataloged in the text. Ibid., p. 547, n. 1. Although the Blechman and Kaplan study purported to go up to the end of 1975, their research actually tailed off with the *Mayaguez* incident in May 1975. This chapter lists two additional incidents for 1975.

17. See n. 16.

18. Blechman and Kaplan, *Force without War,* p. 11. In addition to a macro analysis of the compiled incidents, Blechman and Kaplan included microanalyses of particular incidents authored by various contributors. This latter aspect has been omitted here.

19. Ibid., p. 12.

20. See the background discussion in Fred Hiatt, "Four U.S. Navy Jets Challenge Libya's Sovereignty," *Washington Post,* July 27, 1984, p. 1.

21. Blechman and Kaplan, *Force without War,* p. 16, n. 7. The correlation was 89 percent, with roughly congruent time distribution.

22. Although the United States provided airlift support to Zaire and to Moroccan troops quelling the invasion of Shaba province by ex-Katangese gendarmes in March 1977, this help was not listed as an incident because the airlift was accomplished by civilian charters. See Bernard Gwertzman, "Vance Says Invaders in Zaire Threaten Vital Copper Mining," *New York Times,* March 17, 1977, p. 1; Department of the Air Force, Office of Military Airlift Command History, "Significant Airlift Missions," unpublished memorandum to commander-in-chief, Military Airlift Command, September 15, 1982.

23. U.S. support for Britain during the Falklands War was provided (to the extent the nature of this support has been declassified) only in the North Atlantic area and at Ascension Island.

24. Blechman and Kaplan, *Force without War,* p. 33.

25. Ibid.

26. Ibid.

27. Ibid., p. 36.

28. Ibid.

29. Ibid., p. 46.

30. See ibid., p. 50, table 2–9. Theater nuclear units are included as analogous to strategic nuclear units in measuring levels of force.

31. The only recent incidents with uses of force as high as level 2 were the August 1976 Korean incident, the measures adopted to underscore the Carter doctrine in 1980, the Israel-Syria confrontation over missiles in Lebanon during 1981, the Lebanon crisis accompanying the Israeli invasion of 1982, the Big Pine II demonstration of force in Central America during 1983, the deployment of nuclear missiles to Western Europe in 1983, and the Ocean Venture demonstration of force in the Caribbean during 1984.

32. Blechman and Kaplan, *Force without War,* p. 52.

33. Ibid., p. 57.

34. Ibid., p. 71. As Blechman and Kaplan pointed out, these theoretical distinctions are elaborated by the substantial body of literature in this area. Ibid., p. 71, n. 3.

35. See James Cole, "Zaire Airlift," *Airlift Operations Review* 2 (October–December 1980): 14; Department of the Air Force, "Significant Airlift Missions"; Henri J.G. Depoorter, "Kolwezi," *Military Review* 59 (September 1979): 29; Bruce Palmer, "U.S. Security Interests and Africa South of the Sahara," *AEI Defense Review* 2, no. 6 (1978): 38–39; Edward Sleeper, "Zaire Airlift: Another Perspective," *Airlift Operations Review* 3 (October–December 1981): 21; Crawford Young, "Zaire: The Unending Crisis," *Foreign Affairs* 57 (Fall 1978): 169.

36. Blechman and Kaplan, *Force without War,* pp. 72–73.

37. See, for example, Barbara A. Gilmore, "Chronology of U.S. Naval Events 1981," unpublished document prepared for Operational Archives Branch, Naval Historical Center, Department of the Navy, January 1982.

38. Blechman and Kaplan, *Force without War,* p. 73.

39. Kaplan, *Diplomacy of Power,* p. 334. Kaplan's survey covers the period between 1944 and 1979.

40. Ibid.

41. Blechman and Kaplan, *Force without War,* p. 83.

42. Ibid., p. 87.

43. Ibid., p. 89.

44. Ibid.

45. Ibid., p. 95.

46. Ibid., p. 107.

Appendix 3A:
Bibliography for Incidents

1. Korea, 1975. "U.S. Troop Buildup in Korea Reported," *New York Times,* May 31, 1975, p. 8; see Peter Ward, "North Korea Believed Preparing Attack on the South," *Detroit News,* June 1, 1975, p. 8; see also Ralph N. Clough, *Deterrence and Defense in Korea: The Role of U.S. Forces* (Washington, D.C.: Brookings Institution, 1976).

2. China, 1975. Bernard Gwertzman, "U.S. Has Removed Combat Aircraft Based on Taiwan," *New York Times,* June 8, 1975, p. 1; Dana Adams Schmidt, "Ford Aides Split over Taiwan," *Christian Science Monitor,* June 9, 1975, p. 1; see generally Victor Li and John Lewis, "Resolving the China Dilemma: Advancing Normalization, Preserving Security," *International Security* 2 (Summer 1977): 11.

3. Morocco, 1976. Barbara A. Gilmore, "Chronology of U.S. Naval Events 1976," unpublished document prepared for Operational Archives Branch, Naval Historical Center, Department of the Navy, January 15, 1977; J.B. Finkelstein, "Naval and Maritime Events," *United States Naval Institute Proceedings* 103 (May 1977): 50; see Richard Mowrer, "Saharan Clash Due?" *Christian Science Monitor,* January 5, 1976, p. 18; "Moroccans Detain Soviet Cargo Ship," *New York Times,* January 6, 1976, p. 7; Stephen S. Kaplan, *Diplomacy of Power: Soviet Armed Forces as a Political Instrument* (Washington, D.C.: Brookings Institution, 1981), p. 199.

4. Lebanon, 1976. "U.S. Has Evacuation Plan," *New York Times,* March 30, 1976, p. 4; "U.S. Warning Is Renewed," *New York Times,* March 30, 1976, p. 4; Bernard Gwertzman, "Ford and Hussein Ask Beirut Truce," *New York Times,* March 31, 1976, p. 16; David K. Shipler, "Soviet Warns U.S. on a Lebanon Move," *New York Times,* April 8, 1976, p. 3; Bernard Gwertzman, "Kissinger Warns Syrian Acts Test Israeli Patience," *New York Times,* April 15, 1976, p. 1; Gilmore, "Chronology, 1976"; see generally Adeed Dawisha, *Syria and the Lebanese Crisis* (London: Macmillan, 1980); Walid Khalidi, *Conflict and Violence in Lebanon: Confrontation in the Middle East* (Cambridge: Harvard Center for International Affairs, 1980).

5. Uganda, 1976. John W. Finney, "U.S. Sends Frigate to Kenya in

Show," *New York Times,* July 13, 1976, p. 1; Gilmore, "Chronology, 1976"; Finkelstein, "Naval and Maritime Events," p. 244.

6. Tunisia, 1976. *Keesing's Contemporary Archives,* June 11, 1976, p. 27774; Gilmore, "Chronology, 1976."

7. Korea, 1976. Bernard Gwertzman, "U.S. Crisis Unit Takes Up DMZ Killings," *New York Times,* August 20, 1976, p. A3; Andrew H. Malcolm, "Both Sides Raise Korea Readiness," *New York Times,* August 20, 1976, p. 1; Gwertzman, "U.S. Asks Amends by North Koreans," *New York Times,* August 21, 1976, p. 1; Gwertzman, "U.S. Carries Out a Show of Force at Korean DMZ," *New York Times,* August 22, 1976, p. 1; Shim Jae Hoon, "U.S. Action Hailed by South Koreans," *New York Times,* August 22, 1976, p. 4; Gwertzman, "U.S. Softens Its Reaction to North Korea Regrets," *New York Times,* August 24, 1976, p. 4; "U.S. Still Sending B-52s over Korea," *New York Times,* August 25, 1976, p. 9; Gilmore, "Chronology, 1976"; George S. Brown, *United States Military Posture for FY 1978* (Washington, D.C.: Joint Chiefs of Staff, 1977), p. 48; Office of Military Airlift Command (MAC) History, "Significant Airlift Missions," unpublished memorandum to CINCMAC, September 15, 1982.

8. Uganda, 1977. See notes 1–8.

9. Somalia, 1978. *Keesing's Contemporary Archives,* May 26, 1978, pp. 28989, 28993; Barbara A. Gilmore, "Chronology of U.S. Naval Events 1978," unpublished document prepared for Operational Archives Branch, Naval Historical Center, Department of the Navy, February 15, 1979; see generally Peter Schwab, "Cold War on the Horn of Africa," *African Affairs* 77 (1978): 306–320. An aircraft carrier battle group was moved in connection with this incident, but the movement was apparently designed so as not to send any particular signal to the states involved. See Zbigniew Brzezinski, *Power and Principle: Memoirs of the National Security Advisor, 1977–1981* (New York: Farrar, Straus and Giroux, 1983), pp. 182–183; Cyrus Vance, *Hard Choices: Critical Years in America's Foreign Policy* (New York: Simon and Schuster, 1983), pp. 86–87.

10. Zaire, 1978. See note 35; see also Vance, *Hard Choices,* pp. 89–90.

11. Sea of Okhotsk, 1978. Gilmore, "Chronology, 1978"; see H. Gary Knight, "The Law of the Sea and Naval Missions," *United States Naval Institute Proceedings* 103 (June 1977): 32, 39.

12. Nicaragua, 1978. *Keesing's Contemporary Archives,* December 29, 1978, p. 29374; Gilmore, "Chronology, 1978."

13. Baltic Sea, 1978. Gilmore, "Chronology, 1978"; R.D.M. Furlong, "The Threat to Northern Europe," *International Defense Review* 12, no. 4 (1979): 517; see also Ulrich Weisser and Klaus Jancke, "The Problems in the Baltic: Threat and Response," *NATO's Fifteen Nations* 23 (April–May 1978): 52; Ken Booth, "Law and Strategy in Northern Waters," *Naval War College Review* 34 (July–August 1981): 3, 9.

14. Cuba, 1978. Richard Burt, "U.S. Photo Flights Resume over Cuba,"

New York Times, November 17, 1978, p. A11; Terence Smith, "Carter Says Delay on Mideast Accord Would be 'Serious,'" *New York Times,* December 8, 1978, p. 1; see Raymond L. Garthoff, "American Reaction to Soviet Aircraft in Cuba, 1962 and 1978," *Political Science Quarterly* 95 (Fall 1980): 427.

15. Iran, 1978. Bernard Gwertzman, "U.S. Moving Carrier," *New York Times,* December 30, 1978, p. 1; Drew Middleton, "Difficult Military Decisions Faced by U.S. in Iran Crisis," *New York Times,* December 30, 1978, p. 5; Gwertzman, "U.S. Jets Will Visit Saudi Arabia as Show of Support in Tense Area," *New York Times,* January 11, 1979, p. 1; Richard Burt, "U.S. Strategy on Iran Stirs a Fierce Debate," *New York Times,* January 12, 1979, p. A3; Burt, "69 Marines, 6 Copters Are Ready to Act," *New York Times,* February 12, 1979, p. A8; Gilmore, "Chronology, 1978"; William Pranger and Dale Tahtinen, "American Policy Options in Iran and the Persian Gulf," *AEI Foreign Policy and Defense Review* 1 (1979): 1; Gilmore, "Chronology of Naval Events 1979," unpublished document prepared for Operational Archives Branch, Naval Historical Center, Department of the Navy, January 20, 1980; Brent Baker, "Naval and Maritime Events," *United States Naval Institute Proceedings* 106 (May 1980): 50; William H. Sullivan, "Dateline Iran: The Road Not Taken," *Foreign Policy* 40 (1980): 175; Jimmy Carter, *Keeping Faith: Memoirs of a President* (New York: Bantam Books, 1982). The aircraft carrier battle group dispatched to the Persian Gulf region was turned around before it entered the Indian Ocean. Gwertzman, "Carter, Fearing the Impact on Iran, Tells Navy Unit Not to Head There," *New York Times,* January 3, 1979, p. 1; Gilmore, "Chronology, 1979."

16. Yemen, 1979. Richard Burt, "U.S. Sends Ships to Arabian Sea in Yemen Crisis," *New York Times,* March 7, 1979, p. 1; "Southern Yemen Accuses U.S. of Military Aggression," *New York Times,* March 11, 1979, p. 5; Richard Burt, "Intervention in Yemen War Signals Policy Shift," *New York Times,* March 18, 1979, p. E3; Lewis Ware, "Turmoil in Southern Arabia," *Military Review* 59 (November 1979): 51; Gilmore, "Chronology, 1979"; Baker, "Naval and Maritime Events," p. 52; Brzezinski, *Power and Principle,* p. 447.

17. Cuba, 1979. Bernard Gwertzman, "Carter Plans Latin Command and Steps Up Watch on Cuba," *New York Times,* October 2, 1979, p. 1; "Transcript of President's Speech," *New York Times,* October 2, 1979, p. A18; Richard Halloran, "Marines Will Conduct Maneuvers and Fire Artillery in Guantanamo," *New York Times,* October 3, 1979, p. A15; Hedrick Smith, "Carter Says He Feels Soviet Will Alter Brigade in Cuba," *New York Times,* October 3, 1979, p. A14; Gilmore, "Chronology, 1979"; Baker, "Naval and Maritime Events, p. 222; Carter, *Keeping Faith,* pp. 262–263; Brzezinski, *Power and Principle,* pp. 347–352; Gloria Duffy, "Crisis Mangling and the Cuban Brigade," *International Security* 8 (Summer 1983): 67.

18. Korea, 1979. Richard Hurt, "U.S. Deploys Carrier and Planes to Deter Action by North Korea," *New York Times,* October 29, 1979, p. A12; Gilmore, "Chronology, 1979"; Baker, "Naval and Maritime Events," p. 222.

19. Iran, 1979. Richard Halloran, "Carter Sending 6 More Navy Ships, including Carrier, to Arabian Sea," *New York Times,* November 20, 1979, p. 1; "Excerpts from Speech by Khomeini Broadcast over Tehran Radio," *New York Times,* November 21, 1979, p. A13; Bernard Gwertzman, "Carter Shifts Stand," *New York Times,* November 21, 1979, p. 1; Gilmore, "Chronology, 1979"; Baker, "Naval and Maritime Events," p. 226; Barbara A. Gilmore, "Chronology of U.S. Naval Events 1980," unpublished document prepared for Operational Archives Branch, Naval Historical Center, Department of the Navy, January 25, 1981; Brent Baker, "Naval and Maritime Events," *United States Naval Institute Proceedings* 107 (May 1981): 49; Carter, *Keeping Faith,* passim; Brzezinski, *Power and Principle,* p. 483; James F. Kelly, Jr., "Naval Deployments in the Indian Ocean," *United States Naval Institute Proceedings* 109 (May 1983): 174, 179.

20. Rhodesia, 1979. John F. Burnes, "Rhodesian Peace Force Begins Taking Up Its Positions," *New York Times,* December 24, 1979, p. A3; Burnes, "Monitoring Forces All in Rhodesia Now for Cease-Fire Job," *New York Times,* December 26, 1979, p. 1; Brzezinski, *Power and Principle,* pp. 142–143.

21. Persian Gulf, 1980. See notes 9–13.

22. Korea, 1980. Bernard Gwertzman, "U.S. Urges 'Maximum Restraint' on South Korean Military Leaders," *New York Times,* May 23, 1980, p. 1; Henry S. Bradsher, "Restoring Order in Korea Given First Priority by U.S.," *Washington Star,* May 24, 1980, p. 1; Gilmore "Chronology, 1980"; Baker, "Naval and Maritime Events," p. 212.

23. Thailand, 1980. Graham Hovey, "Carter Orders Airlift of Rifles and Artillery to Thais," *New York Times,* July 2, 1980, p. A5; Henry Kamm, "Thailand Uses Vietnamese Raid to Bolster Alliances," *New York Times,* July 4, 1980, p. A4; "U.S. Airlift to Thailand Begins," *New York Times,* July 6, 1980, p. 12; Richard Burt, "U.S. Warily Expands Southeast Asia Security Role," *New York Times,* July 10, 1980, p. A3; *Asian Recorder,* August 12–18, 1980, p. 15602; *Asian Recorder,* September 16–22, 1980, p. 15653; see also address delivered by Morton Abramowicz, former U.S. ambassador to Thailand, Fletcher School of Law and Diplomacy, December 10, 1982.

24. Persian Gulf, 1980. Bernard Gwertzman, "U.S. Grants Saudi Request to Send Command Aircraft," *New York Times,* October 1, 1980, p. A10; Drew Middleton, "Aid for Saudis: A Risk for U.S.," *New York Times,* October 1, 1980, p. 1; Philip Shabecoff, "Brown Discloses U.S. Sends Saudis Ground Radar and 100 Personnel," *New York Times,* October 6, 1980, pp. 1, A14; Edward C. Burks, "U.S. Orders Guided Missile Cruiser

and 2 Tanker Jets to Persian Gulf," *New York Times,* October 12, 1980, p. 18; Bernard Gwertzman and Richard Burt, "Role of the U.S. in Persian Gulf: How It Evolved," *New York Times,* October 12, 1980, pp. 1, 22; Gilmore, "Chronology, 1980"; Baker, "Naval and Maritime Events," pp. 216, 220; Stephen R. Grummon, *The Iran-Iraq War: Islam Embattled* (New York: Praeger, 1982), p. 62; Carter, *Keeping Faith,* pp. 558–559; Brzezinski, *Power and Principle,* pp. 452–454.

25. Poland, 1980. "NATO Naval Forces Primed in Case Poland Is Invaded," *Christian Science Monitor,* December 9, 1980, p. 2; Bradley Graham, "U.S. Sends Planes to Monitor Buildup on Polish Frontier," *Washington Post,* December 10, 1980, p. 1; John Vinocur, "U.S. to Supply NATO with Radar Planes," *New York Times,* December 10, 1980, p. A11; Carter, *Keeping Faith,* pp. 584–585; Brzezinski, *Power and Principle,* pp. 465–468.

26. Morocco, 1981. Barbara A. Gilmore, "Chronology of U.S. Naval Events 1981," unpublished document prepared for Operational Archives Branch, Naval Historical Center, Department of the Navy, January 1982; Alexander M. Haig, Jr., *Caveat: Realism, Reagan, and Foreign Policy* (New York: Macmillan, 1984), pp. 97–98. This incident, which took place during the waning days of the Carter administration, was managed in coordination with the Reagan transition team.

27. El Salvador, 1981. Office of MAC History, "Significant Airlift Missions," September 15, 1982; see also William LeoGrande, "A Splendid Little War," *International Security* 6 (Summer 1981): 27; Paul Sigmund, "Latin America: Change or Continuity," *Foreign Affairs* 60 (1981): 629.

28. Ecuador-Peru, 1981. Interviews with officials in Division of International Security Affairs, Office of the Secretary of Defense, U.S. Department of Defense, November 1982. I am grateful to Luis Gallegos for bringing this incident to my attention. See also Edward Schumacher, "Behind Ecuador War, Long-Smoldering Resentment," *New York Times,* February 10, 1981, p. A2.

29. Liberia, 1981. "U.S. and Liberia Plan Joint Military Exercises," *New York Times,* April 2, 1981, p. A6; "U.S. Calls Maneuvers with Liberia a Move to Stabilize Its Regime," *New York Times,* April 5, 1981, p. 10; Flora Lewis, "Green Berets Stage a Parachute Show for Liberians," *New York Times,* April 12, 1981, p. 8; Gilmore, "Chronology, 1981."

30. Lebanon, 1981. Bernard Gwertzman, "Not Much Time to Cool Crisis over Lebanon," *New York Times,* May 10, 1981, sec. IV, p. 1; Leslie H. Gelb, "War or Peace in the Mideast," *New York Times,* May 23, 1981, p. 4; Serge Schmemann, "Brezhnev Warns of Mideast Dangers," *New York Times,* May 23, 1981, p. 4; David K. Shipler, "Missile Crisis: Shift by Israel," *New York Times,* May 23, 1981, p. 1; Gilmore, "Chronology, 1981."

31. Gulf of Sidra, 1981. Alan Cowell, "45 Libya Incidents Reported by Navy," *New York Times,* August 25, 1981, p. 1; "News Conference aboard

the Nimitz," *New York Times,* August 25, 1981, p. A10; Gilmore, "Chronology, 1981"; see also William Safire, "Looking for Trouble," *New York Times,* September 25, 1980, p. A27.

32. Central America, 1981. "U.S. General Meets Worried Nicaraguans," *New York Times,* October 2, 1981, p. A5; "Honduran-U.S. Exercise Starts Despite Protest," *New York Times,* October 8, 1981, p. A8; "Four Week Navy Drill Is Begun in Caribbean," *New York Times,* November 7, 1981, p. 48; Haig, *Caveat,* pp. 130–131.

33. Egypt-Sudan, 1981. "Awacs Aircraft Is Sent to Egypt-Libya Border," *New York Times,* October 10, 1981, p. 6; Bernard Gwertzman, "Two Radar Planes Are Sent to Egypt," *New York Times,* October 15, 1981, p. 1; Gilmore, "Chronology, 1981"; William D. Brewer, "The Libyan-Sudanese 'Crisis' of 1981: Danger for Darfur and Dilemma for the United States," *Middle East Journal* 36 (Spring 1982): 205, 211.

34. Middle East, 1981. Richard Halloran, "U.S. Not Adding Troops to War Games in Egypt," *New York Times,* October 14, 1981, p. A12; William E. Farrell, "800 U.S. Paratroopers Open War Games in Egypt," *New York Times,* November 15, 1981, p. 21; Gilmore, "Chronology, 1981"; Joint Chiefs of Staff Supplement, *United States Military Posture for FY 1983* (Washington, D.C.: Joint Chiefs of Staff, 1982), p. 102.

35. Nicaragua, 1982. Richard Halloran, "U.S. Destroyer Monitors Activity in Area of Salvador and Nicaragua," *New York Times,* February 25, 1982, p. 1; Barbara Crossette, "Nicaragua Presses U.S. to Confer Immediately," *New York Times,* April 19, 1982, p. A12; Christopher C. Wright, "U.S. Naval Operations in 1982," *United States Naval Institute Proceedings* 109 (May 1983): 225.

36. Sinai, 1982. David K. Shipler, "670 U.S. Soldiers Arrive in Sinai for Peace Control," *New York Times,* March 18, 1982, p. A3; Carter, *Keeping Faith.*

37. Falklands War, 1982. Richard Halloran, "U.S. Plans Supplies If Fighting Lasts," *New York Times,* May 21, 1982, p. A12; "America's Falklands War," *Economist,* adapted and reprinted in *Baltimore Sun,* March 16, 1984, p. 15.

38. Lebanon, 1982. Richard Halloran, "U.S. Fleet Reaches East Mediterranean for Naval Exercises," *New York Times,* June 24, 1982, p. A15; "U.S. Flotilla in Position If Evacuation Is Needed," *New York Times,* June 10, 1982, p. A20; address by Richard Pipes, former director of Soviet affairs on the National Security Council, Kennedy School of Government, Harvard University, November 3, 1982; Wright, "U.S. Naval Operations in 1982," pp. 50, 225.

39. Somalia, 1982. Richard Halloran, "U.S. Flying Arms to Somalia after Ethiopian Raids," *New York Times,* July 25, 1982, p. 6; U.S. Airlifting Weapons to Somalia," *Washington Times,* August 27, 1982, p. 5; "African

Update," *Africa Report* (September–October 1982): 28–29; International Institute for Strategic Studies, *Strategic Survey, 1982–1983* (London: International Institute for Strategic Studies, 1983), p. 152.

40. Honduras, 1982. Raymond Bonner, "G.I.'s Join Hondurans in Touchy Region," *New York Times,* August 5, 1982, p. 3; Larry Boyd, "US Helps Honduras Beef Up Military Base at Swampy Nicaraguan Border," *Christian Science Monitor,* August 6, 1982, p. 5; "Units Train in Honduras," *Army Times,* August 16, 1982, p. 6; Julia Preston, "With U.S. Help, Honduras Is Upgrading Its Military," *Baltimore Sun,* August 18, 1982, p. E-1; "A Secret War for Nicaragua," *Newsweek,* November 8, 1982, p. 48.

41. Beirut, 1982. Charles W. Corddry, "U.S. Marines Leave Italy for Lebanon Area," *Baltimore Sun,* August 17, 1982, p. 2; John Kifner, "Christian Clash with Syrian Units on Lebanese Road," *New York Times,* August 25, 1982, p. 1; "Reagan Gives Notice on the Use of Marines," *New York Times,* August 25, 1982, p. A8; James F. Clarity, "On the Shores of Beirut's Harbor, U.S. Marines Are Standing Guard," *New York Times,* August 26, 1982, p. 1; Loren Jenkins, "800 Marines Take Positions in Beirut Port," *Washington Post,* August 26, 1982, p. 1; "Marines Leave Beirut; Reagan Thanks Them for 'Splendid Job,'" *Baltimore Sun,* September 11, 1982, p. 2.

42. Beirut, 1982. David B. Ottaway, "Marines Deploy in W. Beirut," *Washington Post,* September 30, 1982, p. 1; "Soviets Observe U.S. Air 'Attacks' in Mediterranean," *Washington Times,* December 2, 1982, p. 8; *Report of the Department of Defense Commission on Beirut International Airport Terrorist Act of October 23, 1983* (Long Commission) (Washington, D.C.: Government Printing Office, 1984), pp. 29, 35–38.

43. Vietnam, 1982. Information from Operational Archives Branch, Naval Historical Center, Department of the Navy; see Wright, "U.S. Naval Operations in 1982," p. 225.

44. Morocco, 1982. Associated Press, "U.S. Plans for Landing Irk Spanish," *Baltimore Sun,* November 9, 1982, p. 2.

45. Oman, 1982. "2,500 G.I.'s Hold Maneuvers in Oman," *New York Times,* December 6, 1982, p. 4; "U.S. Troops in Oman Maneuvers," *Washington Post,* December 6, 1982, p. 4; "U.S. Troops Ending Exercises in Oman," *Chicago Tribune,* December 8, 1982, p. 5.

46. Honduras, 1983. George de Lama, "U.S. Aids Honduras in Military Exercise," *Chicago Tribune,* February 2, 1983, p. 9; Michael Wright, "G.I.'s Join Honduran Soldiers in Maneuvers on Nicaraguan Border," *New York Times,* February 2, 1983, p. 4; Christopher Dickey, "Honduran Troops Jump in U.S.-Aided War Game," *Washington Post,* February 3, 1983, p. 25; James Nelson Goodsell, "Washington's Quiet Military Buildup in Central America," *Christian Science Monitor,* February 22, 1983, p. 1; Fred Hiatt, "U.S. to Escalate Its Military Presence in Central America," *Washington Post,* July 21, 1983, p. 1; Christopher C. Wright, "U.S. Naval Operations

in 1983," *United States Naval Institute Proceedings* 110 (May 1984): 52, 64. For background on administration goals for this and other military moves in Central America in 1983, see Christopher Dickey, "Central America: From Quagmire to Cauldron?" *Foreign Affairs* 62 (America and the World 1983, 1984): 659, 660–662.

47. Sudan, 1983. Walter S. Mossberg and Gerald F. Seib, "U.S. Sends Four AWACs Planes to Egypt and Moves Carrier to North African Coast," *Wall Street Journal,* February 17, 1983, p. 2; "U.S. AWACs Planes Sent to Egypt: Reagan Says Mission Is 'Training,'" *New York Times,* February 17, 1983, p. 1; John M. Goshko, "U.S. Forces in Mideast Said on Routine Exercise," *Washington Post,* February 18, 1983, p. 23; Mossberg and Seib, "U.S. Military Buildup in North Africa Said to Be Prompted by Libyan Actions," *Wall Street Journal,* February 18, 1983, p. 2; Lou Cannon and George C. Wilson, "U.S. Says Libya Eyed Sudan Coup," *Washington Post,* February 19, 1983, p. 1; Bernard Weinraub, "F-14s from Carrier Nimitz Chased 2 Libyan Fighters, U.S. Aides Say," *New York Times,* February 19, 1983, p. 1; see also Walter Pincus and Fred Hiatt, "U.S. Has a Secret Base with 100 Men in Egypt," *Washington Post,* June 23, 1983, p. 2; Richard Halloran, "U.S. Tells of Secret Air Operations in Egypt," *New York Times,* June 24, 1983, p. 9.

48. Nicaragua, 1983. Juan O. Tamayo, "U.S. to Set Up Radar in Honduras," *Philadelphia Inquirer,* March 11, 1983, p. 13; "U.S. Plane Hunting for Guerrilla Radio Station, Rebels Say," *Los Angeles Times,* May 18, 1983, p. 10; "Flights over Salvador Disclosed," *Boston Globe,* May 24, 1983, p. 1.

49. Caribbean Sea, 1983. "U.S. Fleet in Caribbean as a 'Signal,'" *Chicago Tribune,* March 17, 1983, p. 5; "CNO: Navy Committed to Caribbean Stability," *Navy Times,* March 28, 1983, p. 3; International Institute for Strategic Studies, *Strategic Survey, 1983–1984* (London: International Institute for Strategic Studies, 1984), pp. 120, 137.

50. Thailand, 1983. "U.S. Arms Shipment Arrives in Thailand," *Washington Post,* April 21, 1983, p. 7; International Institute for Strategic Studies, *Strategic Survey, 1983–1984,* p. 135.

51. Central America, 1983. "100 Green Beret Trainers Are Due in Honduras Today," *Philadelphia Inquirer,* June 14, 1983, p. F1; John E. Newhagen, "U.S. Troops Stir Debate in Honduras," *Philadelphia Inquirer,* June 16, 1983, p. 20; "U.S. Advisors Train Hondurans," *Chicago Tribune,* June 29, 1983, p. 9; "Projected U.S. Maneuvers to Center on Honduras," *New York Times,* July 21, 1983, p. 4.

52. Lebanon, 1983. William Beecher, "U.S. Sends Carrier to Warn Syrians," *Boston Globe,* June 15, 1983, p. 1; see *Report of Department of Defense (Long) Commission,* p. 30.

53. Central America, 1983. "U.S. Said to Plan Military Exercises in Latin America," *New York Times,* July 19, 1983, p. 1; "Carrier Heads Battle

Group," *Baltimore Sun,* July 20, 1983, p. 1; "Navy Battle Craft Go to Central America," *Washington Times,* July 20, 1983, p. 1; Walter Andrews, "'Blockade' of Central America Will Continue through Summer," *Washington Times,* July 21, 1983, p. 12; Fred Hiatt, "U.S. to Escalate Its Military Presence in Central America," *Washington Post,* July 21, 1983, p. 1; "Projected U.S. Maneuvers to Center on Honduras," *New York Times,* July 21, 1983, p. 4; Charles W. Corddry, "3,000 Troops Due Role in Exercises," *Baltimore Sun,* July 26, 1983, p. 1; Richard Halloran, "Pentagon Details Honduras Action," *New York Times,* July 26, 1983, p. 10; Gerald F. Seib and Walter S. Mossberg, "Reagan's Rationale," *Wall Street Journal,* July 26, 1983, p. 1; William Ringle, "Maneuvers Not Run of the Mill," *USA Today,* July 29, 1983, p. 7; Rick Maze, "8 Ships Deployed off Honduran Coast," *Air Force Times,* August 1, 1983, p. 7; Richard Halloran, "General Details U.S. Role in Honduras Exercises," *New York Times,* August 3, 1983, p. 7; "U.S. Raises Number of Troops Set for Honduran Exercises," *Baltimore Sun,* August 4, 1983, p. 2; Richard Halloran, "U.S. Warships Will Meet Soviet Vessels in Latin Zone," *New York Times,* August 5, 1983, p. 3; James Wallace, "Honduras: U.S. Linchpin in Central America," *U.S. News and World Report,* November 28, 1983, p. 29; Fred Hiatt and Joanne Omang, "U.S. Buildup in Honduras Described," *Washington Post,* February 1, 1984, p. 1; Wright, "U.S. Naval Operations in 1983," p. 64.

54. Chad, 1983. Don Oberdorfer, "'Urgent' Airlift Set of Military Supplies to Forces in Chad," *Washington Post,* July 19, 1983, p. 10; "U.S. Military Aid Arrives in Chad," *New York Times,* July 26, 1983, p. 3; "U.S. Puts Carrier on Standby in Chad War," *USA Today,* August 2, 1983, p. 7; Ian Black, "U.S. Navy Jets Share Skies with Libyans," *Washington Post,* August 3, 1983, p. 21; Gerald F. Seib, "U.S. Sends Military Gear and 3 Instructors to Help Chad Fight Libyan-Backed Rebels," *Wall Street Journal,* August 4, 1983, p. 2; Judith Miller, "Egypt Is Silent about Maneuvers with U.S.," *New York Times,* August 7, 1983, p. 6; Helen Winternitz and Henry Trewhitt, "U.S. Military Mission in Chad 'Limited,' Reagan Tells Congress," *Baltimore Sun,* August 9, 1983, p. 2; David Hoffman, "U.S. to Withdraw AWACS from Chad," *Washington Post,* August 23, 1983, p. 1; Jennifer Seymour Whitaker, "Africa Beset," *Foreign Affairs* 62 (America and the World 1983): 746, 755–757.

55. Lebanon, 1983. William E. Farrell, "U.S. Positioning 2,000 Marines off Beirut Coast," *New York Times,* September 2, 1983, p. 2; John M. Goshko, "U.S. Denies Shelling Means an Escalation," *Washington Post,* September 9, 1983, p. 1; Herbert H. Denton and David B. Ottaway, "U.S. Warship Fires to Halt Shelling of Marines in Beirut," *Washington Post,* September 9, 1983, p. 1; Lou Cannon and George C. Wilson, "Marines Get Broad Powers," *Washington Post,* September 14, 1983, p. 1; Herbert H. Denton, "U.S. Warships Shell Lebanese Army's Foes," *Washington Post,* September

20, 1983, p. 1; Drew Middleton, "U.S. Battleship Steams to Join Fleet off Beirut," *New York Times,* September 21, 1983, p. 16; *Report of Department of Defense (Long) Commission,* pp. 31–32, 40–42; Wright, "U.S. Naval Operations in 1983," pp. 52, 59; Luigi Caligaris, "Western Peacekeeping in Lebanon: Lessons of the MNF," *Survival* 26 (November–December 1984): 262.

56. Korea, 1983. "Weinberger Going to Funerals," *Washington Post,* October 12, 1983, p. 18; see Chalmers Johnson, "East Asia: Another Year of Living Dangerously," *Foreign Affairs* 62 (America and the World 1983, 1984): 721, 739–740.

57. Persian Gulf, 1983. Robert S. Greenberger, "Standby Marines Leave Coast of Lebanon, Reflecting Eased Tensions in Middle East," *Wall Street Journal,* October 12, 1983, p. 2; "Iraqi Plan to Draw U.S. into Gulf Reported," *Baltimore Sun,* October 12, 1983, p. 4; "Behind U.S. Moves near Persian Gulf," *U.S. News & World Report,* October 24, 1983, p. 12; Robert S. Dudney, "American Military Forces: Are They Spread Too Thin?" *U.S. News & World Report,* November 14, 1983, pp. 30, 31; James McCartney, "U.S. Hinting at Action in Persian Gulf Conflict," *Philadelphia Inquirer,* February 23, 1984, p. 1.

58. Grenada, 1983. "Ships Carrying Marines to Beirut Are Ordered to Head for Grenada," *Washington Post,* October 22, 1983, p. 1; Jim Hoagland, "Marines Invade Grenada, Fight Cubans; Reagan Cites Protection of U.S. Citizens," *Washington Post,* October 26, 1983, p. 1; Patrick E. Tyler and David Hoffman, "U.S. Says Aim Is to Restore Order," *Washington Post,* October 26, 1983, p. 1; Hedrick Smith, "Reagan Aid Says U.S. Invasion Forestalled Cuban Arms Buildup," *New York Times,* October 27, 1983, p.1; Joint Chiefs of Staff Supplement, *United States Military Posture for FY 1985* (Washington, D.C.: Government Printing Office, 1984), pp. 83–94.

59. Western Europe, 1983. David N. Schwartz, *NATO's Nuclear Dilemmas* (Washington, D.C.: Brookings Institution, 1983), pp. 193–252; Raymond Garthoff, "The NATO Decision on Theater Nuclear Forces," *Political Science Quarterly* 98 (Summer 1983): 197; Peter Osnos, "Missiles Delivered in Britain," *Washington Post,* November 15, 1983, p. 1; "Components of the Cruise Arrive in Italy," *New York Times,* November 28, 1983, p. 8; International Institute for Strategic Studies, *Strategic Survey, 1983–1984,* pp. 40–41; Leon V. Sigal, *Nuclear Forces in Europe: Enduring Dilemmas, Present Prospects* (Washington, D.C.: Brookings Institution, 1984), pp. 24–53.

60. Lebanon, 1983. Richard Halloran, "Vow by President," *New York Times,* December 5, 1983, p. 1; David B. Ottaway, "8 Marines Killed after U.S. Raid," *Washington Post,* December 5, 1983, p. 1; Lou Cannon and David Hoffman, "Syria Says It Will Hold Flier Until U.S. Leaves Lebanon," *Washington Post,* December 6, 1983, p. 1; Fred Hiatt, "U.S. Initiates 'Instant

Retaliation' Policy in Mideast," *Washington Post,* December 14, 1983, p. 1; William Claiborne, "2 U.S. Ships Retaliate for Syrian Firing," *Washington Post,* December 19, 1983, p. 1; Herbert H. Denton, "Warships Fire after Attack on Marines," *Washington Post,* January 16, 1984, p. 1; Bernard Gwertzman, "President Orders Naval and Air Attacks," *New York Times,* February 7, 1984, p. 1; Don Oberdorfer and Fred Hiatt, "Reagan Says Troops to Relocate Offshore," *Washington Post,* February 8, 1984, p. 1; Herbert H. Denton and Bradley Graham, "Battleship New Jersey Bombards Pro-Syrian Forces in Lebanon," *Washington Post,* February 9, 1984, p. 1; "Reagan to Dispatch Army Units to Train Lebanese," *Baltimore Sun,* February 14, 1984, p. 1; Wright, "U.S. Naval Operations in 1983," p. 59.

61. Nicaragua, 1984. Fred Hiatt and T.R. Reid, "Reconnaissance Flights Planned in Honduras," *Washington Post,* February 9, 1984, p. 1; Doyle McManus, "U.S. Army Pilots Flying Salvador Spotter Missions," *Los Angeles Times,* March 12, 1984, p. 1; Gilbert A. Lewthwaite, "U.S. Flies Unit from Honduras," *Baltimore Sun,* March 13, 1984, p. 1.

62. El Salvador, 1984. Richard Halloran, "U.S. Is Stepping Up Military Activity for Salvadorans," *New York Times,* March 10, 1984, p. 1; Fred Hiatt, "Carrier Group to Be Sent to Latin America," *Washington Post,* March 10, 1984, p. 10; "Reagan's Military Buildup," *Newsweek,* March 19, 1984, pp. 36–39; Alma Guillermoprieto, "New Exercises Begin in Honduras," *Washington Post,* March 21, 1984, p. 19; George de Lama, "U.S. Hikes Salvador Presence," *Chicago Tribune,* March 22, 1984, p. 8; "U.S., Honduras Hold Air Exercise," *Washington Post,* March 25, 1984, p. 6.

63. Sudan, 1984. Bernard Gwertzman, "2 AWACS Aircraft Sent to Bolster Sudan after Raid," *New York Times,* March 19, 1984, p. 1; Bernard Gwertzman, "U.S. Warns Libya against Attacking AWACS over Sudan," *New York Times,* March 20, 1984, p. 1.

64. Central America, 1984. Fred Hiatt, "U.S. Planning New Honduras Military Drills," *Washington Post,* January 11, 1984, p. 1; Fred Hiatt, "U.S. to Build Airstrips in Honduras Exercise," *Washington Post,* March 24, 1984, p. 1; "U.S. Troops Arrive in Honduras," *Washington Times,* March 27, 1984, p. 6; L.A. Jolidon, "A Show of Strength," *USA Today,* April 2, 1984, p. 9; Edward Cody, "Exercises in Honduras Go Forward Despite Ouster of Generals," *Washington Post,* April 8, 1984, p. 21; B. Drummond Ayres, Jr., "U.S. Ships to Aid Salvador Arms-Smuggling Patrol," *New York Times,* April 26, 1984, p. 9; Joanne Omang and Don Oberdorfer, "Ultimate Goal of U.S. Latin Policy Still Unresolved," *Washington Post,* April 29, 1984, p. 1; "GI's Arrive to Open Latin Maneuvers," *Philadelphia Inquirer,* May 17, 1984, p. 15; Richard J. Meislin, "U.S. Winds Up War Games in Honduras," *New York Times,* 9 June 1984, p. 3; Don Hirst, "1000 Deployed to Honduras for Joint Exercise," *Air Force Times,* June 11, 1984, p. 31.

65. Caribbean Sea, 1984. George de Lama, "U.S. Warship Shows Cuba,

Soviets It's in Fighting Form," *Chicago Tribune,* April 30, 1984, p. 6; Joseph B. Treaster, "War Games at Guantanamo, through Cuban Eyes," *New York Times,* May 1, 1984, p. 2; Brad Knickerbocker, "Caribbean War Games Hone Readiness," *Christian Science Monitor,* May 17, 1984, p. 3.

66. Persian Gulf, 1984. Charles W. Corddry, "Missiles Are Sent to Saudis," *Baltimore Sun,* May 30, 1984, p. 1; David Ignatius, "Missile Shipment Puts U.S. Closer to Saudis But Leaves Them Responsible for Defense," *Wall Street Journal,* May 30, 1984, p. 2; Don Oberdorfer and Rick Atkinson, "U.S. Cites 'Concern' over Persian Gulf," *Washington Post,* June 5, 1984, p. 1; Robert D. Hershey, Jr., "Reagan to Offer Plan for Coping with Oil Crisis," *New York Times,* June 5, 1984, p. 1; Charles W. Corddry and Gilbert A. Lewthwaite, "Iran Jets Reported Downed," *Baltimore Sun,* June 6, 1984, p. 1; Rick Atkinson, "U.S. to Protect Shipping in Gulf, Pentagon Says," *Washington Post,* June 8, 1984, p. 26.

67. Nicaragua, 1984. Fred Hiatt and Joanne Omang, "Pentagon Announces New Maneuvers Slated for Central America," *Washington Post,* June 30, 1984, p. 1; Richard Halloran, "U.S. Moves a Carrier into Caribbean," *New York Times,* July 18, 1984, p. 3; Walter Andrews, "Elite Army Unit Enters Honduras," *Washington Times,* July 24, 1984, p. 6; Fred Hiatt, "Battleship Iowa Going to Central America," *Washington Post,* July 27, 1984, p. 7; "U.S. Plans Aid to Back El Salvador," *Washington Post,* August 10, 1984, p. 15; "New Counterinsurgency Exercise Begun by U.S. Army in Honduras," *Washington Post,* August 21, 1984, p. 12.

68. Gulf of Sidra, 1984. Fred Hiatt, "Four U.S. Navy Jets Challenge Libya's Sovereignty," *Washington Post,* July 27, 1984, p. 11.

69. Gulf of Suez, 1984. Rick Atkinson, "Helicopters Enroute to Egypt," *Washington Post,* August 8, 1984, p. 1; Wayne Biddle, "U.S. Says Red Sea Mine Unit Gets Set to Sail," *New York Times,* August 10, 1984, p. 5; George C. Wilson, "3 More Helicopter Mine Hunters Sent to Mideast," *Washington Post,* August 14, 1984, p. 1; "3 Mines Found in Red Sea, Egypt Accuses Syria," *Washington Times,* August 14, 1984, p. 6; Wayne Biddle, "Source of Mines Is Still a Mystery as U.S. Force Heads for Red Sea," *New York Times,* August 15, 1984, p. 1; "Fighting the Mines of August," *Newsweek,* August 20, 1984, pp. 48–49; "More Vessels Join Mine Search," *Washington Times,* August 24, 1984, p. 6.

70. Lebanon, 1984, John Kifner, "3 Navy Ships Arrive off Lebanon as a U.S. Envoy Visits Damascus," *New York Times,* September 24, 1984, p. 1.

71. Central America. 1984. Fred Hiatt, "7 Exercises Going On as U.S. Continues Nicaragua Pressure," *Washington Post,* November 14, 1984, p. 1; Alan McConagha, "U.S., Honduras Plan Military Maneuvers," *Washington Times,* November 19, 1984, p. 1.

Appendix 3B:
Actors, Principal Actions Desired, Modes and Styles of Force Used, and Outcomes

Mode: C = compel; D = deter; I = induce; A = assure; L = latent. A letter in parentheses connotes style of use was indirect: without parentheses connotes style was direct.

Outcome: P = positive; N = negative.

			Outcome	
Incidents and Actors	*Substantive Action Desired of Actor*	*Mode*	*6 Months*	*3 Years*
1. Korea, 1975				
North Korea	Do not use force against South Korea	D	P	P
South Korea	Maintain alliance with United States	A	P	P
2. China, 1975				
China	Continue improved relations with United States	A	P	P
Taiwan	None relevant	—	—	—
3. Morocco, 1976				
Algeria	None relevant	—	—	—
Morocco	Maintain relationships with United States	A	P	P
Polisario insurgents	None relevant	—	—	—
4. Lebanon, 1976				
Christian insurgents	None relevant	—	—	—
Israel	Do not use force in Lebanon	(L)	P	N
Lebanon	Maintain regime authority	(L)	N	N
Muslim insurgents	None relevant	—	—	—
Soviet Union	Do not use or support use of force in Lebanon	(L)	P	P
Syria	Do not use force in Lebanon	(L)	N	N
5. Uganda, 1976				
Kenya	Maintain relationship with United States	A	P	P
Uganda	Do not use force against Kenya	D	P	P

Incidents and Actors	Substantive Action Desired of Actor	Mode	Outcome 6 Months	3 Years
6. Tunisia, 1976				
Libya	Do not use force against Tunisia	(L)	P	P
Tunisia	Maintain relationship with United States	A	P	P
7. Korea, 1976				
North Korea	Do not use force against U.S. forces	D	P	P
South Korea	Maintain alliance with United States	A	P	P
8. Uganda, 1977				
Uganda	Do not use force against U.S. citizens and allow them to leave country	D	P	P
9. Somalia, 1978				
Cuba	Do not use force to invade Somalia	(L)	P	P
Ethiopia	Do not use force to invade Somalia	(L)	P	P
Somalia	Maintain relationship with United States	(L)	P	P
Soviet Union	Do not support Ethiopian invasion of Somalia	(L)	P	P
10. Zaire, 1978				
Angola	Curtail support of Shaba insurgents	(C)	P	P
Belgium	Use force against Shaba insurgents	I	P	P
Cuba	Do not support use of force against Zaire	(D)	P	P
France	Use force against Shaba insurgents	I	P	P
Shaba insurgents	Terminate use of force against Zaire	(D)	P	P
Soviet Union	Do not support use of force against Zaire	(D)	P	P
Zaire	Maintain regime authority	A	P	P

Event / Actor	Goal			
11. Sea of Okhotsk, 1978				
Soviet Union	Recognize U.S. rights of innocent military passage	C	P	P
12. Nicaragua, 1978				
Costa Rica	Maintain alliance with United States	(L)	P	P
Nicaragua	Terminate use of force against Costa Rica	(L)	P	P
13. Baltic Sea, 1978				
Finland	Do not engage in joint maneuvers with the Soviet Union	A	P	P
NATO	Maintain presence in Baltic Sea	A	P	P
Soviet Union	Recognize U.S. rights of innocent military passage	(C)	P	P
Sweden	Maintain presence in Baltic Sea	(A)	P	P
14. Cuba, 1978				
Cuba	Do not allow Soviet Union to emplace offensive weapons in Cuba	(L)	P	P
Soviet Union	Do not emplace offensive weapons in Cuba	(L)	P	P
15. Iran, 1978				
Iran	Maintain regime authority	(L)	N	N
Saudi Arabia	Maintain relationship with United States	A	P	P
Soviet Union	Do not use force against Iran	(L)	P	P
16. Yemen, 1979				
Egypt	Maintain relationship with United States	(A)	P	P
North Yemen	Maintain regime authority	A	P	P
Saudi Arabia	Continue support for North Yemen	A	P	P
South Yemen	Terminate use of force against North Yemen	D	P	P
Soviet Union	Do not support use of force against North Yemen	(D)	P	P

Incidents and Actors	Substantive Action Desired of Actor	Mode	Outcome	
			6 Months	3 Years
17. Cuba, 1979				
Cuba	Unknown	—	—	—
Soviet Union	Do not escalate troop presence in Cuba	(D)	P	P
18. Korea, 1979				
North Korea	Do not use force against South Korea	D	P	P
South Korea	Maintain alliance with United States	A	P	P
19. Iran, 1979				
Iran	Do not injure U.S. hostages or put them on trial	D	P	P
20. Rhodesia, 1979				
Rhodesia	Support cease-fire agreement	I	P	P
Rhodesian insurgents	Support cease-fire agreement	I	P	P
United Kingdom	Provide peacekeeping force	I	P	P
21. Persian Gulf, 1980				
Egypt	Support deployment of U.S. rapid deployment force	I	P	P
Saudi Arabia	Maintain relationship with United States	(A)	P	P
Soviet Union	Do not use force against Persian Gulf region	D	P	P
22. Korea, 1980				
North Korea	Do not use force against South Korea	D	P	P
South Korea	Maintain regime authority	A	P	P
23. Thailand, 1980				
Members of Association of Southeast Asian Nations (ASEAN)	Maintain relationship with United States	A	P	P

Soviet Union	Do not support use of force against Thailand	(D)	P	P
Thailand	Maintain alliance with United States	A	P	P
Vietnam	Do not use force against Thailand	D	P	N
24. Persian Gulf, 1980				
Iran	Do not use force against Saudi Arabia, Oman, or strait of Hormuz	D	P	P
Iraq	None relevant	—	—	—
Oman	Maintain relationship with United States	A	P	P
Saudi Arabia	Maintain relationship with United States	A	P	P
25. Poland, 1980				
Soviet Union	Do not use force against Poland or Western Europe	(D)	P	P
26. Morocco, 1981				
Morocco	Maintain alliance with United States	A	P	P
Soviet Union	Do not intervene in Morocco-Polisario war	(L)	P	P
27. El Salvador, 1981				
Cuba	End support for Salvadoran insurgents	(C)	N	N
El Salvador	Maintain regime authority	A	P	P
Nicaragua	End support for Salvadoran insurgents	(C)	N	N
Salvadoran insurgents	Terminate use of force against El Salvador	(C)	N	N
28. Ecuador-Peru, 1981				
Argentina	Assist in enforcing cease-fire agreement	I	P	P
Brazil	Assist in enforcing cease-fire agreement	I	P	P
Chile	Assist in enforcing cease-fire agreement	I	P	P
Ecuador	Do not use force against Peru	A	P	P
Peru	Do not use force against Ecuador	A	P	P

Incidents and Actors	Substantive Action Desired of Actor	Mode	Outcome 6 Months	Outcome 3 Years
29. Liberia, 1981				
Liberia	Maintain regime authority and reject offer of arms from Libya	A	P	P
30. Lebanon, 1981				
Israel	Do not use force against Syria	(L)	P	N
Lebanon	None relevant	—	—	—
Soviet Union	Do not use force against Israel	(L)	P	P
Syria	Terminate attacks on Christian insurgents	(L)	P	N
31. Gulf of Sidra, 1981				
Libya	Do not contest U.S. rights of innocent military passage	C	P	P
32. Central America, 1981				
Cuba	End support for Central American insurgencies	(L)	N	N
Honduras	Support U.S. actions against Nicaragua	I	P	P
Nicaragua	Do not use force against Honduras	D	P	P
33. Egypt-Sudan, 1981				
Egypt	Maintain regime authority	A	P	P
Libya	Do not use force against Egypt or Sudan	D	P	N
Sudan	Maintain relationship with United States	A	P	P
34. Middle East, 1981				
Egypt	Support deployment of U.S. rapid deployment force	I	P	P
Oman	Support deployment of U.S. rapid deployment force	I	P	P
Soviet Union	Do not use force against Persian Gulf region	(D)	P	P
Sudan	Maintain relationship with United States	A	P	P

35. Nicaragua, 1982				
El Salvador	Maintain regime authority	(A)	P	P
Nicaragua	End support for Salvadoran insurgents	C	N	N
Salvadoran insurgents	None relevant	—	—	—
36. Sinai, 1982				
Egypt	Do not use force against Israel	I	P	P
Israel	Do not use force against Egypt	I	P	P
37. Falklands War, 1982				
Argentina	Negotiate settlement and terminate use of force	(I)	N	N
United Kingdom	Maintain alliance with United States	A	P	P
38. Lebanon, 1982				
Israel	Terminate use of force in Lebanon	(L)	N	N
Lebanese insurgents	None relevant	—	—	—
Lebanon	Maintain regime authority	(L)	P	P
Palestinians	Terminate use of force in Lebanon	(L)	P	P
Soviet Union	Do not use force in Lebanon	(L)	P	P
Syria	Terminate use of force in Lebanon	(L)	P	N
39. Somalia, 1982				
Cuba	Do not support use of force against Somalia	(D)	P	P
Ethiopia	Terminate use of force against Somalia	D	P	P
Somalia	Maintain regime authority	A	P	P
Soviet Union	Do not support use of force against Somalia	(D)	P	P
40. Honduras, 1982				
Honduras	Support U.S. actions against Nicaragua	I	P	P
Nicaragua	Do not use force against Honduras	D	P	P

Incidents and Actors	Substantive Action Desired of Actor	Mode	Outcome 6 Months	Outcome 3 Years
41. Beirut, 1982				
Christian insurgents	Terminate use of force in Beirut	(C)	N	N
France	Provide troops for peacekeeping force	I	P	N
Israel	Do not use force against Palestinians	I	P	N
Italy	Provide troops for peacekeeping force	I	P	N
Lebanon	Maintain regime authority	A	P	P
Muslim insurgents	Do not use force in Beirut	C	P	N
Palestinians	Terminate use of force and withdraw from Beirut	I	P	P
42. Beirut, 1982				
Christian insurgents	Terminate use of force in Beirut	C	P	N
France	Provide troops for peacekeeping force	I	P	N
Israel	Do not use force in Beirut	I	P	P
Italy	Provide troops for peacekeeping force	I	P	N
Lebanon	Maintain regime authority	A	P	P
Muslim insurgents	Do not use force in Beirut	C	P	N
43. Vietnam, 1982				
Vietnam	Do not contest U.S. rights of innocent military passage	C	P	P
44. Morocco, 1982				
Morocco	Maintain alliance with United States	A	P	P
45. Oman, 1982				
Oman	Support deployment of U.S. rapid deployment force	I	P	P
Soviet Union	Do not use force against Persian Gulf region	(L)	P	P

46. Honduras, 1983				
Nicaragua	Do not use force against Honduras	D	P	P
Honduras	Support U.S. policy against Nicaragua	I	P	P
Panama	None relevant	—	—	—
47. Sudan, 1983				
Egypt	Maintain support for Sudan	A	P	P
Libya	Do not intervene in Sudan	D	P	P
Sudan	Maintain regime authority	A	P	N
48. Nicaragua, 1983				
Nicaragua	End support for Salvadoran insurgents	(L)	N	N
Honduras	None relevant	—	—	—
49. Caribbean, 1983				
Cuba	Do not interfere with U.S. interests in Caribbean Sea	(L)	P	P
Grenada	Do not support revolutionary expansion	D	P	P
Soviet Union	Do not interfere with U.S. interests in Caribbean Sea	(L)	P	P
50. Thailand, 1983				
Thailand	Resist Vietnamese incursions	A	P	P
Vietnam	Do not use force against Thailand	D	P	P
51. Cental America, 1983				
Cuba	End support for insurgents in Central America	(L)	N	N
El Salvador	Maintain regime authority	A	P	P
Honduras	Support U.S. policy in Central America	I	P	P
Nicaragua	End support for insurgencies in Central America	(C)	N	N
52. Lebanon, 1983				
Lebanon	Maintain peace treaty with Israel	A	P	P
Soviet Union	Do not support Syrian aggression in Lebanon	(L)	P	N
Syria	Do not attack Lebanese government	D	P	P

Incidents and Actors	Substantive Action Desired of Actor	Mode	Outcome	
			6 Months	3 Years
53. Central America, 1983				
Cuba	End support for insurgencies in Central America	(L)	N	N
El Salvador	Maintain regime authority	(A)	P	P
Honduras	Support U.S. policy against Nicaragua	I	P	P
Nicaragua	End support for Salvadoran insurgents and do not attack Honduras	C	N	N
Soviet Union	End support for destabilization of Central America	(L)	N	N
54. Chad, 1983				
Chad	Strengthen regime authority	I	P	P
Egypt	Support U.S. policy against Libya	(L)	P	P
France	Provide direct support to government of Chad	I	P	P
Libya	Limit military intervention in civil war in Chad	(C)	P	P
Queddei insurgents	Peacefully settle dispute with government of Chad	C	N	N
55. Lebanon, 1983				
Druze insurgents	Do not attack U.S. forces in Lebanon	C	N	—
Lebanon	Strengthen regime authority	I	N	N
Syria	Do not support attacks on U.S. forces	D	N	—
56. Korea, 1983				
North Korea	Do not use force against South Korea	D	P	—
South Korea	Maintain regime authority	A	P	—
57. Persian Gulf, 1983				
Iran	Do not interfere with passage through strait of Hormuz	(L)	P	—

Iraq	None relevant	—	—	—
Oman	Defend maritime rights	A	P	—
Other Gulf Cooperation Council states	Defend maritime rights	A	P	—
Saudi Arabia	Defend maritime rights	A	P	—
58. Grenada, 1983				
Barbados	Resist destabilization in Caribbean area	I	P	—
Cuba	Curtail support for destabilization in Western Hemisphere	(C)	P	—
Dominica	Resist destabilization in Caribbean area	I	P	—
Grenada	None relevant	—	—	—
Jamaica	Resist destabilization in Caribbean area	I	P	—
59. Western Europe, 1983				
Britain	Maintain alliance with United States	A	P	—
France	Maintain alliance with United States	A	P	—
Italy	Maintain alliance with United States	A	P	—
Other NATO member states	Maintain alliance with United States	A	P	—
Soviet Union	Do not launch nuclear attack on Western Europe	D	P	—
West Germany	Maintain alliance with United States	A	P	—
60. Lebanon, 1983				
Druze insurgents	Do not attack U.S. forces in Lebanon	C	N	—
Lebanon	Maintain regime authority	A	P	—
Syria	Do not attack U.S. forces in Lebanon	C	P	—

Incidents and Actors	Substantive Action Desired of Actor	Mode	Outcome 6 Months	3 Years
61. Nicaragua, 1984				
El Salvador	Maintain regime authority	A	P	—
Honduras	Support U.S. policy against Nicaragua	I	P	—
Nicaragua	End support for Salvadoran insurgents	(C)	N	—
Salvadoran insurgents	None relevant	—	—	—
62. El Salvador, 1984				
El Salvador	Maintain regime authority and hold elections	A	P	—
Nicaragua	Do not support interference with Salvadoran elections	D	P	—
Salvadoran insurgents	Do not attack Salvadoran electoral process	C	P	—
63. Sudan, 1984				
Egypt	Support U.S. policy against Libya	(L)	P	—
Libya	Halt air attacks against Sudan	D	P	—
Sudan	Defend territory against Libya	A	P	—
64. Central America, 1984				
Cuba	Curtail support for Central American insurgents	(L)	N	—
El Salvador	Maintain regime authority	A	P	—
Honduras	Maintain alliance with United States	A	P	—
Nicaragua	End support for Salvadoran insurgents	(C)	N	—
Salvadoran insurgents	None relevant	—	—	—

65.	Caribbean Sea, 1984			
	Cuba	Do not attack U.S. interests in Caribbean area	(D)	P	—
	Soviet Union	Do not attack U.S. interests in Caribbean area	(L)	P	—
	States allied to United States in Caribbean area	Maintain alliance with United States	A	P	—
66.	Persian Gulf, 1984			
	Iran	Do not interfere with shipping in Persian Gulf	D	P	—
	Saudi Arabia	Defend maritime rights in Persian Gulf	I	P	—
67.	Nicaragua, 1984			
	El Salvador	Maintain alliance with United States	A	P	—
	Honduras	Maintain alliance with United States	I	P	—
	Nicaragua	Curtail support for destabilization in Central America	D	N	—
68.	Gulf of Sidra, 1984			
	Libya	Do not contest U.S. rights of innocent military passage	C	P	—
69.	Gulf of Suez, 1984			
	Egypt	Maintain safe shipping in Gulf of Suez	A	P	—
	Saudi Arabia	Maintain safe shipping in Gulf of Suez	(A)	P	—
70.	Lebanon, 1984			
	Lebanon	Maintain alliance with United States	A	P	—
71.	Central America			
	Honduras	Maintain alliance with United States	I	P	—
	Nicaragua	Do not support destabilization in Central America	(C)	N	—

Appendix 3C:
Level, Type, and Activity
of Armed Forces

Overall level of force used: see table 3–4.

Naval forces (largest units are shown; carriers are always accompanied by several other ships): CV = aircraft carrier; LPH = helicopter carrier; BB = battleship; SC = surface combatant ship.

Army/Marine ground forces: AR = army; MC = marine corps; (A) = afloat; COM = less than or equal in size to a company; BAT = less than or equal in size to a battalion; BRG = less than or equal in size to a brigade; DIV = less than or equal in size to a division.

Land-based air forces: AF = air force; MC = marine air; W = more than or equal to a wing; S = more than or equal to a squadron but less than a wing; TA = transport aircraft; AWACS = airborne warning and control aircraft (deployed AWACS aircraft are invariably accompanied by several support aircraft).

U = exact size unknown; ? = possibly.

Incident	Overall Level of Force Used	Naval	Ground	Land-based Air	Activity
1. Korea, 1975	3		U AR		Emplacement
2. China, 1975	4			S AF	Withdrawal
3. Morocco, 1976	5	1 SC			Visit
4. Lebanon, 1976	3	2 CV 1 LPH	BAT MC(A)		Presence, evacuation, visit
5. Uganda, 1976	4	1 CV			Presence, visit
6. Tunisia, 1976	5	2 SC			Visit
7. Korea, 1976	2	1 CV	DIV AR	W AF U TA	Presence, demonstration, alert
8. Uganda, 1977	4	1 CV			Presence
9. Somalia, 1978	5	2 SC			Surveillance, presence
10. Zaire, 1978	3		BRG AR	U TA	Transport, alert
11. Okhotsk, 1978	5	2 SC			Presence

Incident	Overall Level of Force Used	Naval	Ground	Land-based Air	Activity
12. Nicaragua, 1978	4	1 CV			Surveillance, alert
13. Baltic Sea, 1978	5	4 SC			Visit, presence
14. Cuba, 1978	5			U AF	Surveillance
15. Iran, 1978	4	1 CV		S AF, U TA, U AWACS	Presence, visit, evacuation
16. Yemen, 1979	4	1 CV		U AWACS	Presence, surveillance
17. Cuba, 1979	3	1 LPH	BAT MC	S MC, U AF	Surveillance, exercise
18. Korea, 1979	3	1 CV	DIV AR	2 AWACS	Presence, visit, surveillance, alert
19. Iran, 1979	3	1 CV, 1 LPH	U AR, BAT MC (A)	U AF	Presence
20. Rhodesia, 1979	4			2 S TA	Transport
21. Persian Gulf, 1980	2	1 LPH	BAT MC(A), BAT AR	W AF, U TA, U AWACS	Presence, visit, exercise, surveillance
22. Korea, 1980	4	1 CV		U AF	Presence
23. Thailand, 1980	5			U TA	Transport
24. Persian Gulf, 1980	4	1 SC		A AF, U TA, 4 AWACS	Presence, transport, surveillance
25. Poland, 1980	5	5 SC		4 AWACS	Surveillance, presence
26. Morocco, 1981	5	3 SC			Presence, visit

27. El Salvador, 1981	5			U TA	Transport
28. Ecuador-Peru, 1981	5		U AR		Surveillance, transport
29. Liberia, 1981	4	1 SC	COM AR		Visit
30. Lebanon, 1981	2	2 CV / 1 LPH	BAT MC(A)		Presence
31. Gulf of Sidra, 1981	3	2 CV			Presence
32. Central America, 1981	3	2 CV	U MC		Exercise
33. Egypt-Sudan, 1981	3	2 LPH	2 BAT MC(A)	2 AWACS	Surveillance, presence
34. Middle East, 1981	3	1 CV	2 BAT AR / BAT MC	S AF / U TA	Exercise, visit, presence
35. Nicaragua, 1982	5	1 SC			Surveillance
36. Sinai, 1982	3		BAT AR	U TA	Emplacement, transport
37. Falklands War, 1982	5			U AF	Logistic and intelligence support
38. Lebanon, 1982	2	2 CV / 1 LPH	BAT MC(A)	U AF	Presence
39. Somalia, 1982	5	1 SC		U TA	Transport
40. Honduras, 1982	5		COM AR	U TA	Transport, construction, visit
41. Beirut, 1982	2	2 CV / 1 LPH	BAT MC		Emplacement
42. Beirut, 1982	2	2 CV / 1 LPH	BAT MC		Emplacement
43. Vietnam, 1982	4	1 CV			Presence

Incident	Overall Level of Force Used	Naval	Ground	Land-based Air	Activity
44. Morocco, 1982	3	U SC	BAT MC		Exercise
45. Oman, 1982	3	1 CV	BAT MC BAT AR?	U AF	Exercise
46. Honduras, 1983	4	2 SC	COM AR	U TA	Exercise, civic action
47. Sudan, 1983	4	1 CV		4 AWACS AF	Presence, surveillance
48. Nicaragua, 1983	5	2 SC		U AF	Surveillance
49. Caribbean, 1983	3	3 CV			Exercise
50. Thailand, 1983	5			U TA	Transport
51. Central America, 1983	5		COM AR		Training
52. Lebanon, 1983	4	1 CV			Presence
53. Central America, 1983	2	2 CV 1 BB	BRG AR BAT MC	U AF U TA	Presence, exercise, surveillance, construction
54. Chad, 1983	4	1 CV		S AF U AWACS U TA	Presence, support
55. Lebanon, 1983	3	1 CV 1 BB	BAT MC(A) BAT MC		Presence, fire support
56. Korea, 1983	4	1 CV		U AF	Presence
57. Persian Gulf, 1983	3	1 CV	BAT MC(A)		Presence

58. Grenada, 1983	3	1 CV 1 LPH	BRG AR BAT MC	U TA	Invasion, occupation
59. Western Europe, 1983	1		BRG AR	U AF	Presence
60. Lebanon, 1983	3	2 CV 1 BB	BAT MC		Air attack, naval and ground fire
61. Nicaragua, 1984	5		U AR	U AF	Surveillance, construction
62. El Salvador, 1984	3	1 CV	2 BAT AR	U TA	Presence, exercise, surveillance
63. Sudan, 1984	5			2 AWACS U AF	Presence, surveillance
64. Central America, 1984	3	SC	2 BAT AR	U TA	Presence, exercise, construction, training
65. Caribbean Sea, 1984	2	1 CV	BRG AR BAT MC	W AF	Presence, exercises
66. Persian Gulf, 1984	4	1 CV		U AWACS U AF, U TA	Support, presence, surveillance
67. Nicaragua, 1984	3	1 CV 1 BB	BAT AR +		Presence, exercises
68. Gulf of Sidra, 1984	4	1 CV			Presence
69. Gulf of Suez, 1984	5	3 SC		U TA	Mine clearance
70. Lebanon, 1984	3	3 SC	BAT MC(A)		Presence
71. Central America, 1984	3	1 SC	BAT AR +	U TA	Exercises

II
Did Vietnam Make a
Difference? Policymaking

4
The Executive Office of the President

Louis W. Koenig

Despite their severe testing by the Vietnam War, the presidency and the political system were remarkable in maintaining their historic continuities. For all of the dislocations it inflicted on American society, the war did not alter the basic constitutional framework. The presidency retained its historic functions of initiative and action in foreign affairs and national security, while Congress persisted in its dual capacities of critical overseer and as supplier of support. The framers intended that both the president and Congress be powerful in foreign affairs and national security and toward that end left the powers of each branch largely general and undefined and somewhat overlapping, thus ensuring competition and struggle between them and forestalling a continuing undue ascendance of one branch over the other. In essence, war making is subject to the play of checks and balances. The Vietnam War did not undo or even soften this formula.

In important degree because of checks and balances, the impact of any war, including the Vietnam War, on the political system is regulated by a cycle evident in U.S. history: fluctuating ascendance and descendance of the presidency and Congress in their respective influence. If one branch is ascendant for a time, it subsequently will experience a decline. The Vietnam War followed the general cyclical pattern of legislative-executive power in modern wars. Like these other wars, Vietnam in its earlier stages expanded the use of presidential power—for example, the progression from the commitment of military advisers to the injection of U.S. combat forces, and the president's initiative in extending the use of U.S. forces into new theaters such as Cambodia and Laos. Later in the war, when it was clear the president could not extract victory, the legislature became more assertive and the executive more circumscribed.

In the early stages of a war, such as Vietnam and Korea, public opinion and Congress support the president. If the war drags on and a successful conclusion is beyond sight, the presidency encounters grave political trouble. The public becomes disenchanted, a mood that quickly overtakes Congress. It is easier for Congress and public opinion to cut and run than for the president, who is encoiled in the daily administration of the war. As victories eluded Union forces, Lincoln became increasingly vulnerable to attack. As Korea and Vietnam ground on endlessly, the political lives of their respective presidential managers became endangered. If anything, both wars numbered presidents among their casualties. The prolonged Korean War was a principal factor in prompting Truman not to run again in 1952, and Vietnam led to a similar declination by Johnson in 1968. Vietnam, which became entwined with Watergate, also counted Nixon among its victims.

Vietnam also matches the historic pattern of warmaking as a joint legislative-executive enterprise. Although the Vietnam War often is characterized as a presidential war, it was, like other U.S. wars, a joint executive-legislative conflict. In fact, the war was sustained by an interbranch partnership of extraordinary duration. For nearly a decade and in presidencies of both major political parties, Congress supported the war and the presidents' conduct of it with substantial annual appropriations. No other U.S. war incurred legislative support of such duration.

As it has in all other wars, the president's power as commander in chief remained intact following the Vietnam War. The framers originally had constituted that power in ways that largely have immunized it against the changing fortunes of war. The framers' magic ingredient was sparse and general language, affording the president a broad terrain of power. Although it may expand and contract to some degree due to changing circumstance, it keeps its essence intact. Vietnam adheres to the experience of past wars, which, whatever their rigors or untoward developments, leave the president with his essential military power. No burst of congressional assertiveness that the war may engender significantly alters it. Lincoln withstood the hostile scrutiny of Congress's Committee on the Conduct of the War, and the War Powers Act of 1973, a creature of the Vietnam War, made no real dent on the commander in chief's power.

The Vietnam War nevertheless had an important impact on the presidency. Although the war did not alter the essentialness of the presidency, it did have significant consequences, particularly for its relationships with other components of the political system. The effect of the war was magnified by its linkages with Watergate and by the circumstances that it coincided with other political and social forces of its day: the civil rights and women's movements and the reform efforts important in the 1970s in Congress and the major political parties. These forces imparted momentum to each other. Vietnam made Congress more assertive in its relationships with the executive branch and made the parties more accessible to left-out groups, including youth, many of whom demonstrated against the war. The war coincided with the advent of television as a pervasive national phenomenon and illuminated the difficulties its presence imposes on policymaking and political leadership.

The effects of the war must be traced over a wide front. In one perspective, they imposed a variety of strains on the presidency. Illegal and unethical conduct, conduct offensive to democracy, was spurred by the war. The war was a nest of syndromes, of hurt national pride, of desperate puzzlement about how to cope with future situations similar to Vietnam. The war touched the president's principal roles and all the major components of the political system with which he interacts: national security decision making, the parties and electoral processes, his relation with public opinion and the media, and, above all, his interactions with Congress. No principal function of the president, no governmental or political component with which he interacted, was untouched by the war.

Strains on Presidential Leadership

The Vietnam War can be perceived as a kind of Pandora's box that unloosed a variety of afflictions and strains on the presidency, some of which it has not altogether escaped. The war lured all three of the presidents who were its principal prosecutors into acts that violate basic norms for conducting the office in a democratic political system. Deception, intimidation, burglary, and assassination are on the list of sins of the Vietnam presidencies. The scale and severity of these infractions exceed those of earlier wars.

Faced with the approaching election of 1964 and anticipating that his principal opposition would come from the right wing, Lyndon Johnson put the war in the best possible light. The some 16,000 U.S. military in Vietnam he called not combat troops but advisers, and if the situation worsened, Johnson said, "I would, of course, go to Congress."[1] Johnson's principal recourse to Congress produced the Tonkin resolution, which gave the president a virtual carte blanche to conduct the war, but he is widely accused of twisting the facts on which the resolution was based, the alleged attacks by North Vietnam on U.S. naval craft. Earlier, under President Kennedy, as events deteriorated in Vietnam, the leader of South Vietnam, Ngo Dinh Diem, was overthrown, with the approval of the White House and the U.S. ambassador in Saigon, and killed.[2]

Richard Nixon long conducted a secret war in Cambodia, unknown to Congress and the public. When the *New York Times* eventually disclosed the details about that war, Nixon established the "plumbers" as a unit of the White House staff to plug future leaks. The plumbers' attempted break-in at the Democratic party's headquarters at the Watergate complex commenced a string of events that led to Nixon's forced resignation from the presidency.

In the decade after the war's termination, dissembling in the handling of foreign and military affairs has become no stranger to the presidency. President Reagan, for example, first justified his invasion of Grenada as necessary to forestall a take-over by a Marxist regime but later cited the need to rescue American students enrolled in the island's medical school.

The presidency and the nation suffered the strain of losing a war, of failing in the objective of keeping South Vietnam afloat as a nation-state. Along with Castro's take-over in Cuba, Vietnam was an early major failure of the cold war policy of containment for checking the thrusts of the Soviet Union and its client states. Prior to Vietnam, presidents had generally prevailed in the major crises of the cold war. In the Truman years, civil war in Greece and a failing economy in Turkey were coped with and the dangers of Communist take-overs averted. A second major challenge materialized with the Korean War, when the threat of South Korea's independence was repulsed.

The failure in Vietnam has left a lasting pall over presidential policymaking. When wars of liberation, as they are known in the Soviet lexicon, overtook Angola, Zaire, and other African states and erupted in Nicaragua and El Salvador, U.S. policymakers and their critics were sensitive to the analogy of Vietnam and its imperative of caution and restraint. "No more Vietnams" seems to many policymakers a mandate to avoid a well-defined kind of disaster, just as "no more Munichs" reechoed among an earlier generation of policymakers.

Nonetheless, like other historical analogies, Vietnam is an uncertain tool for future policymaking. Every event and the policy problems that are its offspring possess unique characteristics. El Salvador and Nicaragua have dimensions that Vietnam did not have, such as proximity to the United States, and policymakers, rather than blindly adhering to "no more Vietnams," are better served if they weigh each situation in its full dimensions. If anything, Vietnam is instructive in warning that the United States should not undertake substantial foreign commitments without knowledge of the people of the other country involved, its culture and history. Vietnam illuminates the dangers of ignorance.

Presidents and their advisers have yet to find a dependable solution for coping with wars of liberation. In this perspective, Vietnam is an unsolved problem that may haunt future presidents who face comparable situations at many points around the globe. Kennedy and his aides were distressed when, during the first month of his presidency, Premier Nikita Khrushchev declared in an eight-hour speech that national liberation wars were a preferred means for advancing the Communist cause, and these "just wars" would have wholehearted Soviet support. Kennedy rushed plans to strengthen the U.S. ability to wage limited conventional and counterguerrilla war. McGeorge Bundy, assistant for national security affairs to Kennedy and Johnson, expressed in 1964 the administration's prevailing view that the United States must stand and fight in Vietnam or lose not only Southeast Asia but the world's faith in its will and ability to cope with the Communist surge in that entire region.[3] As Secretary of State Dean Rusk noted, Kennedy, in increasing the U.S. role in Vietnam, was concerned that he would look weak and vacillating to Khruschev if he did not stand by the SEATO treaty, obligating the United States to come to South Vietnam's support.[4]

Post-Vietnam presidents have had to struggle with the same danger of being misperceived, as well as Vietnam's legacy of nonsolutions for Communist insurgency. These presidents have behaved in characteristic presidential fashion, as they did before Vietnam, when faced with policymaking dilemmas. They remain accessible to competing groups of advisers who advocate alternative ways of handling international crises of the moment. President Carter, for example, zigzagged between two groups of advisers, one led by his national security assistant, Zbigniew Brzezinski, and the other by Secretary of State Cyrus Vance. The Brzezinski group, many of whom were on his staff, had supported the Vietnam War unswervingly. Vance's group was based mainly in the State Department but also included ambassador to the United Nations Andrew Young and Paul Warnke, the arms control negotiator. Many of the Vance group had mildly opposed the Vietnam War, particularly after the invasion of Cambodia, and they looked to diplomacy and negotiation to resolve insurgency and other foreign affairs problems. At times, one or the other camp prevailed. But with the Soviet invasion of Afghanistan, the imposition of martial law in Poland, and the attempted rescue of U.S. hostages in Iran, Brzezinski gained ground, and ultimately Vance resigned.

The Reagan administration too was divided by conflicting counsel concerning responses to upheavals in Central America, Grenada, and Lebanon. While civilian conservatives in the Defense Department often advocated intervention, the Joint Chiefs of Staff were frequently a moderating influence, a position doubtless spurred by memories of Vietnam.

Doubt over how to cope with insurgency led Richard C. Lugar, chairman of the Senate Foreign Relations Committee in the Reagan era, to assert that as a result of the Vietnam War, "The United States has been and continues to be uncertain about the use of force in the conduct of American foreign policy." Lugar noted that prior to that involvement, "some widely shared assumptions were held about the national interest and potential threats to it."[5] Vietnam shattered that consensus.

Lugar's search for the strands of a new consensus drew conflicting counsel from the secretaries of state and defense, which derived chiefly from their contrasting evaluations of the Vietnam experience. Defense Secretary Caspar Weinberger, clearly mindful of Vietnam, contended that military intervention anywhere in the world should occur only as a "last resort," with full public backing, and "with the clear intention of winning." In the Vietnam War, these conditions were not satisfied, and the armed forces reaped the bitter harvest. Secretary of State George Shultz, in contrast, mindful of both Vietnam and earlier U.S. wars, contended that "there is no such thing as guaranteed public support in advance" and that no-win situations must not automatically disqualify hard-to-win situations. Shultz maintained that a great power must be prepared to use force to buttress diplomacy.[6] The fact that this dispute was aired so publicly implies that President Reagan himself had not resolved the issue of when and when not to use force, which the heritage of Vietnam poses.

A basic function of the president is to explain the complex reality of the world and its problems to the citizenry. The president is uniquely situated to discharge this function with legions of expert aides and vast resources of information. Franklin Roosevelt's painstaking elucidation of the ominous state of the world in World War II invaluably prepared the public undertaking for the trials ahead.

But in both the Vietnam War and the post-Vietnam era, the presidents' performances as explicator of international problems and policy responses typically have been ineffectual or largely shunned. Kennedy employed martial rhetoric, Johnson dissembled, and Nixon and his aide Kissinger, confident of their talents, conducted foreign policy with the secrecy and privatism of an imperial court. The Christmas bombing of North Vietnam is typical of major policy changes made without public explanation. Former Senator J. William Fulbright, a leading critic of the Vietnam War, has observed in retrospect, "The biggest lesson I learned from Vietnam is not to trust Government statements. I had no idea until then that you could not rely on Government statements." He likened the Reagan administration's course in Central America and its lack of provision of "solid information" as a reprise of Vietnam. "They fit the facts to fit the policy," he said of officials' statements on Vietnam and Central America.[7]

The Vietnam War casts a shadow of doubt on a presidential type long celebrated by historians and in public memory and acclaim: the charismatic chief executive. This type is an ambitious goal setter and high achiever in domestic and foreign affairs. As charismatic presidents like Lincoln, Wilson, and Franklin Roosevelt suggest, a common outlet for their leadership gifts is war making. In the Vietnam and post-Vietnam eras, a charismatic type like Kennedy sustained the Bay of Pigs invasion and nuclear confrontation with the Soviet Union, and he launched the first large-scale commitment of U.S. forces in Vietnam. A charismatic successor, Reagan, has not shrunk from dispatching military forces to combat or to situations of likely combat in Grenada, Lebanon, and Central America.

Midway in the Vietnam War, Walter Lippmann cautioned that the nation had reached a point where it clearly needed "deflationary" leadership and policies—presidents who would diminish their political promises and scale down their overseas commitments. The costly, ongoing disintegration of presidential policies in Vietnam underscored the value of prudent restraint. Needed were future presidents who offered competence rather than charismatic aggressiveness.[8] Admittedly, such prescription flies in the face of the public's historic preference for the imagery of strong leaders. Put another way, the problem posed, in both the Vietnam War and throughout the decade of its aftermath, is how the nation can have an activist liberal president, or an activist conservative president, whose strivings will not include involvement in war.

Presidential Relations with Other Actors

National Security Advisory System

During the Vietnam War, power and decision in military and foreign affairs moved markedly from the executive departments to the White House. A principal beneficiary was the assistant to the president for national security affairs. The post was transformed from a modest role in the Truman and Eisenhower presidencies to a position whose influence on policymaking often exceeded that of the secretaries of state and defense. Kennedy and Johnson commenced the trend with the expanding roles of McGeorge Bundy and Walt W. Rostow, respectively, as their national security assistants, and Nixon enlarged it in close partnership with his national security assistant, Henry Kissinger. Prosecuting the Vietnam War was an abiding preoccupation of these presidents and their aides. The assistant was advantageous to the president in that he did not need Senate confirmation and could not be required to testify on Capitol Hill—in contrast to cabinet secretaries. The bureaucracies over which the secretaries presided were prone to forge alliances with members of Congress, to the detriment of presidential policymaking, while the White House staff was free of those encumbrances and more responsive to the president.

Like his predecessors in the Truman and Eisenhower administrations, McGeorge Bundy, the first of the wartime national security assistants, functioned basically as a facilitator, managing the flow of the president's personal, day-to-day foreign affairs and defense business from the departments to his desk. Bundy accrued a sizable, highly competent NSC staff. The staff had undergone marked expansion after the Bay of Pigs fiasco, which prompted Kennedy to centralize staff work increasingly in the White House under Bundy. The NSC staff gained direct access to information in the White House Situation Room, which was also then established and which became a focal point for departmental cables to and from the State and Defense departments and the Central Intelligence Agency (CIA). As the Vietnam War ran its course, the NSC staff and its practices were solidified and extended, and they continued easily into the post-Vietnam era. The enduring NSC staff has provided an institutional base for a strong presidentially oriented staff in foreign affairs.[9]

Not surprisingly, as U.S. control of the Vietnam War's outcome weakened, the country's commitment was increasingly questioned, and pressures to conclude the war mounted, the post of national security assistant, given its pivotal relationship with the president and the war, underwent important changes. The state of the war at any given moment markedly affected the shaping and reshaping of the national security assistant's role. Consequently Bundy's successor, Rostow, functioning in an interval when Johnson felt driven to escalate the U.S. commitment and subsequently when outcries against the war were rising, played a different role from Bundy. Rostow was convinced of the merits of the war, was intellectually reassuring to Johnson, and became a weighty influence on policy. He conducted his duties in ways that maximized his prowar influence. Unlike Bundy, who functioned as an honest broker, Rostow was the advocate, who was less inclined to see that the president was apprised of the arguments on all sides of the issue, including Vietnam issues.[10]

In the Nixon era, the post of national security assistant took on additional dimensions, influenced by the necessity facing the president of extricating the United States from what had become an unpopular and unwanted war. Unlike Bundy and Rostow, Henry Kissinger as national security assistant became a premier diplomatic negotiator on the war and other foreign policy matters. With Nixon, he shared an unquenchable thirst for monopolizing and secretly managing foreign policy issues. The war lent itself to that preference. Fashioning a truce with the North Vietnamese and imposing it on South Vietnam were complex and sensitive enterprises, protracted in their execution. In negotiating the war's issues, Kissinger excelled at using back channels, which he employed to exclude State Department officials, who normally would be involved, from sharing in or even becoming apprised of the nation's principal communications with North and South Vietnam. In time, Kissinger became a prime public spokesman on the war and other foreign policy and, with Nixon's approval, largely obliterated the distinction between the respective functions of the secretary of state and the national security assistant.[11] In Ford's presidency, with Vietnam diplomacy entering a new phase of intensity, Kissinger became secretary of state and carried with him his near monopoly of knowledge of the status of the war's negotiations and developing policies.

In Carter's post-Vietnam presidency, the high-flying model of the national security assistant that was a progeny of the war persisted. Initially, Carter, put off by Kissinger's superstar act, opted for a restoration of cabinet government, decentralization, and open policy processes. But in little time, Carter abandoned this formulation and reinvoked the model provided by Johnson and Nixon in the Vietnam War: of the president as a prime policy initiator and activist manager of foreign affairs, aided by a professionally skilled and assertive national security assistant, in his case, Zbigniew Brzezinski. Carter could make this transition readily since the key elements of the Vietnam model were all in place. The substantial NSC staff, created in the war, was continued in the postwar period, its members now selected by Brzezinski. The NSC's committee structure, which Kissinger had used defly during the war to consolidate his power over the State and Defense departments, remained, and Brzezinski quickly adapted it to his purposes. Like his predecessors in the Vietnam War, Brzezinski provided the president a daily briefing on foreign affairs–national security developments, and he enjoyed ready access to the Oval Office. He was also a highly visible policy spokesman, but unlike Kissinger, he did not conduct most major diplomatic negotiations. Like Rostow, Brzezinski was a policy advocate, committed to a hard line toward the Soviet Union.

Ronald Reagan also brought to the presidency the conviction that the power-centered national security assistant of the Vietnam era should not be duplicated in his incumbency. The national security assistant, initially Richard Allen, was dropped a rung on the hierarchical ladder, which deprived him of direct access to the president. Instead he reported to Edwin Meese, who with James Baker and Michael Deaver constituted the troika of top White House staff. A key aid in Reagan's governorship, Meese was unschooled in foreign affairs.

Again the effort to modify the structural heritage of the Vietnam War was abandoned. Following Allen's resignation, Meese surrendered his dominion over foreign policy, and the powerful national security assistant of the Vietnam War was restored. First William ("Judge") Clark and subsequently Robert McFarlane and John Poindexter functioned in that capacity. Their emergence coincided with the increased personal activism of President Reagan in foreign affairs and duplicated the pattern of the Vietnam War of lodging the primary management of foreign affairs in the White House. Like Kissinger, Clark, McFarlane, and Poindexter became public defenders of administration policy, managers of the considerable professional staff of the NSC, daily briefers of the president, and overseers of the NSC's committee structure. The prominent roles played by McFarlane and Poindexter in developing and implementing the policy of selling arms to Iran indicates the extent to which the national security assistant has retained a position of influence. Indeed, in the Iranian arms sales affair, the NSC staff assumed operational responsibilities normally reserved for executive departments.

The Party and Electoral Systems

The Vietnam War contributed toward making important changes in the party and electoral system in which the presidency functions. Johnson's presidency became a casualty of the war and its impact on electoral politics. In 1968, when he was expected to run again, the Gallup poll disclosed, ominously for his candidacy, that 69 percent of the public favored pulling out of Vietnam.[12] Senator Eugene McCarthy of Minnesota challenged Johnson's renomination by charging that under his stewardship, the presidency had become excessively personalized and its powers abused. Although Johnson defeated McCarthy in the New Hampshire primary, 48.5 percent to 42 percent, the senator's strong race was startling. Within days, Robert Kennedy announced his candidacy, and Johnson terminated his. Clearly the consensus of the Democratic party, which Johnson so much valued, had been eroded by the war. The National Democratic Convention in Chicago, which nominated Hubert Humphrey, was enlivened by war protesters on the convention floor and in demonstrations outside that provoked clashes with the police.

Humphrey won the nomination as the choice of party leaders and without a victory in any primary. Deeming themselves deprived of an effective voice by the established party leaders and procedures, the Vietnam War dissenters provided the leverage that prompted the Democratic party to adopt reforms for choosing delegates to the national nominating convention and for opening up the procedures by which other party business is conducted. The reforms moved control of delegate selection from handfuls of party stalwarts to mass participation. A principal instrumentality of this change was the party primary. The first Democratic presidential nominee produced by the reformed procedures was George McGovern (1972), a severe critic of the Vietnam War who called for its immediate termination. His success in the primaries owed much to the organizational work of the young war protesters. His Republican rival, Richard Nixon, who was more constrained in discussing the war, won a landslide victory. The outcome was a warning bell of the widening chasm between the newer war, social, and racial issue liberalism of the Democratic party elites and the more conservative attitudes of the general population.[13]

The Democratic reforms shifted the party away from the traditional predominance of party leaders and subleaders as convention delegates to major representation for previously left-out groups — blacks, women, and youth — the last provided for largely because of the intensity of the antiwar protests.

In contrast to the Democrats, the Republican party remained largely unreformed. The left-out groups gained some increases in representation among convention delegates, and the majority of delegates from both parties have, since the presidential election of 1972, been chosen by primaries and caucuses. But unlike the Democrats who enlarged national party control over delegate selection in the states and enforced demographic quotas and affirmative action, the Republicans retained the traditional confederate legal structure of their party.[14] The sturdy decentralization of the party and the long-prevailing concept that the national party is simply an association of state parties increased Nixon's freedom of maneuver with the Vietnam War issues in his 1968 and 1972 campaigns.[15]

More important than these structural characteristics was the rightward shift of the Republican party. Nixon sought to capitalize on the shift in promoting a "new American majority" founded on policies responsive to the concerns of blue-collar labor, ethnic groups, the suburbs, the Southeast, and the Southwest. Typically these groups were disaffected by the antiwar protests, youth living styles, civil rights policies, and other issues. Nixon's policies of Vietnamization and the Nixon doctrine enabled the United States to pull back honorably from its military commitments, including the Vietnam War. Simultaneously, Nixon provided aid to other countries, such as Iran and South Korea, to enable them to shoulder responsibility for their own defense. Nixon's approach was expected to appeal to his domestic constituencies who welcomed the termination of the war. But his contribution to what some were calling the emerging Republican majority went up in smoke with Watergate.

Jimmy Carter provided the faltering Democrats a reprieve by reintegrating much of the party's disintegrated coalition founded by Franklin Roosevelt, and by using the party reforms established during the Vietnam War to wrest the nomination from the liberal reformers. He set his administration on a conservative course and adjourned the politics of confrontation so long practiced by the war protesters and civil rights advocates.

Carter's inability to cope with economic issues—inflation, unemployment, and energy shortages—helped usher in the even more conservative presidency of Ronald Reagan. Public opinion polls of 1980 disclosed popular concern with a perceived U.S. decline in relation to the Soviet Union and discontent with repeated affronts in international affairs to "national honor."[16] Both candidates campaigned on cold war platforms in 1980, which in effect moved the consensual midpoint to the right and left the McGovernite opponents of the Vietnam War and their successors virtually excluded.[17]

In campaign addresses, Reagan extolled the Vietnam War as a "noble cause" and characterized the Democrats as "dominated . . . by the McGovern wing," while the public was "sick and tired" of leadership that "tells us why we can't contain the Russians."[18] Reagan's 1984 campaign featured patriotic and cold war themes and credited his foreign policies with enabling the country to "stand tall" again in international affairs. His massive electoral victories disclose that the great body of Americans' yearnings for a return to national pride and patriotism were achieved through Reagan's presidency, and the values and virtues that were derogated by the Vietnam-nurtured counterculture have been restored. A consequence of Vietnam is a conservative restoration, which in the Reagan years is denoted by militancy in foreign affairs and a decline in the social activism of the Vietnam era.[19]

Public Opinion and the Media

Studies consistently have shown that nearly two-thirds of the public used television during and since the Vietnam War as their chief source of news, with newspapers a distant second.[20] The war was also the first to be regularly reported on television, and its blood and gore became a staple of nightly viewing. The president, too, was a focus of television, which it defined as the center of government action.

Television brought great political profit to masters of the medium like Kennedy and Reagan, but it also made the president a ready blame object, as Vietnam demonstrated, if policies went awry. When Walter Cronkite, the nonpareil newscaster, came to doubt the government's statements that the United States was winning the Vietnam War, he journeyed to Vietnam to see for himself, and he broadcast his findings to the nation in a special report: the war had in fact become a bloody stalemate, and military victory was beyond reach. President Johnson, after viewing the broadcast, turned to his aides and said, "It's all over." "We always knew," an aide explained, "that Cronkite had more authority with the American people than anyone else."[21] Although various factors doubtless contributed to his decision, Johnson, soon after Cronkite's report, announced that he was ending air and naval bombardment in most of Vietnam and that he would not run again for president.

An enduring legacy of Vietnam and Watergate is the widespread loss of confidence in the believability of the president. Although Ford and Carter strove to rid the office of that albatross and to run open administrations, restoring the presidency's pre-Vietnam credibility was no easy task. Carter's press secretary, Jody Powell, was surprised by the style of reporters' questions, which had the air of an inquisition seeking to unveil a dark secret. The press's manner was attributable, he thought, to Vietnam and Watergate, whose "wounds will take a lot longer to heal than I anticipated."[22]

If there is anything more potent than the media in influencing the state of public opinion with which the president must function, it is events themselves and their reflection in popular perceptions. For a time after the Vietnam War, public opinion constituted a relatively dovish consensus, which forced the president and Congress to sustain a reduction in the military establishment and in alliance commitments. This consensus was especially prevalent among voters under thirty and among opinion leaders, such as those of an upper socioeconomic status. But the Iranian hostage crisis and the Soviet invasion of Afghanistan in 1979 obliterated this heritage of Vietnam, and Gallup polls disclosed a landslide shift to support for rebuilding military readiness to protect U.S. interests abroad. Various polls showed a greater willingness to defend the nation's allies and to spend on defense than on any other kind of spending. A political vulnerability of the Vietnam War was its remoteness from the United States, but the 1980 polls revealed that proximity was a declining factor in the willingness to defend a country; Japan and the Persian Gulf, for example, faired nearly as well as Western Europe in attracting over two-thirds of the public willing to use force in their behalf.[23]

Sharing Power: The President and Congress

Since the Constitution allocates substantial power over foreign policy to both the executive and legislative branches, the state of relationships between them vitally affects how foreign policy is made and conducted. A major casualty of the Vietnam War was bipartisan foreign policy, whose roots reached back to World War II.

The Vietnam War also revived the historic Hamiltonian-Madisonian conflict that sporadically has simmered and boiled since the Constitution's inception. The president, in initiating and escalating the commitment of U.S. forces in Vietnam and in claiming a broad constitutional mandate to do so, acted out the Hamiltonian model. Opponents of the Vietnam War, however, asserted the Madisonian view: Congress is not limited to overseeing the executive and evaluating the quality of his performance; it is also responsible for developing its own policy, and the executive is duty bound to carry it out.

Once having embraced Madison's concept of its proper role, Congress asserted it imaginatively, particularly in contriving the War Powers Act of 1973, which was passed over Nixon's veto midway in the Watergate crisis when he was severely weakened politically. Under the resolution, the president can undertake emergency military action in the absence of a declaration of war, subject to reporting and consultation requirements, time limits, and possible intervention by Congress at any time. Congress can order an immediate removal of the forces by adopting a concurrent resolution, which is not subjective to presidential veto.

In the post-Vietnam era, the president's fortunes in sharing power with Congress can, for convenience, be seen in the near term (the Ford and Carter presidencies) and the further term (the Reagan presidency). In both intervals, Congress has pursued the Madisonian concept against a backdrop of shifting events and different presidents endowed with varying political skills and resources.

President Ford demonstrated that under the right circumstances, the War Powers Act could be no serious obstacle to the function of commander in chief, when Cambodian naval units seized a U.S. cargo ship, the *Mayaguez,* in 1975, soon after Vietnam fell. U.S. forces raided Cambodian territory, and the crew and vessel were retrieved. Public opinion polls showed strong support for the president, and Congress, as it is wont to do in the face of successful military action and obvious public approval, acclaimed the president's action. (Reagan's invasion of Grenada is also of this genre.) Ford complied with the notification requirements of the War Powers Act, although he cited his own authority as president as legal justification for his action.

Ford was less successful in Angola, which since 1974 has been beset by several local factions vying for power. A Soviet-backed faction, the Popular Movement for the Liberation of Angola (MPLA), prevailed over a rival faction, backed by the United States and China, in taking over the government. The Soviets imported thousands of Cuban troops into Angola, and Ford urgently appealed to Congress for funds to aid the pro-U.S. faction that continued to fight. Simultaneously he declared that U.S. troops would never be sent. But the Senate, as its debate on the measure repeatedly disclosed, was bent on "avoiding another Vietnam," and it rejected the president's request. For a time, the Ford administration supported its favored Angola faction with military supplies from available funds.[24] Secretary of State Kissinger voiced his displeasure with Congress by declaring that Americans, and especially the young, "have been traumatized by Vietnam as we were by Munich," causing a lack of will to stand up to the Soviets.[25]

Senator Dick Clark, still riding on Congress's mood of greater self-assertion generated by the Vietnam War, introduced an amendment to the foreign aid authorization bill to prohibit covert aid to Angola. The Senate rejected a plea by Senator Robert P. Griffin that the executive branch be granted "the flexibility necessary to carry out U.S. foreign policy" and adopted the amendment. While Senator Edward M. Kennedy warned of "another Vietnam on the continent of Africa" if "step-by-step increments" of U.S. money and manpower were committed, Ford reproached Congress for perpetrating "a deep tragedy for all countries whose security depends on the U.S."[26]

From another perspective, Ford and Kissinger too were under the spell of Vietnam. Nathaniel Davis, assistant secretary of state for African affairs, who advised against a covert operation, which, he said, would be matched by a counterescalation, felt that only quick, massive, decisive U.S. intervention would turn the tide. But, Davis was impressed, Kissinger and Ford were "not for that."[27]

The guerrilla warfare in Angola raged on into the Carter administration, and the mood of Congress, a carry-over from Vietnam, to restrict the president persisted. Carter determined to continue arms aid, but with existing appropriations running low, he was blocked by a second Clark amendment that permanently prohibited aid "of any kind" to promote military operations in Angola. Although the president protested that such constraints crippled his conduct of foreign policy, he avoided a confrontation with Congress.[28]

Zaire became a further test case when armed contingents from Angola, including Cuban troops, invaded it. Long supportive of U.S. policy in central Africa, Zaire pleaded for U.S. military assistance. But Carter responded meagerly, providing only modest amounts of equipment, spare parts, and medical supplies and no weapons or ammunition. Zaire President Mobutu bitterly condemned Carter for having "capitulated" to the Soviet-Cuban alliance, while administration officials acknowledged that their caution reflected a concern that any deeper involvement would stir memories of Vietnam and provoke a strong reaction from Congress and the country.[29] There were roughly similar scenarios in countries of the strategic Horn of Africa—Somalia, Sudan, Ethiopia—with local instabilities and Soviet and/or Cuban intervention.

It was during the near-term of the post-Vietnam era that Congress employed, in addition to the War Powers Act, several techniques for making its assertiveness more effective. Congress has long attached conditions to foreign aid; it sharpened their use during the Vietnam War, especially in its later stages, and in the post-Vietnam period the practice has been compounded. During the Carter administration, restrictions were imposed on twenty-six nations, including Afghanistan, prior to the Soviet invasion.

In the further term since the Vietnam War, with his emphasis on military means for attaining his foreign policy objectives, President Reagan has had many encounters with the War Powers Act. His reports to Congress, called for by the resolution, cover the commitment of a military force to the Sinai to carry out the peace treaty between Egypt and Israel (1982), the deployment of 1,200 marines to Lebanon as part of a multinational peacekeeping force (1982), the dispatch of military aircraft to aid Chad in its conflict with rebel and Libyan forces (1983), and the U.S. invasion of Grenada (1983). Like his predecessors, Reagan treated the reports as optional rather than mandatory. As combat intensified in Lebanon in 1983, the marines sustained casualties, and public support weakened, Congress adopted a resolution in September invoking previously unused provisions of the War Powers Act by passing a resolution authorizing the marines to remain in Lebanon for up to eighteen additional months. In signing this legislation invoking the War Powers Act, Reagan took pains to question its constitutionality and to declare that he would not be bound by its terms.[30] But by his signing, the president accorded the War Powers Resolution greater political status than it had ever attained in the decade of its existence.

On balance, the War Powers Act looms as a likely influence chiefly when the president, in using military force, cannot achieve prompt success; if public support meanwhile weakens—the Vietnam scenario—congressional opponents will invoke the resolution in attacking the president's policies. The act's utility has been enfeebled severely by *Immigration and Naturalization Service v. Chadha*, which in effect holds the legislative veto unconstitutional since it deprives the president of his constitutional role in lawmaking.[31]

Congress's appropriations power remains its most powerful limitation on presidential use of the armed forces, as it was before and during the Vietnam War. This thesis is supported by the legislative histories of the Reagan administration's policies concerning El Salvador, Nicaragua, and other Central American countries. Although Congress approved all economic development aid for El Salvador that Reagan requested in 1983, it cut his requests for military aid by 40 percent for fiscal 1983 and by 25 percent for fiscal 1984.[32] It also scaled down the administration's requests for aid to the Nicaraguan rebels, with a cap of $24 million imposed for 1984. In 1986, the administration's request for $100 million in aid to the rebels was approved by Congress only after public and acrimonious debate. These congressional debates, as well as Reagan's dispatch of military advisers to El Salvador, awakened memories for some of comparable steps leading toward irreversible U.S. involvement in Vietnam.

Despite a decade-long trend of increasing congressional assertiveness, constitutional constraints on Congress continue to ensure the preeminence of the president in foreign policymaking. Also as in the past, however, effective long-term policy requires the president to gain congressional support.

Conclusions

The Vietnam War, although vivid in national memory, has not altered the essence of the presidency, its empowerment and conduct. Impressed with the need for a strong chief executive in foreign affairs, the framers endowed the president with generous constitutional authority, including a monopoly of direct official action in foreign affairs. Although Vietnam has made presidential power more susceptible to legislative challenge, the foundation of that power, laid out by the framers, remains intact. Consequently, just as Jefferson, McKinley, and other pre-Vietnam presidents deployed the armed forces into combat and situations of potential combat, Reagan did so in Lebanon, Grenada, and Libya.

Vietnam affirmed the traditional public impatience with protracted, inconclusive war making and sharpened Congress's techniques for constraining the president's exercise of power. When he requires legislative support, he is more likely to obtain half a loaf than the full measure of his requests.

As a historic phenomenon, Vietnam is itself vulnerable to limitations. As time passes, it becomes weaker in public memory. Its effects can be modified by changes in the international and domestic environments. The Soviet invasion of Afghanistan was one such modifier, an abrupt reminder that the Vietnam analogy was no all-purpose tool for coping with every thrust and hazard in world affairs. Similarly, Vietnam is modifiable by the onset of new charismatic presidential leadership, such as Reagan's, which helped sustain his combat initiatives in foreign affairs.

The Vietnam War and the changes in the Democratic party that it helped engender have altered the state of interparty competition for control of the presidency. Since the Kennedy-Johnson era, the Republican party has won every presidential election, except for Carter's triumph in 1976. According to public opinion polls and analyses by its own leaders, the Democratic party, as a fertile source of antiwar critics, has acquired in the electorate's eyes an image of insufficient commitment to the defense of U.S. interests abroad. Reagan profitably exploited that image in the 1980 and 1984 elections.

According to opinion polls, the public is eager for the United States to strike a more assertive posture abroad, in contrast to the relative quiescence that characterized the immediate post-Vietnam era of Ford and Carter. The public's longing smoothed the way for legislative concurrence in Reagan's program of arms expansion in his presidency's early years. But, paradoxically, the public, apparently under Vietnam's spell, abhors engagement in a protracted war. That preference has modified Reagan's policies concerning Nicaragua, El Salvador, and Lebanon. In his administration's later years, it has stiffened congressional resistance to his program of arms expansion.

A principal consequence of the Vietnam War is Congress's discovery that it can use its appropriation power with decisive effect—as a veto or modifier of the president's management of foreign affairs. By every sign, the appropriation power will continue to be a major instrument of future congressional assertion. It provides leverage for the bargaining and compromise that have become commonplace in the areas of joint legislative-executive policymaking. Television, whose political profitability to legislators was securely established in the Vietnam War, remains undimmed. Now as then, it is a source of national political recognition for legislators and a means of building constituency support.

On balance, Vietnam endures as an object lesson to presidents that warns that if they become committed to waging an extended unwinnable war, they risk incurring severe political costs, including the possible sacrifice of their reelection. As yet, their chief insurance (but not assurance) against these unwanted consequences is the coupling of Congress and the president as the joint initiators of combat. That course was followed successfully in the two world wars. If the president is perceived to be the solitary initiator of the war, the deluge of future blame will fall entirely on his shoulders. A prudent president, as the Vietnam War instructs, will be solicitous to associate Congress with his decision to initiate combat.

Notes

1. Chester Cooper, *Lost Crusade* (New York: Dodd, Mead, 1970), pp. 193–194.

2. *The Pentagon Papers* (New York: New York Times, 1971), pp. 215–232.

3. Townsend Hoopes, *The Limits of Intervention* (New York: David McKay Company, 1973), pp. 13–19.

4. Malcolm W. Browne, "Two Hawks and a Dove: How They Look at the Indochina War Now," *New York Times,* April 30, 1985, p. A6.

5. Bernard Gwertzman, "Senator Lugar Seeks to Define Policy Abroad," *New York Times,* January 24, 1985, p. 1.

6. Excerpts of Weinberger's and Shultz's views are in *New York Times,* November 28, December 9, 1984.

7. Bernard Gwertzman, "Senator," *New York Times,* April 30, 1985, p. A6.

8. Bruce Mazlish and Edwin Diamond, *Jimmy Carter: An Interpretive Biography* (New York: Simon and Schuster, 1979), p. 261.

9. I.M. Destler, "National Security Advice to U.S. Presidents: Some Lessons from Thirty Years," *World Politics* 29 (January 1977): 155.

10. Hoopes, *Limits of Intervention,* pp. 59–60.

11. I.M. Destler, "National Security Management: What Presidents Have Wrought," *Political Science Quarterly* 95 (Winter 1980–1981): 578–586.

12. Robert C. Goldwin, ed., *Political Parties in the Eighties* (Washington, D.C.: American Enterprise Institute, 1980), p. 6.

13. Walter Dean Burnham, *The Current Crisis in American Politics* (New York: Oxford University Press, 1982), p. 299.

14. Nelson W. Polsby, *Consequences of Party Reform* (New York: Oxford University Press, 1983), p. 54.

15. Goldwin, *Political Parties in the Eighties,* p. 119.

16. Burnham, *Current Crisis,* p. 288.

17. Thomas Ferguson and Joel Rogers, *The Hidden Election: Politics and Economics in the 1980 Presidential Campaign* (New York: Random House, 1981), pp. 217–218.

18. Ibid., p. 219.

19. Allan E. Goodman and Seth P. Tillman, "10 Years Later, Lessons of the Vietnam War," *New York Times,* March 24, 1985, p. E23.

20. Austin Ranney, *Channels of Power: The Impact of Television on American Politics* (New York: Basic Books, 1983), pp. 19–20.

21. Ibid., pp. 4–5.

22. Michael Grossman and Martha Kumar, *Portraying the President* (Baltimore: Johns Hopkins Press, 1981), pp. 10–11.

23. Bruce Russett and Donald R. DeLuca, "'Don't Tread on Me': Public Opinion and Foreign Policy in the Eighties," *Political Science Quarterly* 96 (Fall 1981): 381–389.

24. David Binder, "Angola Reported Getting $50 Million in U.S. Arms," *New York Times,* December 12, 1975, p. 1.

25. Address, April 17, 1975, *Department of State Bulletin,* May 5, 1975, p. 560.

26. James L. Sundquist, *The Decline and Resurgence of Congress* (Washington, D.C.: Brookings Institution, 1981), pp. 286–287.

27. Nathaniel Davis, "The Angola Decision of 1975: A Personal Memoir," *Foreign Affairs* 57 (Fall 1978): 114, 123.

28. Bernard Gwertzman, "Carter Cites Limits on Policy in Angola," *New York Times,* May 24, 1978, p. 1.

29. Graham Hovey, "U.S. Will Send Zaire $13 Million Package of 'Nonlethal' Help," *New York Times,* April 13, 1977, p. 1.

30. *Congressional Quarterly Almanac, 1983,* pp. 109–110.
31. *Immigration and Naturalization Service v. Chadha,* 462 U.S. 919 (1983).
32. *Congressional Quarterly Almanac, 1983,* p. 111.

5
Domesticating Foreign Policy: Congress and the Vietnam War

Wallace Earl Walker

Wars agitate Congress. In the grand arena of institutional politics, large-scale wars have intensified the legislative-executive struggle for dominance in policymaking. The great containment struggle waged by the United States from 1941 to 1966—what most call World War II and the cold war—was an exception. The Vietnam War was not.

Following the Revolutionary War, the Confederation and the Constitutional Congresses were the dominant institutions in the federal establishment. The brilliant maneuvering of Thomas Jefferson and the populism of Andrew Jackson provided but fleeting exceptions to this rule.[1] During the Civil War, President Abraham Lincoln turned the presidency into the ascendant branch in the federal government. Motivated by Lincoln's unprecedented assertions of power, Congress reasserted its policymaking authority after the Civil War and continued to rule through the end of the nineteenth century.[2] The same pattern is evident during and after World War I: executive branch preeminence followed by congressional reassertion of power. As E.S. Corwin and Theodore Lowi have shown, there is a cyclical nature to presidential power, and since the Great Depression and World War II, presidents have aggrandized power to turn government into an active, reforming force at home and abroad.[3]

External threats to national security invite a presidential response because only the chief executive possesses the necessary resources and horizons to react. Historically, such responses have entailed an expansion of power, as exemplified by Lincoln's blockade of the South during the Civil War and Franklin Roosevelt's lend-lease agreement with Great Britain. These executive assertions of power threaten the institutional arrangements established by the Constitution. Congress has no choice but to reassert itself after such episodes; to fail to do so is to risk irrelevance in foreign affairs and, ultimately, in domestic concerns as well.

Thus the great containment struggle was anomalous. Although Congress did seek in a tentative way to reassert itself immediately after World War II in such areas as aid to Greece and Turkey, the Marshall Plan, and the 1947

National Security Act, the arrival of the cold war in 1947 and 1948 almost immediately seemed to relegate Congress to the role of a minor actor. Congress did not seek to reestablish its authority after the Korean War. Thus the rise of the Soviet empire, the threat of nuclear war, and the necessity for the United States to play a dominant role in world affairs provided the executive branch with a tailor-made situation for national security policy dominance. In fact as Arthur Schlesinger has noted, a global foreign policy swallowed up congressional power.[4]

This chapter will explain how Congress reasserted itself during the Vietnam War and immediately after. It will consider congressional reactions not only to the war itself but also to subsequent presidential initiatives in foreign policy and then will review the implications of this resurgence in foreign policy formulation and implementation. Essentially, I will argue that congressional reactions to the war itself were less significant than the statutes it imposed on the executive branch as a result of the Vietnam War. Those statutes have dramatically restrained the presidency in conducting foreign policy. The result of these laws is the domestication, the democratization, and the destabilization of national security policymaking.

Congressional Reactions to the Southeast Asian War

Congress supported the war in Vietnam. Indeed Congress and Presidents Lyndon Johnson and Richard Nixon served as partners for that war. As Leslie Gelb has observed, the weight of congressional actions regarding Vietnam both "reinforced the stakes against losing and introduced constraints against winning."[5] Thus, from the early 1950s through the introduction of U.S. combat troops into Vietnam and until their withdrawal in 1973, Congress as an institution backed presidential initiatives in Southeast Asia and routinely appropriated funds for the war.

It is equally fair to say, however, that Senate doves were outspoken in their opposition to the war from the first introduction of ground troops. The incursion of U.S. troops into Cambodia in April 1970 was perhaps the seminal event that crystallized broad congressional opposition. Once troops were withdrawn from Southeast Asia and U.S. prisoners of war were released in 1973, Congress moved quickly to end U.S. involvement. A chronology of major events relating to U.S. policy in Southeast Asia appears in table 5–1.

Congressional concern for not "losing Southeast Asia" to Communist influence dates to the early 1950s. Most congressmen felt that the United States should support united action there but were opposed to the introduction of combat troops. This disposition was clearly evident in the Eisenhower administration's consultations with senior members of Congress in April 1954 over the use of U.S. combat support to relieve the beleaguered French

Table 5–1
Congressional Response to Vietnam: Significant Events

April 1954	Senior members of Congress object to the use of air and naval power to assist the French at Dien Bien Phu.
September 1954	SEATO becomes operative with Senate approval
August 1964	Congress readily passes the Gulf of Tonkin Resolution
May 1965	Congress quickly passes President Johnson's appropriations request for combat operations in South Vietnam
May 1966	Senator William Fulbright's hearings legitimate opposition to war
August 1967	Senator John Stennis's hearings advocate heavier use of combat power
Spring 1968	Further hearings before Senator Fulbright's Foreign Relations committee are televised and promote opposition to the war
March 1968	Senate hawks resist the introduction of 206,000 more troops into Vietnam
April 1970	Cambodian invasion stirs congressional opposition
January 1971	Cooper-Church amendment bans further combat operations in Cambodia; Gulf of Tonkin Resolution is repealed
May 1973	Congress prohibits the reintroduction of forces into Vietnam after August 15, 1973
September 1974	Congress resists President Ford's request for restoration of aid cuts
April 1975	Congress refuses to provide further aid to Vietnam; Secretary Kissinger declares Congress a "coequal branch" in foreign policy

fortress at Dien Bien Phu. It was also evident in the Senate's approval of SEATO during that same year.[6]

With the deterioration of the political situation in South Vietnam in the early 1960s, the increased success of the Vietcong guerrilla movement, and the reaction of North Vietnam to increased U.S. military presence in Southeast Asia, Congress was more than willing to sustain President Johnson's initiatives. After the alleged attack by North Vietnam on the U.S. destroyer *Maddox* in August 1964, Johnson won support for the Tonkin Gulf resolution by a House vote of 414–0 and a Senate vote of 88–2. The following spring Johnson again handily won congressional support by declaring that his proposal for $400 million to support military operations in Vietnam would constitute a referendum on his policies.[7]

Subsequent congressional votes were equally supportive. In early 1973 the *Congressional Quarterly* calculated that from 1965 through the end of 1972, over 95 percent of congressmen present and voting approved war-related appropriations on the final votes in each chamber.[8] To put the matter another way, of the 113 recorded votes on the Vietnam War in this period, almost all sustained presidential initiatives.[9]

Congressional hearings did create difficulties for the chief executive in managing the war. In fact these hearings tended to whipsaw the president in one direction and then another. Within one year after the Tonkin Gulf resolution, Senator William Fulbright, chairman of the Foreign Relations Committee, began to have serious doubts about his support for the resolution and for U.S. actions in Vietnam. Hearings held by his committee in 1966 and 1968 provided legitimacy for those opposed to the war and later prompted opposition to the war.[10] Simultaneously Senate hawks were squeezing the president from another direction. In 1967 hearings before Senator John Stennis's Armed Services Committee, the administration was criticized for not using sufficient force to end the war. Yet Senate hawks were unwilling to support the introduction of more ground troops into Vietnam after the 1968 Tet offensive.[11]

After the Cambodian incursion, Senate doves were able to gain congressional support for some of their initiatives.[12] In January 1971 the Cooper-Church amendment to the Foreign Assistance Act banned the further use of ground combat troops in Cambodia. Also in that month, Congress repealed the Tonkin Gulf resolution. After the Christmas bombings of 1972 and the return of all U.S. prisoners, Senate doves were able to win passage of a bill that prohibited the reintroduction of U.S. combat forces into Vietnam after August 15, 1973.[13]

In 1974 Congress heavily cut administration requests for military aid to South Vietnam. In the face of a coordinated and massive North Vietnamese military assault in South Vietnam, President Ford objected to these cuts, but Congress would not restore them.[14] In April 1975 Congress refused to provide any further military aid to South Vietnam. These actions eroded the morale of the Saigon government and also withheld U.S. support for a rapidly deteriorating situation. By May, the North had overrun all of South Vietnam.

Thus, Congress sustained support for military prosecution of the Vietnam War as long as U.S. troops were engaged in combat or held prisoner. Once U.S. troops had departed, Congress cut aid almost immediately and ended it altogether soon after.

Congressional Reaction to Executive Ascendancy in Foreign Policy

Congressional reactions to the Vietnam War itself were less significant than congressional reassertiveness in foreign affairs. The impact of the war on presidential hegemony (and congressional subservience) in national security policymaking was profound. Without question the war shattered the post–World War II myth of executive infallibility in foreign and defense affairs and the consensus on containing communism. Thereby the war promoted a total restructuring of government procedures in policymaking.[15]

Congressional resurgence in policymaking in general and in national security policymaking in particular during the 1970s was stunning in both its speed and its breadth. Listed in table 5–2 are the more significant pieces of legislation that followed the demise of popular support for the war in early 1968.[16] Beyond these landmark statutes were a host of other congressional actions that impinged upon the formulation and conduct of foreign policy during the 1970s and early 1980s. Former Senator John Tower has counted over 150 such restrictions on executive influence in the 1970s alone.[17] The following list notes but a few of these limitations on executive policy formulation:

Nixon and Ford years (1969–1977): 1973, 1974, and 1975 Jackson-Vanik and Stevenson amendments linking U.S. trade with the Soviet Union to Jewish emigration; 1974 arms embargo on Turkey; 1975 restrictions on the mobility of Hawk missiles sold to Jordan; 1976 Tunney amendment prohibiting covert or overt operations in Angola. Also in this period the following: cut or reduced presidentially proposed military

Table 5–2
Post-Vietnam Statutes that Transformed Foreign Policymaking

1970	Legislative Reorganization Act	Increases congressional oversight by expanding congressional staff and enhancing the power and responsibilities of the General Accounting Office and the Congressional Research Service
1972	Case Act	Requires details on all executive agreements be submitted to Congress
1973	War Powers Resolution	Requires presidential reporting on use of troops overseas and subsequent support for such troops remaining beyond ninety days
1973 and 1975	CIA restrictions	Hughes-Ryan Amendment of 1973 requires all CIA operations to be reported; 1975 resolutions create Select Committees on Intelligence in both chambers
1974	Budget and Impoundment Control Act	Promotes greater congressional control over the budget and restricts presidential reapportionment and impoundment of funds
1974	Freedom of Information Act Amendments	Make agency documents more easily available by reducing the hurdles erected by executive bureaucracies
1974 and 1976	Amendments to Arms Export Control Act	Provide for notice of foreign arms sales and opportunity for Congress to veto such sales
1976	National Emergencies Act	Restricts presidential use of national emergency legislation and requires him to advise Congress on any action he takes under this legislation
1976	Harkin amendment	Creates a human rights coordinator in the State Department, requires annual reports for each country receiving security assistance, and places security aid restrictions on countries violating human rights

assistance to numerous countries for human rights violations; U.S. withdrawal from the International Labor Organization; temporary withdrawal of U.S. funds to UNESCO; and a mandated delay on the construction of a U.S. naval base at Diego Garcia.

Carter years (1977–1981): Restrictions on the Panama Canal Treaty and arms sales to Israel, Saudi Arabia, and Egypt; prohibition on imports of chrome from Rhodesia; resolutions opposing Carter initiatives to withdraw U.S. troops from South Korea and to normalize relations with Vietnam and China; and influence on the final SALT II accords

Reagan years (1981–present): Restrictions on actions in El Salvador and Central America and prohibition on continued aid to the contra rebels in Nicaragua.

The Vietnam War was the central cause of congressional resurgence in the 1970s. Analysts list a host of other explanations that clearly contributed to this new congressional assertiveness, among them the Watergate scandal; impoundment of funds by the Nixon administration; a new generation of congressmen impatient with established internal norms of seniority and policy procedures; the several-fold increase in congressional staff; détente between the Soviet Union and the United States; U.S.-Soviet parity in nuclear forces; and the new salience of such economic issues as energy and international trade in foreign policy.[18] Yet for all analysts, the public rancor and congressional frustration over the conduct of the Vietnam War remain either the most significant explanation for congressional resurgence or are listed as equally prominent with Nixon's impoundment of funds and Watergate. Some even argue that Watergate and the impoundments were the result of the sense of isolation and paranoia enveloping the White House over public reaction to Nixon's prosecution of the Vietnam War.[19]

Thus, most explanations seem ultimately to wind their way back to Vietnam as the central cause of congressional resurgence in foreign policy in the 1970s. As Congressman Lee Hamilton and House International Relations Committee staff director Michael Van Dusen have observed: "The new assertiveness and activism of Congress have stemmed from many factors. But to any member whose service goes back to 1965, there is no question that Vietnam was the single most important event in that transformation."[20] Thus by 1965, forces other than Vietnam had created a smoldering resentment among legislators over presidential aggrandizement of power in foreign affairs, and the presidential conduct of that war provided the spark that inflamed Congress. Absent the Vietnam War, Congress may well have sought to restrict presidential power in foreign policymaking, but it seems doubtful that it would have gone as far or as fast in reasserting itself.

Implications of Congressional Resurgence

This congressional reassertion of power has had three effects on national security affairs: domestication (how the executive branch must work with Congress), democratization (how Congress influences national security policy), and destabilization (how national security policy must now be characterized).

Domestication

Post–World War II presidents used two very different approaches to policy-making. On domestic issues, intensive labor was required to design a new initiative, to dramatize the need for change, to build a supporting coalition inside and outside Congress, and to appease constituencies likely to be harmed by the proposal.[21] The success rate for such initiatives was never very high; the presidents, however, did not expect easy victories.

They did expect to be more successful in national security affairs. In this realm, the president possessed a more plentiful range of options: propaganda initiatives available through the U.S. Information Agency, arms sales or economic aid to foreign governments, secret executive agreements, CIA covert action, or military intervention. The choices in national security policymaking required deciding what to do in initiating a new policy or what response was appropriate for a crisis; the options in both areas were usually unappealing. Once the decision was made, the president needed only to explain his policy to perhaps half a dozen senior congressmen and provide a few cryptic public announcements.[22]

This distinction between domestic and national security policymaking no longer applies.[23] The statutes listed in table 5–2 have deprived the president of his readily available options. To cite but a few examples, the Arms Export Control Act makes foreign military sales subject to congressional approval, and the Case Act no longer permits secret executive agreements. National security policymaking must now be conducted largely in the open.

Furthermore, Congress has disaggregated into what might be called member-centered government. In other eras, Congress was dominated by the political parties. In the early 1900s, party government gave way to committee government in Congress.[24] As a result of the 1970 Legislative Reorganization Act, the Budget Act, and numerous other resolutions, Congress has disaggregated even further. Member-centered government is characterized by vastly reduced power of party and committee leaders and by increased resources and influences for individual members of Congress.[25] This fragmentation has forced the president to search for fresh coalitions on virtually every foreign policy initiative in order to achieve his ends. His failure to build such coalitions and to appease opposing constituencies affects his reputation at home and his credibility abroad. Allied and neutral nations are increasingly less disposed to negotiate with an administration unable to obtain congressional support for its initiatives. Indeed, Congress has become a principal obstacle to coherence in U.S. national security policy.[26]

Presidential comments on the difficulty in conducting U.S. affairs under these conditions confirm the domestication of national security policy. Gerald Ford has observed that he attempted to consult with Congress as required by the War Powers Act in the 1975 *Mayaguez* rescue effort, but the incident occurred during a congressional recess:

> Not one of the key bipartisan leaders of Congress was in Washington. . . . This, one might say is an unfair example, since the Congress was in recess. But it must be remembered that critical world events, especially military operations, seldom wait for Congress to meet. In fact most of what goes on in the world happens in the middle of the night, Washington time.[27]

Jimmy Carter and former Vice-President Walter Mondale have been equally critical about coordinating with Congress on foreign affairs.[28] Thus, in an era of member-centered government, presidential consultation with Congress during periods of crisis borders on the impossible. The president can no longer confidently negotiate with a small number of congressmen as President Eisenhower did in 1954 over the siege at Dien Bien Phu.

In many ways the burdens on presidents pale in comparison to the demands on cabinet and subcabinet officers. Francis Wilcox has counted sixteen committees in the Senate that call for foreign policy testimony from the administration. It is more often the case than not that cabinet secretaries, their deputies, and their under secretaries and assistant secretaries must provide essentially the same testimony two or more times before various congressional committees. For example, initiatives on foreign military sales often require testimony before the House International Affairs Committee, the Senate Foreign Relations Committee, the House Armed Services Committee, and the Senate Armed Services Committee. In fact former Deputy Secretary of State Warren Christopher has calculated that he and Secretary of State Cyrus Vance spent more than 25 percent of their time dealing with the Congress.[29]

Congressional intervention in national security affairs does have certain advantages, which presidents are often loathe to advertise. Because policymaking is now more open and the executive branch is no longer viewed as infallible, the president needs protection.[30] There is much to be said for a presidential strategy that blames intractable foreign policy issues on congressionally initiated statutes, which are said to shackle the president in the conduct of foreign policy. Presidents can condemn Congress for its intransigence in some policy matter. Thus presidents can blame the deteriorating situation in Angola on congressional restraints over covert activity or the frustration over Turkish base rights on legislative restrictions on foreign military sales.

Democratization

Paralleling the domestication of the foreign and defense policy processes have been the increasing activism and influence of new players heretofore excluded from the system. These players, who operate from both inside and outside Congress, are positioned to take advantage of existing congressional repertoires for authorization, budgeting, and oversight, and thus they have been able to affect congressional influence on national security matters.

The authorization process in the area of national security affairs is now much more detailed. Prior to the 1960s, Congress would authorize, for example, a new weapons system and then appropriate funds for the purchase of an entire set of weapons. Now each year the House and Senate Armed Services committees must authorize each new ship, airplane, and tank, and then the House and Senate Appropriations committees must appropriate funds for every one of these weapons.[31] Passage through this legislative labyrinth provides numerous opportunities for changing or deleting a program such that the end result is often unrecognizable from the initial proposal.

To fund all national security agencies and programs, the budgeting process must be negotiated. The 1974 Budget Act provides for new budget committees in each chamber and for a new repertoire for moving funding requests through the Congress. This new repertoire has impeded and constrained national security policies. As often as not, no budget is passed, and programs must survive on continuing resolutions or previous-year funding levels.

The oversight process is less routinized but equally accessible to outside interests. Further empowered by the 1970 Legislative Reorganization Act and Budget Act, the legislative and government operations committees in both chambers have become much more active in conducting oversight since the Vietnam War. For instance, congressional committees monitor both the reports on human rights behavior of foreign governments that receive security assistance and reports on executive agreements. More oversight has meant more executive accountability, but it has also meant that executive officials are required to spend more of their time calculating congressional reactions before they initiate or implement policies. Thus, in the aggregate, the authorization, budgetary, and oversight processes have been modified by the post-Vietnam reforms initiated by the Congress and have opened up national security affairs to review and influence more fully than at any other time in U.S. history.

Not only have the policymaking processes been altered, but the players have changed as well. Inside the Congress, the House has become as influential in national security affairs as the Senate. The statutory reforms listed in table 5–2 give the House as much influence over such issues as executive agreements and foreign military sales. More committees are also involved. The Budget committees and the select committees on Intelligence are new additions. Older committees, such as the Commerce and Interior committees, have expanded their domains to include such issues as foreign trade, energy, and transnational pollution. Subcommittees of the House Foreign Affairs Committee, such as the Asian and Pacific Affairs Subcommittee, chaired by Congressman Stephen J. Solarz (D–N.Y.), have amassed considerable influence in the foreign policy community.[32] All of this attention on national security affairs has meant more openness and more conflict as each committee and subcommittee seek to stake out its domains. More openness and more conflict result in more influence for congressmen, who can now intervene in many more ways, and for outside interests groups, who find national security policymaking conducted more openly.

There are two other new sets of players within the Congress, each of which has been shaped by the Vietnam War. The first is a new generation of congressmen who are disposed to member-centered government.[33] A number of them became politically active in reaction to the Vietnam War, and they see themselves as liberals committed to the idealism of John Kennedy and the Great Society programs created by Lyndon Johnson. They tend to view U.S. involvement overseas with skepticism, if not outright resistance. For instance, Congressmen Michael Synar (D–Okla.) and Bruce Morrisson (D–Conn.) were both actively involved in the antiwar movement, and both have been cautious about U.S. intervention in Lebanon and Central America.[34]

The second set of new players on Capitol Hill are congressional staffers. During the 1970s, their numbers increased several-fold. Now virtually every member has at least one legislative assistant whose full-time, or at least principal, concern is national security affairs. Committee staffs have grown enormously too. Whereas in 1947 when Francis Wilcox served on the Senate Foreign Relations Committee staff with only three clerks, today the committee has some sixty staff members, most of them highly trained professionals.[35] The principal preoccupation of these staffers is to find racy issues for their subcommittee chairman, issues that will add to their patron's stature or influence. Such issues are willingly provided by interest groups preoccupied with their own special concerns.[36]

Outside the Congress, many more groups now actively influence national security affairs than before the Vietnam War. The Freedom of Information Act Amendments and the Case Act provisions have provided such groups sufficient intelligence to advise both the Congress and the executive on a host of issues. Ethnic organizations representing Greeks and Jews, for example, have played an increasingly active role in foreign arms sales to Turkey and to Arab countries. Most commercial interests are now represented by full-time lobbyists working out of trade associations or out of newly created Washington headquarters. Much of this lobbying has become much more aggressive and tends to be based on temporary coalitions that create temporary "war rooms" to organize their efforts on issues coming before the White House or Congress.[37]

Still a third set of new outsiders includes ideological groups and think tanks representing all facets along the political spectrum. The Heritage Foundation, the Hoover Institute, the Committee on the Present Danger, the Nuclear Freeze Political Action Committee, and the Center for Defense Information have allied themselves with various supporters on Capitol Hill.[38]

The final cluster of outside groups seeking influence on national security affairs in Congress are foreign governments, which used to limit their representation to the executive branch. Aware that congressional sensibilities need to be stroked, foreign leaders now seek to spend as much time on Capitol Hill as they do in the White House. Furthermore, foreign embassies, such as Jordan, Israel, and Canada, openly lobby congressmen on such issues as security assistance and fisheries treaties.[39] Embassies or designated lobbyists such as those representing Korea and South Africa also seek to build grass-roots support. As one observer noted, the efforts of such embassies "to influence American opinion [have] become less surreptitious and far more sophisticated and subtle."[40]

Thus groups outside the Congress have become more agitated, and new players inside the Congress have become more polarized on foreign and defense policy.[41] Agitation and polarization have promoted democratization in national security policymaking as groups inside and outside Congress demand the attention of political executives and congressmen.

Destabilization

The Congress has responded to this clamor by becoming involved in everything and therefore, perhaps, incapable of acting on anything. Thus the result of domestication and democratization of U.S. national security policy is destabilization.

In member-centered government, no issues are considered sacrosanct. All are subject to intervention or at least frantic, episodic review through the authorization, budgetary, or oversight processes.[42] Impasse often results when the president is deprived of freedom of action and is unable to sustain more than a few initiatives in foreign affairs or when the Congress is predisposed to suspicion of presidential initiatives in all facets of national security affairs. Thus, treaties go unratified—as in the 1979 fisheries agreement with Canada—or are ratified with debilitating side payments by the president and with direct Senate involvement in the negotiations—as in the

Panama Canal Treaty. Other manifestations of this impasse are numerous country-specific restrictions on foreign economic and security aid, restrictions that weaken U.S. relationships abroad (such as the foreign aid restrictions on Turkey after the Cyprus invasion) or humiliate foreign governments (as in congressional restrictions on Hawk missiles sold to Jordan).

Statutory constraints have limited the president's ability to forge a new consensus on foreign affairs and to guarantee to allies or friendly third world nations U.S. support. The Harkin amendment's emphasis on human rights has polarized the government, resulting in dramatic diplomatic shifts on this issue from the Carter to the Reagan administrations. The War Powers Act and CIA restrictions have impeded the U.S. ability to sustain a military or paramilitary intervention, thereby creating doubts about the reliability of U.S. response in a crisis. Allies must now hedge against the unwillingness of the United States to intervene or rapid U.S. withdrawal regardless of the consequences.[43] Potential adversaries, superpower and third world alike, are no longer faced with what one senior foreign policy official confidentially called the "long shadow of military force" to back up U.S. negotiating stances.

Just as congressional frustration over the handling of the Vietnam War begat the War Powers Act, that act begat the Weinberger doctrine, which has imposed a number of preconditions on the use of military force, among them, clearly defined political and military objectives, a commitment to winning, and clear support of the Congress and the public.[44] Such preconditions have created considerable strain in the national security establishment with, at one time, Secretary of State George Schultz and the national security adviser, Robert McFarlane, critical of the defense secretary and these preconditions.

Thus U.S. national security policy is destabilized, with no consensus over what aims should be pursued and what means are appropriate. Clearly the congressional reaction to the Vietnam War has played a central role in creating this state of affairs.

Conclusions

The Vietnam War brought executive-legislative relationships over national security policy full circle. The unusual quiescence of Congress after World War II and Korea ended during and after the Vietnam War. This chapter has advanced three propositions about institutional relationships in national security affairs. First, Congress supports presidential actions while U.S. troops are engaged in combat. Second, aggregate congressional support does not stifle the dissent of individual congressmen opposed to the war or its conduct. Finally, as wars conclude, Congress responds by reasserting its power in relation to the executive branch.

What Congress learned from the Vietnam War—if institutional recognition of developments can be called learning—is that presidential power cannot go unchecked if Congress is to retain its constitutional powers. What presidents have learned—or should have learned—is that they must forge alliances on Capitol Hill. Arrogance in the face of these constitutional provisions will, in the end, deprive presidents of their initiative in national security affairs.

Another conclusion from the post–Vietnam War period is that a consensus sustained by a theme in national security affairs is crucial to executive-legislative relations. Neither President Carter nor Reagan has attended to this requirement to build a new consensus around some new strategy, preferring instead to focus on specific episodes or issues in national security affairs. Members of the Reagan administration have privately stated that they should not articulate such a policy because the details invite criticism as outsiders compare performance with aspirations. What neither administration seems to have realized is that absent such a grand strategy and consensus for that strategy, as there was for containment before Vietnam, success in specific policy areas is much more difficult to achieve. This is so because congressional supporters find presidential policy initiatives easier to promote if they can make the case that these intitiatives sustain national strategy and thereby serve the national interest.

One must also conclude that a coherent and cohesive foreign policy seems unlikely under conditions of congressional resurgence unless Congress confines itself to the role of developing consensus on the broad parameters of grand strategy and pressing the executive branch to develop and implement specific policies within that grand design. Such limitations are not likely in the near term; yet the result is likely to be great risks to U.S. prestige and influence abroad. Destabilized foreign policymaking is synonymous with drift, not mastery. Drift by the United States means a free world without leadership, a condition not likely to promote international arrangements supportive of U.S. goals and interests.

In the arena of grand politics, where the Constitution decrees executive-legislative struggle, the beginning of the Vietnam War was another executive peak in the cycle followed by still another instance of congressional resurgence during and after the war. In this sense, little has changed.

In another sense, everything has changed. In foreign policymaking, congressional resurgence to executive power during and after the Vietnam War was qualitatively different. New laws, new organizations, and new processes have fundamentally realigned national security affairs. These shifts have promoted member-centered government in which many members of Congress have become actively involved in defense and foreign policy issues. Congress is now an equal partner, and in some cases the dominant partner, in national security policymaking. The results to date of this new partnership have been the domestication, democratization, and destabilization of U.S. foreign policy. For those who worry about the United States and its worldwide responsibilities, congressional resurgence matters a great deal indeed.

Notes

1. James Young, *The Washington Community: 1800–1828* (New York: Harcourt Brace & World, 1966), and John Ward, *Andrew Jackson* (London: Oxford University Press, 1953).

2. E.S. Corwin, *The President: Office and Powers* (New York: New York University Press, 1957), pp. 229–231, and Woodrow Wilson, *Congressional Government* (Gloucester, Mass.: Peter Smith, 1973).

3. Corwin, *President,* pp. 234–262, 306–313, and Theodore Lowi, *The End of Liberalism* (New York: W.W. Norton, 1969), pp. 157–190.

4. Arthur Schlesinger, *The Imperial Presidency* (Boston: Houghton Mifflin, 1973), p. 206.

5. Leslie Gelb, *The Irony of Vietnam: The System Worked* (Washington, D.C.: Brookings Institution, 1979), p. 25.

6. James Sundquist, *The Decline and Resurgence of Congress* (Washington, D.C.: Brookings Institution, 1981), pp. 113–114, and George Herring, *America's Longest War* (New York: Wiley, 1979), pp. 31–32.

7. Alton Frye and Jack Sullivan, "Congress and Vietnam: The Fruits of Anguish," in *The Vietnam Legacy,* ed. Anthony Lake (New York: New York University Press, 1976), p. 198.

8. *Congressional Quarterly Weekly Report,* June 27, 1973, p. 115.

9. Frye and Sullivan, "Congress," p. 199.

10. Sundquist, *Decline,* p. 241; Frye and Sullivan, "Congress," p. 199.

11. Gelb, *Irony of Vietnam,* pp. 158, 176.

12. Francis Bax, "The Legislative-Executive Relationship in Foreign Policy," *Orbis* 20 (Winter 1977): 889.

13. Edward Haley, *Congress and the Fall of South Vietnam and Cambodia* (London: Associated University Presses, 1982), pp. 29–31, 41–42.

14. Earl Ravenal, "Consequences of the End Game in Vietnam," *Foreign Affairs* 43 (July 1975): 651.

15. Hrach Gregorian, "Assessing Congressional Involvement in Foreign Policy," *Review of Politics* 46 (January 1984): 94–95.

16. Data for tables 5–1 and 5–2 and the list of restrictions that follows have been gleaned from virtually all the sources cited in these notes.

17. John Tower, "Congress versus the President," *Foreign Affairs* 60 (Winter 1981–1982): 234.

18. Sundquist, *Decline,* p. 238; Gregorian, "Assessing Congressional Involvement," p. 95; Francis Wilcox, "Cooperation vs. Confrontation," *Atlantic Community Quarterly* 20 (Fall 1984): 261; Lee Hamilton and Michael Van Dusen, "Making the Separation of Powers Work," *Foreign Affairs* 62 (Fall 1978): 23; Lawrence Dodd and Richard Schott, *Congress and the Administrative State* (New York: Wiley, 1979).

19. Gelb, *Irony of Vietnam,* p. 348; Herring, *America's Longest War,* p. 25.

20. Hamilton and Van Dusen, "Making the Separation of Powers Work," p. 18.

21. Aaron Wildavsky, "The Two Presidencies," in *Classics of the American Presidency,* ed. Harry Bailey (Oak Park, Ill.: Moore, 1980), pp. 162–172.

22. On the differences between domestic and foreign policymaking before the Vietnam War, see Thomas Cronin, *The State of the Presidency,* 22d ed. (Boston: Little, Brown, 1980), pp. 145–154.

23. James Chace, "Is a Foreign Policy Consensus Possible?" *Foreign Affairs* 57 (Fall 1978): 15–16; Douglas Bennett, "Congress in Foreign Policy," *Foreign Affairs* 57 (Fall 1978): 47–48; and Ralph Carter, "Foreign versus Domestic Policy" (paper delivered to the American Political Science Association meeting, Washington, D.C., August 30–September 2, 1984).

24. Dodd and Schott, *Congress,* p. vii.

25. For further discussion of this phenomenon, see Wallace Earl Walker, *Changing Organizational Culture* (Knoxville: University of Tennessee, 1986), esp. chaps. 3, 7.

26. David Abshire, "Lessons of Vietnam," in *Vietnam Legacy,* p. 406.

27. Gerald Ford, *A Time to Heal* (New York: Harper & Row, 1979), p. 252.

28. Sundquist, *Decline,* pp. 299–300.

29. Warren Christopher, "Ceasefire between the Branches," *Foreign Affairs* 60 (Summer 1982): 1000.

30. Bennett, "Congress," p. 43.

31. Holbert Carroll, "The Congress and National Security Policy," in *The Congress And America's Future,* ed. David Truman (Englewood Cliffs, N.J.: Prentice-Hall, 1965), p. 166.

32. Christopher Madison, "Solarz's Brash Style Tempers His Quest for Influence in the Foreign Policy Area," *National Journal,* October 26, 1985, pp. 2413–2417.

33. Wilcox, "Cooperation," p. 261.

34. Myra Macpherson, "Vietnam, the 1960s: A Welter of Conflicting Legacies," *Washington Post,* April 15, 1985.

35. Wilcox, "Cooperation," p. 269.

36. Michael Malbin: *Unelected Representatives* (New York: Basic Books, 1980).

37. Based on personal interviews in Washington, D.C., in summer 1982. In the case of the waiver restrictions passed by Congress in 1981 to answer Canadian objections to the Alaskan Natural Gas Pipeline, such a "war room" was organized and proved effective. On coalitional lobbying more generally, see Bill Keller, "Coalitions and Associations Transform Strategy, Methods of Lobbying in Washington," *Congressional Quarterly Weekly Report,* January 23, 1982, pp. 119–123.

38. Wallace Earl Walker and Andrew Krepinevich, "No First Use and Conventional Deterrence: The Politics of Defense Policymaking," in *The Presidency and National Security Policy* (New York: Center for the Study of the Presidency, 1984), pp. 355–377.

39. Interview with a foreign embassy officer, Washington, D.C., summer 1982; Hamilton and Van Dusen, "Making the Separation of Powers Work," p. 18; and John Felton, "Hussein Courts Wary Congress, But Arms Sale Is Uphill Struggle" *Congressional Quarterly Weekly Report,* October 5, 1985, pp. 2018–2020.

40. Sanford Ungar, "South Africa's Lobbyists," *New York Times Magazine,* October 13, 1985, p. 82.

41. On the issue of polarization, see Ole Holsti and James Rosenau, "Vietnam, Consensus and the Belief Systems of American Leaders," *World Politics* 32 (October 1979).

42. Charles Stevens, "The Use and Control of Executive Agreements," *Orbis* 20 (Winter 1977): 905.

43. Ravenal, "Consequences," pp. 658–660.

44. George Church, "Lessons from a Lost War," *Time,* April 15, 1985, pp. 41–42, and Richard Harwood and Haynes Johnson, "Vietnam, the War's Final Battle," *Washington Post,* April 14, 1985.

6
Vietnam and the U.S. Army: Learning to Cope with Failure

John P. Lovell

The U.S. armed forces in general and the army in particular were and continue to be profoundly influenced by the experience of Vietnam. An understanding of how and why this influence has been manifested is dependent less upon a detailed review of the particulars of the Vietnam experience than it is upon a recognition of the factors that have contributed to or impeded learning by the military in the years since the war drew to its humiliating conclusion.

The Vietnam experience is reflected in varying degrees in modifications of structure that have been made in U.S. military organization, in strategic and tactical doctrine, in choices that have been made in weaponry and equipment, in military training, and in personnel practices. More fundamentally, in terms of the consequences of the experience for the future relationship of the military to the civilian sector of the government and to the society at large, the Vietnam experience is reflected in the professional values and self-image of members of the armed forces.

To the extent that experience or lessons from the past become assimilated into organizational structure, doctrine, practices, values, and beliefs, one may speak of "organizational learning."[1] The implication is not that the organization is necessarily getting wiser or more effective, but only that it has made adjustments in response to experience. The lessons that organizations such as the branches of the military have chosen to accept or reject reflect the realities of bureaucratic politics (that is, who controls organizational resources, who makes decisions, and who has the boss's ear) and not simply logical deductions from a systematic appraisal of experience. Moreover, the learning process is dynamic. As circumstances change and changes are made in key personnel, the lessons learned may change.

This chapter examines the learning process for a twenty-year period beginning in 1965, the year of the transition from a U.S. military advisory role in Vietnam to the commitment of combat units. No effort is made to deal exhaustively with the subject. Although some reference is made to the other armed services, the discussion centers on the army, which was assigned the major combat role in Vietnam and became the focal point for critical attention during and after the war. The focus is on the evolution of lessons that the army derived at various stages about the nature of the conflict in Vietnam, about the appropriate role for the U.S. military in such conflicts, and, more generally, about the current state of health of the U.S. military profession and changes, if any, that are required. There is virtually no discussion of the effects of Vietnam on weapons technology or equipment, although modifications that have been made in the design and armament of helicopters, for instance, and in communications equipment reflect the combat experience in Southeast Asia. Nor are changes in tactics or intelligence gathering resulting from the combat experience discussed. Similarly, there is little discussion here of the debate that has emerged in the post-Vietnam era regarding the command structure used in Vietnam.[2]

Although the identification of transition points is necessarily inexact, four phases in the evolution of the response of the U.S. Army to the Vietnam experience can be distinguished. The first, which began prior to the commitment of U.S. combat units to Vietnam in 1965, can be labeled the "can-do" phase of organizational learning. Phase 2, beginning in 1969 and continuing into the mid-1970s, may be described as the phase of armed forces agonistes, a painful but creative period of heated debate about the war in Vietnam and its effects on the military profession. Phase 3, which was evident to some extent as early as the final withdrawal of U.S. forces in 1973 but was fully apparent by 1975, is one of denial of the Vietnam experience. More precisely, this was a time of turning inward by U.S. military professionals, avoiding discussion or reexamination of the Vietnam experience, while their leaders sought to rebuild a doctrinal consensus with an alternative focus. Phase 4, which had begun by 1979 and continues to the present, is one of revisionism regarding the lessons of Vietnam (even as some military professionals continue in the phase of denial). It is revisionism that has contributed to, as well as drawn inspiration from, a revival of professional self-esteem within the military. A brief discussion of each of these phases will serve as the basis for extracting some general propositions about what kinds of lessons the army has tended to draw from the Vietnam experience and why.

Learning to Cope with the Vietnam Experience

Phase 1: Can-Do Lessons

In the aftermath of a 1961 Kennedy presidential directive on counterinsurgency, the U.S. Army launched a feverish study of relevant historical experience and theory, including the writings of Mao Zedong, Che Guevara, and General Giap. The commitment of U.S. combat troops in 1965 represented the Americanization of the war and a de facto downgrading of the counter-insurgency concern. However, the army chief of staff, General Harold K. Johnson, described the army's "third principal mission" (after deterrence and readiness to fight successfully a conventional war) as that of promoting "stability and progress in the modernization process of emerging nations."[3] Army professional journals continued to be filled with articles optimistically supportive of such a mission. As early as 1962, some Americans had been sending bleak reports from the field lamenting poor performance by South Vietnamese military units and warning against overly sanguine claims by U.S. officials in Saigon of progress in the counterinsurgency efforts.[4] However, the overwhelming majority of articles that military authors shared with a largely military readership in journals such as *Military Review* and *Army* in the mid-1960s expressed a conviction that obstacles being encountered in the counterinsurgency effort could and would be overcome. Guarded optimism, with an emphasis on the centrality of the nation-building mission, remained the dominant motif in U.S. military writings even as the media turned sour on the war, beginning especially with the Tet offensive of early 1968.[5]

Phase 2: Armed Forces Agonistes

The intensity of the 1968 presidential and congressional election campaigns in the United States accurately reflected the frustration and anger that a substantial portion of Americans now felt regarding the costly and inconclusive war in Vietnam. "Why don't we do what is required to *win* or else bring the troops home?" was a typical refrain.

The campaign pledge of Richard Nixon to achieve peace with honor became translated into policy beginning in 1969 through a carrot-and-stick approach to peace negotiations with the North Vietnamese that was heavy on the stick. The announcement was made that U.S. ground forces would be withdrawn from Vietnam gradually as South Vietnamese armed forces assumed the major role for ground combat, but bombing by the United States was intensified. The relaxation of targeting restrictions for bombing that accompanied the intensified bombing campaign was welcomed by most military officials, who had chafed under previously imposed restrictions. So also were later policy decisions to move against enemy sanctuaries in Cambodia and to mine the harbors of Haiphong (decisions that military leaders had advocated years earlier).

If the political climate had improved in these respects, from the vantage point of military professionals seeking to turn the tide of the war decisively in their favor, in other respects the U.S. armed forces were experiencing a period of anguish, the depth of which varied by service. In the air force, for example, the early 1970s were a time of concern about retention of skilled personnel and about the adverse effects on recruitment, morale, and discipline of the turbulence within the larger society. There was anxiety also about the proclivity of the Congress to cut the defense budget. The prevailing view among top-ranking air force officers, however, was that the war in Vietnam had reaffirmed the decisive effect of air power, once debilitating targets restrictions were removed (as they were in facilitating the December 1972 bombing of North Vietnam).[6] Thus, for the air force, the early 1970s were less a time of trauma and soul searching than they were of seeking to maintain and upgrade the organization's capacity to play a vital role in the nation's defenses.

During the same period, the navy entered a period of turbulent but dramatic reform, presided over by the youngest man ever to be appointed as chief of naval operations (CNO), Admiral Elmo R. "Bud" Zumwalt, Jr. The problems of enlisted discontent and racial strife that provoked Zumwalt's searching review of working conditions and leadership practices had been festering for years prior to the commitment of naval forces to Vietnam. However, Zumwalt's concern about the deleterious effects on morale and performance of "mickey mouse" practices (as he termed them) had been heightened by his command of naval forces in riverine operations in Vietnam from 1968 to 1970, just before his appointment as CNO. Moreover, continuing crises with which the navy had to deal despite the changes wrought in response to the fabled Z-grams (Zumwalt's announcements) included ones with a Vietnam focus (for example, racial conflict on board the carrier U.S.S. *Kitty Hawk,* en route to the Gulf of Tonkin).[7]

Marine corps units had been the first U.S. military units to be committed to combat in Vietnam in 1965. By the early 1970s, the corps was faced with major problems of morale and discipline. One consequence was a skyrocketing of desertion and AWOL (absent without leave) rates, from 17.8 per thousand in fiscal year 1964 to 89.2 per thousand in fiscal year 1974.[8]

If formal reports from that period are to be believed (given the demands for favorable reports, there is reason for skepticism), the rates of desertions and unauthorized absences in the army in the mid-1970s were roughly half of those that the marine corps was experiencing. Nevertheless, in most respects the army's problems were similar to those of the marine corps: recruitment problems, serious morale problems in overseas and stateside units, racial strife, mounting drug usage, and a widespread feeling among soldiers that their combat accomplishments had gone unrecognized and that antimilitary sentiment was rampant in American society.

Many army professionals believed that the problems had grown to ominous proportions. Writing in *Military Review* in mid-1972, an army officer who had served with the Ninth Infantry Division in Vietnam and more recently in Washington with the office of the army assistant vice-chief of staff itemized the multiple elements of the organizational crisis of the times:

It is a crisis of confidence, born of an "unwon" war, of charges of mismanagement and incompetence attendant to that war, of increasing manifestations of public antimilitarism, and of doubts about the role of ground forces in the era of the Nixon doctrine.

It is also a crisis of conscience, stemming from charges of war crimes and official coverups, service club and post exchange kickbacks and embezzlement, misconduct by the Army's top police official, and allegations of self-serving careerism in the professional officer corps. Finally, it is a crisis of adaptation, as the traditionally hierarchical and disciplined armed service attempts to come to terms with the "Age of Aquarius"—a revolution in American styles, manners and morals.[9]

It is unnecessary to discuss the crises in detail; the travails of the U.S. military in the 1970s have been described elsewhere.[10] Here I note simply the pattern of military response to the crisis atmosphere that prevailed; in effect, the pattern represents the second phase (armed forces agonistes) of the learning response to the Vietnam experience.

There was a good deal of variation in the attitudes and beliefs that military personnel at the time displayed, with differences particularly evident according to the vantage point from which individuals viewed the war in Vietnam and its consequences. In the enlisted ranks, sharp differences of attitude and behavior pitted draftees against career noncommissioned officers (NCOs, who typically were older than draftees) in ways that were deleterious to morale and discipline, not only in Vietnam but also elsewhere (most notably Europe). Drug usage and racial strife aggravated the differences. Junior officers responded to the atmosphere of turbulence with frustration. In much higher numbers than had been true a few years earlier, they opted out of the military at the first opportunity.[11]

Field-grade officers also were frustrated. A disturbing number of able and experienced majors, lieutenant colonels, and colonels were resigning, some with an accompanying public expression of their grievances.[12] Some field-grade officers remained on active duty despite high levels of frustration because they had invested some fifteen to twenty years in a military career.

To some extent that frustration turned to anger among officers in the early 1970s. It often was directed at those who seemed to be making the task of the military more difficult: the mass media, civilian political leaders, student antiwar protesters, and their academic mentors. But some of the anger was directed internally. The turmoil and ferment of the times provided the occasion for open, critical debate of assumptions and practices regarding the conduct of the war that those at middle and low levels in the military hierarchy long had accepted silently, if sometimes grudgingly. In that sense, it was a creative period for the military profession, and the professional journals of the armed forces for roughly a four-year period beginning in 1970 make fascinating reading.[13]

The nature of the debate called into question the leadership at flag-rank levels of the armed forces. Some internal critics argued that the U.S. military had failed in Vietnam and that needed reform could occur only when the officer corps acknowledged the failure and its root causes. Frequently mentioned among the latter were short command tours that had fed careerism and "ticket punching" and had hampered the cultivation of unit cohesion. The quantifiable measures of readiness and performance such as body counts also were viewed widely as having led inexorably to the falsification of reports and perhaps to a disregard of the distinction that might have been made between combatants and noncombatants.[14] Other internal critics argued, however, that the failure to achieve ultimate policy objectives in Vietnam ought not lead military professionals to conclude that therefore all of the tactics and practices applied in the Vietnam war were mistaken ones.[15]

A 1974 survey of U.S. Army general officers who had held command positions in Vietnam at some point in the years 1965 through 1972 showed that personal anguish was not peculiar to those at lower rungs in the military hierarchy. Indeed, some general officers shared the critical view of strategic guidance and top-level leadership that their subordinates expressed. As noted by Douglas Kinnard, author of the survey and himself a brigadier general who had served in Vietnam: "[The replies to survey questions] show a noticeable lack of enthusiasm, to put it mildly, by Westmoreland's generals for his tactics and by implication for his strategy in the war."[16]

The depth of their own concern, augmented by the cries of their subordinates for reform, led flag-rank officers to the conviction that some major changes in organizational structure and practice had become imperative (although not necessarily change in the direction or magnitude advocated by officers at lower grades). Those who occupied the key billets were experiencing criticism and demand for change from above as well as from below, and the former proponents of change (that is, the president, civilian leaders in the Pentagon, and members of Congress) were in control of resources to a degree that severely limited the options military leaders could consider.

The years 1969 through 1974 were the "dark days" in the fortunes of the military establishment, as Lawrence Korb has observed, despite the paradoxical fact that these were years of ferment and creativity in the military profession.[17] The Pentagon suffered a cut of nearly 40 percent in buying power from fiscal year (FY) 1968 to FY 1974. All arms of service were affected. In this time span, the number of long-range bomber, fighter-attack, and fighter-interceptor squadrons in the air force was reduced from 169 to 110. The navy experienced a slight increase in submarines, but the number of surface ships declined by more than a third, from 902 in 1968 to 593 in 1974. The marine corps was reduced from 4 divisions to 3, with the army suffering cuts that forced it to deactivate 6 divisions (from 19 to 13).[18]

As a means of accommodating force reductions, the White House and the

Pentagon changed from a "two and one-half war" to a "one and one-half war" worst-case assumption. Previously the notion had been that the United States must and could prepare to fight a major war in Europe and another in Asia, and still cope with a major conflict elsewhere. The new policy guidance was to prepare for a major war, which it was presumed would break out in Europe if at all, and a minor war somewhere else.[19]

Whereas active duty military forces were cut during these years, the funding of National Guard and reserve units was increased. Because it was estimated that six reservists could be funded in a given year at the cost of funding a single active duty soldier, the rationale was that the total force available for the most feared contingency, all-out war with the Soviet Union, could be maintained at relatively stable levels while cutting total defense costs.[20] A similar rationale of "more bang for the buck" accompanied a shift to investment in nuclear warheads and delivery systems while active duty personnel were being cut.

Doubtless the policy change during this period that had the most important enduring consequences for the armed forces, particularly the army, was the shift from a mixed system of conscription and voluntary recruitment to an all-volunteer system. The handwriting already was on the wall for such a change in 1969 with the appointment by President Nixon of a commission headed by former Defense Secretary Thomas Gates to investigate the feasibility and desirability of an all-volunteer force. In the same year, the army launched a study of the all-volunteer concept. As the director of the study noted subsequently:

> In September 1970, pressure was exerted on the military services from the highest levels to show support for and progress toward the President's goal to end the draft. Suddenly and dramatically, in October 1970, the Army Chief of Staff announced full support for the volunteer concept and . . . appointed Lieutenant General George I. Forsythe as his special assistant to direct the effort [to prepare for the transition].[21]

Perhaps the historical trend away from mass mobilization armies would have led to an abandonment of military conscription even if the United States had not become embroiled in an unpopular war in Vietnam.[22] However, as casualties increased in Vietnam, inequities of the draft became a focal point of mounting criticism, demanding a policy response. Reporting to the president in 1970, the Gates commission termed conscription a costly and inequitable form of taxation.[23] In 1971, Congress sought to reduce the reliance on conscripts by enacting a large increase in the pay of newly recruited military personnel. Subsequent legislation brought an end entirely to conscription, and the all-voluntary force was initiated in 1973.

The prospective transition to an all-volunteer force provided further urgency to the need to take action to improve dangerously low levels of morale and discipline in the military in the early 1970s. Army officials felt under particular pressure to effect change. The marine corps could remind its recruits, "We never promised you a rose garden"; but the army needed more than "a few good men"; it needed thousands, even with personnel reductions that were occurring. Following a conference of key commanders in 1970, the army chief of staff, General William Westmoreland, announced that new measures were being introduced in an effort to make life more attractive to soldiers. There would be no more bed checks; it would be easier for GIs to obtain weekend passes; 3.2 beer would be permitted in the barracks and in mess halls; and commanders were directed to make themselves more readily available to soldiers with grievances.

Changes such as these became a new source of consternation to many army officers and NCOs who were dealing on a daily basis with disciplinary problems that ranged from disobedience of orders into combat in Vietnam to violence in the barracks in Europe. However, it was the residue of earlier problems that raised the most serious questions about the quality of military leadership and the integrity of the officer corps. The most shocking breakdown of discipline had come at My Lai in March 1968, where the killing of unarmed Vietnamese men, women, and children by U.S. soldiers clearly violated not only generally accepted norms of moral conduct and of international law but also explicit guidelines for the treatment of civilians and prisoners that had been distributed to all personnel throughout the U.S. Military Assistance Command in Vietnam (MACV).

Months later, a letter from a Vietnam veteran who had learned about the atrocities from soldiers who participated in them reached General Westmoreland. Court-martial proceedings were brought against Lieutenant William Calley, leader of the platoon that had carried out the killings at My Lai, and Westmoreland ordered a full inquiry to determine why there had been no earlier report of the atrocities or disciplinary action against the violators. Responsibility for the investigation was assigned to a panel headed by Lieutenant General William R. Peers, an officer widely respected for his integrity. The results of the Peers inquiry, accompanied by a forthright memorandum from Peers to Westmoreland, suggested that the atrocities committed at My Lai had their roots in a major failure of army leadership.

Just how widespread the problem was, and what its full dimensions were, Westmoreland determined to discover. He decided to commit the army, as he put it, "to an honest, 'no-holds barred' self-examination."[24] Such top-level guidance encouraged those at lower levels to generate proposals for reform and change.

Doubtless the most significant officially sponsored result of the Westmoreland directive was a study initiated by the Army War College of the moral and ethical climate of military professionalism in the army.[25] A member of General Westmoreland's staff summarized the study:

In general, it discovered that the majority of the Officer Corps perceived a stark dichotomy between the appearance and reality of the adherence of senior officers to the traditional standards of professionalism, which the words duty, honor and country sum up. Instead, these officers saw a system that rewarded selfishness, incompetence and dishonesty. Commanders sought transitory, ephemeral gains at the expense of enduring benefits and replaced substance with statistics. Furthermore, senior commanders, as a result of their isolation (sometimes self-imposed) and absence of communication with subordinates, lacked any solid foundation from which to initiate necessary corrective action.[26]

Numerous changes were initiated as a result of the findings of this and related studies of problems in the army. A leadership board, chaired by Brigadier General Henry E. Emerson, was established at Fort Bragg, North Carolina; the board in turn sent three-man leadership teams to army installations throughout the world to hold discussions with those in command positions at various levels, with the goal of improving the quality of army leadership. Professional ethics received major emphasis, with the curricula revised at virtually all service schools in the army to include instruction on professional ethics. (Similar curricular changes were made in the other services.) Guidelines were disseminated for the stabilization of tours of duty for brigade and battalion commanders at eighteen months and company commanders at twelve months. An officer personnel management system (OPMS) was developed, designed to provide "for the professional development of each officer in an atmosphere of constructive competitive advancement."[27] A committee to review the system of military justice was established; and a directorate of discipline and drug policies was created, under the leadership of Brigadier General Robert G. Gard.

When General Westmoreland gave official encouragement to critical self-examination in the army, he emphasized, "We are looking to the future, learning from but not being mesmerized by the past."[28] General Donn A. Starry observed from his 1978 vantage point as commander of the army training and doctrine command (TRADOC) between 1970 and 1973 at the Pentagon, "There was the strong feeling that, after every war, armies always set out to figure out how they might have fought the last war better. There was an even stronger determination to avoid that pitfall, and this time to look ahead, not back."[29]

Phase 3: Turning Inward

To describe the next phase of the army response to Vietnam as one of denial of the experience is accurate in terms of the focus of organizational activity in the mid-1970s but perhaps misleading in terms of the outlook of army leadership. Numerous studies of various facets of the war were initiated, including a series of monographs by senior officers who had held important posts in

Vietnam and a more extensive scholarly series of studies undertaken by the Army Center of Military History.[30] Moreover, in personal terms as well, the senior army leadership found that Vietnam continued to be much on their minds.

General Paul Gorman has noted this concern to be the case, for example, in frequent conversations that he had in the mid-1970s as deputy to the TRADOC commander, General William E. DePuy.[31] DePuy, who according to David Halberstam in the early 1960s had been "considered by most civilians in the Pentagon the brightest general they had ever met," had served in Vietnam as assistant chief of staff for operations to General Westmoreland, and then as commander of the First Infantry Division.[32] He had returned to Washington to become special assistant to the army chief of staff for counterinsurgency and then assistant vice-chief of staff before his appointment as commander of the newly created TRADOC.

However vivid the continuing recollections of Vietnam might be personally to an army leader such as General DePuy, there were several compelling reasons in the mid-1970s why post-mortems on Vietnam were to be avoided. For U.S. military professionals in the mid-1970s to have reexamined the war critically would have given the appearance, in DePuy's somewhat irreverent terms, of "revisionism, alibis, self justification, rearranging the deck chairs on the Titanic, opening old wounds, [or] severe mental retardation, given public attitudes."[33]

Moreover, DuPuy and other army leaders had become convinced that reorientations of strategy and doctrine were long overdue. In World Wars I and II, the United States had been able to rely on the mobilization of previously untrained personnel to serve as soldiers. In meeting the escalating demands as the army expanded during the Vietnam era, a similar pattern had been followed. Such an approach was inadequate to anticipated future needs in the minds of key army leaders. The army director of manpower and forces wrote in 1972 that what was needed was "a revolution in military thought in our country," based on the acknowledgment that "the whole threat-strategy-requirements-mobilization framework in which we have all been raised and trained is no longer applicable."[34]

General DePuy expressed similar views to members of the Infantry Officer Advanced Course at Fort Benning, Georgia, in November 1975: "We're now living through a major historic turning point in the history of the U.S. Army . . . a transition from the old Army [of World Wars I and II, Korea, and Vietnam] to a new one that none of us have really seen yet, but you are going to see a lot more of it than I will."[35]

In short, those who had responsibility for shaping army doctrine and training practices in the 1970s had to adapt to a vastly altered environment and set of requirements. They had to look beyond Vietnam to future contingencies. Given resource constraints, throughout most of the 1970s this adaptation became translated by army planners into preparing to fight in Europe.

Such an orientation was deemed desirable also because of the concern with remedying the neglect of equipment and force levels in Europe that had been a consequence of the Vietnam commitment and of undertaking much-needed modernization. Moreover, various proposals were being discussed in Congress for effecting major reductions in troop strengths in Europe, which implied severe reductions in the size of the U.S. Army. Only if the rationale for the current army mission in Europe could be argued successfully could such a dire contingency be forestalled.

If further encouragement to a European focus were needed, it was provided by President Nixon in his State of the World message to Congress on May 3, 1973, declaring the "year of Europe," a theme echoed in subsequent weeks by national security adviser Henry Kissinger. The Nixon message served to underscore a policy emphasis that had been evident virtually from the time of the promulgation of the Nixon doctrine in 1969. For example, a 1970 review of military strategy for the NSC by a team headed by Deputy Secretary of Defense David Packard noted explicitly that Europe was the region of top priority for U.S. strategic interests.

The 1973 army reorganization (termed Operation STEADFAST) further reflected the high-level commitment of the army to preparing to fight in Europe, with attendant downgrading of the counterinsurgency mission. It was acknowledged in the document that became the core of army doctrine for its operations, field manual FM 100-5, *Operations,* published in 1976:

> Because the US Army is structured primarily for [battle in Central Europe against forces of the Warsaw Pact] and has large forces deployed in that area, this manual is designed mainly to deal with the realities of such operations. The principles set forth in this manual however, apply also to military operations anywhere in the world.[36]

In his TRADOC command, General DePuy became the driving force behind the revising of all important army field manuals, including FM 100-5, the capstone.[37] The core group of officers charged with drafting FM 100-5 had their convictions regarding priorities confirmed by the Arab-Israeli War of 1973. In particular, the lethality of conventional weaponry used in the 1973 war provided convincing evidence that the United States needed to be prepared for a "come-as-you-are" war in which victory or defeat might hinge upon the capability to win the first battle.[38] Doubtless the criticism that the Pentagon had received—for example, in widely discussed Brookings studies in 1973 and 1974—for basic strategic and force planning in NATO on the assumption of a protracted rather than short-but-intense conflict contributed to the reorientation of army thinking.[39]

Army leaders who sought to effect change, however, encountered resistance. General Starry confessed to a colleague in 1972, "I'm terribly frustrated at the horrible inertia around me."[40] In later reflections on reform efforts of the time, he recalled:

At this point, it was apparent that the reformers [that is, those who were designing the reorientation of army strategy and force structure] had to begin anew. It became apparent that considerable internal consensus building would be necessary as organizational development proceeded. So, for two and one-half years, school commandants, representatives of the Army staff, major commands, supporting organizations and other services were gathered at frequent intervals, and what we now know as Division 86 [which restructured army divisions to accommodate heavier armament and equipment appropriate to the NATO mission] was hammered out at Fort Leavenworth, Kansas.[41]

Consensus building was only partially successful. A divisive issue was that of the orientation of the army almost exclusively for war in Europe. Internal critics were troubled about the readiness of the army to cope with more probable contingencies, such as conflict in the third world. Writing in *Military Review* in 1977, an officer serving as chief of the joint and combined operations committee on the faculty of the Command and General Staff College expressed his deep concern about the issue. Data showed a trend in the 1970s in army schooling toward substantial reductions in the hours of instruction devoted to the study of low-intensity conflict. "Coupled with the Special Forces training emphasis being shifted to resistance forces in support of conventional operations," he noted, the data suggest that army disavowal of low-intensity conflict as a legitimate mission for the armed forces "could be the end product of the nonbenign neglect which to date has progressed quite far along."[42] The harshness of the criticism was unusual, but the author clearly had a point. The relative neglect of the study of conflicts in the third world was no mere oversight. It was the army of the 1970s' version of "no more Vietnams."

For several years, the top-level decision to turn the attention of the army sharply away from the Vietnam experience was largely successful, sustained not only by the disinclination of many of those who had served there to want to review the experience but also by the mood of the country at large, which, particularly after the highly publicized accounts of the fall of Saigon and Phnom Penh in 1975, turned away from Southeast Asia.

To the extent that they alluded to the experience at all in the middle to late 1970s, military professionals often tended to see Vietnam as having been an experience that left the American people with an ugly image of its military establishment. This sense of being held in low esteem, despite opinion polls to the contrary, was the mirror image of views held by a small group of critics on the political Left who, even as Congress made cuts in the defense budget and the size of the armed forces, continued to express their concerns about the alleged militarization of American society.

Some individuals knew better. Writing in 1970, air force Colonel Richard Rosser saw the trend as one neither toward militarism nor toward mounting antimilitary sentiment. Rather, he predicted that U.S. civil-military relations in the years ahead would have three prime characteristics: "a restricted role for the military; the primacy of domestic politics; and amilitarism among the young [that is, not antimilitary sentiment but merely apathy]."[43] Rosser was essentially accurate in his predictions. Americans in the 1970s tended to become preoccupied with domestic affairs, and young Americans displayed little hostility toward the military, only apathy. The military, however, turned inward.

Phase 4: Vietnam Revisionism
and the Revival of Military Self-Esteem

Efforts by top military leaders following the withdrawal of U.S. forces from Vietnam to revive organizational pride and self-confidence were augmented fortuitously by the emergence of revisionist interpretations of the Vietnam experience and by a revival of patriotism. By the late 1970s and early 1980s, the military had moved largely beyond the denial phase to look again for lessons from Vietnam, finding these in a form compatible with the revisionist mood.

An important early initiative leading to this fourth phase in the organizational response to the Vietnam experience was that provided by the army chief of staff, Creighton Abrams, in 1973. Concerned about restoring a feeling of self-worth among army personnel, Abrams directed that a strategic assessment group be organized "to determine if there was a legitimate role for conventional strategy and for the Army in the post-Vietnam world." The report of the thirteen-member Astarita group, as it was known informally (after its chairman, Colonel Edward F. Astarita), provided strong affirmation to the question under consideration. The report shifted the focus of organizational attention away from the frustrations of Vietnam to the deterrence and readiness mission of the army elsewhere, especially Europe. In 1981, General John Vessey, the army vice-chief of staff, would look back at the Astarita report as a turning point in the development of the post-Vietnam army.[44]

The European focus of the energies of the army was consistent with a back-to-basics emphasis in military training and education that became particularly prominent in the late 1970s and early 1980s. Prompted especially by evidence that officers as well as enlisted personnel who had entered the army during the Vietnam era had failed to acquire some of the fundamental skills of soldiering, the back-to-basics movement, like that in civilian education, had some elements also of an attack on educational frills. As noted in a 1975 report by a TRADOC OPMS task group, officer education should "focus on fundamental skills to the exclusion of 'nice to know' material in the limited resident training time available." The Army Command and General Staff College altered its curriculum to conform to the group's additional recommendation that the program be designed "to prepare officers specifically for their next immediate assignment" (rather than more long-range preparation, as had been the case).[45]

The Army War College resisted a narrowing of its educational focus initially, but by 1980, a shift was evident in the direction of emphasis on purely military subjects such as land warfare and military strategy, with some reduction in time devoted to domestic policy issues and study of the policy process.[46] Those who promoted such change argued that in its eagerness to retain a favorable image in the society at large, the army and its educational institutions had become too civilianized. "We are becoming more narrowly professional in our approach," Colonels Zeb Bradford and Frederick J. Brown observed in 1977. "This is long overdue."[47]

Although military professionals were not devoting much attention in this period to Vietnam, their attention was redirected to the topic in 1976 by the publication of General William Westmoreland's *A Soldier Reports.* The book put emphasis on the "shackling" of professional military men in Vietnam by civilian leadership; on the defeat inflicted on the enemy at Tet, only to have it thwarted largely due to distorted media accounts; and on traitorous conduct of antiwar protesters. A reviewer in the Army War College journal, *Parameters,* recognized that the book was clearly an apologia, but he observed:

> Members of the armed services, particularly those who served in Vietnam, will find the book absorbing, for it affords an informed and coherent context in which their own isolated experiences will take on new life and significance. We can all be grateful for this distinguished soldier's report.[48]

Also in 1976 appeared the first North Vietnamese accounts of the war. General Dung Van Thien's *Our Great Spring Victory* was brought to the attention of General Fred C. Weyand, army chief of staff, by his assistant, Lieutenant Colonel Harry G. Summers, Jr., who noted its importance. Here was evidence of the design of enemy strategy, including perhaps an awareness of the eroding commitment of the U.S. government and public to the war.

In two army journals in 1976, General Weyand and Lieutenant Colonel Summers (who had been in the Astarita group) attacked the "Vietnam mythology that the war was illegal, immoral and unjust." They also rejected the "myth" that the United States had to withdraw from Vietnam because of defeats on the battlefield. The authors stressed the vital continuing role for conventional ground forces in U.S. strategy. They advised readers not to ignore the Vietnam experience; rather, it could be seen as a reaffirmation of the necessary link of a democratic army to its people; only when the people understand and support the commitment of armed forces can it be justified.[49]

The 1977 publication of Kinnard's *The War Managers* was important in revealing broad dissatisfaction among military commanders who served in

Vietnam with the gradualist approach to fighting the war and widespread disenchantment among them with civilian management of the war.[50]

The U.S. bicentennial in 1976 had fostered a revival of patriotism, ushering in a mood of growing receptivity to more favorable portrayals than in the past of the rationale for the U.S. commitment to Vietnam. Thereafter the first important revisionist accounts of Vietnam from journalists and academic writers began to appear, among them books by Braestrup (1977), Lewy (1978), and Gelb and Betts (1979). Karnow (1983) has provided a more recent synthesis with added importance because of the television documentary based on the book. The accounts are revisionist in rebutting the view that the United States entered Vietnam in pursuit of ignoble goals, in rejecting interpretations of the escalation of the U.S. involvement that laid the blame to deceitful or ignorant civilian or military advisers ("the system worked"), and in acknowledging failures or distortions on the part of the mass media.[51]

President Carter's attempt early in his administration to withdraw U.S. troops from Korea was further evidence of the continuing "no more Vietnams" syndrome and of the European orientation of strategy. The resistance to the move by Generals Singlaub (clumsily) and then Vessey (quietly and successfully) had the effect of arousing sympathy elsewhere in the military and of reminding military planners of the strategic importance of Northeast Asia.

The abortive effort by the Carter administration to pull U.S. troops out of Korea was but one of several incidents cited by critics of alleged weakness by the United States at a time when greater strength and resolve were needed. The Iranian hostage crisis had the effect of triggering a resurgence of jingoism and of further eroding Carter's political support. The seeming inability of the administration to do more than protest and cancel U.S. participation in the Olympic games in 1980 following the Soviet invasion of Afghanistan fed popular desires for a restoration of U.S. military strength.

A pattern of U.S. military decline in relation to Soviet strategic gains had been the object of expressions of alarm since the mid-1970s by groups such as the Committee on the Present Danger and the United States Strategic Institute (the latter with a membership largely of retired military personnel, including several admirals and generals). Such groups received an increasingly attentive hearing in the media and in the Congress in the late 1970s; after Iran and Afghanistan, the political climate was altered profoundly in a direction favoring the rebuilding of U.S. military might. The overwhelming victory of Ronald Reagan at the polls in 1980 illustrates the change, and his 1984 reelection affirmed that the mood remained favorable to support of the military (although not to major budget increases).

It was in this context of mounting popular support for the military that the most significant reexamination of the Vietnam experience by the army occurred. The genesis of the reexamination, however, came several years earlier. For example, from the end of the U.S. involvement in Vietnam, Major General DeWitt C. Smith, Jr., had had the conviction that the army needed to try to understand the war. Upon assuming the position of commandant of the U.S. Army War College in 1974, Smith initiated measures designed to encourage students and faculty to reexamine and to write about the war. These efforts were only partially successful, given the reluctance of many military officers at the time to relive the Vietnam years. Nevertheless, beginning in academic year 1975–1976, an elective on Vietnam was introduced into the War College curriculum, and speakers such as William C. Westmoreland, James Gavin, Edward Lansdale, and Robert Komer were brought in to discuss various facets of the war.

At the Pentagon, a decision was made by the army chief of staff to commission a massive study of the war, gathering data while most of those who had participated in levels of responsibility from company commander to top commands still were on active duty. In 1979 the first volumes began to appear of the study, undertaken by the BDM Corporation under contract with the army. The study provided an abundance of useful information (in more than 3,500 pages) but not an easily discernable central theme. Major General Smith, having read some of the writings of Colonel Harry Summers and impressed with his insight, arranged to have Summers assigned to the Strategic Studies Institute at the Army War College with the primary assignment of tapping the BDM data for a book on the Vietnam experience. It was in his own search for a theoretical framework within which to bring order to the analysis that he was asked to undertake that Summers turned to the classic study *On War,* by Carl von Clausewitz, and there he found what he believed to be the key to interpreting the American experience.

A draft of the resultant Summers study was critiqued by an internal editorial board at the War College and subsequently by officials in the Pentagon. There was some resistance to publication of the study, principally on grounds that its publication might merely open old wounds. But in April 1981, the army chief of staff, General Edward C. Meyer, approved publication. Meyer had a copy of the study, *On Strategy,* sent to all general officers in the army (with a copy also to the White House). Subsequently the book became widely adopted as a text in military educational institutions of each of the armed services.[52]

The Summers book has provided an interpretive framework that has enabled the military, after several years of neglecting the subject, to reexamine the Vietnam experience. The book adopts much of the revisionist critique of the role in the war of the media, the White House, the civilian secretary of defense and his staff, and the antiwar movement. At the same time, Summers gently chides the military for seeking scapegoats in lieu of accepting their own measure of responsibility for failure to achieve victory in Vietnam. The military, Summers argues, must acknowledge that in a fundamental sense it failed and thereby contributed to the failure of U.S. efforts in Vietnam.

The 1984 publication of General Bruce Palmer's *The 25-Year War* provided important reinforcement to this interpretation.[53] This reinforcement is not entirely coincidental since Summers drew upon Palmer's expertise in writing his own book. Especially notable in both accounts is the stress on the importance of clear political objectives as the foundation for strategy, and therefore for the commitment of military force. Because Palmer's book includes not only criticism of civilian political leadership but also of military leadership, including the Joint Chiefs of Staff, it is accorded somewhat greater credence among military personnel who served in Vietnam at the battalion level or below than is accorded to the Westmoreland interpretation, for instance. Many veterans of the Vietnam experience have some reservations about General Westmoreland's role in Vietnam even as they share some of his views regarding failures of civilian leadership that served to thwart the military effort.

The interpretation of the Vietnam experience as a failure in strategic design and in clarity of policy objectives has not gone unchallenged, even within the army. A recent book by Colonel William Darryl Henderson, for example, contends that the "strategy school" neglects an operational shortcoming that was at least of equal importance in contributing to failure: the lack of cohesion among combat units. Whereas "the organization, policies, and leadership . . . created North Vietnamese Army resiliency to hardship, danger, and outside influences . . . their opponents [U.S. soldiers] were significantly affected by almost all elements within their environment."[54]

The Henderson thesis is unsettling in its implications for army leadership at all levels. In contrast, the Summers-Palmer theses are ones in which failure can be acknowledged more readily by army officers because the interpretations include description of an impressive pattern of successes. The failure, in the Summers-Palmer view, was a fundamental one: inability to grasp the nature of war in Clausewitzian terms. Nevertheless, the U.S. military personnel who fought in Vietnam at the platoon, company, or battalion level are able to accept the Summers-Palmer indictment and hold their heads high, through a favorable assessment of performance by U.S. units at the tactical level.

Moreover, the strategic critique of the Vietnam experience discussed the army mission in terms consistent with the back-to-basics approach. On the other hand, it is precisely this emphasis that arouses some debate among officers who argue that the army ought to be doing more to cultivate breadth and depth of expertise, particularly in order to cope with the complexities of conflict in the third world.

Such concern among internal critics remains severe despite some actions that reveal a broadening of the focus of the army's energies beyond NATO–Warsaw Pact scenarios. The publication in 1981 of Army Field Manual FM 100-20, *Low Intensity Conflict,* and in 1982 of a revised version of FM 100-5, *Operations,* signaled a growing awareness among army leadership of the need of the army to prepare for contingencies in addition to an outbreak of a world war in Europe. The emphasis on Central America by the Reagan administration has provided cues for such breadth of readiness that the army scarcely could ignore. The creation in recent years of light divisions also represents a swing of the pendulum back from the heavying up of divisions that occurred in the early post-Vietnam era when virtually all attention was focused on NATO.

Congressional resource support of the military has diminished in the past few years (for example, denying the full funding the army requested for building light divisions). Yet the popular mood in the country remains supportive of the military, providing a climate favorable to the revisionist reexamination of the Vietnam experience. The dedication of the Vietnam Veterans Memorial as a national monument on Veterans Day 1982 provided a powerful symbol of the degree to which the nation had come to accept the military role in Vietnam as an object of pride rather than shame. A statue of four fighting men was placed near the wall and dedicated on Memorial Day 1984. The surprise appearance of General Westmoreland at that ceremony and the warmth of the reception he was accorded by assembled veterans was further testimony to the change that had occurred in attitudes.

The generally sympathetic outlook toward the military was evident even in popular commentary on the curious 1984–1985 trial of Westmoreland versus CBS. The 1982 CBS documentary that provided the grievance that led General Westmoreland to file suit missed an opportunity to highlight some valuable points about the capacity of governments for self-deception, as well as for deception of the public. Instead CBS sought to structure the documentary in terms of the alleged misdeeds of a prominent villain. The inconclusive outcome of the trial, when, upon the advice of his attorneys, Westmoreland dropped the charges, left open doubts about the command pressures generated in Vietnam for favorable intelligence reports; but there is little evidence that the image of the military as a whole thereby suffered. In a sense, therefore, as Colonel Summers has pointed out, General Westmoreland, in this instance as well as earlier, has taken the blame for the military for the failure to achieve victory in Vietnam.

Conclusions and Policy Implications

The Military Response to Vietnam: Positive Consequences

Perhaps the most important point to be made is that the U.S. military has come to acknowledge failure in Vietnam in terms that preserve a fundamentally healthy relationship of the military to the civilian sector of the government and to the society at large. As Major General DeWitt Smith emphasized in a speech to a civilian and military audience at the Army War College in June 1975:

> This is no disillusioned Army after Indochina and Algeria! Nor even the Army of Cromwell. This is no Nazi Germany! Nor even a land of kings, or especially of military oligarchs. This is a land of an Army with 200 years of demonstrated faith in ideals; 200 years, not of perfection but of moving up the road of human progress—together.[55]

Beyond this fundamental conclusion, one can observe at least four other important consequences of the Vietnam experience that have been positive for the U.S. Army, and therefore for the United States.

First, the U.S. Army version of "no more Vietnams" is an emphatic conclusion that the commitment of armed forces abroad should occur only in pursuit of political goals that enjoy broad public support in the United States. The promulgation of the Weinberger doctrine in November 1984 reveals top-level endorsement of such a view.

The notion that the armed forces of the United States should be committed to battle only in pursuit of publicly approved policies leaves open the questions of what level of support is sufficient and at what stages and by what means the determination of public support is to be made. Nevertheless, one may regard as healthy the recognition by military professionals in a democracy that armed forces exist ultimately as servants of the citizenry and that military force is an instrument to be available to the government to carry out political objectives established through democratic processes.

A closely related second consequence of the Vietnam experience has been a renewed concern among U.S. military professionals not merely with tactical doctrine but also with strategic thought, as embodied, for instance, in the writings of Clausewitz. Optimally, this renewed concern will enable military professionals to make their appropriate contribution to the design of military strategy rather than abdicating this responsibility to civilian strategists.

Third, despite the dismal outcome for the United States, the war in Vietnam has served to revalidate a role for conventionally armed military forces in a nuclear age. Although such revalidation has proved to be of particular practical significance to the army and the marine corps in the quest for resources, the lesson is one that is of general importance in an age in which abstract theorizing on the basis of available technology might point to a different conclusion.

Fourth, the aftermath of Vietnam has been one in which the armed forces have given reemphasis to professionalism, particularly to the central importance of professional ethics. Because the erosion of integrity in the armed forces can have devastating consequences for the nation, the nation as a whole is the beneficiary of the reemphasis on military professionalism.

Counterpoint: Some Inadequacies of
the Lessons of Vietnam

Significant though the consequences are, a thorough assessment of the policy implications of the response of the military to Vietnam must acknowledge also some inadequacies of the response. More precisely, one must note the selectivity of learning from experience that occurred and the cosmetic or partial nature of some of the reforms initiated in response to deficiencies brought to the light by the Vietnam conflict. Thus for each of the four points made above, there is a counterpoint.

Linking the Commitment of Force to Political Objectives. To the extent that a lesson learned from Vietnam by the U.S. Army is articulated in the Weinberger doctrine, the expectation is that

> if we do decide to commit forces to combat overseas, we should have clearly defined political and military objectives. And we should know precisely how our forces can accomplish those clearly defined objectives. And we should have and send forces needed to do just that. As Clausewitz wrote, "No one starts a war—or rather, no one in his senses ought to do so—without first being clear in his mind what he intends to achieve by that war, and how he intends to conduct it."[56]

Commendable as such conditions for force commitment are in the abstract, actual foreign policy decision making is filled with an ineradicable element of uncertainty. No guarantee can be provided that, in time of crisis, a president confronted with the necessity to act in protection of national interests that he believes to be threatened will be certain that his actions will command public support or that forces committed to meet the threat will be adequate to the task. Thus, one must be concerned that the lesson learned by the U.S. military after Vietnam about the link between force commitments and broadly supported political goals includes a sensitivity to political complexity and policy uncertainty.

The heightened awareness among U.S. military professionals of the relationship of military force to political purposes was rekindled through the painful experience of risking death in combat at the bidding of civilian political leaders, some of whom violated the trust that had been placed in them by the society not merely for clarity of judgment but even for integrity. In short, much from the Vietnam experience served to foster suspicion and distrust by the military of civilian political leaders. Similarly, many in the military found in their own personal experiences in Vietnam grounds for hostility toward the mass media and toward antiwar activists.

As a consequence, just as the civilian sector of the society continues to abound with various stereotypical views of the military mind, so one continues to find in the armed forces a variety of stereotypes regarding elements of the civilian sector: politicians, the mass media, the antiwar movement (and more recently, the nuclear freeze movement). Stereotypes are most readily dissolved through an extended working relationship. However, simplistic notions deleterious to the smooth functioning of the political process may be perpetuated as a generation moves up the military hierarchy with less Washington experience, on the average, than was characteristic in recent decades.

Vietnam in Strategic Perspective. The military of the 1980s displays a renewed concern about strategic thought, largely as a result of assessments of the Vietnam experience such as those provided by General Palmer in *The 25-Year War*. However, to conclude that "American direction and conduct of the war and the operational performance of our armed forces, particularly during the 1962–69 period, generally were professional and commendable" is potentially to gloss over a multitude of misjudgments and errors in those years.[57] A critical reexamination of the record could prove beneficial to military performance in the future. Palmer himself notes, "Engrossed in U.S. operations, we paid insufficient attention to our number one military job, which was to develop South Vietnamese armed forces that could successfully pacify and defend their own country."[58] Others have been more harsh in their assessment. Robert Komer notes:

> We consistently underestimated the strengths of the enemy and overestimated those of our GVN [South Vietnamese] allies.
> Politically, we failed to give due weight to the revolutionary dynamics of the situation, the popular appeal of the Viet Cong, the feebleness of the Diem regime, or the depth of factionalism among traditional Vietnamese elites.[59]

Komer makes clear that such failures were not peculiar to the U.S. military but were characteristic as well—if not more so—of civilian policy officials. Nevertheless, the point at hand is that the danger of lessons of Vietnam that contrast strategic failure with tactical success is that the latter becomes exaggerated to the neglect of important performance deficiencies.

Moreover, even if the record of U.S. military units in combat with those of the enemy were as impressive as some accounts contend, there remains the point made by a North Vietnamese colonel to Colonel Harry Summers in a conversation in Hanoi in April 1975: to have "won every battle," as some Americans claimed, was irrelevant.[60] Despite the deference now being paid to the writings of Clausewitz and the enthusiasm for revisionist explanations of the U.S. experience in Vietnam, there is little evidence among army professionals that they have fully grasped this point.

As I suspect Harry Summers would agree, the writings of Clausewitz provide a guide to interpreting the Vietnam experience that is incomplete.

As with most other books that enjoy the fate of becoming fashionable, *On Strategy* runs the risk of becoming the source of easily remembered platitudes about the war in Vietnam. Much of the experience, particularly that during the advisory phase and the guerrilla warfare elements, may be thereby neglected. Surely much remains to be learned by the military from the Vietnam experience. With few exceptions, the hope of Lieutenant General DeWitt Smith that the Summers book would serve as a catalyst for the reexamination of Vietnam by others in the military has yet to be realized.[61]

Furthermore, although the military displays more strategic consciousness than was evident a decade or two ago, one must ask about the quality of strategy that can be anticipated. Are professional military officers getting the kind of education that fosters creativity, sensitivity to nuance, tolerance of ambiguity, and capacity for critical inquiry that will enable at least a core group of them to play an essential role in the development of strategic thought? Are those who challenge prevailing orthodoxy and inject fresh ideas into strategic discussions rewarded by the system of evaluation and promotion?

The answer to these questions may be "yes." Some encouraging innovations have been introduced at the Army Command and General Staff College (CGSC), for example. The reintroduction at Fort Leavenworth, after nearly half a century, of a one-year program of instruction to supplement the regular year-long CGSC course represents a commitment by the army to attempt to develop at least a cadre of officers well educated in the theory as well as the practice of war and warfare. The granting of accreditation for the program at the master's-degree level is evidence of the care that those who have developed the program have taken to ensure that it meets requisite educational standards of rigor.

One notes with concern, however, the response of army commissioned officers below flag rank to a recent survey. Forty-nine percent of some 14,000 respondents expressed agreement with the statement, "The bold, original, creative officer cannot survive in today's Army."[62]

Of concern also is the fact that strategic planning appears to be largely NATO oriented, despite claims of global scope to the contrary. It is true that there has been a broadening of focus, especially represented by the recent enthusiasm for developing a doctrine and a force capability to cope with low-intensity conflict. But low-intensity conflict remains largely a concept in search of a definition and a theory.[63]

An additional point that merits emphasis is that even if one assumes that U.S. military professionals in the aftermath of Vietnam have become more sophisticated strategic thinkers than in the past, it does not necessarily follow that U.S. military strategy will be designed and executed effectively. As noted by a variety of critics ranging from General David C. Jones to Edward N. Luttwak, the armed forces are structured in a way that impedes rather than facilitates the design and implementation of effective strategy. The structural problem predates Vietnam but was highlighted in that war and in subsequent conflicts.[64]

Revalidation of the Role of Conventional Forces in a Nuclear Age. The most probable occasion for the commitment of U.S. military forces in the foreseeable future would appear to be a conflict in which nuclear arms are not used, despite the necessary continuing concern for the maintenance of forces to deter—and if necessary to wage—nuclear war. Vietnam reaffirmed the importance of conventional forces. Nevertheless, the lessons drawn in this regard may be partial or misleading. Those who argue that the army was misled in getting drawn directly into a counterinsurgency role (as opposed to an advisory role) in Vietnam have a point. But so also do those who argue that the army failed to be attentive to the political dynamics of the struggle in Vietnam and continues to be insufficiently attentive in training and doctrine to the dynamics of revolutionary change in the third world. To a large extent, the two groups are talking by one another.

There are, nevertheless, some recent encouraging signs in the army of sustained analysis of third world conflict and training for a U.S. military role, as required, in such conflict. For example, at the request of General Paul Gorman, then commander of the U.S. Southern Command, in 1984 the Combined Arms Operations Research Activity at Fort Leavenworth, Kansas, developed an Absalon training simulation designed to prepare trainees for operating in a guerrilla warfare environment. Absalon was used in Honduras and more recently has been introduced into instruction at the U.S. Army Command and General Staff College. The Center for Army Lessons Learned has been established at Leavenworth. In addition, the army chief of staff has directed TRADOC to undertake a study of low-intensity conflicts worldwide, with special emphasis on identifying lessons learned from conflicts in Central America.[65]

Military Professionalism after Vietnam. Vietnam generated a crisis in U.S. military values and beliefs, especially a crisis in military ethics. The ensuing efforts at reform have had salutary effects. However, no thoughtful military professional would deny that important problems in this realm remain. Among the most fundamental is that of reconciling the conflicting demands and perspectives of bureaucratic management with those of the outlook and values of the traditional warrior-leader.

The tensions generated by these conflicting demands and values are ones that the Vietnam experience exacerbated rather than originated; such tensions were evident to some extent even early in the nation's history. A century and a half ago, for example, Alexis de Tocqueville contrasted the outlook of the U.S. Army in a newly industrialized democratic society with that of the aristocratic officer corps of armies in feudal societies. Honor, the core concept in feudal armies, referred primarily to physical courage and personal loyalty. In democratic societies, military officers continued to espouse a form of honor; but unlike their aristocratic forebears, they displayed a concern with promotion to higher grades that was "eager, tenacious, and continual," explicable as the individual's primary source of social status.[66]

The counterpart of the American military man's quest for promotion, Tocqueville observed, was the American civilian's quest for wealth. As he put it, "The Americans will describe as noble and estimable ambition that which our medieval ancestors have called base cupidity."[67] Such ambition has the redeeming virtue, in Tocqueville's view, of supporting a desire for peace, whereas the military quest for ceaseless promotion gives vent, he argues, in a longing for war.[68]

This historical record provides little support for either the proposition that a quest for wealth promotes peace or for the argument that a desire for promotion leads the military to long for war. One may reject these propositions, however, and still acknowledge that Tocqueville has identified perceptively some potentially troublesome characteristics of behavior of career military personnel in a democracy.

Post–World War II analysis of the U.S. military reveals an indebtedness to Tocqueville's insights. In *The Soldier and the State,* for instance, Samuel Huntington warned that military professionalism in a democratic society tends to be eroded if the military abandons its distinctive conservative values, traditions, and beliefs in an effort to become more closely identified with the liberal, commercial ethics of the civilian sector.[69] In *The Professional Soldier,* Morris Janowitz discussed the erosion of the traditional concept of honor, which had been fundamental to the self-image, and particularly self-esteem, of military professionals.[70]

The emphasis of the U.S. armed forces on management techniques and doctrine has increased several-fold in the decades since the Huntington and Janowitz works were published, with resultant strains in military-professional ethos and self-image. As numerous critics have observed, some of the important miscalculations by U.S. military officers in the prosecution of the war in Vietnam are attributable to a naive application to the battlefield of the formulas of management textbooks.[71]

Similarly, revolving-door personnel practices in combat command and staff assignments, designed to ensure that a maximum number of career military personnel got the right experience, reflected the institutionalization of careerist ambition to a degree that might have startled even Tocqueville.

Military officials have been cognizant (in varying degrees) of these problems. The writings of scholars such as Janowitz, Moskos, and Segal are relatively well known in the military and have served to heighten consciousness of tensions between the traditional view of the military profession as a calling and more recent emphasis (for example, with the shift to an all-volunteer force) on mercenary incentives.[72] Charles Moskos especially has highlighted the implications of alternative institutional and occupational models of military organization. In lectures and in seminars at the Army War College every year from 1972 to 1984, Moskos brought the issue to the attention of a generation of officers, many now in key positions in the army.

The army has taken a variety of steps in an effort to restore institutional pride and a sense of professionalism among its members. Particularly noteworthy are the introduction of thirty-month command tours (subsequently reduced to twenty-four months) and of the system of unit replacement rather than individual replacement introduced by army chief of staff Edward Meyer. These changes represent a variation on the traditional regimental system that the British Army has found successful and a response to recommendations made by numerous critics of the erosion of unit cohesion in the U.S. Army during the Vietnam War. On the basis of reforms such as those instituted by Meyer, a recent internal commentary contends that "the U.S. Army is presently undergoing more substantive change than at any time since the period 1938 to 1941."[73]

The question remains, however: Have remedial measures proved adequate? Most fundamentally, have they proved adequate to the restoration to the armed forces of a sense of integrity and mutual trust that are the by-products of effective leadership? A 1979 study of a sample of enlisted soldiers in armored and infantry units found 52 percent of respondents who felt "that they cannot count on their officers and senior NCOs to look out for the soldiers' interest and 20 percent more [who] are unsure." Twenty-eight percent of respondents went as far as to say that "most officers and senior NCOs cannot be trusted and 23 percent more [of respondents] are unsure."[74]

More recently, extensive surveys have been conducted of army general officers (333 of whom responded) and commissioned officers below the rank of general (some 14,000 of whom responded). Forty-five percent of the general officers expressed the view that "senior Army leaders behave too much like corporation executives and not enough like warriors," and 68 percent of the junior officers and field-grade respondents expressed agreement with the proposition that "the officer corps is focusing on personal gain rather than selflessness."[75]

Of course, survey results can be misleading in failing to plum the full complexity of problems and therefore in leading to the fallacious conclusion that simple solutions lie readily at hand. Discontent with failures of leadership and the misapplication of managerial aphorisms during the Vietnam era have led armed forces officials in recent years to reemphasize the distinction between leadership and management. However, as the astute among them recognize, and as Janowitz noted a quarter of a century ago, the dilemma for the modern military official is not that of choosing between the cultivation of warrior-leader qualities and the skills of the manager. Both are needed. Rather, the challenge is that of developing and using managerial skills commensurate with the requirements of technological and organizational complexity while fostering and maintaining the capacity for the exercise of human leadership.

No amount of enlightened reform can succeed fully in transforming the careerist ambition of military personnel into devotion to duty that is totally selfless. Nor should those who select a military career be expected to view it solely as a calling, with a complete disinterest in the material incentives that are associated with an occupation. On the other hand, most of those who have selected such a career would agree with the sentiments pungently expressed by Colonel Dandridge Malone, that if all that is unique about the life of a soldier can "be called just another job . . . then, by God, I'm a sorry suck-egg mule."[76] The continuing challenge of the post-Vietnam era for the U.S. armed forces is that of adapting institutional practices in ways that enable the military to maintain high standards of recruitment and retention in an all-volunteer force, while affirming the distinctive values and traditions that will enable military organizations to be effective instruments of deterrence and, if needed, of combat.

Summing Up

In short, some of the lessons learned from Vietnam have been partial lessons or, perhaps, the wrong lessons. But why should the military be immune in this regard? Selectivity and distortion characterize the learning process in varying degrees in all organizations. In theory, organizations (and governments) have the capacity to reduce or compensate for the biases and memory lapses that afflict the efforts of individuals to learn from experience. Institutionalized structures to promote multiple advocacy and procedures for crosschecking individual interpretations of experience can, in theory, be established in organizations. In practice, such systematic means of reviewing the past seldom are characteristic of governments or of the organizations that comprise them. On the contrary, lessons are assimilated to the extent that they are perceived by organizational officials to be consonant with the prevailing political climate, advantageous in relationship to resource constraints and requirements, and adaptable to the missions and technologies that favorably distinguish the organization from its key bureaucratic competitors.

As the response of the U.S. Army to Vietnam indicates, the lessons of experience are susceptible to modification as key organizational officials change, as the political climate becomes transformed, as resources become more abundant or more scarce (for example, through increases or cuts in the defense budget), and as competition with rival organizations intensifies, lessens, or takes new forms. An important implication of the dynamic is that the policy guidance provided to the military from the executive branch and from the Congress (explicitly and implicitly, through the allocation of resources) helps to shape the response that the military makes to major experiences such as the involvement in Vietnam. Military leaders must assume primary responsibility for ensuring that organizational performance and individual professionalism are reviewed critically and standards raised in the aftermath of a painful and costly experience such as Vietnam. But the responsibility for creating the climate and providing the incentives that make needed change probable lies with the civilian sector of the government and with the society at large.

Acknowledgments

I am grateful for the support and encouragement of this research that have been provided by the Strategic Studies Institute and particularly by its director, Thomas R. Stone. The research was greatly facilitated by the assistance of the staff of the library of the U.S. Army War College, the staff and archivists of the U.S. Army Military History Institute, and my secretary, Rita A. Rummel.

I have benefited from comments by several individuals on a draft of the paper, including Colonel Stone; Colonel Albert W. Baker; Colonel William P. Boyd; Graham A. Cosmas; General (ret.) William E. DePuy; General (ret.) Paul F. Gorman; Douglas Kinnard, brigadier general (ret.); Max G. Manwaring; Colonel Paul L. Miles, Jr.; Charles C. Moskos, Jr.; William J. Olson; Colonel George K. Osborn; Dr. Alan Ned Sabrosky; Colonel (ret.) Donald P. Shaw; Jerome N. Slater; Lieutenant General (ret.) DeWitt C. Smith, Jr.; Dr. Lewis S. Sorley III, lieutenant colonel (ret.); Colonel William O. Staudemaier; Colonel Harry G. Summers, Jr.; Major General Frederick F. Woerner, Jr.; and Colonel Charles A.P. Woodbeck.

My understanding of issues and events discussed in the chapter also has been enriched by discussion with a number of other individuals who participated in events described or have themselves studied these issues. They include Colonel (ret.) Dwight L. Adams; Archie D. Barrett; Joseph J. Coffey; Colonel John A. Cope, Jr.; Lieutenant Colonel Thomas W. Fagan; Lieutenant Colonel Kenneth E. Hamburger; Colonel David G. Hansen; Colonel (ret.) William L. Hauser; Colonel (ret.) Charles F. Kriete; Colonel (ret.) Arthur F. Lykke, Jr.; Major General Jack N. Merritt; Brigadier General (ret.) Roger Nye; Colonel Jim R. Paschall; and Colonel John P. Stewart. Of course, I alone bear responsibility for whatever errors of fact or interpretation remain.

Notes

1. The formulation is similar to that of Ravenal, who observed: "The learning of a collective . . . is different from the learning of an individual or a narrow decision-making group. Lessons must be internalized in some enduring, objective, consistent, and therefore predictable way. They may be institutionalized, embodied in new or revised procedures, preparations, dispositions; or they may take the form of new constraints or conditions that are added to the policy process." Earl C. Ravenal, *Never Again: Learning from America's Foreign Policy Failures* (Philadelphia: Temple University Press, 1978), pp. 27–28.

2. For example, see David C. Jones, "What's Wrong with the Defense Establishment?" in *The Defense Reform Debate,* ed. Asa A. Clark IV et al. (Baltimore: Johns Hopkins University Press, 1984), chap. 16. Also see Paul F. Gorman, "Toward a Stronger Defense Establishment," in *The Defense Reform Debate,* chap. 17; Archie D. Barrett, *Reappraising Defense Organization* (Washington, D.C.: National Defense University Press, 1983); Edward C. Meyer, "The JCS—How Much Reform Is Needed?" *Armed Forces Journal* 119 (April 1982): 82–90; Edward N. Luttwak, *The Pentagon and the Art of War* (New York: Simon and Schuster, 1984).

3. Harold K. Johnson, "The Army's Role in Nationbuilding," *Army Information Digest* (November 1965), reprinted in *U.S. Army War College Commentary* (December 1967, special edition entitled, "The Army's Third Mission"): 3. (*USAWC Commentary* is the forerunner of *Parameters.*)

4. Halberstam found that the senior advisers operating in the Mekong delta "were the fulcrum between the Saigon command, with its illusions about the war and its sense of responsibility to its superiors in the Pentagon, and the reality in the field where the junior officers, the captains and the lieutenants, were discovering their ally did not want to fight and that the enemy was winning." David Halberstam, *The Best and the Brightest* (New York: Random House, 1969), p. 202. Similarly, Bruce Palmer has noted that the resignation from the army of Lieutenant Colonel John Paul Vann was triggered by the frustration he experienced in attempting to get his superiors to acknowledge the crisis situation experienced in the delta. Bruce Palmer, Jr., *The 25-Year War: America's Military Role in Vietnam* (Lexington: University Press of Kentucky, 1984), p. 22.

5. This is not to say that authors were universally uncritical in their views of progress in the war. Some were remarkably candid and concerned. For example, Special Forces adviser Robert B. Rheault noted that "the long-range program of winning the loyal support of the Montagnard population for the government of Vietnam has largely failed. The Vietnamese-Montagnard rift has *not* been closed, and many Vietnamese harbor justifiable suspicions of U.S. motives and objectives in the highlands. . . . The Montagnard problem will not go away, nor can it be deferred to be dealt with 'later.' It must be dealt with positively and soon, or it will be too late." Robert R. Rheault, "The Montagnard Problem," *U.S. Army War College Commentary* (July 1966): 21–29. Rheault was highly regarded in the army when the article was written. Three years later he retired from the service, disillusioned at his experience in a controversial episode as commander of U.S. Special Forces in Vietnam. See "Col. Robert Rheault, ex-Green Beret," *Life,* November 14, 1969, pp. 34–39.

6. For example, see George J. Eade, "Reflections on Air Power in the Vietnam War," *Air University Review* 25 (November–December 1973): 2–9.

7. See Elmo R. Zumwalt, Jr., *On Watch: A Memoir* (New York: Quadrangle, New York Times Book Co., 1976), esp. pt. III.

8. Data are from Defense Department and congressional sources as reported by Alan Ned Sabrosky, *Defense Manpower Policy: A Critical Reappraisal,* monograph no. 22 (Philadelphia: Foreign Policy Research Institute, 1978), p. 18. For a more detailed treatment of the problems experienced by the marine corps during the 1970s, see Allen R. Millett, *Semper Fidelis: The History of the United States Marine Corps* (New York: Macmillan, 1980), esp. pp. 577–622.

9. William L. Hauser, "Armies and Societies: Three Case Studies," *Military Review* 52 (July 1972): 4. The points are developed in detail in Hauser's book, *America's Army in Crisis: A Study in Civil-Military Relations* (Baltimore: Johns Hopkins University Press, 1973).

10. For example, Hauser, *America's Army in Crisis;* Robert G. Gard, Jr., "The Military and American Society," *Foreign Affairs* 49 (July 1971): 698–710; Stuart H. Loory, *Defeated: Inside America's Military Machine* (New York: Random House, 1973); Ward Just, *Military Men* (New York: Knopf, 1970); Haynes Johnson and George C. Wilson, *Army in Anguish* (New York: Pocket Book by arrangement with the *Washington Post* from a series September–October 1971, 1972).

11. The trend that seemed ominous to many more senior officers was described by David H. Hackworth: "Back in the early 1960s a thought struck me with . . . intensity . . . . What extraordinarily fine officers are joining our ranks! How bright and eager! What an abundance of good sense, enthusiasm, dedication and purposeful idealism these young men have brought with them. . . . I am no longer so optimistic, for too many of the good ones are gone." Hackworth, "Cerebrations: Bluster, Insensitivity Cost Army Good Men," *Army* 20 (November 1970): 56–58. (After a second tour of duty in Vietnam, Hackworth retired from the army; see note 12.) See also James H. Short, "Young Soldiers Fade Away," *Military Review* 49 (October 1969): 44–53. William L. Hauser, "Professionalism and the Junior Officer Drain," *Army* 20 (September 1970): 16–22; Julius T. Crouch, "The Black Junior Officer in Today's Army," *Military Review* 52 (May 1972): 61–67.

12. For example, see D.H. Hackworth, "Soldier's Disgust," *Harper's* 245 (July 1972): 74–76; Josiah Bunting, "The Conscience of a Soldier," *Worldview* 16 (December 1973): 6–11.

13. The following sample of articles from *Military Review* illustrates the point. Donald F. Bletz, "Military Professionalism: A Conceptual Approach," 51 (May 1971): 9–17; Ramon A. Nadal, "Status Quo: Enemy of Leadership," 51 (June 1971): 24–30; Richard J. Stillman, "Creativity: Stymied or Stimulated?" 51 (December 1971): 67–72; Frederic J. Brown, "The Army and Society," 52 (March 1972): 3–17; John J. Madigan III and Pat C. Hoy II, "The Dialectical Imperative: Civil-Military Confrontation," 53 (November 1973): 41–54; Paul B. Parham, "The American Military Profession: An Egalitarian View," 54 (November 1974): 18–29. For historical perspective on the creative output of the journal in the early 1970s, see Forrest R. Blackburn, "Military Review 1922–1972," 52 (February 1972): 52–62.

14. For an extensive critique of the problem, see Lewis Sorley, "Prevailing Criteria: A Critique," in *Combat Effectiveness: Cohesion, Stress and the Volunteer Military,* ed. Sam C. Sarkesian (Beverly Hills: Sage, 1980), chap. 2.

15. For example, Richard G. Stilwell, "Evolution in Tactics: The Vietnam Experience," *Army* 20 (February 1970): 14–23; Zeb B. Bradford, Jr., "US Tactics in

Vietnam," *Military Review* 52 (February 1972): 63–76; Edward C. Logelin, "The US Army: Success Unrecognized," *Army* 22 (January 1972): 6.

16. Douglas Kinnard, *The War Managers* (Hanover, N.H.: University Press of New England for the University of Vermont, 1977): p. 45.

17. Lawrence J. Korb, *The Fall and Rise of the Pentagon: American Defense Policies in the 1970s* (Westport, Conn.: Greenwood, 1979), chap. 2.

18. Ibid.

19. As Jordan and Taylor note, "In reality, the change was not all that dramatic, for, despite declaratory policy, the U.S. had earlier never even approached the kinds and levels of forces needed for two and a half wars." Amos A. Jordan and William J. Taylor, Jr., *American National Security: Policy and Process,* rev. ed. (Baltimore: Johns Hopkins University Press, 1984): p. 75.

20. The army has frozen its active duty strength at 781,000. The increased emphasis in recent years on reserve forces (including National Guard) has resulted in building the reserve force to numbers almost equal to the active duty army, with the reservists due to outnumber active duty personnel by fiscal year 1988. See George C. Wilson, "Reservists Soon to Outnumber U.S. Soldiers on Active Duty," *Washington Post,* April 12, 1985, pp. A1, A14. Also Bill Keller, "Reserves Move to the Forefront of Defense," *New York Times,* March 10, 1985, p. 3E.

21. Jack R. Butler, "The All-Volunteer Armed Force—Its Feasibility and Implications," *Parameters* 2, no. 1 (1972): 17–29.

22. Such an argument is made by Morris Janowitz, "Volunteer Armed Forces and Military Purpose," *Foreign Affairs* 50 (April 1972): 427–443. Also Richard V.L. Cooper, *Military Manpower and the All-Volunteer Force,* report prepared for the Defense Advanced Research Projects Agency, R-1450-ARPA (Santa Monica, Calif.: Rand, September 1977).

23. President's Commission on an All-Volunteer Armed Force, *The Report of the President's Commission on an All-Volunteer Armed Force* (Washington, D.C.: Government Printing Office, February 1970).

24. William C. Westmoreland, "An Army Taking Stock in a Changing Society," *Army* 21 (October 1971): 19–22.

25. The 1970 professionalism study is on file in the library of the U.S. Army War College, Carlisle Barracks, Pa.

26. Paper prepared by Jerry M. Solinger, quoted by W.R. Peers, *The My Lai Inquiry* (New York: W.W. Norton, 1979), p. 249. See also Seymour M. Hersh, *Cover-Up* (New York: Random House, 1972).

27. Westmoreland, "An Army Taking Stock."

28. Ibid.

29. Donn A. Starry, "A Tactical Evaluation—FM 100-5," *Military Review* 58 (August 1978): 2–11.

30. Examples of the monograph series are James L. Collins, *The Development and Training of the South Vietnamese Army, 1950–1972* (Washington, D.C.: Department of the Army, 1975), and James L. Collins and Stanley R. Larsen, *Allied Participation in Vietnam* (Washington, D.C.: Department of the Army, 1975). The first volume in what is intended as a comprehensive collection of historical studies of the U.S. Army in Vietnam by the U.S. Army Center of Military History is Ronald H. Spector, *Advice and Support: The Early Years, 1941–1960* (Washington, D.C.: Army Center of Military History, 1983).

31. Paul F. Gorman, conversation with author, June 1, 1985. Gorman commanded a battalion and served as operations officer of a division in Vietnam before returning to the United States to become deputy chief of staff of the Army Training and Doctrine Command when TRADOC was created as part of the army reorganization of 1973.

32. David Halberstam, *The Best and the Brightest* (Greenwich, Conn.: Fawcett Crest, 1972), p. 656.

33. William E. DePuy to author, July 1, 1985.

34. Donn A. Starry to Frederic J. Brown, March 31, 1972, Donn A. Starry collection, box 1A, personal correspondence 1969–1972, U.S. Army Military History Institute, Carlisle Barracks, Pa. The letter was sent in acknowledgment of receipt of Brown's article, "The Army and Society," *Military Review* 52 (February 1972): 3–17.

35. William E. DePuy, address to Infantry Officer Advanced Course, Fort Benning, Ga., November 1, 1973, transcript on file in William E. DePuy collection, addendum J to oral history transcript, archives, Military History Institute.

36. FM 100-5, quoted by Donald B. Vought, "Preparing for the Wrong War?" *Military Review* 57 (May 1977): 16–34.

37. W.E. DePuy, commander, U.S. Army Training and Doctrine Command, to commanders of TRADOC subordinate commands, memorandum, October 10, 1974, subject, "Field Manuals," on file in Starry collection, box 1B, personal correspondence 1973–1974, Military History Institute.

38. Robert A. Doughty, "The Command and General Staff College in Transition, 1946–1976," special study project, CGSC, June 1976, distributed by Defense Technical Information Center, Defense Logistics Agency, Cameron Station, Alexandria, Va., chap. 3. Also Donn A. Starry, "To Change an Army," *Military Review* 63 (March 1983): 20–27.

39. Edward R. Fried et al., *Setting National Priorities: The 1974 Budget* (Washington, D.C.: Brookings Institution, 1973). Also Richard D. Lawrence and Jeffrey Record, *US Force Structure in NATO: An Alternative* (Washington, D.C.: Brookings Institution, 1974). Lawrence was an army colonel who was a federal executive fellow at Brookings in 1972–1973.

40. Starry to Brown, March 31, 1972.

41. Starry, "To Change an Army," p. 26.

42. Vought, "Preparing for the Wrong War?" p. 30.

43. Richard F. Rosser, "American Civil-Military Relations in the 1980s," *Seaford House Papers: 1970* (London: Royal College of Defense Studies, 1970), reprinted in *Military Review* 52 (March 1972): 18–31.

44. The Astarita report was classified secret. An unclassified study that was prepared initially in 1974 at the behest of Secretary of the Army Howard Callaway was published seven years later at the suggestion of the army vice-chief of staff, General John W. Vessey, Jr. Harry G. Summers, Jr., *The Astarita Report: A Military Strategy for the Multipolar World,* occasional paper (Carlisle Barracks, Pa.: U.S. Army War College, Strategic Studies Institute, April 30, 1981).

45. U.S. Army Training and Doctrine Command, Officer Personnel Management System Task Group Report, quoted by Doughty, "Command and General Staff College," p. 62.

46. For details, see Harry P. Ball, *Of Responsible Command: A History of the*

U.S. Army War College (Carlisle Barracks, Pa.: Alumni Association of the U.S. Army War College, 1983), chap. 21.

47. Zeb B. Bradford and Frederic J. Brown, "Implications of the Modern Battlefield," *Military Review* 57 (July 1977): 3–11. There were others who warned that narrowing the focus of professionalism was unwise. Examples include William J. Taylor, Jr., and Donald F. Bletz, "A Case for Graduate Education," *Journal of Political and Military Sociology* 2 (Fall 1974): 251–267; Sam C. Sarkesian and William J. Taylor, Jr., "The Case for Civilian Graduate Education for Professional Officers," *Armed Forces and Society* 1 (February 1975): 251–262; Donald B. Vought and John Binkley, "Fort Apache or Executive Suite? The US Army Enters the 1980s," *Parameters* 8 (June 1978): 21–34; and Alfred H. Paddock, Jr., "Does the Army Have a Future? Deterrence and Civil-Military Relations in the Post-Vietnam Era," *Parameters* 8 (September 1978): 51–57.

48. Review by Lloyd J. Matthews in *Parameters* 5, no. 2 (1976): 88–90. See also William C. Westmoreland, "Vietnam in Perspective," condensed from an address delivered April 11, 1978, at the US Army Command and General Staff College, *Military Review* 59 (January 1979): 34–43.

49. Fred C. Weyand and Harry G. Summers, Jr., "Vietnam Myths and American Military Realities," *Commander's Call* (July–August 1976): 1–13; reprinted in *Armor* (September–October 1976).

50. Kinnard, *War Managers.*

51. Peter Braestrup, *Big Story: How the American Press and Television Reported and Interpreted the Crisis of Tet 1968 in Vietnam and Washington,* 2 vols. (Boulder, Colo.: Westview, 1977); Guenther Lewy, *America in Vietnam* (New York: Oxford University Press, 1978); Leslie H. Gelb with Richard K. Betts, *The Irony of Vietnam: The System Worked* (Washington, D.C.: Brookings Institution, 1979); Stanley Karnow, *Vietnam: A History* (New York: Viking, 1983). A useful critical review of recent interpretations of the U.S. experience in Vietnam is provided by Paul M. Kattenburg, "Reflections on Vietnam: Of Revisionism and Lessons Yet to Be Learned," *Parameters* 14 (Autumn 1984): 42–50. A more extensive treatise, which makes a number of useful distinctions among varieties of revisionism in the interpretation of recent U.S. foreign policy, is Richard A. Melanson, *Writing History and Making Policy: The Cold War, Vietnam and Revisionism* (New York: University Press of America, 1983).

52. Harry G. Summers, Jr., *On Strategy: The Vietnam War in Context,* prepared for the Strategic Studies Institute, U.S. Army War College (Washington, D.C.: Government Printing Office, 1981). The book has been published commercially as *On Strategy: A Critical Analysis of the Vietnam War* (New York: Dell, 1982).

53. Palmer, *25-Year War.*

54. William Darryl Henderson, *Cohesion: The Human Element in Combat* (Washington, D.C.: National Defense University Press, 1985), p. xvi.

55. DeWitt C. Smith, Jr., remarks at Twenty-first Annual National Strategy Seminar, U.S. Army War College, published in *Parameters* 5, no. 1 (1975): 2–5.

56. Caspar W. Weinberger, address to the National Press Club, Washington, D.C., November 28, 1984; news release from the Office of the Assistant Secretary of Defense (Public Affairs).

57. Palmer, *25-Year War,* p. 155.

58. Ibid., p. 179.

59. R.W. Komer, *Bureaucracy Does Its Thing: Institutional Constraints on U.S.-GVN Performance in Vietnam* (Santa Monica: RAND, prepared for the Defense Advanced Research Projects Agency, R-967-ARPA, August 1972), p. 5. Emphasis in the original.

60. Summers, *On Strategy,* p. 21.

61. DeWitt C. Smith, Jr., discussion with author, May 23, 1985. Among the exceptions is Henderson, *Cohesion,* although it deals only partially with the Vietnam experience.

62. Quoted by Benjamin F. Schemmer, "Internal Army Surveys Suggest Serious Concerns about Army's Senior Leaders," *Armed Forces Journal International* 122 (May 1985): 18–19.

63. Countless quantities of time and energy continue to be expended in Pentagon-generated efforts to devise a truly useful and authoritative doctrine for low-intensity conflict. This situation exists despite the fact that the term was introduced many years ago. A detailed critical discussion of the subject at a workshop in Chicago in 1979 attended by military professionals, civilian officials, and scholars yielded some potentially helpful results. See Sam C. Sarkesian and William L. Scully, eds., *U.S. Policy and Low-Intensity Conflict* (New Brunswick, N.J.: Transaction Books, 1981), especially the introductory essay by Sarkesian and the chapter by George K. Osborn and William J. Taylor, Jr., "The Employment of Force: Political Constraints and Limitations." For a more recent discussion of the subject by Sarkesian, see "Low-Intensity Conflict: Concepts, Principles, and Policy Guidelines," *Air University Review* 36 (January–February 1985): 4–23. The army has attempted to codify operational guidance in a field manual, FM 100-20, *Low-Intensity Conflict.*

64. See note 2.

65. For an awareness of recent developments at Fort Leavenworth, I am indebted especially to conversations with Colonels Richard Sinnreich and Robert Herrick.

66. Alexis de Tocqueville, *Democracy in America,* trans. George Lawrence, ed. J.P. Mayer, Anchor Books ed., 2 vols. (Garden City, N.Y.: Doubleday, 1969), 2: chap. 18.

67. Ibid., p. 621.

68. Ibid., pp. 647–651.

69. Samuel P. Huntington, *The Soldier and the State: The Theory and Politics of Civil-Military Relations* (Cambridge: Belknap Press of Harvard University Press, 1957).

70. Morris Janowitz, *The Professional Soldier: A Social and Political Portrait* (New York: Free Press, 1960, 1971), chap. 11.

71. Such a criticism is made in detail, with emphasis on the cultural roots of the U.S. military proclivity for high-technology solutions, by Donald Vought, "American Culture and American Arms: The Case of Vietnam," in *Lessons from an Unconventional War: Reassessing U.S. Strategies for Future Conflicts,* ed. Richard A. Hunt and Richard A. Shultz, Jr. (New York: Pergamon, 1982), pp. 159–190. See also Summers, *On Strategy;* Palmer, *25-Year War;* and Richard A. Gabriel and Paul L. Savage, *Crisis in Command: Mismanagement in the Army* (New York: Hill and Wang, 1978).

72. See, for example, Charles C. Moskos, Jr., "The All-Volunteer Military: Calling, Profession, or Occupation?" *Parameters* 7, no. 1 (1977): 2–9; Moskos, "From

Institution to Occupation: Trends in Military Organization," *Armed Forces and Society* 4 (Fall 1977): 41–50; Morris Janowitz, "From Institutional to Occupational: The Need for Conceptual Continuity," *Armed Forces and Society* 4 (Fall 1977): 51–54; David R. Segal and Joseph J. Lengermann, "Professional and Institutional Considerations," in *Combat Effectiveness,* pp. 154–184.

73. Huba Wass de Czege, "How to Change an Army," *Military Review* 64 (November 1984): 32–49.

74. Stephen D. Wesbrook, "The Alienated Soldier: Legacy of Our Society," *Army* 29 (December 1979): 18–23.

75. Schemmer, "Internal Army Surveys," pp. 18–19.

76. Dandridge M. Malone as quoted by James Fallows, "A Military without Mind or Soul," *Washington Monthly* 13 (April 1981): 12–27. See also D.M. Malone and Donald D. Penner, "You Can't Run an Army Like a Corporation," *Army* 30 (February 1980): 39–41.

7
The Vietnam Experience and the Intelligence Community

John M. Oseth

To appreciate the impact of the Vietnam experience on the intelligence community, it is helpful to view the war from two very different angles.[1] The first sees Vietnam as a total societal experience: a span of years in which new and multidimensional dynamics changed American society and politics—and the business of governing—in important ways. The war is seen here as a phenomenon imbedded in a larger era, one of several forces (such as the civil rights movement) that altered the American political landscape forever. The second angle of vision considers Vietnam, the war itself, as an episode: a case study in the making and executing of national security policy and in the role of intelligence in decision making. On this level the war is seen as a discrete case in problem solving for the nation's leaders and the apparatus of government.

Both perspectives provide important insights into what the intelligence community has become and also into its future challenges and prospects. When the entire era, the 1960s and the 1970s, is surveyed, emerging international realities and major pressures for sociopolitical change in the United States stand out not just as context for the war but as forces that were crystallized by the war and sharpened in their impact on the intelligence community. This viewpoint sees much change occurring in U.S. intelligence as a result of the confluence of those forces. Indeed, it suggests that when the Vietnam experience can be appraised fully and objectively, we may find that it had greater effect on U.S. intelligence agencies than on the U.S. policy instruments most deeply involved in the combat, the armed forces.

The second perspective, examining Vietnam as an episode in policymaking and policy application, finds the war illustrating organizational and operational difficulties that still concern the intelligence community today. At the highest level of generality, these problems can be framed as simple questions: How do we define a policy problem? Who does it? How successful are we at connecting the best information and analysis with the process of decision making at all levels? What tools, especially covert ones, can be used to achieve policy goals? In this view, Vietnam exemplified some central deficiencies that will be at the heart of the intelligence challenge in the future.

The ultimate question emerging from this bifocal analysis is whether the persisting challenge highlighted by the second viewpoint can be addressed adequately by an intelligence community that has undergone the changes wrought by the Vietnam experience and outlined by the first perspective. That question cannot be answered definitively here; it is beyond the bounds of the inquiry, and in any event the story is far from completed at this point. But awareness of the problem may itself prove valuable in the years ahead.

Perspective I: The Vietnam Era

Central Characteristics and Trends

Institutions operate within contexts that both shape them and are shaped by them. The characteristics of the Vietnam era, roughly the years between 1960 and 1975, are set out in general terms elsewhere in this book. For our purposes, however, it is important to highlight several themes that were especially important to the intelligence community.

First, the international scene became much more diverse and complex. Contacts between and among nations multiplied, communication networks expanded, and interpenetration of societies and economics deepened. New actors emerged with diverse outlooks and interests: former colonies seeking full rights as nation-states; poor nations seeking political independence and larger shares of the world's material wealth; middle nations rising to economic and political power rivaling that of the advanced societies. Nonstate actors became prominent: international businesses, transient revolutionaries and terrorist bands, and regional associations of countries established for specific (notably economic) purposes. Lines between the major blocs became less distinct, though the two superpowers retained their military preeminence. Around the world, the proliferation of technology, especially in its military applications, made outbreaks of violence in previously localized trouble spots more dangerous and thus more relevant to far-flung superpower interests. And all this—plus the Vietnam War itself—was brought home to American living rooms by advanced communications networks with great immediacy and little accompanying attempt to make the picture coherent.

In all these ways and more, the world was becoming harder to understand and less amenable to the analytical frameworks applied, inside and outside the government, in the first fifteen years after World War II.[2]

At home, meanwhile, there was growing introspection and criticism of how the United States used its tools of power abroad. For many Americans, a sense of moral imperative was increasingly influencing views on the use of force and on U.S. purposes and actions in international affairs. Growing international interdependence, the need to avoid nuclear conflict between the superpowers, and rising concern about socioeconomic causes of international violence seemed to relegate tools of military power to a position of secondary importance. Intelligence capabilities, notably those involving intrigue and manipulation, were similarly disadvantaged by this dimension of the emerging public consciousness.

As the Vietnam War dragged on, moreover, there was palpable loss of confidence within and outside government concerning the ability to understand what was going on, in Southeast Asia or elsewhere, and the capacity to do something about it. The light had appeared, and then disappeared, at the end of the war's tunnel so often that by 1970 almost no official assessment of the war's progress was accepted at face value. That all-too-evident inability to understand and influence what was happening suggested to many that this incapacity had broader ramifications across the entire U.S. national security posture. The limits of power became an important theme in policy analyses and a major focus of informed discussion among the public at large.

In the U.S. polity, finally, both Congress and the public were developing a new sense of their rightful roles, potentials, and efficacy. The Vietnam War crystallized a sense in Congress that the legislature had to become more assertive in national security and foreign policy matters generally in order to live up to the Constitution's expectations about shared and balanced power. Public protest against the war gave that movement a great deal of energy, but it also drew strength from a perceived need to redress decades of drift toward an imperial—and imperious—presidency. There were demands for new institutions forcing executive collaboration and consultation with Congress on national security matters. The War Powers Act was one result. There were also instances in which an aroused Congress dictated specific national security policies, such as the prohibition of covert U.S. involvement in Angolan civil strife or in the 1975 cessation of U.S. aid to the Thieu regime in Saigon.

Those among the public who had opposed the war saw their activism finally vindicated in these measures. Determination to widen the channels for influence, and to make the democratic system work even on the most important national security issues, grew substantially. Measures were enacted specifically to open up the processes of government to public monitorship; the Freedom of Information Act was notable here. In all these ways, the Vietnam era saw major pressures for public and congressional participation in policy-making and appreciable advances in their ability to shape and regulate the behavior of the United States abroad.

Effects on the Intelligence Community

These dynamics produced three effects with respect to the intelligence agencies.

First, three presidential adminstrations (Ford, Carter, and Reagan) developed formal rules and collaboration routines permitting greater congressional, judicial, and public scrutiny and control of intelligence activities and facilitating closer oversight of the intelligence agencies by executive branch authorities. This regulatory impetus was felt in all operational areas: in intelligence collection activities, in counterintelligence (protecting against or seeking to exploit the collection operations of foreign services), and in the covert action area (attempts to influence events abroad, not just to report on them). The result, many feel, was a regime of rule and oversight that restrained and burdened the nation's intelligence effort in harmful ways.

Second, in the same period of time, the decision-making elite—those who are attentive to and influential in the arena of national security policy—appreciably widened, and a variety of authoritative sources of information and analysis arose to compete with executive expertise for the attention of this expanded establishment. If it ever had a monopoly over the most important government information channels, the intelligence community lost it irretrievably in this period, with concomitant loss of credibility, influence, and power. Newly active segments of the public and the Congress literally were bombarded with media and academic analyses and opinions about the war and about world affairs in general. Moreover, conflict within the government over official Vietnam assessments had sharpened internal bureaucratic tensions that now emerged more persistently than before, presenting new challenges in the effort to make the community function as a community.

Finally, the rise of technology, and American fascination with it, was manifested in the intelligence business. Classic clandestine espionage of human sources was deemphasized. Technological and technology-dependent sources of collection were favored in the all-important bureaucratic competitions for limited dollars and manpower. As a result, the U.S. intelligence effort in essence disarmed itself for some critical missions, especially in third world societies and against the terrorist threat.

Regulatory Ethos and Apparatus. After the Vietnam War, four perspectives on intelligence capabilities contended against one another in an extended public debate that was unprecedented even in this most open of societies.[3] The first held that lively and aggressive intelligence agencies are an imperative of international life, mandated by external realities that had grown more complex and more threatening. This viewpoint defended all operational capabilities of the intelligence community—foreign intelligence collection, counterintelligence, and covert action—and insisted that national security required their enlargement.

A second viewpoint recognized the nation's need for security but argued that actions by the United States to cope with security challenges had to align with basic ideals of fair play and decency. Adherents of this perspective insisted that the United States must eschew some of the capabilities routinely employed by its less principled adversaries or else the strategic struggle between competing value systems would be lost in the fog of overzealous combat. The practices of clandestine spying, involving secret collection activities beyond the law in other societies, were of some concern, though many observers understood the need to learn about events, trends, and personalities in other countries. Attempting to manipulate those events, trends, and personalities seemed to raise normative issues of a more serious order. CIA covert action operations drew special criticism, especially after congressional investigations in 1975 and 1976 exposed a long history of U.S. involvement in foreign coups, civil wars, politics, and even assassination plots against foreign leaders. Even those who had no objection to clandestine espionage criticized these secret, manipulative activities as unworthy of fundamental American ideals.

Another perspective in the U.S. debate wanted to impose constraints on intelligence operations that would prevent government intrusion on individual liberties at home. Civil liberties activists in particular sought to confine intelligence activities by rules — derived from constitutional protections — that were applied to domestic law enforcement operations, attacking intelligence agency practices that had been allowed for years by the executive, the Congress, and the courts under a national security rationale. They rejected the intelligence professionals' argument that hostile, foreign threats justified greater latitude for U.S. intelligence-counterintelligence operations than is permitted for activities directed by law enforcement officials against domestic criminals. The need to protect Americans from government intrusion and abuses should not, in their view, be subordinated to the need to protect against perceived foreign threats. Government power, whether used against perceived internal or external threats, had to be confined by rules respecting individual rights.

Finally, a fourth perspective sought to develop and institutionalize new operational oversight measures that would rein in a presidency and its tools of prerogative and power and hold the executive accountable for its actions. This argument had deep constitutional and legal groundings, aside from the growing public skepticism, even cynicism, about the presidency engendered by Vietnam and the Watergate episode.

The competition among these perspectives played out in several forums. The most visible was the arena of public debate, where serious controversy started around 1970 with revelations about military intelligence surveillance of civil rights and antiwar demonstrations. This often-inflamed public inquiry continued through the mid-1970s with spectacular exposés of CIA and FBI activities, notably assassination plots and domestic spying on such prominent figures as Martin Luther King, Jr. Formal congressional investigations and hearings about such operations provided both a platform for opposing views and a continuing source of information about government intelligence and security agencies. The rise of investigative journalism added fuel to the fire. In the late 1970s, serious attempts were made in the Congress to enact detailed charter legislation that would have stated operational constraints and oversight procedures as a matter of law. That movement kept the contending arguments in the headlines daily, and as events developed, much of Washington was captured by the reform momentum.

The legislative effort moved slowly, however, and reform activists branched out in other directions. Civil libertarians in particular took their views to the courts, alleging infringement of constitutional rights and often seeking huge sums in money damages from government employees. These lawsuits stemmed from an earlier case that was interpreted to allow claims against officials in their personal capacity, where government actions may have violated the privacy rights of individuals. For an intelligence profession already demoralized by a drumfire of criticism from all sides, these suits raised the prospect that government agents and their supervisors could be held liable in the event that a judge, with the benefit of hindsight, found their actions had violated someone's constitutional rights.

The Ford, Carter, and Reagan administrations attempted to accommodate these pressures for change, though each balanced the competing values differently. Each president issued his own charter for the intelligence agencies, in the form of executive orders that announced operational rules and constraints and also established formal oversight mechanisms. The Carter order, published in 1978 at the height of the reform momentum, was the most detailed and restrictive. In 1976 President Ford's charter essentially had repeated prohibitions that were already in force, and President Reagan's 1981 order had as its avowed purpose the restoration of intelligence capabilities that the reform had confined. In all cases, however, when the charters were combined with separate rules promulgated by the attorney general for the FBI, a significant regulatory regime was put in place that intelligence professionals resented and many others believed was profoundly disabling.[4]

In the new regime, approval procedures for many sensitive activities tightened. Approval authority tended to move upward in the channels of executive bureaucracy, away from the operators, and also outward to involve agency general counsel and the attorney general himself. Rules about what could and could not be done multiplied. In the Carter administration especially, the impetus to confine operations within well-established boundaries was strong. The rights of individuals were given special standing in executive regulations, as operatives were told, for instance, to use the least intrusive operational techniques available if the rights of Americans might be implicated. President Carter also spoke frequently of the need for intelligence activities to be kept within the bounds of moral decency. Covert action operations declined to a low ebb in his administration, to the great concern of intelligence professionals and many others who believed that the United

States had to take a more activist approach to shaping events in an increasingly dangerous and unpredictable world. The Carter administration also significantly reduced the CIA's clandestine service, letting go many of the agency's most experienced espionage hands, as well as covert action operators.

In 1980 the congressional charter movement finally produced a statute that streamlined the congressional oversight procedures, reducing the number of committees involved but also requiring the executive to keep the House and Senate intelligence committees fully and currently informed about intelligence activities. This legislative charter was much abbreviated in comparison to earlier proposals. But the intent of Congress to be seriously involved in watching over the intelligence agencies was clear, and the oversight process now had statutory basis. The working of that process has been highlighted, indeed headlined, from time to time since 1980. The extraordinary outcry in 1984 over the CIA's covert mining of Nicaraguan ports and over whether congressional committees had been adequately informed about that operation is illustrative. Recurrent debates in Congress about U.S. aid to guerrillas in Central America provide further evidence of legislators' continuing desire to affect the ways in which intelligence capabilities are used.

In summary, the product of the regulatory ethos that emerged in the aftermath of the Vietnam experience included:

Substantial segments of the public that had become attentive to intelligence activities and concerned about controlling them (this included, in some quarters, an abiding suspicion of human intelligence and counterintelligence operations).

Routinized congressional oversight of specific operations and recurrent legislative efforts to influence the use of intelligence capabilities.

More elaborate, and many still say unduly confining, rules about what kinds of operations could be undertaken and about how they were to be controlled.

Diminished capabilities for classic human espionage and covert action operations.

Vigorous media scrutiny and Freedom of Information Act procedures that raised the chances that sensitive information, such as the identity of intelligence sources and personnel, might be exposed, with adverse consequences for the nation's security.

Larger Establishment and the Problems of Dissonance. As attentive and mobilized segments of the public and an aroused Congress began to exploit new avenues of policy influence, the decision-making arena—the circle of influential knowledgeables—in Washington and elsewhere widened appreciably. There was also a vast proliferation of information sources and repositories of policy-relevant expertise available to support advocacy of all persuasions on the full array of national security issues.

The news media and private think-tanks especially assumed markedly magnified roles as reporters and analyzers of international affairs and U.S. security problems. In essence they became a second channel of expertise that competes with the intelligence community for influence in policy councils and for the public mind.[5] In the latter case—the competition for influence outside the executive branch—the intelligence community is severely disadvantaged. The intelligence underpinnings of policy are subjected to the constant pressure of outside critics whose concerns are often unanswerable because of secrecy needs or the pressures of time and other priorities within the government. As contending and seemingly plausible analyses are pressed forward, the credibility of intelligence community work is inevitably undermined. The fabled Team A–Team B exercise of the mid-1970s, in which a team of outside experts was formed to prepare analyses publicly challenging CIA estimates of Soviet strategic objectives and military strength, was but one manifestation of this erosion of confidence in official studies. There are, of course, good reasons for challenging analysts' work; vigorous review and criticism can improve the ultimate product.[6] But the point here is that in the post-Vietnam years, the emergence of alternative, unofficial sources of policy-relevant analyses essentially routinized a competitive system, not a synergistic system of review and debate.

Proliferation of highly vocal and professionalized expertise and highly visible information communicators also had another effect. It created a veritable fog of argumentation that often obscured issues instead of illuminating them. Some observers have pointed out that the decline of foreign policy consensus in the post-Vietnam years is in no small part attributable to this persistent, even insistent, disarray in the viewpoints of reputed experts and influential people.[7]

The extra pressures thus placed on the intelligence community in the post-Vietnam years are manifold. News media now literally cover the earth, bringing events quickly and directly to an expanded consumership and disseminating reports far more widely than the intelligence agencies can. This reporting can be inaccurate and irresponsible, to be sure, but much of it is quite good by any standard. Attentive publics accustomed to this kind of service find it hard to understand why the government often seems less informed and less capable. Government officials also are tempted to rely on outside sources that seem more responsive than the intelligence community, which is, after all, a bureaucracy with all the associated deficiencies of large organizations.

Furthermore, news organizations and think-tanks seek not just to inform, as do the intelligence agencies, but to inform visibly with great impact. They have none of the intelligence professionals' scruples about separating their reporting and analysis from policy prescriptions. Indeed, much of their research and analytical work is produced precisely to promote certain policies, and that can make their work more appealing to officials struggling to make and justify hard decisions.

Finally, although the intelligence agencies serve government officials, they cannot reach the wider establishment now active in national security affairs. Even when they perform their duty well, their work may be overshadowed by the analyses available in the alternative public channel. Their effectiveness depends not on the quality (clarity, congency, timeliness) of their product but on the cast of players active on a particular subject or issue and on the relative influence those players wield. This is a far cry from the situation that obtained in 1947 when the National Security Act laid the foundations for the modern intelligence community. The presumption then was that a rationalized intelligence effort serving officials in Washington would rationalize the policy product. Since Vietnam, the information-expertise glut and the expansion of the policymaking establishment have combined to undermine that fundamental presumption. As a result, the problem of connecting the best information with the policy process has been greatly complicated.

As if these difficulties attending emergence of the outsider information channel were not frustrating enough for intelligence professionals, two kinds of dissonance problems within the community became especially acute in the aftermath of Vietnam. One centered on the natural tensions between national and departmental intelligence, and the other stemmed from a heightened concern that analytical dissent be protected and, indeed, recognized in community products. Both are issues with long histories, but the Vietnam experience brought them to sharp focus and added impetus to the long-term search for remedies.

One of the earliest and most astute observations about the postwar U.S. intelligence community pointed to the natural tension between national and departmental intelligence.[8] National intelligence here means community-subscribed analyses and estimates produced by interagency consultation and bargaining—produced, in other words, by politics in the classic sense, in Washington. Departmental intelligence is that produced by the line policy departments for their own uses and needs. The centralizing impetus reflected in the 1947 National Security Act's creation of the CIA has survived in the analytical world in the process of developing national intelligence estimates and other studies propounding agreed community views. It is reflected also in the executive charter defining roles and missions for the intelligence agencies, which gives the director of central intelligence (DCI) full responsibility for producing and disseminating national foreign intelligence.[9]

But agencies within the intelligence community also produce analyses that support the policy responsibilities of their parent departments. The State Department's Bureau of Intelligence and Research produces intelligence related to U.S. foreign policy that the secretary of state needs for the execution of his responsibilities; the agencies of the Department of Defense produce "military and military-related intelligence" for the defense secretary's responsibilities; and so forth throughout the community.[10] Students of the intelligence business knew early that department analyses would tend to gravitate toward positions that support departmental policy (and especially budgetary) interests and that this could degrade the quality of national intelligence products or, at least, make them harder to develop. Suspicions about military intelligence have run especially deep, in part because of the strong superior-subordinate dynamic in the military.[11] For many observers, the Vietnam War highlighted this disability because of constant disarray in departmental intelligence positions. Military assessments of the war tended to be more optimistic concerning progress and the efficacy of military activity, while others had more doubts.[12] Even Secretary of Defense McNamara became increasingly disenchanted with the performance of his Defense Intelligence Agency and turned finally to the CIA for support he considered more objective and more reliable, not only about the war in Indochina but also concerning larger perspectives on the Soviet Union.[13]

These developments intensified the search for a better way to organize the community's analytical effort in support of the president's need for a unified, coherent perspective on major international events and trends. When James Schlesinger took over from Richard Helms as DCI in 1973, one of his main goals was to improve the national estimate process. His tenure lasted only six months, but his successor, William Colby, had similar concerns. He abolished the Office of National Estimates and the Board of National Estimates, the high-level forum in which community intelligence products had been developed from contrasting departmental positions. He replaced them with national intelligence officers (NIO) having functional or regional responsibilities for both collection and production within their areas of expertise. The aim was to sharpen national estimates by eliminating the diluting effects of cross-boundary bargaining and to connect producers more closely with the users of the products. The NIO system has strong supporters, but there remains real concern about whether it permits political bias to affect analytical work and whether it can provide sufficient central, or cross-boundary, management and evaluation of the national effort. Former DCI Stansfield Turner has argued that the NIO organization ought to be expanded to permit better national-level management of the total analytic effort, central and departmental.[14]

A related concern intensified by the Vietnam experience was the preservation of upward channels for analytical dissent within the community. Even aside from divergent perspectives on the nature of the war, there was a furious intracommunity debate about estimates of enemy strength, generated by some CIA analysts and others who charged that their data and analyses were suppressed by their superiors. Years after the war, this debate emerged in full flower on the public record as a result of a CBS television program that alleged a conspiracy, led by former General William Westmoreland, to understate enemy strength in intelligence reporting coming from the theater of war. Although this episode was important in its own right, it represented only one way in which the question of how to recognize dissent has emerged. It surfaced at national level, too, in the Team A–Team B exercise, where special channels were created to give visibility to alternative views. The process of coordination and bargaining that produced community-wide estimates has always tended to work toward consensus, or toward compromise of differences. This has tended to rob the resulting studies of clarity and cogency, as important differences are papered over in adroit use of agreed language. The long-standing practice of including dissenting views as footnotes to a majority text also was viewed as unsatisfactory, since footnotes might never be read, and in any event they hardly could do justice to the substance of opposing views. But everyone knew that the business of national-level analysis could not dissolve into uncoordinated circulation of disparate views. Some mechanism had to be found that would serve the twin needs of coherence and debate.

The Reagan administration's resolution of this problem has been to emphasize competitive analysis. While the DCI has the authority to produce national estimates on behalf of, and with the cooperation of, the community, he also was told to ensure that "appropriate mechanisms for competitive analysis are developed so that diverse points of view are considered fully and differences of judgment within the intelligence community are brought to the attention of national policymakers."[15]

Some observers remain unconvinced that these mechanisms have in fact permitted dissent on major issues to become visible, pointing out that the prevailing pressures are still toward consensus and, consequently, dilution of the national-level product.[16] But the concern for sharpening analysis that was heightened by the Vietnam experience also remains high, and the search for ways to promote debate without sacrificing coherence, cogency, and timeliness likely will remain high on the community's agenda.

Rise of Technology. Following World War II, classic espionage operations had their heyday on both sides of the cold war. Spying is as old a practice as diplomacy itself, of course, but in the United States there had been no formal institutionalization of the effort in peacetime until the modern intelligence community was established in 1947. Although signals intercept and photographic techniques were available and employed in the early years, the great bulk of intelligence collection was by humans.

As collection technologies matured, however, new institutions grew up around them, notably the National Security Agency and the Defense Department's reconnaissance offices.[17] When the intelligence community's prime targets, the closed societies in Eastern Europe, the Soviet Union, and China, became more difficult to penetrate with human sources, the technical disciplines stepped in to fill the void. Gradually they came to dominate the U.S. collection effort. By the late 1970s many regarded classic espionage as a cold war anachronism.[18] In the Carter administration, Stansfield Turner, the DCI, reduced the espionage service drastically, in part to make room for younger people but also because he believed it was time to recognize the dominance of technology. A number of observers argued against this on the ground that technological sources of collection cannot report on some critical matters as well as human sources can. There was particular concern about diminished coverage of third world societies and about the incapacity of technical systems to monitor the movements and intentions of international terrorists and revolutionaries. Later, the Reagan administration began to revitalize the human espionage establishment because of growing concern about information gaps in those areas. But the rebuilding of an espionage establishment cannot be accomplished quickly; it will require sustained attention in the years ahead.

The Vietnam experience did not account directly for the decline of classic espionage or the rise of technical collection sources. But the combat theater did provide a practical exercise in which the application of technical collection systems could be (and was) tested and validated. Imagery-producing systems, signals intelligence units, and remotely monitored acoustic and movement sensors were widely and profitably employed. The human source effort, meanwhile, produced a glut of dubious and often only accidentally relevant reports. Much of an entire generation of the professional national security establishment passed through that practical exercise and had their ideas about intelligence formed by it. By any measure, it was hardly a showcase for the human intelligence discipline. One prominent participant, General Bruce Palmer, now argues that overreliance by the United States on signals intelligence and declining interest in human collection were major deficiencies in the prosecution of the war.[19] But this was not so clear at the time, and the fascination with technological systems grew even more intense as the United States withdrew from the war and concentrated on a more traditional intelligence concern, the Soviet threat to Europe and NATO.

As Washington entered upon the ballyhooed "year of Europe" following the Vietnam cease-fire in 1973, the United States renewed its earlier interest in nuclear arms control negotiations and returned to the problem of managing the central strategic relationship with the Soviet Union. The intelligence community redoubled its effort to develop technical collection systems that could see into closed societies and listen beyond borders that had become virtually inpenetrable for human sources. These systems provided reliable documentary proof—photographs, communications texts, and so on—of the Soviet military capabilities that threatened European and U.S.-NATO security. And those contributions earned them the lion's share of attention and resources within the intelligence community and in the policy establishment.

Moreover, the decade of open discussion about U.S. intelligence agencies that was fueled by Vietnam-related sentiments had two particularly debilitating effects on the human espionage effort. On the one hand, it demoralized American operatives and curbed their initiative. On the other hand, the profusion of leaks and revelations that emerged from the various formal inquisitions deterred foreign sources, both individuals and intelligence services, from cooperating with the United States for fear of ultimate exposure. Classic espionage was losing its place in Washington and its most precious asset: credibility with potential agents abroad.

At the end of the Vietnam era, then, there were marked changes in the way the intelligence community operated and was organized in comparison to the early years after World War II. It was more constrained and regulated. It was under great pressure from competing information and expertise channels within and outside the government. And it was struggling to find the proper balance among techniques of collection. These changes and challenges cannot be attributed only to the war. Rather, they were the product of an era in which the Vietnam War was a major phenomenon, generating or energizing forces that also drew strength from the civil rights movement, from fear of nuclear war, and from student unrest in the universities, among other sources. Whether those forces would have coalesced with such effect in the intelligence arena if Vietnam had never occurred is a question about which we can only speculate. But it is certain that developments in the intelligence community cannot be understood adequately without an appreciation of the larger context in which the war was a central episode.

Perspective II: Vietnam as Episode

Taking a narrower viewpoint than the one that considers Vietnam as part of a larger societal experience, one can focus on the operational reality of the war and the role of intelligence in shaping decisions about it. The discussion that follows highlights key features of the intelligence effort in Vietnam and relates them to several issues: the quality of intelligence produced, its connection to decisions at all levels of the government, and the ability to shape events abroad with a hidden hand, the covert action tool. The overarching thesis is that the war illustrated larger and endemic difficulties that still define the intelligence challenge for the United States.

The Operational Reality

Before the United States became massively involved in Vietnam, the intelligence community had done fairly well there with a modest but thoroughly professional CIA reporting effort and community assessments that were in many ways remarkably prescient. Reporting was sensitive to the many dimensions of the instability plaguing Saigon, and analyses produced from that reporting were typically on the mark.[20] But all this changed soon after Washington made its commitment of combat troops to the war.

The immediate judgment of the military leadership in the burgeoning Saigon command was that the intelligence then available was inadequate.[21] There was not enough of it, and what was available was frequently untimely, unreliable, or unsuited to the needs of tactical units. In developing remedies, the tendency from the start was to create a large and complex organization that would supply all intelligence needed to fight the war. What resulted was a large headquarters staff in Saigon, with a wide variety of U.S. units operating throughout the country and in all collection disciplines and with tactical intelligence units and staffs assigned to combat formations at battalion level and higher. This large and lively organization funneled streams of reports upward through military channels and laterally to adjacent units. Each intermediate headquarters used the reports for its own operational purposes and to support a myriad of analyses that were in turn similarly disseminated widely up, down, and laterally. All this paralleled a similar effort on the Vietnamese military side. And both military efforts were paralleled by the reporting of U.S. and Vietnamese civilian agencies: intelligence services (the CIA and its Vietnamese counterparts, as well as host country police-security forces) and other agencies operating field programs or having representatives out among the population (notably the U.S. Agency for International Development). The U.S. advisory apparatus attached to Vietnamese tactical units and to local government authorities also had its own reporting duties, and these products were made widely available to analysts and decision makers trying to understand the war.

The CIA's station chief in Saigon was nominally in charge of the U.S. intelligence effort as the senior intelligence adviser to the ambassador. But it became literally impossible to integrate the activity of the operational colossus that emerged, and in no event could he control the reporting activities and analyses of in-country agencies outside the local intelligence community. Washington, meanwhile, was beset by analytical disarray. It is no wonder that Richard Nixon and others could declare, years later, that one of the major reasons for U.S. failure in Vietnam was that the apparatus supporting the president never understood what was happening there.[22] Aside from the national-level dissonance and coordination problems, even within the theater of operations there were few energies or institutions working effectively toward coherence or unity of management. Rather than integration and synergy of operations and analysis, there was instead dispersion and disaggregation of authority with a cacophony of voices speaking out at once about different slices of the Vietnam problem and a myriad of agencies at all levels taking action based on that fragmented advice.

Bureaucratic interests began to play importantly, affecting the reporting and analytical focus of intelligence elements. Military concerns were naturally tactical and combat oriented. Nonmilitary agencies treated other aspects of the problem while also addressing the military dimension in terms most relevant to their own operational interests (the huge pacification apparatus, for instance, was much more concerned about the Vietcong infrastructure than were combat elements, which constantly sought to engage military formations in stand-up battles). Organizational interests and missions also affected the judgments of decision makers at all levels, military and civilian, tactical and strategic, about which intelligence authorities to pay attention to. The result was that the early and primarily CIA sensitivity to on-the-ground realities was soon displaced by massive operational proliferation and narrow, uncoordinated focus on specialized bureaucratic missions.[23]

Understanding the Problem

In part the confused operational reality reflected the way Americans always have tended to structure their thinking about and organization of the intelligence business. In the American scheme of things, a number of analytical and organizational distinctions are important: between political and military features of the world, between civil and military authority, between intelligence and law enforcement activities, between combat actions and internal security operations, and between tactical and strategic intelligence, to name just some of the most prominent. Separate agencies, expectations, and operational rules have grown up to deal with discrete problems falling on one side or the other of these distinctions. But the problem in Vietnam was not divided up so neatly into discrete compartments. It was a multidimensional whole that could not be permanently disassembled into parts for the sake of bureaucratic missions or operational convenience. To reduce it analytically and operationally into parts without also at some point putting it back together again handicapped U.S. policymakers by giving them assessments that were incongruent with reality.

This tendency is still with us. Viewed most generally, it works this way. Military agencies produce military intelligence—enemy order of battle, doctrine, likely battlefield intentions, and so forth—and they develop experts who specialize in describing indicia of military strength and capability. Nonmilitary agencies, notably the CIA and the State Department, produce analysis that takes account of political and other factors as well as purely military ones: the strength of the regime, popular sentiment, economic performance, social grievances, and so forth. They develop specialists in those subjects who, like the military intelligence experts, push their analyses forward in policy councils. These separate repositories of expertise see different aspects of reality, but they do not, on their own motion, tend to coalesce into a coherent analytical whole. This can be especially perplexing for decision makers who sense that the real issues they address run across the analytical boundaries that separate the intelligence effort into compartments.

This factionalization of intelligence may account in some measure for the growth of large official and unofficial advisory groups supporting the president—analytical experts at the NSC, for instance, or trusted advisers in the outside foreign policy establishment who can take the broader view.[24] What is clear is that the overcompartmentalization of intelligence—the drawing of operations and analysis toward the center of bureaucratic missions—still plagues the intelligence and policymaking communities. After the 1983 bombing of the marine barracks in Lebanon, the official inquiry into the tragedy concluded in part that the U.S. military commanders on the ground did not have effective human intelligence support (which is controlled primarily by the nonmilitary agencies of the intelligence community). It also concluded that greater efforts were required to fuse intelligence from all sources, to make the analytical picture coherent and to take cognizance of all possible sources of information and expertise. Without that multidimensional support, the military command's concept of the surrounding environment had, over time, become outdated and insufficiently attuned to increasing threats.[25]

Aside from the problem of composing a coherent picture of the policy challenge for decision makers to act on, the Vietnam episode illustrates another difficulty: inevitable intrusion of decision makers' preexisting beliefs and ideas. Scholars have long pointed to the importance of the belief systems of leaders: their attitudinal orientations and prior experiences that filter or color incoming information. They are in essence preprogrammed for receptivity to some kinds of information but not for other kinds. Focusing at the top of government, James Rosenau has categorized these belief systems in terms of worldviews brought to their positions by the nation's leaders.[26] Also important are their policy preferences, which may lead them to select certain reports or analyses over others although the merits do not objectively support that choice.[27] And there is also some opinion that third world societies in general may be incomprehensible to Americans, rendering it extremely difficult for Americans to report sensibly about them.[28]

Although these observations often focus on the national-level Washington community, Vietnam also shows that they may apply as well to levels of decision making much closer to the operational challenge. The great debate about enemy strength in Vietnam can be understood in this light.

The outlines of the debate are well known, thanks most recently to the celebrated suit brought by former General William Westmoreland against CBS alleging that a 1982 program, "The Uncounted Enemy: A Vietnam Deception," had maligned his reputation. The question raised by the program was whether Westmoreland knowingly had deceived Washington by directing his intelligence subordinates to reduce their estimates of enemy numbers. Westmoreland indignantly denied that he had done this, but the program pursued the thesis that there had been a conspiracy to keep the estimates low. The out-of-court settlement of Westmoreland's suit fell short of resolving that debate, but the case did reveal how Westmoreland's ideas about the nature of the war had set parameters for the work of his intelligence people.

In the theater of combat the problem was, How many enemy are there? Behind that question were other more subtle ones: Who is the enemy, and what is the nature of this conflict? In principle, certainly, those underlying questions are ones that intelligence officials ought to answer. But in this case, the commander answered them by reporting as enemy only those who conducted organized combat against U.S. forces. This drew attention to battlefield developments, a natural concern of the theater commander. But it left out of the calculation all the shadowy infrastructure activists and part-time guerrillas who were counted in some CIA assessments. Although Westmoreland may not have excluded them in order to avoid political difficulties with his superiors, as CBS hypothesized, his own view about the nature of the war did influence importantly the way the war was described in military intelligence analyses and in reports of operational progress. The connection between the decision maker and the provider of information and knowledge worked exactly backward from the way it often is described in the abstract. Intelligence professionals know that this is nothing new; it may even be inevitable. But for those who seek to have intelligence lead the way, rationally, toward solutions to policy problems, this aspect of the Vietnam syndrome may be the most enduring and troublesome dimension of all.

The Covert Action Legacy

Much of Vietnam was highly visible to everyone. Combat operations of all sorts were covered in depth by official briefings, statements, and reports, and television and print journalists covered them energetically. Firefights were eminently observable; commanders and their troops were accessible and often talkative; and the truly massive dimensions of the U.S. effort and its effects were plain to see. In fact, the main concern of some U.S. officials, particularly as media coverage of combat seemed to inflame public debate about the war, was that there was too little publicity and credit given to U.S. initiatives away from the battlefield. Economic and rural development progress, pacification achievements, and other indicators of accomplishment were ignored in the media's fixation on news about combat deaths, corruption among high Vietnamese officials, and the inefficiencies of the huge and unwieldy war machine that grew up as the U.S. presence expanded. The problem as seen from this standpoint was not that U.S. activity and achievement should be shielded from public scrutiny but that it should be examined fairly and in its totality.

But there were other parts of the war that no one wanted publicized. Among these were activities that translated the CIA's covert action capability, or manipulative operations in which U.S. sponsorship was hidden, from its peacetime cold war uses into an adjunct to hot war combat. The full length and breadth of these operations is not a matter of public record, but it is known that they began long before U.S. combat troops were sent to the war. In the early 1960s the CIA expanded its counterinsurgency program worldwide and, in the wake of the Bay of Pigs disaster, moved to upgrade and professionalize its capabilities for paramilitary action. In Southeast Asia the agency took over the previously military responsibility for training and advising Laotian tribesmen organized to fight against North Vietnamese troops located in or going through that country. From modest beginnings this became the largest paramilitary effort in U.S. history. In 1962 the CIA also began a small paramilitary program in Vietnam. This was eventually turned over to military control, but the agency continued to assist U.S. military covert activities against North Vietnam, and to conduct its own operations in Vietnam and elsewhere.[29]

As the U.S. presence in Vietnam expanded, the momentum of these activities was the same as the momentum of the rest of the war: toward bigness, costliness, bureaucratization, overt militarization, and multiple agency involvement (both U.S. and Vietnamese). All of these characteristics pushed operations inevitably toward clumsiness, on the one hand, and toward openness, on the other. Although the 1950s had seen a significant increase in the use of covert action around the world, the energies of the war magnified and intensified that trend. Activism, pressure to show results, and can-do thinking permeated decision making about this instrument of policy. Along the way U.S. officials lost sight of its place as an exceptional and adjunct, not a central, means of pursuing national goals.

A number of dynamics specific to the Vietnam situation combined to produce an ill-starred legacy for post-Vietnam covert action. The pressure toward more and bigger operations, with more participants and with more visible effects, together with the persistent investigative activities of journalists all over Southeast Asia, guaranteed that some would be exposed. CIA sponsorship of the secret war in Laos, for instance, was widely known for years. Moreover, the association of these operations with an unpopular war did not work to their credit. But even beyond these factors, the apparent militarization of the capability — its devotion to wartime and paramilitary uses — occurred at a time when public esteem for military activities was at an all-time low. Years after the war, this stigma remained, and it probably explains the provisions in successive presidents' executive orders that carefully restrict authority to engage in covert action to the CIA.

It was a time, additionally, when secrecy was widely abused in the war — to cover, for instance, U.S. bombing activities in Cambodia that started in 1969, unbeknown to Congress and the American public (official records were falsified to maintain the secret). When such deceptions became known, all secret tools of policy were tarnished. Secrecy seemed, to many, to connote deviousness, duplicity, and dishonor and to embrace activities that would not be undertaken if subjected to normal channels of approval and supervision. A capability that was by definition covert was naturally suspect at the outset. In the light of these public impressions, it is probably not coincidental that the official term now applied to this capability is *special activity,* not *covert action.*

Two other interrelated features of the war worked further to stigmatize the covert action capability in the public mind. One was U.S. association with Vietnamese counterpart agencies, which had far fewer scruples than the Americans about humane behavior. The other was the internal, domestic focus of the effort to deal with the Vietcong, essentially a police function absorbed into the war effort. The Phung Hoang, or PHOENIX, program illustrated both problems. Under direction of CIA officials in MACV, PHOENIX advisers (almost all military) worked with Vietnamese agents to identify and neutralize the enemy's clandestine political-military command and administrative cadre in South Vietnam, the Vietcong infrastructure. PHOENIX activities involved intelligence gathering, police work (arrests and interrogations), and strike operations that looked a great deal like military sweeps and ambushes. Neutralization of suspected Vietcong agents often involved firefights and killings. Throughout his later tenure as DCI and the one-time head of the program, William Colby found himself and his agency on the defensive against criticism alleging gestapo tactics and murders under the PHOENIX program. And though it is not truly a CIA covert action in classic terms, PHOENIX figured prominently in the debate of the 1970s about the proper bounds for CIA covert action. It was a distraction and a distortion, but its effect on a debate previously uninformed about the capability was telling.[30]

For the covert action capability, then, the lessons of Vietnam included these: big paramilitary operations are hard to keep covert; involvement of multiple agencies in planning and implementation is likely to produce clumsiness and leaks; an alert press will pursue eagerly all evidence of secret government activity; and an attentive public and Congress will ask hard questions about the character of official behavior.

All of these lessons had been evident much earlier, after the CIA-orchestrated Bay of Pigs fiasco. They also have emerged since Vietnam in, for instance, the open debate about covert aid to anti-Sandinista guerrilla fighters in Central America. The issues surrounding them will be with us for as long as the United States is a nation that strains to uphold democratic values at home, because it cannot do that—protect values at home—without also working to protect them in the world at large. In the Vietnam legacy a lingering question for the United States is how to engage with the world to serve those values; as a nation it has yet to come to terms with the covert action capability as a tool in the arsenal of freedom.

Conclusion

The intelligence community emerged from the Vietnam era much changed from the early cold war years; some endemic disabilities of the community were illustrated sharply by the Vietnam episode. Together these propositions define the intelligence challenge ahead for the United States: to deal with Vietnam-like situations and indirect security threats while operating within regulatory and organizational frameworks that reflect values and political dynamics outside a narrow national security calculus.

Prominent analysts within and outside government now believe that the conflict situations most likely to confront the United States and the other nations of the world in the years ahead will look more like Vietnam than a world war. As long as a military balance of sorts is held between East and West, full-scale war between the blocs is unlikely. Fear of superpower confrontation and escalation will tend to limit regional conflicts where U.S. and Soviet interests are clearly implicated. But in the third or developing world, combustible forces are at work: high population growth, the dislocating effects of economic, social, and political change, and the introduction of alien values and modes of behavior. Ancient hatreds, hegemonism, and irredentist designs inflame many regional interactions. Terrorists of all stripes—from international revolutionaries to local bandits—cross borders with ease and lash out unpredictably. The Soviet Union and its surrogates continue to seek international advantage by encouraging and manipulating revolution and regional strife. Local causes of violence are thus mixed with regional dynamics and the forces of global competition. Even challenges traceable to Moscow are more frequently indirect than direct. Intense international propaganda campaigns and vigorous intelligence efforts, for instance, are aimed at disarming the United States without a fight.

The question for the future is whether an intelligence community much changed by the Vietnam experience can overcome the difficulties evidenced in that war and recurrent since. Vietnam can be either a portent of inescapable events to come or a learning experience that better equips us to deal with the future. For the intelligence community, the Vietnam experience did make a difference, but it is not yet clear how that difference will affect the strategic competition in the remainder of the century. Inquiries such as this book may serve to clarify that issue and to point the way toward sensible remedies.

Notes

1. *Intelligence community* is used here in its official sense, as outlined in the president's charter for the intelligence agencies: executive order 12333, "United States Intelligence Activities," *Federal Register,* December 8, 1981, p. 59941 (cited hereafter as EO 12333). Agencies included in the community are the Central Intelligence Agency; reconnaissance offices within the Department of Defense; the Bureau of Intelligence and Research of the State Department; the intelligence elements of the armed forces, the Federal Bureau of Investigation, and the departments of Energy and Treasury; and the staff elements of the director of central intelligence.

2. See James N. Rosenau, "Fragmegrative Challenges to National Security," in Terry L. Heynes, ed., *Understanding U.S. Strategy* (Washington, D.C.: National Defense University Press, 1983), p. 65.

3. For detailed analysis of this debate, see John M. Oseth, *Regulating U.S. Intelligence Operations: A Study in Definition of the National Interest* (Lexington: University Press of Kentucky, 1985).

4. The development of rules for the FBI is traced in James T. Elliff, *The Reform of FBI Intelligence Operations* (Princeton: Princeton University Press, 1979).

5. Bernard Brodie analyzed and compared these two channels of information in *War and Politics* (New York: Macmillan, 1973), pp. 209–215.

6. William Colby makes this point in Roy Godson, ed., *Intelligence Requirements for the 1980s: Analysis and Estimates* (Washington, D.C.: National Strategy Information Center, 1980), p. 170.

7. See I.M. Destler, Leslie H. Gelb, and Anthony Lake, *Our Own Worst Enemy: The Unmaking of American Foreign Policy* (New York: Simon and Schuster, 1984), esp. chap. 2.

8. Sherman Kent, *Strategic Intelligence for American World Policy* (Princeton: Princeton University Press, 1949), pp. 78–115.

9. EO 12333, sec. 1.5k.

10. See especially ibid., sec. 1.9, 1.10.

11. See the summary of critical perspectives in James H. Dixon and Associates, *National Security Policy: Institutions, Processes and Issues* (Washington, D.C.: National Defense University Press, 1984), pp. 186–189. See also John M. Collins, *U.S. Defense Planning: A Critique* (Boulder, Colo.: Westview Press, 1982), pp. 130–131.

12. See Brodie, *War and Politics,* pp. 194–195, and Stafford T. Thomas, *The U.S. Intelligence Community* (Lanham, Md: University Press of America, 1983), pp. 67–69.

13. See Lawrence Freedman, *U.S. Intelligence and the Soviet Strategic Threat* (Boulder, Colo.: Westview Press, 1977), p. 43.

14. Stansfield Turner, *Secrecy and Democracy: The CIA in Transition* (Boston: Houghton Mifflin, 1985), p. 266. On the rationale for and critique of the NIO system, see Mark M. Lowenthal, *U.S. Intelligence: Evolution and Anatomy* (New York: Praeger Publishers, 1984), pp. 35–37.

15. EO 12333, sec. 1.5k.

16. Allan E. Goodman, "Fixing the Intelligence Mess," *Foreign Policy 57* (Winter 1984–1985): 160, 178.

17. For discussion of these techniques, see Amrom Katz, "Technical Collection in the 1980s," in Roy Godson, ed., *Intelligence Requirements for the 1980s: Clandestine Collection* (Washington, D.C.: National Strategy Information Center, 1982), p. 101.

18. See, for example, Robert F. Ellsworth and Kenneth L. Adelman, "Foolish Intelligence," *Foreign Policy 36* (Fall 1979): 147; and Herbert Scoville, "Is Espionage Necessary for Our Security?" *Foreign Affairs 54* (April 1976): 482.

19. Bruce Palmer, *The 25-Year War: America's Military Role in Vietnam* (Lexington: University Press of Kentucky, 1984), p. 167.

20. See ibid., pp. 162–163. See also Walter Laquer, *A World of Secrets: The Uses and Limits of Intelligence* (New York: Basic Books, 1985), pp. 180–182.

21. Joseph A. McChristian, *Vietnam Studies: The Role of Military Intelligence, 1965–1967* (Washington, D.C.: Government Printing Office, 1974), pp. 4–11.

22. Richard Nixon, *No More Vietnams* (New York: Arbor House, 1985), pp. 46–47. See also Harry G. Summers, Jr., *On Strategy: The Vietnam War in Context* (Carlisle Barracks, Pa.: U.S. Army War College, 1981).

23. Nixon, *No More Vietnams*, p. 56.

24. For an examination of the advisory process at work on critical Vietnam decisions, see Larry Berman, *Planning a Tragedy: The Americanization of the War in Vietnam* (New York: W.W. Norton, 1982).

25. *Report of the DOD Commission on Beirut International Airport Terrorist Act, October 23, 1983,* December 20, 1983, pp. 5, 9–10, 39–41 (hereafter cited as *Long Commission Report*).

26. See, for example, Rosenau, "Fragmegrative Challenges," pp. 73–77.

27. For a recent episode in which policy preferences were alleged to have shaped choices about intelligence, see John Horton, "Why I Quit the CIA," *Washington Post,* January 2, 1985, p. A15.

28. See Howard J. Wiarda, *Ethnocentrism in Foreign Policy: Can We Understand the Third World?* (Washington, D.C.: American Enterprise Institute for Public Policy Research, 1985).

29. U.S. Senate, Select Committee to Study Governmental Operations with Respect to Intelligence Activities, *Foreign and Military Intelligence,* S. Rept. No. 94–755, 94th Cong, 2d sess., 1976, p. 147. See also Stanley Karnow, *Vietnam: A History* (New York: Penguin Books, 1984), pp. 363–364; and Ray S. Cline, *Secrets, Spies, and Scholars: Blueprint of the Essential CIA* (Washington, D.C.: Acropolis Books, 1976), pp. 214–215.

30. On the place of the PHOENIX program in the military apparatus, see Thomas W. Scoville, *Reorganizing for Pacification Support* (Washington, D.C.: U.S. Army Center of Military History, 1982), pp. 78–79. For a perspective that figured prominently in the 1970s debate, see Victor Marchetti and John D. Marks, *The CIA and the Cult of Intelligence* (New York: Alfred A. Knopf, 1974), pp. 244–246; and Ralph W. McGehee, *Deadly Deceits: My 25 Years in the CIA* (New York: Sheridan Square Publications, 1983), pp. 140–145.

8
The Media

Charles Mohr

A noted Kentucky editor of another era once commented that although daily journalism matters much to its practitioners, it matters little to others. A daily article, he wrote, "goes up like a rocket but comes down like a stick, its coruscations lost forever in the blackness of illimitable space." It is an ironic misfortune that this is not true for Vietnam war correspondents. They are never allowed to forget what they wrote, or at least what some people think they wrote. It is the harshest critics of journalism who have tended to attribute to the media (a word that few in journalism like) a much more important role in the course and outcome of the Vietnam War than most journalists would do or, I think, most historians are likely to do.

Still, journalism unquestionably played a role of some significance in Vietnam itself and in the turbulent domestic scene in the 1960s and early 1970s. Some journalists liked to say, "You don't lose wars in the newspapers." That remains sound as far as it goes. But the Vietnam War was not lost in any conventional sense of that word. The U.S. armed services failed without being defeated militarily, an even more galling frustration that reporters who accompanied them on the battlefield are especially well able to understand. It is clear that myth has tended to displace historical reality in contemporary perceptions of Vietnam journalism. What is much less clear is whether the media, the Pentagon, and the executive branch of government learned or have remembered much and whether remedies for a sometimes awkward relationship can be applied in a future conflict of the magnitude of Vietnam.

The sins and failures of the media in Vietnam are worth examining. However, it is necessary to separate mere failures in journalistic art, lapses in professional excellence, from the more complex and emotional question of whether journalism unintentionally or intentionally poisoned the well.

The media undercovered the early phase of the conflict from 1961 to 1965. More surprisingly, it is possible to argue that the media continued to undercover Vietnam at the height of U.S. involvement from 1965 onward. The blame is mostly that of editors and publishers. Individual reporters were industrious enough, for the most part eager to be in the field. But there were not many of them early on and probably never enough. When I first went to Vietnam in May 1962, the legendary Homer Bigart was close to finishing a special six-month temporary assignment for the *New York Times;* the *Times* did not open a permanent one-person bureau until that summer. For most of 1962–1963, there were fewer than a half-dozen resident correspondents (including British and French wire service agency reporters) and one staff photographer for the Associated Press. The television networks, weekly news magazines, and most of the major newspapers mostly covered Vietnam by visiting reporters. Such visits became increasingly prolonged as the 1963 Buddhist crisis and other developments increased journalistic demands, but this did not constitute a truly appropriate institutional commitment to the story.

It is also true that most of the press corps early and late were young, relatively inexperienced in journalism, and without prior experience in war correspondence. But it is also true that it was some members of this youthful group who had by far the most distinguished Vietnam careers. Several older men and women with considerable war experience pitched up in Vietnam early. With the exception of Keyes Beech of the *Chicago Daily News* and perhaps a couple of others, these older hands did not distinguish themselves; to adapt a cliché, they were covering the last war.

All war correspondence is difficult, including coverage of more conventional conflicts such as the 1973 Israeli-Arab war. Clausewitz's famous dictum on friction applies to correspondents as well as to commanders. What seems so simple becomes, in war, quite difficult. Mechanics is perhaps the least of it. A reporter who cannot communicate, who is unable to "file," will find aptitude or even brilliance useless. In Vietnam, however, a cooperative Military Assistance Command, combined with remarkable ingenuity by the best reporters, made Vietnam a notably convenient war to cover in physical terms. Empty medical evacuation helicopters and underloaded supply helicopters often got reporters into the thick of firefights within minutes. On the day after heavy North Vietnamese shelling of the marine outpost of Khe Sanh began, I was able to ride directly from Saigon to Khe Sanh on a plane loaded with 155 mm shells and empty body bags. Communications proved to be merely tedious, not impossible.

There is little question that the Vietnam press corps did exceptionally well in first-hand combat reporting, perhaps better than reporters in previous wars. Yet such shot-and-shell narrative (what television people these days call "boom boom") is only a small part of the task. In late 1966 I covered a night action by two patrol boats that resulted in a Medal of Honor for one petty officer. It was a wonderful newspaper story but small in significance.

The proper aim of war correspondence is clarity and coherence; it is to give readers and viewers some faint idea of the progression of events. This may never be easy. A reporter hypothetically privileged to have access to all of the operational reports reaching a senior commander might still be confused. Personal recklessness in combat is no substitute for clear thinking. Stories that recognized the significance and intentions of the Israeli canal crossing in 1973 were more important by orders of magnitude than eyewitness combat narrative. But if coherence is difficult in other wars, it was an even more elusive goal in Vietnam.

Conventional methods of military scorekeeping did not work in Vietnam. The problems were detecting long-range trends, sifting grains of relevance from the chaff of drearily reminiscent episodes, endlessly repeated in detail that varied only slightly. It is not so much that the press failed to grasp the meaning of most or even many of those episodes. It was unaware of and absent from the great majority of them. Even with a greatly expanded pool of personnel, it would have been physically impossible for the media to cover most of the events of the war.

In a fundamental sense, though, journalism did not do badly. It had trouble following the progress of pacification programs. In this regard, cynical but well-merited scoffing at the computerized hamlet evaluation system was not a satisfactory substitute for independent assessment. After 1965, reporters almost certainly concentrated too much on U.S. combat units and too little on the South Vietnamese army and regional forces. In large part because of journalists such as Robert Shaplen of the *New Yorker,* the labyrinth of South Vietnamese internal politics was well covered. The real political story of the war, the contest for the hamlets, was underreported.

In retrospect, however, important segments of the media, which through excellence exercised an unasked influence over their colleagues, were right about most trends and at most turning points in the war. In the early 1960s, Homer Bigart, David Halberstam, Neil Sheehan, and Malcome Browne recognized and devastatingly chronicled the basic weaknesses in Vietnamese bourgeois society that crippled prosecution of the war and contributed to the ultimate collapse more than a decade later. Within months of the commitment of U.S. combat troops, reporters such as Peter Arnett began to recognize that "counter-escalation" by North Vietnam, with less cost at the margin, was going to be a fundamental problem and that the force levels Lyndon Johnson was willing to permit were insufficient. It was Vietnam-based reporters who instantly saw Kissinger's Vietnamization program, conceived at the Pierre Hotel in late 1968, as a plan to postpone, but also to guarantee, failure.

The reporters, of course, did not develop this insight about the dismal long-run prospects of the war by themselves, by any means. They were in the most basic sense reporters. To the extent that they did become increasingly sophisticated, they did so by mining the knowledge of a wide range of U.S. field advisers and, to a lesser extent, thoughtful commanders of combat units and such Vietnamese realists as pacification commander Major General Ngyuen Duc Thang. The real issue for Vietnam-based reporters was almost never whether the war was immoral, or unjustifiable in terms of international law. The consuming argument was pessimism versus optimism, the debate on how well the war was being prosecuted. The harsh critics make a mistake on this point. Journalism did not create the pessimist-optimist debate; it described it and made it public. If it is true that most reporters became pessimists early, it is also true that few of them could match the mordant realism of such advisers as the late John Paul Vann or the agonized uncertainties of the more thoughtful field-grade officers or even the then-secret musings of McNamara and McNaughton as later revealed in the Pentagon Papers.

In this regard, it is useful to draw again the distinction between myth and reality. Much of journalism is distressingly related to mere stenography. The officials and the mission certainly were covered. Far more space and time was consumed by reporting the usually optimistic appraisals and forecasts of MACV and the embassy than in the pieces that cast doubt on those appraisals. That the credibility of these pronouncements diminished among readers and that the artfulness of these sales pitches was never very high cannot fairly be attributed to the press, which reported them faithfully and perhaps too exhaustively. The more violent contemporary critics of the media profess to recall a journalism in which authority was cruelly and contemptuously flouted. They should go back and read the material. The prize-winning reporting of 1963 was good, but it was also mild, at times nearly timid, in tone. It did not have a devastating effect on domestic public opinion or much effect at all on policymakers. If policymakers had their hands tied by reportage, they showed few signs of it until after January 1968. Clearly the prophets of optimism had the upper hand (to their own later discomfort) in 1967, the "victory year." It was not so much the practice to shoot the messengers of bad news as to ignore them.

The sore point, and possible exception, is Tet. Here, too, myth has tended to supplant reality. One charge of the most embittered critics is that the 1968 Communist offensive was a military victory for the allied side but was reported as a defeat by journalism, thus suffocating public support for the war in the United States. I agree that much of the public misperceived the tactical realities of the Tet offensive and tended to draw sweeping—although not necessarily mistaken—conclusions about the futility of the war soon after it began. I also agree in part with former war correspondent Peter Braestrup's conclusion in his book on Tet journalism, *Big Story,* that Tet was an event that tended to overwhelm journalism and the conventional tools and practices of the media. I do not think any reasonable person can argue that the coverage of Tet was without significant shortcomings; however, the thesis that the media managed to conceal a victory and convert it into an irreversible psychological setback is probably not sound.

The domestic audience did not wait for press analysis before drawing its own sweeping conclusions: that the public had been misled by official optimism and that years of war had not weakened the Communists. And the press, on the whole, did not draw such conclusions. I know of no case (and Braestrup's exhaustive research supplies none) in which Vietnam-based reporters called Tet a military defeat. Almost all, in fact, regarded that as a physical impossibility because of the force ratios involved. About a week after the offensive began and when much of the Chinese sector of Saigon was still being fought over, the *New York Times* remarked that the enemy offensive was embarrassing precisely because it had lasted "so long." Such a conclusion was based on a belief that the enemy had been far too weak to undertake a conventional, head-on contest with U.S. and South Vietnamese forces in cities and towns.

The real indictment seems to be that journalists did not instantly declare it an unambiguous allied victory and thus squelch war revulsion in the United States. After much reflection, I cannot see how the media could have done this. General Fred Weyand, then a corps commander, and General Abrams, the deputy commander, warned journalists early not to draw sweeping conclusions. Journalists were constantly harangued about next-wave attacks, some of which materialized. It was, for instance, not until May that losses were most extensive, when more than 1,100 Americans were killed in action in two weeks. For much of the early period, the countryside and the pacification effort was physically denied to journalists. Nevertheless, television particularly drew some silly conclusions. Saigon was described as being generally in ruins; in fact, destruction was quite limited.

My own opinion, reached in 1968 and adhered to since, is that Tet was a tactical defeat of major proportions for the Vietcong and the North Vietnamese but that it did not constitute a strategic victory for the United States. Having lost much of the Vietcong, the North Vietnamese found other ways to continue the war. The setback was not fatal.

In short, lapses in journalistic excellence were probably not the main root of withering support for the war, although that does not excuse them. In *The 25-Year War,* Bruce Palmer remarks that the military and government failed to recognize the criticality of the time factor. After fewer than three years of combat by U.S. forces, the public was getting impatient, and Tet made them hopelessly impatient. Cheer-leader journalism could not have concealed, or much ameliorated, the passage of time.

That conclusion provides a convenient bridge to a discussion of the discouraging implications of the Vietnam experience for the future. Paradoxically, I am neither encouraged nor discouraged about the future. A workable press-military relationship is possible in any future conflict, but it will not be achieved because of institutional memories of Vietnam.

As entrenched as they have become, some of the myths about Vietnam journalism can, and probably will, be overcome in a future conflict. Perhaps the worst of these myths is that a bitterly hostile tension is the natural state of affairs and existed between the press and the military at the time of the war. That is not true. Those who covered the war (I did so for about four and one-half years over an eleven-year span) encountered almost no hostility from troops and officers in the field. In fact, we were met by an almost unblemished hospitality. Even the relation with the command was not poor. When I was covering the battle of Hue in 1968 and flying out of the city to file at the Phu Bai base, General Abrams, who had been assigned to supervise the counterattacks in I Corps, used to poke his head into the office where I was writing and engage in a conversational briefing. He asked more questions than he answered, although he answered all that I asked.

One reason for the current belief that press-military relations should naturally be adversarial is a belief that reporters constitute a sort of intolerable physical nuisance to unit commanders in combat. This has never been true in the past. Reporters learned how to walk with battalion and company commanders in the field and to wait for war's friction to provide the opportunities for pause and conversation. We were not going anywhere and did not require running commentary during the course of a firefight (we soon learned to understand the radio traffic on our own, anyway). I covered the divisions of Israeli Major General Ariel Sharon in two Israeli wars. That he once talked for four hours about how he crossed the Suez Canal was due more to Sharon's gregarious volubility, not my persistence. Self-assured, competent soldiers do not fear reporters. Nor do war correspondents tend to paint soldiers as baby killers or to denigrate soldiering at all.

Although I know that it need not be so, I have gradually had to accept as true that this generation of field-grade officers and even some general officers with Vietnam experience have, through a sort of mutation of real past experience into a more virulent folk memory, become extremely wary of journalists. Before the myths of natural hostility and intolerable nuisance are overcome, they will have to be disproved in practice. This may be difficult.

Journalism has certainly not changed much for the better in twenty years. It remains an imperfect instrument. Superficial changes have probably been for the worse. The nuisance factor may have become more real. Smaller newspapers and local television stations that two decades ago would never have considered staff coverage of major foreign events now have the economic resources and the professional initiative to do so. The advent of rucksack journalism by young freelancers looking for a war was noticeable by the early 1970s; it is now widespread. By the time of the Grenada operation in 1983, the sheer numbers of journalists and quasi-journalists clamoring for a place on aircraft constituted a real physical problem. A major operation in, say, Nicaragua would probably trigger an awesome demonstration of mob journalism. There are no easy or equitable solutions. I would commend the Pentagon to the unashamed policy of enlightened favoritism long exercised by the Israeli Defense Forces. There is an almost undeniable need for war to be covered by journalism; it may not be necessary for everyone to be treated the same way.

That the early Vietnam War reporters were inexperienced was not a fatal flaw. But in any future conflict, there will be an even smaller pool of experience. This applies not only to reporters but to the military, which, contrary to myth, did a good job of press relations in Vietnam but appears to have forgotten most of the lessons.

Still another potential and unavoidable problem, not much encountered in Vietnam, is behind-the-lines coverage. American journalism has increasingly, although properly, begun covering other people's wars and sending reporters to the capitals and outback of potential enemies of the United States. There was no safe way to cover the Vietcong (or we would have done it). In a Central American conflict, the first and most vivid accounts will come from U.S. journalists in Managua. This is bound to be frustrating to some military officers, administration officials, and, especially, to vocal press haters.

It may be trite, but is also true, to observe that journalistic values have changed in some ways. Vietnam certainly contributed to a code of skepticism, which was professionally rewarded by the peculiar circumstances of that war. But the Watergate scandal and a general erosion of respect for authority, which is by no means all bad, resulted in the late 1970s in a prosecutorial attitude in many reporters. The coverage of air strikes on Libya in early 1986 made me conclude that in a crisis, this tends to diminish, but there are bound to be bitter tensions between many younger reporters and that minority of professional officers who, because of their hostility toward the press and their insistence on painting all military affairs in the most favorable light, we used to call "Star Spangled Gas Bags." A recent example occurred when a Pentagon official said that speculation that the air force had demanded a slice of the Libyan action was an insult to young pilots, a wonderful example of non sequitur.

These future problems cannot be managed or planned for. Seminars on military-press relations do not do any real harm, but they probably do little good. Only pragmatic adjustment in actual operational situations will provide solutions to problems in new military circumstances. There may be painful moments, but the adjustments will probably be attained because there are no fundamental reasons to prevent a workable relationship.

9

The Vietnam War and Higher Education

Vincent Davis

The Vietnam War has had an enduring impact on educational institutions and practices at all levels in the United States, particularly on higher education, and especially with regard to the teaching of internationally oriented subjects and foreign languages.

The Vietnam War was actually several different conflicts for different combinations of participants at different time periods; the crucial period (in terms of impact on American thinking), however, was from President John F. Kennedy's escalation in 1962–1963 to the final U.S. withdrawal under President Gerald R. Ford in 1975. Although the war was only one of several highly important developments that combined to catalyze profound transformations in the national and international systems, it was arguably the most important of those catalysts. Many, maybe most, of the transformations would have occurred eventually in any case—but perhaps at a much later time and in a quite different form. In this sense, it might be more accurate to assert that the Vietnam War vastly accelerated and heightened rather than actually caused a set of important consequences.

Before the Vietnam War

World War II ended just before fall classes were to begin in 1945 on U.S. campuses. Impatient servicemen generated massive political pressure to be discharged into civilian status almost instantly in order to resume their interrupted private lives. For most of them, this resumption included taking advantage of the provisions of the GI Bill for college educations and other forms of additional schooling. National political leaders were anxious to accommodate these returning heroes, and campuses across the United States suddenly were assaulted by the most overwhelming demand for their ministrations ever before experienced. Campus structures of all kinds were hastily converted into dormitories and classrooms. The biggest bottleneck was in finding sufficient numbers of available and qualified instructors. This post-war boom launched the greatest expansion of colleges and universities in U.S. history.

In those boom years, local campuses acquired ambitions for national stature. Teachers' colleges became universities; young doctoral degree faculty members demanded opportunities to teach graduate students as a crucial element in their own self-esteem and career advancement. Research became the new religion, and new professional journals were launched to publish the explosion in research results. Although much of that work was highly perishable, the growth in research provided the breeding ground for extraordinary new advances in science and technology.

In the broadest and most general terms, higher education in the United States during the 1945–1960 period faithfully reflected the basic moods and trends in the larger society. Never mind the seriousness of the cold war and the hot wars included within it, particularly in Korea. Never mind the growing magnitude of the Soviet challenge and its new dimensions, particularly the diversion of the main arenas away from Europe into emerging third world theaters. Never mind that virtually all of the basic assumptions, policies, and strategies devised by the United States for managing the postwar world were being discredited significantly or undermined by new developments, domestic and international. Managing was itself a key conceit. Americans saw themselves as highly successful managers, having coped successfully with the Great Depression of the 1930s and World War II to lead the great economic booms of the postwar years. Management skills were embodied and taught in graduate schools of business and public administration; masters' programs in business administration and public administration had become the new rage. All problems were assumed to have acceptable and achievable solutions. Problems thus were perceived to be momentary inconveniences, to be endured until the solutions soon appeared. This updated version of the traditional American can-do spirit attacked all older conventional wisdom and all established authorities. The old institutions and old authorities were perceived as obstacles standing in the way of straight-line efficiency between problems and solutions.

One of the most striking characteristics of this period was the extent to which higher education joyfully promoted this diffuse sense of optimism. Colleges and universities clearly were caught up in the general euphoria, with unlimited optimism about endless growth and development in the future. Professors surely enjoyed more income and general social prestige than in earlier times. Indeed, professors during this period increasingly were seen as among the emerging affluent elites.

How did this boom period in higher education affect academe's political roles and general relations between government and the academic community? It is in the nature of intellectual life to harbor dark forebodings of the future, to criticize social institutions and practices, and to issue Cassandra-like warnings of dire circumstances ahead. Eric Goldman noted that this phenomenon was evident again in the late 1950s:

> For the most part, intellectuals were glum, warning. They kept insisting that the decisions made in the Crucial Decade were not enough in either foreign or domestic affairs. . . . The intellectuals satirized and gloomed and warned, and the general public did not listen. The general public . . . was harking to . . . the incessant wheels of upward mobility.[1]

This disdainful posture was the traditional stance of academics. Everett Carll Ladd, Jr., and Seymour Martin Lipset contended that this was a valid generalization in both the United States and Europe for perhaps two centuries or more: "the intellectual community, of which faculty are a part, is inherently questioning, critical, socially disruptive." Ladd and Lipset cited supporting commentaries from the writings of such commentators as Alexis de Tocqueville, Lewis Namier, Whitelaw Reid, Raymond Aron, and Daniel Patrick Moynihan.[2]

One of the most extraordinary characteristics of American higher education for perhaps half a century, however, was the extent to which the generalizations of Goldman, Ladd, Lipset, and others did not fit either the institutions or the individuals in the academic community. The central argument here is that one of the important consequences of the Vietnam War was to reestablish the traditional estrangement between government and academia but that something much more akin to frequently cordial cooperation existed for at least fifty years—from roughly the end of the Taft administration in early 1913 to the end of the Kennedy administration in late 1963.

Cordial connections between the government and academic communities perhaps began in the United States as early as 1862 when the Morrill Act established the land-grant university system. Academicians certainly were supportive of President Woodrow Wilson, who, after all, was one of their own. Indeed, most academic specialists in international relations spent most of the two decades following World War I in efforts designed to support the spirit of Wilson's Fourteen Points and the League of Nations. Virtually all kinds of academicians were strongly supportive of President Franklin D. Roosevelt during the New Deal period of the 1930s, and this support continued throughout World War II when the physical and human resources of American campuses were contributed eagerly to the overall national mobilization.

These cordial ties grew even stronger and more substantial after World War II. Research laboratories at the larger American universities often derived most of their resources from federal programs, particularly in physics but also in chemistry and in the aeronautical, agricultural, and biological sciences, as well as in many engineering fields. Significant numbers of scientists and engineers moved back and forth at fairly frequent intervals between government and campus labs, often holding professorial appointments. Graduate students in these same categories depended heavily on federal support. Federal subsidies for higher education took many direct and indirect forms, such as tax deductions for financial contributions.

As the cold war became an increasingly serious concern, international relations specialists were particularly responsive to the perceived needs of federal agencies for research and other assistance from campus-based scholars. Centers or institutes for this kind of work already existed at some prominent universities, and more of them were created after 1945. Many received direct or indirect federal support; for example, the Center for International Studies at MIT and the East-West Center at the University of Hawaii were launched and originally financed by the CIA. If university and college researchers did not receive federal support collectively through the centers and institutes on their campuses, they often got such support directly as individuals in the form of Department of Defense–affiliated grants and contracts. One of these, the Institute for Defense Analyses (IDA), was created as a consortium of some of the most prominent universities in the United States, including a number of the Ivy League schools. Although the presidents of the participating universities were board members for IDA, it was established explicitly to do research for the Department of Defense. The Advanced Research Projects Agency (ARPA) was another Pentagon entity heavily involved in using campus-based research professors, either on contracts or occasionally in ARPA's own offices as part-time consultants.

A related phenomenon was the emergence of contract research organizations. The most prominent of these cold war think tanks was the RAND Corporation, headquartered in Santa Monica, California, and with large offices in Washington, D.C. Researchers often moved back and forth between those organizations and professorial appointments on prominent campuses, including Bernard Brodie, Alexander George, Paul Hammond, and Albert Wohlstetter. International relations professors tended to regard their think tank colleagues, such as Herman Kahn, as full-fledged members of the academic community. In one case, this phenomenon came full circle when the RAND Corporation launched a fully accredited graduate program offering doctoral degrees. The cold war cordiality between academe and defense-related government agencies led the academic accreditation organizations to create this new form of incipient competition for themselves by letting nonuniversities penetrate the degree-granting business. A later case was the accreditation of the Defense Department's Defense Intelligence College for a master's degree program.

In summary, the new policies of active U.S. involvement in the world were widely supported by public opinion in general and by academic activism on the campuses as the United States emerged from World War II into the cold war years. Just as the nation was emerging from the isolationism that had characterized it during the 1930s, academe was emerging from its ivory tower. The United States was becoming engaged fully in international endeavors in its role as leader of the non-communist world, and the academic community became a closely cooperating partner in supporting this ballooning sense of global activism. International relations scholars were often the chief architects of foreign and defense policy initiatives as the United States adopted global roles. Professors and some academic administrators took leaves of absence from their campuses to work full time in important policy positions in Washington. By the 1960s, economists and political scientists (especially specialists in international relations) seemed almost as abundant as lawyers in Washington, and historians and other kinds of academicians were in growing evidence.

Indeed, it became quite fashionable for professors to do this kind of government-related work in the 1950s and early 1960s. Significant involvement by a young faculty member in the RAND Corporation, for example, was a prestigious badge of honor that could help significantly in moving up the academic ladder to the rank of tenured full professor. One notable example was Graham Allison, whose career as an international relations specialist was launched by a RAND-associated project and largely sustained him up to his appointment at a young age as dean of the John F. Kennedy School of Government at Harvard University.

Closely associated with these trends was the post-1945 emergence of the private foundations—particularly the so-called big three (Ford, Rockefeller, and Carnegie Foundations)—in heavily funding international relations research by campus-based scholars. These philanthropic organizations made major contributions to scholarly research in connection with forming and shaping the cold war policies and practices of the United States.

That persistent consensus on national self-confidence, affluence, and a purposeful march into the future was the most striking characteristic of the 1945–1960 period in the United States. This oblivious optimism almost completely overwhelmed any tendency to confront the problematic implications of major shifts in many categories that were undermining the basic assumptions, expectations, and resulting national policies formed during the early years of this period. Significant anxieties, doubts, and a sense of lost direction began to emerge by the end of the 1950s, but these soon were dispelled by the dramatic election of John F. Kennedy in 1960. Fifteen years later, when the tragic involvement of the United States in Southeast Asia had ended, these doubts had crystalized into a rejection of the old consensus in a different United States.

Consequences of the Vietnam War

The Vietnam experience had three major consequences on higher education: decreased funding for higher education, estrangement of academic institutions from the government, and decreased emphasis on the liberal arts.

Decreased Funding

Higher education became a boom industry after World War II. From 1950 to 1984, college enrollments increased by a factor of four to a total of approximately 12 million students. The number of institutions of higher education increased by almost 60 percent to a total of over 3,000. The national system of higher education in 1984 employed 2 million people and accounted for about 3 percent of the gross national product.[3] In the mid-1970s, all of these growth indicators experienced a substantial leveling off and in many cases turned downward. Growing deficits at all levels of government, resulting largely from the fact that President Lyndon B. Johnson elected to fight the Vietnam War on the cheap, caused reduced funding for higher education. When, after a decade of rising inflation, President Ronald Reagan decided to fight inflation by cutting taxes and government services, the federal deficit ballooned. As a result, education became the target of heavy spending cuts.

Two kinds of demographic shifts reinforced this shift from fiscal prosperity to fiscal poverty. First, based on projected declines in campus enrollments in the 1980s—reflecting the passage of the baby boom generation through the education system—legislators concluded that universities and colleges were overbuilt and overstaffed. Hence the higher education system needed less rather than more money. This conclusion failed, however, to account for the ravages of inflation on the educational system. Second, as elderly people increased as a percentage of the population, political support for continued high taxes and high spending for education waned.

A first-order consequence of the Vietnam War was reduced funding for higher education, which led to second-order effects, such as sinking faculty morale, drive, motivation, and incentives. Professors found themselves trapped in the overworked and underfunded syndrome. They were increasingly unable to seek relief by moving elsewhere because most institutions were in the same dire circumstances. Many professors became less efficient and less dedicated; they withdrew, gave less time to undergraduate students, had fewer graduate students to assist them, and conducted less research.[4] Many dissatisfied faculty members—particularly the younger research professors who found ready markets for their talents beyond campus borders—spent more and more time away from their institutions. In addition to a significant brain drain problem,[5] increased resort to consultation and externally funded research created a variety of conflict of interest problems.[6]

Educational institutions also sought new means to generate more money. They more aggressively recruited so-called nontraditional students, as in continuing education programs.[7] They lowered academic standards, making it easier to admit more students and to avoid flunking them out.[8] They made greater use of nontenured part-time faculty members, who were typically willing to work without job security and for lower pay.[9] And they went into business, becoming builders, landlords, auctioneers, and speculators.[10] In spite of these efforts, between 200 and 500 colleges and universities went defunct by the mid-1980s.[11] Substantial numbers of private schools merged with state university systems as public institutions; this happened, for example, at Temple University in Philadelphia and at the University of Pittsburgh; the previously private University of Buffalo became the State University of New York at Buffalo; the previously private University of Kansas City became the University of Missouri at Kansas City; and the University of Louisville gradually moved into Kentucky's system of public institutions. But this trend soon ran its course as states could no longer absorb any more financially troubled campuses and did not need any more in any case.

Most disturbing among these trends were the new permissiveness and the accompanying erosion of academic standards, which, though first evident in the 1950s, were accelerated substantially during the Vietnam War. By the end of 1984, one comprehensive study reported that colleges were offering more than 1,100 majors and programs, with more than half of these in occupational fields. Given that many institutions had large campuses with expensive-to-maintain and therefore deteriorating physical plants, alongside heavy debt obligations, the report summarized: "Virtually all institutions of higher education, public and private, are dependent on some form of enrollment-driven funding and hence tend to serve the changing whims of demand rather than student needs." The proliferation of majors and degree programs was a reflection of market forces—trying to provide whatever the paying customers wanted even when the institutions did not think students were well served by this short-term job-oriented approach. The traditional liberal arts education was the primary victim. By 1984, only 36 percent of the annual number of awarded bachelor's degrees were in the arts and sciences, compared to 49 percent in 1971. Some professional accrediting associations reinforced this trend by mandating that as much as 80 percent of a student's undergraduate courses be related to his or her vocational or professional career preparation.[12] Meanwhile, the earlier prevailing permissiveness and lowering of academic standards at precollegiate levels produced the widely publicized decline in Scholastic Aptitude Test scores in the late 1970s.[13]

Notwithstanding all the techniques used for ameliorating the new hard times on the campuses, however, these problems that originated in the Vietnam War period were still very much a fact of life in the mid-1980s. As *The*

Economist magazine reported, "Belt-tightening and penny-pinching have become the watchwords in the groves of academe."[14]

Estrangement from Government

Perhaps the most profound and potentially far-reaching impact of the Vietnam War on American higher education was the academic community's estrangement from the government community. A relatively close and cordial relationship between these two communities began to develop with the passage of the Morrill Act in 1862, gained ground during the Wilson administration, accelerated again during the Franklin D. Roosevelt administration, and reached new heights of close cooperation during the 1945–1960 period. The relationship began to turn sour as the Vietnam War became more bitterly divisive, particularly on campuses where many students—not infrequently with the support and connivance of friendly faculty members—used their academic standing as a means to evade military service. Indeed, popular resistance to the war did not loom large until substantial numbers of middle-class and upper-middle-class college students faced the prospect of service in Vietnam.

The turn-around perhaps began in the mid-1960s with an article appearing in an obscure magazine, *Ramparts,* published in California for the market represented by dissident students. This article attacked Michigan State University for a project that allegedly supported U.S. actions and policies in Vietnam. The professors involved had as much difficulty in overcoming this stigma in their future careers as citizens (including professors, entertainers, and government officials) previously had experienced in overcoming the stigma of being labeled Communists or Communist sympathizers. It was a kind of McCarthyism in reverse.

One of the most publicized instances accelerating the turn by the academic community against almost everything associated with the U.S. government, particularly government activities involving other countries, was Project Camelot. This was an ongoing research project using academic scholars from the United States, working on an unpublicized contract with the U.S. Army, designed to forecast the likelihood of insurgencies and rebellions against Latin American governments, particularly in Chile. This episode was memorialized and criticized in the most caustic terms in various papers and articles, some of which were collected in a volume edited by noted sociology professor Irving Louis Horowitz.[15]

The turnaround in academic attitudes seemed to occur almost overnight during the late 1960s. The change was evident, for example, at the International Studies Association (ISA), a professional society for scholars and others who did teaching or research in this field. Suddenly members began telephoning to be assured that ISA had never taken any money in any fashion, directly or indirectly, from even presumably benign government agencies such as the Department of State. Anything resembling any form of support from the U.S. Department of Defense or, far worse, the intelligence agencies and particularly the CIA, was the kiss of death for academic people. Major debates, ordinarily acrimonious, erupted at professional society meetings and conventions between those who continued to feel that scholars could work legitimately with and for government agencies and those who felt that anything resembling such a connection was a mortal professional sin for which there was no redemption.

Tempers eventually calmed, but even in the mid-1980s there tended to remain a distinct coolness on the part of those professors who thought that scholars should gain no support from and have very little contact with government agencies—at least, agencies of the U.S. government—toward those professors who felt less strongly about this matter. As for institutional policies, Harvard president Derek Bok took the lead in 1979 in proposing that universities and colleges should maintain a neutral posture on major social issues and controversies and should "not [try] to reform society."[16] Later, during 1982–1983, Bok and Harvard took the lead in formulating major policy statements that prohibited professors from undertaking any kind of sponsored research (whether sponsored by government, industry, or any other institution) if the results of the research could not be published fully in the open academic literature.[17] The Harvard statements, sometimes with minor modifications, were adopted by a number of other universities and colleges. The overall idea was that the schools should protect their autonomy, although it was a rather forlorn hope to think that universities and colleges, certain to feel the impact of major government policies and social trends, should somehow stand separately aloof. It was a worthy ideal largely unworkable in practice.

The National Association of State Universities and Land-Grant Colleges, the main organization representing most of the large state universities, tried to begin repairing some of the damage with the issuance of a brochure in 1983–1984, *In the National Interest: Higher Education and the Federal Government: The Essential Partnership*. The problem, however, has tended to be more serious for private schools than for the state schools and more serious for schools elsewhere than for those close to Washington, D.C. The rift had not been patched up adequately or healed over to the satisfaction of all key parties by the mid-1980s. It was a major lingering consequence of the Vietnam War turmoil, altering for the foreseeable future an earlier pattern stretching back a hundred years or more.

Decreased Emphasis on the Liberal Arts

Another impact of the Vietnam War, though less direct, was the erosion of emphasis on traditional liberal arts and sciences curricula. High-level concern about this matter was voiced in 1978 when New York University president

John C. Sawhill delivered the keynote address at the 1978 College Board National Forum. One press report began: "Materialism is toppling liberal arts education, once on academia's highest pedestal, university officials were told today."[18] Harvard Arts and Sciences dean Henry Rosovsky, speaking to the same group, sought to turn around the academic permissiveness beginning perhaps three decades earlier. He said that students make "many poor choices" and do not know what they do not know. "You can't just give an 18 or 19-year old a [college] catalogue and expect him to make the right choices." He added that Harvard planned to put more structure and requirements back into undergraduate education.[19] But when *U.S. News & World Report* surveyed the national educational scene in 1983, it found that nothing had changed. Universities and colleges were adding even more courses and programs in fields such as business and computer science that were vocationally oriented, meeting student demands to be taught subjects of immediate value in the job market after graduation.[20] In late 1984, President Reagan's chairman of the National Endowment for the Humanities, former philosophy professor William J. Bennett, cited heavy evidence of the major decline of arts and humanities courses and programs and called for a major new reemphasis.[21]

In the spring of 1985, CBS volunteered to assist in the kind of campaign that William Bennett wanted, donating $750,000 to help launch a "Corporate Council on the Liberal Arts" to be administered through the American Academy of Arts and Sciences headquartered near Harvard University. Other large corporations pledged support in substance and spirit.[22] Bennett's appeal was strengthened by prestigious organizations issuing basically identical statements. General education (as contrasted to vocationally oriented studies) was suddenly in vogue.[23]

Despite displays of genuine concern, the heart of the matter was not a group of distinguished people issuing such reports and appeals, nor was it a matter of adequate funding from corporations or elsewhere. Rather, the heart of it was the doubt and anxiety originally provoked in the thinking of college students by all of the social moorings loosened by the Vietnam War. These doubts made them determined to minimize at least the risks under their own control, given that the other dangers were more than enough to live with. One major risk that they thought they could reduce was the threat of a bleak job market, and they perceived that the best way to achieve this goal was to emphasize job-oriented courses in their college programs. Unless and until evidence persuaded the students that well-paying jobs could be obtained on the strength of a degree in ancient history or the fine arts or a foreign language, other efforts to shift students toward revived liberal arts and humanities curricula were likely to be unavailing.

Directly related to this shift away from the liberal arts was an increasingly severe failure to develop knowledge on international relations. This trend is certainly one of the most disturbing legacies of the war, particularly for those believing that national security could be threatened seriously by such a failure, a failure that many indicators suggested to be severe at the level of the general public and at the level of specialized expertise available as a national resource.

The field of international relations, or international studies as it came to be called over recent years, first emerged as a definable body of knowledge around the turn of the century when the United States, in the wake of its victory in the Spanish-American War, assumed a larger and growing role in world affairs. In its broadest dimensions, the field could include almost anybody and everybody, from any academic discipline, who sought to develop or use knowledge fairly closely pertaining to the relations between nations. The field became fashionable after World War II as the United States assumed a dominant role on the world stage. The Ford, Rockefeller, and Carnegie foundations began to provide substantial sums for research support and other forms of institutional and individual assistance. Centers of international studies sprang up and prospered. The Ford Foundation, the dominant factor in this support, invested more than $306 million in international studies support from 1951 to 1978. But these numbers are highly misleading. From 1960 through 1970, Ford committed an average of about $27 million per year. Starting in 1970, the annual support from Ford suddenly dropped and by 1978 was down to an annual average of $3 million to $4 million. Actually relatively little of this funding was for research in any direct sense. Most of it was for institution building. Funding for actual research fell from around $5 million in 1965 to essentially zero by 1975.[24]

Much the same happened with federal support. In the late 1960s, Secretary of Health, Education and Welfare John Gardner took the lead in promoting a new piece of supportive legislation, the International Education Act. At about the same time in the Senate, an amendment to the Higher Education Act of 1965 provided a U.S. foreign service corps somewhat along the lines of the military Reserve Officers Training Corps programs but including graduate education support as well as undergraduate studies. In effect, it was a federal scholarship program for highly qualified students seeking civilian careers in various kinds of foreign affairs work for diverse government agencies. A third bill was designed to create a new National Social Science Foundation, providing support for the social sciences, including international studies, apart from the research support provided to the laboratory and physical sciences through the National Science Foundation. The first two bills were enacted, but money was never appropriated for the programs. As for the third, Congress decided to channel money for the social sciences through the existing National Science Foundation; the support proved to be highly limited in amount and scope.

Federal agencies—the Department of State, the Arms Control and Disarmament Agency, the Agency for International Development, and the Department of Defense among them—also had provided various forms of support for campus-based international studies scholars and institutions, but that too dwindled to a trickle after about 1970—a cut of 52 percent measured in constant dollars adjusted for inflation, from 1967 to 1976. The total was $32.6 million in 1976, from twenty different federal agencies.[25]

Title VI of the National Defense Education Act of 1958 was designed to provide support for the study of foreign languages and specific geographic areas. Ultimately incorporated as an amendment to the Higher Education Act, Title VI was never funded at anywhere close to the authorized levels; in most years, $12 million to $15 million was appropriated, although $75 million was authorized. Further, those appropriations also experienced a steady decline. Private corporate giving to international studies was always negligible, ordinarily amounting to well under 2 percent of all gifts and grants from this sector.

In summary, the so-called neoisolationism that was one important expression of public bitterness toward the Vietnam War began to be felt in the field of international studies in about 1970, when virtually all sources of support for this field began to dry up overnight. By 1986, nothing had happened to reinstitute the support, although there were glimmers of growing concern, such as President Carter's establishment of the Commission on Foreign Language and International Studies in 1978, assigned to survey the magnitude of the problem and to make recommendations. Little became of this effort.

Anecdotes abound to emphasize the dramatic failures of the United States to educate itself about world affairs. To illustrate the shortfall in foreign language studies, it was noted often that more people teach English in the Soviet Union than there are Americans who study the Russian language in the United States. If ignorance by Americans of the rest of the world could be more profound in any other area than its failure to study foreign languages well, that other area probably would be geography. National Geographic Society president Gilbert Grosvenor in 1985 noted that Americans are ignorant of basic geographic facts about their own nation; surveys by the Department of Geography at the University of Kentucky revealed an abysmal ignorance even of the basics of the state's geography on the part of Kentucky college students.[26]

The period starting in about 1970 thus represented a fifteen-year loss on almost all fronts in gaining and teaching important knowledge about the world to Americans, some of whom eventually would be the diplomats, generals, admirals, intelligence officials, business and banking executives, congressmen, and presidents of the United States in the future. The loss was acute in released time for research by university-based scholars, research fellowships for those same scholars and their graduate students, the acquisition of critical library resources (for example, publications from other countries in languages other than English), the basic costs of disseminating and sharing the findings within the international studies community, and salaries for essential support personnel.

The ramifications of these trends for U.S. national security are not difficult to imagine. International studies research, knowledge repositories, and knowledge dissemination represent a basic national security resource. It was a severely depleted resource as of 1986, without much hope of immediate revival. Allan R. Millett published a study in 1977 showing that not even the subject of national security policy itself was taught on many campuses, with substantial resistance—as part of the anti-Vietnam War backlash—to adding such courses on the many campuses where they did not exist.[27] Although the situation had begun to improve by the mid-1980s, the field of national security policy has not yet become a growth industry in American higher education.

Conclusion

The people still in charge of the Western security system were old enough to have been inspired, motivated, and energized by the original circumstances calling this system into existence after World War II. Soon a new generation—called the successor generation by the Atlantic Council—without this personal remembrance and experience will have to move into the positions of leadership to guide the Western security system in changing but still threatening circumstances.[28] It will be necessary to transmit to the members of this new generation a knowledge of the original heritage plus the new circumstances.

Virtually all of this next generation will necessarily be products of the American educational system, a system weakened by the combined consequences of the Vietnam War. Today this system is incapable of providing more than a cursory understanding of international relations for more than a handful of students. This seriously eroded national capability, a direct consequence of the national backlash against the Vietnam War, could prove to be the war's most bitter and ironic lesson and stumbling block. This bleak prospect is ironic because one reason for the badly flawed U.S. experience in Southeast Asia was the lack of regional experts.[29]

The only optimism in this sea of dark ignorance about the world was a personal grant from W. Averill Harriman in the amount of $10 million to Columbia University's Russian Institute in 1982 and a drive by Harvard University launched in 1983 to raise $5 million for its own Russian Research Center. The idea was that if the United States did not have a repository of experts and knowledge about any other country in the world, then it should at least have this with regard to the primary challenger and threat—after former Secretary of State Cyrus Vance and many others had expressed grave concerns about the dwindling number of Soviet experts in the United States.[30]

Joseph Lurie, director of International Education at Adelphi University, published an informal study in 1981, *America—Globally Blind, Deaf and Dumb.* That title stands well enough as a conclusion to this chapter, given that it was the circumstance that helped to get the United States into the Vietnam War and then was the even more severe circumstance that the war ramified.

Notes

1. Eric Goldman, *The Crucial Decade—and After: America, 1945–1960* (New York: Vintage Books, 1960), pp. 303, 305.

2. Everett Carll Ladd, Jr., and Seymour Martin Lipset, *Academics, Politics, and the 1972 Election,* Domestic Affairs Studies Series (Washington, D.C.: American Enterprise Institute, 1973), pp. 6–7.

3. From "Involvement in Learning: Realizing the Potential of American Higher Education," report drafted by the National Institute of Education's Study Group on the Conditions of Excellence in Higher Education (1984). For a commentary on this report, see Jonathan Yardley, "Translated, This Jargon Says Our Colleges Are Dreadful," *Washington Post,* November 19, 1984, pp. 24–25.

4. See Hugh Gardner, "Faculty in Jeopardy: Caught between Declining Enrollments and an Oversupply of New Ph.D.s, Academia Is in Trouble," *Nutshell: The Magazine for the College Community* (1978–1979).

5. Harvard University, for example, issued a policy statement on May 20, 1983, "Guidelines on Research Conducted with Industry."

6. See "The Tempest Raging over Profit-minded Professors," *Business Week,* November 7, 1983, pp. 86–91; and "Commercial Science: Money Doesn't Talk," *Economist,* July 28, 1984, p. 73.

7. See Edward B. Fiske, "Problems Arise as Colleges Recruit Students Overseas," *New York Times,* February 24, 1980, p. 1.

8. See Edward B. Fiske, "The Marketing of the Colleges," *Atlantic* (October 1979): 93–98, and his "A New Kind of Shortage: Students," *New York Times,* November 11, 1979, sec. 12, p. 1.

9. Gene I. Maeroff, "Colleges, Pressed for Students, Grow Less Selective," *New York Times,* April 4, 1980, p. A12.

10. "Money-shy Colleges Go 'Moonlighting,'" *U.S. News & World Report,* November 26, 1979, pp. 73–76.

11. Fiske, "New Kind of Shortage," p. 1.

12. "Involvement in Learning." See also Yardley, "Translated."

13. For information on declining test scores, see an Associated Press report in many newspapers in September 1979; for example, see *Lexington (Ky.) Herald-Leader,* September 9, 1979, p. A-7.

14. *Economist,* December 10, 1983, p. 26, in an article using the nine-campus University of California system to illustrate the key points, "California's Enfeebled Faculties."

15. Irving Louis Horowitz, ed., *The Rise and Fall of Project Camelot* (Cambridge: MIT Press, 1967). This book was reprinted and reissued in various forms later, gaining wide circulation. Horowitz continued writing numerous pieces critical of links between scholars and government.

16. Stacy Jolna, "Bok Urges Harvard to Protect Autonomy," *Washington Post,* March 10, 1979, p. A9.

17. See, for example, "Guidelines on Research Conducted with Industry" (Cambridge: Harvard University, May 20, 1983).

18. Patricia McCormack, "Materialism 'Toppling' Arts Education," *Lexington (Ky.) Herald-Leader,* October 30, 1978, p. A6.

19. Patricia McCormack, "Harvard Dean Calls for Reforms," *Lexington (Ky.) Herald-Leader,* October 31, 1978, p. C-1.

20. "Liberal-Arts Colleges Bow to the Future," *U.S. News & World Report,* May 23, 1983, p. 67.

21. Christopher Connell, "Reagan Official Decries Lack of Faith in Humanities," *Lexington (Ky.) Herald-Leader,* November 26, 1984, p. A-2.

22. Gene I. Maeroff, "Shifting Away from the Liberal Arts," *New York Times,* March 26, 1985, p. C-1.

23. For an interesting commentary on the ferment stirred up by these reform proposals, see Ann Hulbert, "Curriculum Commotion: How Real Is the General Education Revival?" *New Republic,* May 6, 1985, pp. 27–31.

24. These data were taken from the congressional testimony of Rose L. Hayden, director of the International Education Project at the American Council on Education, before the Subcommittee on International Security and Scientific Affairs, House Committee on International Relations, March 22, 1978.

25. Ibid.

26. See Nancy Ross, "Ignorance of Geography Poses Future Dangers, Expert Warns," *Lexington (Ky.) Herald-Leader,* April 25, 1985, p. B-4.

27. Allan R. Millett, *American Education in National Security Policy,* Position Papers in the Policy Sciences, no. 2 (Columbus: Ohio State University Mershon Center, August 1977).

28. See Atlantic Council, Working Group on the Successor Generation, *The Successor Generation: Its Challenges and Responsibilities* (Washington, D.C.: Atlantic Council, 1981) and its *The Teaching of Values and the Successor Generation* (Washington, D.C.: Atlantic Council, 1983).

29. In fact, there was only one, Barnard Fall of Howard University, if true expertise requires intimate knowledge of the local languages, personal knowledge of its leaders, frequent and extensive research visits to the place, and substantial archival research. I participated in 1965 in an effort within the Office of the Secretary of Defense to persuade Secretary Robert S. McNamara to invite Professor Fall for a talk, but McNamara had persuaded himself that no one originally a French citizen was likely to have objective views on Vietnam. No senior U.S. leader ever asked Fall to serve as a consultant during the Vietnam War, and thus the deep knowledge of this

only true expert was lost in any case, and then eventually lost forever as a result of his death while back in Vietnam on another research trip in 1967.

30. On the Harriman grant to Columbia, see Fox Butterfield, "Harriman Donates $1 Million for Soviet Study," *New York Times,* October 7, 1982, p. 1; on the Harvard campaign, see Fred Hiatt, "Harvard Drive Seeks New Soviet Scholars," *Washington Post,* May 17, 1983, p. A-8.

III
Did Vietnam Make
A Difference?
The Use of Force

10
The Relative Importance of Force

William P. Bundy

In evaluating the relative importance of force in U.S. foreign policy, we must focus primarily on the role of force, or the threat of force, in situations where policy has a range of apparent options, either to improve affairs in terms of its national interests or to anticipate, deter, or deal with threats to those interests. In practice the latter has been by far the more common type of situation, at least as perceived by policymakers and the public. Although the United States has often been described in the postwar period as an imperial power, most notably by Raymond Aron, I contend strongly that although its interests have certainly been imperial in scope and sweep, its objectives have not. One can persuasively argue that the United States has never acted to enlarge its control of territories or governments abroad, save temporarily and as an adjunct to securing or preserving their independence from external control.

Vietnam is a good case to test this assertion because there the United States used force in a situation in which clear national commitments—as in the case of hostile armed action against the NATO area, Japan, Korea, or the ANZUS nations (Australia and New Zealand)—were absent. (I deliberately omit the Organization of American States treaty obligation—never automatic and now much attenuated and open to interpretation—and that remnant of SEATO, Thailand, a special case.) Not only are such threats in a separate category in the policymaking process—with contingency plans at the ready and, in most cases, forces already in place with congressional approval—but the experience since Vietnam has been that public support for these core commitments has held firm and may indeed have increased. One of the valid and enduring lessons of Vietnam is that there should be a constant reassessment as to what interests are truly vital, downgrading those that are not. A national corollary is that the ones that survive the test should be reaffirmed.

If it is what is loosely called the Vietnam syndrome that we are assessing, its symptoms will be found little, if at all, in the responses to perceived threats in these core areas. Since 1973 and 1975, each of these alliances has had its tests; in none has there been a flagging of U.S. policy or public support that one could plausibly trace to the impact of the Vietnam experience.

The cases that concern us here, then, are those that arise in the grey areas, where commitments are not clear—where the "long twilight struggle," as John Kennedy called it, goes on with the Soviet Union—and where threats to U.S. interests may come from other sources as well, with mixed cases in between. Almost all such cases arise in the third world.

Throughout the postwar period, the primary threats in third world areas have been from the Soviet Union and those ideologically aligned with it or under its control, many with their own special objectives and motives, such as North Korea, North Vietnam, and Cuba. In the 1950s and 1960s the basic U.S. policy of containment also embraced China. In the 1970s major threats came from sources where the immediate Soviet hand was minimal (Khomeini in Iran, and Islamic fundamentalist forces generally) or limited to supplies and training without real control of policy (Qadaffi and most terrorist groups). Finally, U.S. policy has sought to prevent, limit, or if possible settle conflicts that could spill over to affect major U.S. and Western interests (Iran-Iraq today). Indeed, threats to secure and reasonably priced raw materials, oil above all, have been a major factor in U.S. policy, especially in the 1970s.

As the sources of threat have been varied, so have their tactics. These have ranged from outwardly orthodox relations with military and economic aid programs to political penetration, to outright subversion and takeover, and finally to terrorism and armed action, often by proxy, all supported constantly by vast and interlinked covert operations, together with overt intelligence, influence, and information activities.

On the U.S. side, with a large defensive mission, the mix of actions has been significantly different. There has been much more stress on orthodox political ties, along with a dominant private role in trade ties, cultural links, and personnel exchanges; participation in and encouragement of alliance structures and other closely knit bilateral and regional groupings (the United States has allies and friends and a few clients but no proxies); and bilateral and multilateral economic aid to poorer countries, with the bilateral route preferred for countries with security problems.

In the next category—military assistance and training, often accompanied by training teams and advisers—U.S. programs have been much more widespread, but also much less intense, than those of the Soviet Union.[1] In the nature of U.S. society, programs for intelligence and information activity generally, and covert operations specifically, have always been on a much smaller scale than Soviet activities of these types.

In short, from the early cold war period on, the United States has marshaled a wide range of measures short of the use or threat of force. One of the constant and recurring questions is whether it has done nearly as well as it might have in the use of these assets to help third world nations preserve their independence and to influence them generally in directions compatible with U.S. interests. Although there have been cases where the choice between force and no force is starkly precipitated—as in Korea in 1950—in the great bulk of the cases where force may become an option, there are substantial and often neglected options for action below that level. The effect of Vietnam on the availability of these options, in terms of attitudes within the executive branch and in the Congress and public, is thus a necessary part of discussing the impact of Vietnam on the relative importance of force.

Force embraces several options. One may be the encouragement or pressing of an allied or friendly nation to act, coupled with logistic or other forms of support. In a sense, encouragement is not a use of force, but the distinction would often be lost on much of the rest of the world, including adversaries of the United States, just as the United States ties in Cuban actions to the Soviet Union. But at least the action is on its face—and almost always genuinely—that of an independent sovereign nation.

Next in the scale is U.S. covert support for paramilitary operations but without direct participation by U.S. personnel. Whether such support meets the traditional criterion of plausible deniability—a condition now much harder to satisfy than in the 1950s, partly, it may be argued, as a result of Vietnam—it is at least a twilight zone use of force in which the United States plays a key role, and usually an initiating one.

In earlier postwar periods, there was a next level: U.S. advisers or forces directly participating in military actions but without official announcement or (usually) acknowledgment. Examples are the teams used in Laos in 1960–1961 in support of the right-wing forces of Phoumi Nosavan, the early 1962–1963 U.S. advisers in Vietnam who on occasion flew in the pilot's seat and pushed the button, and perhaps the role of U.S. nominal advisers in Cambodia, at least for a time after 1970. Today such activity would fall within the provisions of the War Powers Act of 1973 and thus has practically disappeared as a realistic option.

Finally is the use of regular U.S. forces. Short of explicit commitment to combat, such use may range from a show of force designed to demonstrate concern and resolve but without a defined military mission; to technical forces stationed to police an area and preserve a cease-fire (the Sinai since 1975); to deployment designed to deter some activity, such as bringing in arms; to blockade or quarantine (the Cuba missile crisis); or to a defensive or security deployment designed to cauterize a situation (Lebanon in 1958, the Dominican Republic in 1965–1966, and Lebanon again in 1982–1983). Even this list is not exhaustive and deliberately omits the rare inclusion of U.S. forces in international peacekeeping operations under the United Nations or other multilateral organizations.

In the case of Vietnam, practically every level of activity was tried in one way or another. How did the Vietnam experience affect the views of policymakers, the Congress, and the public toward the use of means? And how did it affect attitudes and practice in the use of force? These questions could be approached in many ways, from seeking to analyze the impact of Vietnam on national feelings in the broadest sense to attempts to assess poll and other data on specified questions. The approach in this chapter is the study and assessment of what was actually done and decided, or not done or decided, and why.

On their face the questions involve largely historical causation: tracing what was due to Vietnam as opposed to what was already the case or might have evolved in any event. But assessing how much of a given change was Vietnam related may in the end be far less important than to try to assess what the current and prospective picture looks like. Thus this chapter addresses how force was viewed and used in U.S. postwar policy before the impact of Vietnam; the cases between 1973 and 1984 where force was, or might have been, a preferred option; and where the United States appears to stand today and may be headed.

Use of Force Prior to Vietnam

Is the United States prone to the use of force? Some would point to the record of the twentieth century, up to about 1933, as indicating a clear affirmative answer. Over and over again—in defeating the Philippine rebellion, in Cuba, in Central America, in Mexico—the United States used force to restore or ensure order or to install congenial regimes—and all this, at least in hindsight, in situations where no shift in any broader balance of power was threatened.

In the second third of the century, the record has been quite different. Apart from World War II, vast in threat and scale, local or regional U.S. interventions using force have been not only defensive in their objectives but selective and related to visible or at least widely perceived threats. During the Truman administration, the United States declined to intervene (beyond military aid) in the Chinese civil war, a decision sharply attacked at the time but surely even less likely, since Vietnam, to be criticized by serious historians. It met Soviet pressure on Iran—the refusal to evacuate Azerbaijan—by diplomatic action through the United Nations, and it reacted to the forced installation of a Communist regime in Czechoslovakia by moving to form the NATO alliance but not by any action on the ground—the first of many cases where Soviet action in Eastern Europe has gone unchallenged. Communist threats in Greece and the Philippines were handled successfully by military aid and advice (on a large scale in Greece), combined in both cases with effective political action in societies where the United States has strong ties through immigration or history. Even in response to the direct threat of the Berlin blockade, recommendations for a probe up the autobahn were rejected in favor of an improvised airlift that succeeded beyond any initial expectation in keeping the city supplied so that a clearer (but still not wholly satisfactory) agreement could be reached.

In part these choices reflected the postwar dissolution of U.S. military power. Then the clear-cut conventional aggression in Korea—in an area of (belatedly realized) strategic importance and at a time of acute cold war tension—galvanized the emerging framework of U.S. and other Western effort. By 1953, when Eisenhower took over, the United States had, in addition to continued nuclear superiority, a wide network of bases throughout the world and conventional forces and mobility that generally exceeded the outreach capabilities of the Soviet Union or China beyond areas contiguous to them.

Yet Eisenhower declined the gambit in Indochina in the spring of 1954 when the fall of Dien Bien Phu was imminent and might have been prevented by U.S. intervention.[2] To meet a perceived threat of Communist takeover in Iran, no threat of force was used, although Winston Churchill spoke longingly of "a splutter of musketry"; rather a handful of U.S. and British agents worked covertly with strong, willing, and respected local opposition forces to topple the Soviet-leaning regime and restore the shah in an almost bloodless coup. (Pushing on a swinging door is quite different from trying to budge firmer ones, a distinction not always noted in later efforts of this sort.)

Whether this was a use of force, the line was clearly crossed by the covert paramilitary action against Jacobo Arbenz in Guatemala in 1954, and was so seen in Latin America. Yet that Guatemalan operation, small in scale and quickly over, stands out in hindsight as virtually the high point of interventionist tendencies in an administration that had almost everything going for it: an extremely popular president admired particularly for political and military judgment and experience, bipartisan consensus and deference to the executive at postwar (or all-time) peaks, and a variety of capabilities (furnished by a willing Congress and accepted by diffident media) available for use in third world situations.

Certainly military force played much less of a part in the Eisenhower administration than one might have supposed, for reasons astutely analyzed recently.[3] Its conclusion that Eisenhower approached the option of force with extreme care is buttressed by many examples—the Vietnam denouement, the recurrent crises over the islands offshore of Taiwan, and the vehement and principled opposition to the 1956 Suez expedition of Britain, France, and Israel.[4] As the last in particular demonstrated, Eisenhower gave great weight to long-term strategic calculations and to the norms of international behavior laid down by the UN Charter. Both, in this case, outweighed a third basic element in his policies, allied relations.

Thus, the only overt use of U.S. forces in the Eisenhower administration—in Lebanon in 1958—stands out almost as the exception that proves the rule. Assessing the coup in Iraq as likely to lead to greater Soviet opportunities (a kind of domino effect), and in a situation where an advance commitment to the President of Lebanon had been made, the action was taken in response to that president's request. But what one is inclined to single out particularly is that the forces on the ground that might have been opposed or disruptive were extremely weak: a quick U.S. entry in substantial force (14,000 men) could cauterize the situation, and there were the makings of an early political resolution of the local situation. As nearly as any such operation can be, this one promised to be, and was, both risk free and with a built-in exit.

Eisenhower's restraint in the overt use of force related only in small part to two doctrinal features of his administration. One was the initial formulation of massive retaliation as a means of deterring, and if necessary countering, all threats, including those in peripheral areas (the third world in later parlance), with its corollary (enshrined for a time in NSC national policy papers) that nuclear weapons should be regarded as being as usable as conventional ones. Even in the 1950s the emptiness and impracticality of this answer to local conflicts, especially cases of indirect aggression, became progressively clear.[5]

The second feature was the stress on firm diplomatic commitments (called by some *pactitis*), designed to deter hostile action and in reaction to the mistake of Secretary Dean Acheson's defining a Pacific defense perimeter in early 1950 that omitted Korea. Yet, again, the spread of new defense pacts never operated in practice to limit attempts to strengthen nations so that they could stand on their own feet. On the contrary, the Eisenhower administration went in heavily for all forms of aid and support to potentially threatened nations; large-scale economic aid and other measures that amounted to nation building lacked only that later label.

Eisenhower's view of force became somewhat less clear after 1958, an important break point in his tenure. Sputnik had shaken American confidence and made Khrushchev conspicuously bolder, notably in the pressure on Berlin that began in late 1958. Concern over Soviet-related threats increased worldwide, leading to enlarged U.S. aid programs and a new unleashing of the CIA, especially in East Asia. With Iran and Guatemala as apparently successful models, the covert approach was pushed beyond effective limits, with a paramilitary fiasco in Indonesia in 1958 and a political action one in Cambodia at the same time.

In his last year, Eisenhower moved to strong support of the right-wing general Phoumi Nosavan in Laos; a fair-sized conflict was underway by January 1961, and U.S. advisory teams were present in combat roles. As he left office, Eisenhower advised Kennedy strongly to make a stand in Laos, with U.S. combat forces if necessary.[6]

Convinced by 1960 that Castro was making Cuba truly Communist and a latent threat to the neighborhood, Eisenhower authorized the covert training of an exile force of Cubans, a project just ripened by January 1961. As it then stood, the force was very small (it was much enlarged by Kennedy before it went into the Bay of Pigs), and it may be that Eisenhower envisaged the use of U.S. forces if the exile force proved unequal to the task and got into trouble. But there is no evidence that he ever considered taking on Castro frontally, with overt military force, from the outset. As with Sukarno in Indonesia, the covert approach was a way of avoiding public debate (or more than minimum congressional consultation); yet what was put in train concerning Laos and Cuba was bound to break out into the open.

Thus, in his last phase, Eisenhower was moving in directions that portended more use of force. But if his administration is taken as a benchmark of official and public attitudes toward the option of force, before Vietnam, it must still be judged that both were restrained. With perhaps the freest hand and greatest personal prestige of any other postwar president, Ike was very cool for the most part.

President Kennedy almost at once came to reject the outgoing president's advice to make a stand in Laos, turning instead to negotiation. At the Bay of Pigs, he got the worst of both worlds: unwilling to disband the expanded but still small exile force in visible retreat but equally unwilling to commit U.S. forces. His response was partly because he felt the reactions and long-term consequences in Latin America would outweigh a short-term gain in Cuba itself and partly because a confrontation over Cuba could have had negative effects in the much more important Berlin crisis. In effect the CIA, as often before and after, was asked to make bricks without straw.

The widespread attitude of skepticism to rejection of large-scale covert operations, which surely has colored heavily the current running debate on the contras in Nicaragua, derives at least as much from that debacle as from anything related to Vietnam. After 1961 the CIA was never in the same exempt position it had held in the 1950s: everything it did became open to attack. The lid then loosened was almost bound to come off in short order, with or without the essentially auxiliary role the agency played in the Vietnam War, including Laos.

But these initial decisions on Laos and Cuba were far from indicating a turning away from the possible use of force in third world situations. On the contrary, they tended to accentuate the Kennedy administration's new emphasis on conventional forces generally, initially to meet the Berlin crisis but with a strong new thrust on counterguerrilla training under the label of counterinsurgency. The impact of counterinsurgency thinking on the actual conduct of the Vietnam War has been considerably exaggerated in some recent military writings.[7] But it was certainly important, then and for the future, that limited wars with substantial guerrilla components were specifically envisaged as a likely mission.

The dominant crises of the Kennedy administration were Berlin and the confrontation over missiles in Cuba. In the former, the building of the Berlin wall was accepted without a military response (surely difficult to envisage), and in the end steady diplomacy and a firm allied posture caused the Soviets to pull back. The Cuba missile crisis was pivotal. In the short term it turned the Soviets more passive, but in the longer term it contributed greatly to the massive Soviet military buildup of the latter 1960s and 1970s.[8] On the U.S. side, the lift to confidence, energy, flexibility, and consensus was reflected in the prompt military aid to India in the 1962 Sino-Indian War[9] and in a wider frame by the limited détente with the Soviet Union symbolized by the Test Ban Treaty of 1963.

Until the Diem crisis of the fall of 1963, Vietnam moved only gradually to the fore; by comparison with Berlin and the missiles in Cuba and Soviet relations generally, it was back-of-the-stove business. Then, although 1964 was a year of recovery from Kennedy's assassination, it also became a time of peak national self-confidence, with every foreign crisis except Vietnam seeming to recede, and an upbeat economic situation. In any analysis of Vietnam decisions, this background is of crucial, and sometime neglected, importance in distinguishing Vietnam from most other situations where third world crises compete with strong domestic or other foreign concerns.

The initial commitments of U.S. combat forces in Vietnam in early 1965 were from the first intensely controversial, and this surely played a part in the initial outcry over the deployment of U.S. forces in the Dominican Republic in May 1965. Based on apparently shaky evidence of a political Communist threat, that operation became, under the guiding hand of Ellsworth Bunker, effective in restoring political stability; it seems fair to judge that civil conflict of some sort had been imminent and that the outcome, however paternalistic and later resented by Latin Americans and many Dominicans, had many constructive elements.[10] Probably the association with Vietnam has been largely responsible for the failure of much U.S. liberal opinion to see it, even to this day, in anything but black terms. From the Dominican intervention onward, Vietnam colored everything that was done in other third world situations, at least if these resembled Vietnam procedurally or substantively.

Analytically the Dominican occupation met the same criteria as the Lebanon one in 1958: opposing forces were negligible, and there was a built-in political exit, although it took much longer to reach this time. Essentially it was a cauterizing operation in a category that also includes Grenada in 1983, suggesting that if a use of force can be quick, effective, almost bloodless, and locally constructive, it will command widespread support or at least not arouse serious continuing divisions.

Although the timing and style of the Dominican operation contributed to a liberal view that President Johnson was trigger happy or force prone, this was hardly borne out by his handling of other situations. In the Congo, he worked largely through the United Nations, except for one airlift rescue; when hostilities threatened over Cyprus in 1964 and 1967, he used threats to withhold aid to keep Turkey from attacking and made determined diplomatic efforts to resolve the issue; and in the run-up to the 1967 Six-Day War between Israel and its neighbors, the U.S. response to Nasser's provocative closing of the Gulf of Aqaba was at the diplomatic level, when a threat of allied naval action might, arguably, have had some deterrent effect and eased the crisis.

While Vietnam raged, President Nixon had to deal with two situations where the United States came close to the use of force. In September 1970, when Jordan was under attack by the Palestinians within and threatened with intervention from Syria in their support, Israel was encouraged to make preventive tank deployments that probably operated to deter Assad; U.S. forces were conspicuously available in support of the action. In the India-Pakistan War of 1971, information suggesting that India might attack West Pakistan led the Nixon administration to deploy the carrier *Enterprise* to the Bay of Bengal, an action that may or may not have affected India's intentions but that certainly left a legacy of bitterness. In general, though, Vietnam overshadowed everything else, from 1965 to the conclusion of the Paris agreements in January 1973.

Effects of Vietnam

Any catalog of the war's lessons is bound to be incomplete and subjective—and it does not matter, at least for the moment, whether specific conclusions have been fair or consistent. But to single out a few, the American public, Congress, and those directly involved—or substantial parts of all three—came to believe that:

1. The national interests at stake in Vietnam were not and had not been vital, or worth the human and other costs of the war. For many this had important corollaries. To the extent these national interests were deemed to rest on prior U.S. commitment, through the SEATO Treaty and the history of strong U.S. support for South Vietnam, this indicated that such commitments, and close aid ties, tended to suck the United States into unwise conflicts. Judgments of cumulative regional consequences (domino theories) were usually exaggerated. And apparent Communist hostility, threat, and cooperation (China) could be exaggerated, or changed by national factors. Third world conflicts should be seen at least as much in local and regional terms as in terms of an overall East-West balance.

2. U.S. political and military objectives had not been clear and consistent, either as presented to the public and Congress or within the command structure.

3. Those conducting the war had made serious errors of judgment—notably of the South's cohesion and capacity and the North's willpower and stamina.

4. There have been serious errors of strategy and tactics, notably the emphasis on gradual pressures as opposed to hitting hard and fast, constraints on air power, and decisions to confine the ground war (with rare or limited exceptions) to South Vietnam.

5. Successive governments, but especially the Johnson administration, had deceived the American people and the Congress as to its intentions and actions and as to the progress of the war.

6. There should have been, before or at some early point in the U.S. force commitment, either a declaration of war or at least a debate on 1950–1951 NATO lines. Congress, at least until 1971, was entirely too passive and must hereafter be involved much more directly and constantly where issues of U.S. actual or potential use of force were involved.

7. The methods used in the war were excessive, inhuman, immoral, or at least too repulsive to accept, especially as portrayed by live television coverage.

8. Television, and the media generally, overplayed the dark side of the war and by express and implied criticism had a drastic effect on U.S. support for the war, and thus on a watching Hanoi's resolve to hang on. The same is true for critics of the war—or, conversely, only the media and critics had exposed the true nature of the war and in the end got the United States out. Television, as displayed in Vietnam, had become a new dimension in any use of force, at least by the United States.

In most cases, these conclusions became firmer as time went on. On the other hand, two others lost force. In the light of events since 1973, few would now argue that:

9. A genuine negotiated compromise would ever have been possible—or at least one that did not leave, as the Paris agreements did, regular North Vietnamese forces in the South.

10. Hanoi and its leaders were less ruthless and implacable than the U.S. government portrayed them. The voices of the boat people have been heard, and the complete takeover of the South has negated the image of an independent southern NLF.

In sum, there may be widespread agreement that the war was indeed a case of North Vietnamese military action to take over the South and that resistance to this had warrant in principle—that the war was even, in

President Reagan's word, noble. But even many who believe this would agree with two broad conclusions from the listing of specific lessons: that force is a blunt and dubious instrument in tangled third world situations and that the United States is not much good at handling complex or prolonged engagements in areas not initially familiar. Clearly and almost universally, the bottom line remains one of rejection and revulsion; the war was by any standard a national tragedy not to be repeated at almost any cost.[11]

This experience made an enormous difference for U.S. behavior, reaching into every corner of life and thinking. Its overall impact has been incalculable: all around still are the evidences of reactions to the war and of reactions to those reactions. It is impossible to imagine what the course of U.S. foreign and security policy in the late 1960s, the 1970s, and today would have been without Vietnam. To insert the assumption that it did not happen at all is hard enough; to assume some alternative course of action and outcome for Vietnam and the region is beyond at least my imagination.

Moreover, there were links between Vietnam and much else that became pervasive in the 1970s. In time, the onset of inflation in the United States was traced persuasively to the failure to fund the war fully. Preoccupation with Vietnam and a sense of national weakening undoubtedly contributed to the turn to détente, or at least to the overselling of its possibilities and later disillusionment. And the Vietnam experience led directly to the Nixon doctrine of 1969, emphasizing greater reliance on regional strong nations, and thus contributing, for example, to the close embrace of the shah from 1972 on.

More dramatically, the White House burglary capabilities used at Watergate were originally created in response to the leaking of the Pentagon Papers, although anyone familiar with Richard Nixon's career would say that his demons had much older and deeper roots. In 1974–1976, as the results of an internal CIA housecleaning were leaked, key among these was the revelation of covert CIA (and especially FBI) operations directed at domestic critics of the war (Operation CHAOS). Already tarnished by the media view of its auxiliary operations in Vietnam, the CIA underwent major intelligence investigations, emerging with some limiting ground rules and much tighter congressional supervision, eventually centered in the Senate and House Intelligence committees.

Finally, Vietnam left the armed forces, and especially the army, in deplorable condition. It led directly to the ending of the draft. And in the immediate post-Vietnam mood, Congress was not ready (and was indeed not asked) to approve the kind of military budgets that would have started to remedy the ten-year diversion of investment money to operations, let alone the new and lasting impact of higher personnel costs, which went from 46 percent of the FY 1968 military budget to 61 percent of the FY 1976 budget. Most basically, in the wake of Vietnam, the United States let up in its defense effort, although there remains acute controversy over the degree and importance of the let-up and over its relative impact on conventional and nuclear force elements.

The list of identifiable consequences related to Vietnam is long. The greatest of all was the effect on the nation's own view of itself—national self-confidence—which in turn fed into a dominant view in the rest of the world, including the Kremlin, that the United States was in a relatively low state. Inevitably this remade the politics of foreign and national security policy (to the extent the two can ever be separated). The differences over the war were sharper with time rather than less, and the 1970s and early 1980s became a time of acute tension and increasing division among Americans, on foreign policy even more than on domestic issues, with the two major parties increasingly dominated by their most liberal and conservative elements, respectively.[12] The earlier dominance of bipartisan consensus, or at least giving the executive the benefit of the doubt, was not merely lost but replaced by its opposite, instinctive opposition, often extending to presidents of the same party as the critics.

In terms of process, Watergate in particular had an enormous impact. It compounded the distrust of the executive that had emerged during Vietnam, dramatized and increased the power of Congress, and for a time gave a big boost to liberal forces particularly influenced by Vietnam and critical of it, especially in the pivotal 1974 and 1976 elections. If there had been any chance that the sharply more critical media during Vietnam might have become more moderate, Watergate removed that chance, feeding the furor over CIA operations and much else. Vietnam and Watergate were, at least in the 1970s, hard to separate.

Process and substance in foreign and security policy go hand in hand. But since changes in process are easier to identify, let us list the visible procedural changes that came after 1973 and were due to Vietnam or to the post-Vietnam political atmosphere. Clearly tied to Vietnam were:

1. A congressional ban on further military operations in or over Indochina, the first such legislation in U.S. history.

2. The War Powers Resolution, passed over Nixon's veto in November 1973, providing that U.S. forces could not be put in situations of imminent hostility for more than sixty days without specific congressional approval by both houses and that any such action must be fully reported to Congress. By any standard, this was a major change in the historic role of Congress, whose constitutionality continues to be hotly debated.

Less directly, but still substantially, related were:

3. Legislation establishing congressional oversight of covert operations, plus one earlier specific ban on any form of U.S. aid in Angola (the Clark

amendment). Congressional control of covert operations is now accepted as a given, however uneven its application.

4. Specific congressional review of arms sales of any significant size, with greatly expanded use of conditions relating to specific countries (Turkey) and to human rights factors.

5. Generally more intensive congressional scrutiny of aid programs and their implications for involving the United States.

In short, the whole setting for the making of foreign policy, especially in third world situations, has become since 1973 totally different than it was in the 1950s and 1960s. The lessons drawn from Vietnam and the changes in the policymaking process related to it would seem to point to a drastic turning away from the use or threat of force in third world situations. Let us look at the cases since 1973 where force was, or might have been, considered as a U.S. option.

Use of Force Since Vietnam

In examining the record since 1973, one has to deal immediately with the 1973 Middle East war and the drastic oil price rise (and temporary embargo) that accompanied it. These events had little or nothing to do with Vietnam.[13] Their impact on U.S. policy in the Middle East, on public attitudes toward Israel in particular, and—for many years—on the U.S. economic situation and overall U.S. confidence was enormous.

The immediate U.S. response to the Egyptian attack across the Suez Canal was (after a short wait) to send major military aid to Israel and then—as the tide turned in Israel's favor—to reject a brief Soviet proposal to send Soviet or U.S. and Soviet forces to secure a cease-fire, giving bite to the rejection by a limited U.S. nuclear alert. Although neither of these was an actual use of force, they could readily have foreshadowed more direct U.S. engagement if the Israelis had been less successful. Yet the actions were strongly supported and not thereafter criticized save marginally. Congress supported immediate replacement of Israeli equipment losses and in the years to come acted repeatedly to increase aid levels to Israel, in many cases beyond administration wishes.

Clearly the 1973 war even more than the 1967 one deepened the U.S. commitment to Israel.[14] In this respect Israel has been a striking exception in a period otherwise marked by overwhelming public and congressional reluctance to make or enlarge U.S. commitments and by a withering or narrowing of some that are still nominally on the books.

After the 1973 war, as Kissinger's diplomacy contributed to three disengagement agreements, in Egypt, in the Golan Heights, and finally, in 1975, in the Sinai, the United States became progressively more involved. Not only did it initiate massive aid programs to Egypt (and for a time even Syria) to balance in part the aid to Israel, but it also provided U.S. technicians as part of the Sinai observer force. Congress, to be sure, gulped hard at this last but eventually accepted it as more deterring than involving.

In short, from 1973 on, the Middle East seemed to become to a large extent an area where intensified concerns for Israel—as well as for oil supplies and the general stability of an area very much in Soviet sights— outweighed the Vietnam syndrome. The concern for oil supplies and prices could in itself have raised the possibility of using force, and in 1974 there were high-level threats of U.S. action in the event of a total embargo strangling Europe and Japan as well as the United States. But these threats excluded the use of force in any lesser oil contingency, by implication rejecting the urging of a few that the United States should go in and settle the issues of price and availability by force. Any action of this sort would surely have been an enormous gamble even in terms of its immediate objectives, not to mention its impact on relations with the Arab world and with U.S. allies.[15] That the option attracted little support, in either the administration or the public, seems hard to attribute to Vietnam.

Just before Nixon's forced resignation in mid-1974, Greece and Turkey went to war over Cyprus. While U.S. diplomacy may have been faulty, no more than in 1964 or 1967 was it a case where a threat of U.S. force could have been relevant. What did matter, in both the short and long term, was that Congress, with the bit in its teeth generally, imposed a conditional embargo on military aid to Turkey, with the effect, as many saw it, of weakening ties and losing base facilities for a time, while not furthering a negotiated settlement that would in any case have been very difficult to achieve.

In the spring of 1975 came the final debacle in Vietnam itself. Although there was dispute over the usefulness of last-minute U.S. aid, renewed U.S. intervention was not considered. But even if many, perhaps most, Americans had by this time written Vietnam off, the dénouement, and especially the evacuation of Saigon, was still a sickening event that deeply depressed an already beleaguered nation.[16] Very shortly, the seizure by Kampucheans of the crew of the merchant ship *Mayaguez* seemed a last straw, and the Ford administration's forceful response was greeted with approval and relief. But this was only a blip on a screen that showed to all the world a badly damaged United States.

Over the next five years there ensued not only the rapid and complete North Vietnamese conquests of Laos and Kampuchea but new Communist takeovers in Angola, Ethiopia, South Yemen, and (in two stages) Afghanistan, plus the overthrow of the shah and the humiliating hostage crisis of 1979–1980. It has been easy for many Americans to accept in high degree the conclusion summarized most recently by Richard Nixon:

Our defeat in Vietnam sparked a rash of totalitarian conquests around the world as we retreated into a five-year, self-imposed exile. In crisis after crisis in Africa, the Mideast, and Central America, critics of American involvement abroad brandished "another Vietnam" like a scepter, an all-purpose argument-stopper for any situation where it was being asserted that the United States should do something rather than nothing. While we wrung our hands and agonized over our mistakes, over 100 million people were lost to the West in the vacuum left by our withdrawal from the world stage.[17]

Unquestionably, Soviet confidence and assertiveness were at high levels throughout the 1970s and especially after 1975. One could debate how much this traced to the achievement of strategic nuclear parity, ratified by the 1972 SALT I agreements; to the broader implications of détente in accepting the Soviet Union as a genuine worldwide superpower;[18] or to the steady increase in Soviet conventional military capabilities, especially for outreach operations. When the correlation of forces appears to be moving in their favor, the Soviets are almost bound to seize opportunities and on occasion help to create them; 1958–1962 had been a foretaste.

Others would argue in the opposite direction, pointing to the failure to achieve increased U.S. trade ties, symbolized by the Jackson-Vanik amendment of 1974, or to the way the Soviet Union was neatly cut out of Middle East diplomacy and saw its influence there reduced. Weighing all factors, the Soviets, from early 1975 on, surely saw few disincentives to the exploiting of opportunities in the third world and judged the United States to be in real trouble, of which the impact of Vietnam was a part, and thus unlikely to react sharply in either local situations or more generally.

Yet if one looks at the actual cases usually cited and asks whether there was any realistic possibility of meeting the situation by the use or threat of force (either by the U.S. itself or by its allies), what answer might one get? I for one am not persuaded that a hypothetical mainstream-activist U.S. president, working with a willing Congress and an accepting public, would have been disposed to invoke force, or able to use it effectively, in any of these cases.

Angola was the first in time and perhaps the most debatable. Ford and Kissinger never truly took the issue to the country but did provide substantial covert aid to two anti-Communist groups, with the knowledge of Congress, which then, when the crunch came, with both South African and Cuban forces actively engaged, voted (overwhelmingly) to refuse appropriations — and added the Clark amendment to nail down the lid. So far as the record shows, direct U.S. involvement was never considered. The idea of fighting alongside South Africa would surely have foreclosed effective public support for any such action. The blunt fact was that the Soviet Union had discovered in a willing Cuba a new proxy approach for which no answer was at hand.[19]

The takeovers by Communist regimes in Ethiopia (1974–1977) and

South Yemen (1978) were conducted internally, offering no occasion for out-side intervention; nor can one see how either could have been deterred.

More debatable was the policy followed when Ethiopia in early 1977 moved into the Soviet camp, with the result that Somalia turned to the West for aid, obviously intending to use it in the 1977 campaign to retake the long-contested Ogaden region. If the United States had provided the aid Siad Barre of Somalia asked, it would have become involved in a war that clearly vio-lated Africa's postcolonial ground rules and (as in Angola) on a side that could have won only with massive aid and probably direct intervention. Such a course was not widely suggested at the time.

When Ethiopia, with massive Soviet help and Cuban forces, retook the Ogaden in early 1978, the only attainable objective became avoiding invasion of the recognized boundaries of Somalia. At this point Zbigniew Brzezinski earnestly urged deployment of a U.S. aircraft carrier off Somalia to show will and concern, especially to the neighboring countries hostile to Ethiopia. Every other senior official in the Carter administration was opposed to such a show of force, and Carter sided with them.[20] Painful and open to domestic at-tack as this passive posture was, the reasons for it would in my judgment have persuaded other presidents.

Afghanistan and Iran presented much graver issues. In his memoirs, Secretary Vance regrets that the United States did not react more strongly to the initial coup of April 1978 in Kabul; any such reaction, however, could surely have been only in terms of diplomatic posture.[21] Afghanistan had always been considered beyond the reach of U.S. power or even effective pressure.[22] When the signs mounted that the Soviets might move to take con-trol, there were many U.S. protests but none backed by any convincing threat of concrete action. In their memoirs, both Vance and Brzezinski regret not having made clear to the Soviets that the United States would take the kind of actions actually taken—the grain embargo and the Olympic boycott were perhaps the most significant—but the Soviet imperatives behind the invasion were almost certainly strong enough to have outweighed any concern over such measures.[23] If there was a miscalculation, it did not affect the decision. After the invasion, none of the measures taken or considered raised a serious threat of the use of force. There was a small and limited increase in naval and logistic support deployments and proposals for renewed military aid to Pakistan and initiating arms sales to China, but neither was carried through at that time.

Iran was geopolitically the most damaging loss to the U.S. and Western position in the third world in the postwar period though not (as of mid-1987) a corresponding gain in the Soviet position. One can debate whether the shah might have been stiffened to use his army to the full. Quite probably, if this had been the clear-cut U.S. advice, his next question would have been whether U.S. forces would be available to help bail him out or at least counter any Soviet response. Is it possible to visualize any postwar mainstream president giving such a commitment? I doubt it. What was certainly not in the cards was a repeat of 1953; then the masses had been with the effort to restore the shah, but by 1978 they were on the opposite side. Thus, while less confused U.S. advice and political influence might have helped a transition to a constitutional monarchy or a less extreme regime, even such a hope was probably slim.

Force was a much more realistic option when the hostages were taken in November 1979, and there were indeed contingency plans if the hostages had been harmed, perhaps even if they had been put on trial to humiliate the U.S. further. Two U.S. carriers were kept at hand from December 1979 onward and eventually participated in the abortive rescue attempt of April 1980.

Judging that tragic effort is too much a question of operational plans and tactics to be useful here. A more basic question is whether there might have been—as some have since suggested—a strong threat of military action at the very outset, possibly backed by an outright declaration of war (as was separately proposed by George Kennan).

Such a strong threat was not publicly urged by any significant figure in those early days after the hostages were seized. What could have been undertaken is not clear. Khomeini is an unpredictable leader, and if he had not caved in to the threat alone, carrying out any significant military action would have surely had substantial risks. As with proposals for the shah to use his army the year before, it would have been a throw of the dice but this time with the lives of the hostages at stake.

At neither time did the possibility of using or threatening major force become a widespread issue in the United States. Would this have been different at earlier times in the postwar period, so that we see here an effect of Vietnam? I doubt it. A sense of national defeat and humiliation can be just as profound—and devastating in the political arena—even if critics do not offer persuasive alternatives to what was done; witness the "loss" of China in the late 1940s.

What, then, might be a fair summary of this series of U.S. setbacks, many also Soviet gains, that marked the period from 1975 to 1980 in what came to be called an "arc of crisis"? In almost every case, there was room for debate about earlier U.S. policy toward the country affected.[24] But however the situation reached the crisis level, the proximate issue for U.S. policymakers was how to respond then. Undoubtedly the series of cases fed on each other and had substantial negative impact on U.S. interests. In no case was there a reasonably clear-cut or promising use of force option as the situation stood at the time for decision. Thus, I doubt that any postwar president would have acted differently at that stage.

What of the situation since 1980, and especially in the Reagan administration? This period has been marked by a great concern about the Soviet threat in all its aspects, including the kind of third world situations on which we are focusing. But has the relative importance of force been affected?

Let us look first at the attitudes that lay behind the massive military buildup of recent years and then briefly at its nature. From 1976 onward, U.S. opinion—first among conservatives and then more generally—became increasingly concerned about the deteriorating military balance with the Soviet Union and the string of Soviet gains. Significant improvements in Soviet outreach capabilities had been evident, especially in the long-distance supplying and equipping of Cuban and local forces in Angola and Ethiopia. Otherwise the change in the military balance played only a background role in the Soviet-Cuban successes. But it was natural that the two became linked and that redressing the balance came to be seen as essential not only in the larger framework of East-West relations but in meeting and countering damaging actions from any source (mostly but not solely with Soviet ties) in the third world.

Thus the pace of U.S. defense spending began to pick up in 1979, rising to a projected 5 percent real annual increase in Carter's departing budget and then to annual real increase rates of more than 7 percent in the first four Reagan years. The buildup placed special emphasis on strategic nuclear forces (although these never accounted for more than the 15 percent or so of the total defense budget, which had been the norm through the early 1960s) and on naval forces, with the army and air force getting slightly lesser shares that were applied substantially to advanced equipment and much more adequate operating and maintenance funds.[25]

During this period, a command was fleshed out for conducting limited operations in the Middle East, now called the Central Command, and additional forces were earmarked for this contingency. In striking contrast to the budgets of the last major U.S. buildup, in the early 1960s, however, there was relatively little emphasis on greater airlift and sealift, on increased army manpower, or on special light and mobile forces. Edward Luttwak faults the buildup for excessive emphasis on the navy and especially on big carriers—calling these choices "strategically unsound" in themselves—and for failure to make a determined effort to move toward "land-power parity."[26] Most certainly the buildup has not given limited uses of force in third world areas a high priority, although the capabilities for such action have presumably increased to some extent as part of wider improvements.

Whether this is honest strategic thinking, interservice competition and comparative advocacy (as Luttwak argues), or deference to a Congress and public that might feel strengthening forces tailored for limited war made it more likely the United States would get into such wars without good reason, the outsider cannot say. But I believe this is an objective picture of the nature of the Reagan buildup. If so, it fits neatly with at least one thoughtful analysis of U.S. public opinion in recent years. On the basis of extensive in-depth polls, William Schneider classifies the public into two broad groups, internationalists (generally better educated) and noninternationalists. The former are divided, often sharply, into liberals and conservatives, with troop commitments high on the list of issues that divide them. The latter, almost half of the public, tend to want at the same time "peace" and "strength." They are aligned with conservatives in favoring, at least from 1975 to about 1983, substantially increased defense budgets but with liberals when it comes to actual U.S. involvement. Schneider sums up, "The basic impulse is defensive; the public wants to see the United States beef up its military power in order to protect itself from a growing Soviet threat, not in order to assume an interventionist role in world affairs."[27]

This analysis rings true. Obviously it is far too simple, not taking account of the many important groups of Americans who may exert strong pressure for or against interventionist policies in particular situations. Their reasons may include religion, ethnic status, national background, or any combination of the factors that make U.S. society so much more pluralistic than any other. It may well be that the increasing self-consciousness of such groups forms a major barrier to achieving a consensus in support of local interventions. There have been sea changes in the last fifteen to twenty years—some related to Vietnam but a great many not—and the changed habits of Congress and the media stimulate and reflect these.

Let us come back to specific cases to see what can be deduced from them. Since 1981 there have been three cases where force was clearly a U.S. option: Cuba and Central America (treated as one), Lebanon after the 1982 war there, and Grenada in the fall of 1983. No, halfway, and yes have been the answers given. Why, and with what relationship to Vietnam?

No newly elected administration likes to face an early decision on the use of force, especially if the campaign included charges of trigger happiness in the incoming president. Moreover, a central and urgent domestic agenda always affects big foreign decisions where force is not virtually compelled. Thus, when in early 1981 Alexander Haig, as secretary of state, pressed on his NSC colleagues and on the president a program of fairly drastic pressures on Cuba over its role in Central America—as practically the first order of business—he was bucking a lot of history.

The debate that ensued has now been narrated in blunt (and subjective) terms in Haig's memoir of his tenure.[28] It is instructive and rife with overtones from the Vietnam experience. Haig's program itself was designed to get away from the "incrementalism" that he and many others had seen as the great mistake in Vietnam. This time, he argued, the United States should not "tangle ineffectively with the puppets" but get at "the puppet masters," being prepared to "commit ourselves at a high level of intensity from the beginning, with all the risk that this entails." It was a case backed by persuasive evidence that the Cubans had trained the dominant Sandinista group and guided them to power and had provided large-scale aid and advisers to Nicaragua itself and to the rebels in El Salvador, who had just failed in their attempted final offensive and might therefore be all the more vulnerable to a reduction in their outside support.

What Haig actually proposed is not stated in his memoirs as clearly as one would like. Beyond "noticeably higher levels of U.S. aid" and "reasonable numbers of military advisers" in El Salvador, already underway, its keystone appears to have been putting a navy carrier group or two on station between Cuba and the Central American mainland to show "keen U.S. interest . . . and our ability to blockade Cuba if that became necessary." At the same time army and air force units were to be reinforced and brought to high readiness.

Haig says he never contemplated "direct military action," noting that to land marines in Central America would have fallen squarely under the War Powers Act and judging that Congress would have given its consent only "in case of catastrophe." Yet he goes on, cryptically, that military strength was a major U.S. asset and that "a credible willingness to apply it to the degree necessary simply could not be disregarded." Quarantine or blockade? Attack on Cuba itself? U.S. ground forces in Central America? Apparently only the first but with threats of the other two. By April 1981 the State Department, he says, was "close to producing a plan . . . to seal off the export of arms from Cuba to Central America." This must have been the essence of the proposal.[29]

By all accounts, especially his, Haig ran into opposition from the White House staff on the ground that any such program would arouse intense public and congressional controversy that would inevitably sidetrack the Reagan domestic program.[30] But there was also acute internal disagreement:

> The Secretary of Defense genuinely feared the creation of another unmanageable tropical war into which American troops and American money would be poured with no result different from Vietnam. . . . Our forces, he [Weinberger] argued, were already spread too thin. . . . The Joint Chiefs of Staff resisted a major commitment. I . . . sensed, and understood, a doubt on the part of the military in the political will of the civilians at the top to follow through to the end in such a commitment.[31]

Thus Haig's program was watered down to the point of ineffectuality.

Instead, the administration tackled the problem in Central America by a combination of political advice, economic aid, and limited military assistance on the gound—a low-key program—coupled after late 1981 by covert support for the Nicaraguan contras. In the spring and summer of 1983, it conducted military maneuvers in Honduras and temporary naval deployments off Nicaragua and El Salvador, while also participating in the Contadora negotiating process and in occasional bilateral contacts with Nicaragua. In

May 1985 it moved to impose a trade embargo on Nicaragua, still in a pattern of pressure accompanied by repeated statements that the use of U.S. forces was not contemplated.

In all this, the shadow of Vietnam hung heavy. The cases are strikingly different in key respects: U.S. national interests in this neighboring area are very great historically and now — and the potential weight of the United States in usable military force is significantly greater than it was against North Vietnam. But resemblances will be seen by many, not only in the administration's incrementalism but in its failure, with rare exceptions, to explain its purpose and actions frankly, including resort, in the case of support for the contras, to concealment if not outright deceit. If the reader looks back at the list of lessons from Vietnam in this chapter, it will be at once apparent that each of the first eight lessons has been operative or debated once again over Central America. Moreover, almost all the congressional restraints arising from Vietnam — the War Powers Act in particular — have had to be watched constantly, a result applauded by some and deplored by others.

Yet one has to ask whether an administration not thus constrained would have been disposed to more harder and faster. Even before Vietnam, neither Eisenhower nor Kennedy was prepared to take Castro on frontally, the inevitable thrust of Haig's proposal. And if one assesses the possible use of force in El Salvador, it may be true that a determined United States could have concluded the situation there in fairly short order — as Edward Luttwak has argued[32] — but the long-term consequences would surely be debatable. As the mythologizing of the overthrow of Salvador Allende in Chile suggests, any U.S. use of force today in Central or South America faces a heavy burden of proof simply in regional terms. The immense aversion to Uncle Sam in arms was evident well before Vietnam and has its own dynamic, one that now seems sure to operate in virtually any case short of a major action originating outside the hemisphere.

Lebanon was, and is, a very different case. The deployment of the marines near Beirut in September 1982 flowed directly from a basic U.S. policy decision not to acquiesce in Israel's invasion as it developed but rather to seek to restore an independent Lebanon freed of all foreign forces. Those who essentially opposed that basic decision would not have sent the marines, who were deployed initially to permit an orderly evacuation of the PLO apparatus and deny Israel the totally humiliating expulsion sought by Sharon. The marine force was left in place to try to contain the consequences of the massacres in the Palestinian camps and thus to help Amin Gemayel take hold as president of Lebanon. It was a vastly different case than would have been presented by a clearly perceived threat to Israel itself.

Several aspects stand out. First, in the face of the Syrian, local, and Israeli force strengths and armaments, the operation could not have been a cauterizing one. Even if the initial 1,800 men had been deployed with a large reserve force visibly ready to come if needed, such a reserve force would have had to be several divisions. The much greater force requirement reflects a basic change since the 1950s and 1960s: the size and sophistication of local forces, notably but far from solely in the Middle East.

Second, the enemy was varied and hard to relate to a national government. Whatever the Syrian (or Iranian) hand, it was concealed enough to be hard to identify for reprisal purposes. This was terrorism on a grand and often highly organized scale, but still terrorism, conducted by fanatically motivated groups.

Third, the mission was defensive and essentially political—the most difficult and frustrating possible.

So although it may have given Gemayel more of a chance than he would have had otherwise, the operation was in the end painful and fruitless, at best a good try in a no-win situation. Clearly it has left its own trail of (often conflicting) lessons.

By contrast, Grenada seems, in hindsight, an easy case. I believe any other U.S. president would have responded roughly as Reagan did, given the danger to several hundred Americans, the political background, and the inconsequential opposition. Politically the arguments for quick cauterizing action were considerably stronger than in the Dominican case in 1965, and the newness and fragility of the Grenada ministate were in contrast to the long-established status of the Dominican Republic. Although international law was strained, if not breached outright, the special features were enough so that even this factor has had little lasting impact. The first Grenada elections since the invasion are, of course, far from showing that lasting democracy and political stability have been the result, but the chances are surely greater than before. In short, it was a quick success, without wider risks and with a built-in political exit: the 1958 Lebanon model closer to home. But it is a rare and fading species, as subsequent debate has recognized.

What about that debate, dramatically joined in the fall of 1984 in the head-to-head opposing views of the president's two senior advisers?[33] I am on Secretary Shultz's side, conditioned by the earlier and somewhat parallel debate between MacArthur, on the one side, and Marshall, Bradley, and Acheson on the other, in the pivotal 1951 Russell hearings concerning Korea. Conceivably Secretary Weinberger would, if pressed, accept the definition of winning or victory stated by General Bradley in those hearings: "you vary from being willing to accept a rather small thing that you start out to correct up to an objective that we set in World War II of unconditional surrender. There are many variations in between the two."[34] Conceivably he does not mean to imply that the pursuit of victory means using any means or weapons available or to interpret his requirement that force be used only as a last resort to preclude any form of preventive action no matter how clear the impending threat. But even such modifications would leave in place an apparent requirement of reasonably assured public support in advance and of continuing congressional support. This requirement alone would repeal a lot of historically wise decisions, starting with the first response to Korea in June 1950.

But I doubt if either speech is or could be the last word, even in indicating how the Pentagon and State Department would react to the next concrete case. Taken at face value, Weinberger's speech would suggest much less willingness to use or invoke force than was the case during or before Vietnam. Indeed it is practically a codification of the lessons drawn by many military men. But like most other codifications of inherently complex (and emotional) matters, it is a good deal clearer than life. Defining when the United States would use force is a bit too much like stating a defense perimeter in public, something no senior official has done since Acheson's much-criticized 1950 speech.

Conclusions

Where then do Americans stand in national attitudes toward the use or threat of force as an instrument of policy in the kinds of situations discussed here? I have argued Vietnam did not truly strip gears that would otherwise have meshed neatly, although its impact on the policymaking process is profound. Few, if any, postwar presidents would have chosen clearly more forceful responses to the situations that have actually confronted the United States since Vietnam. Where policy has been more restrained than in past periods, notably Central America, the reasons have to do largely with factors not related to Vietnam.

The underlying point is that even if Vietnam had been a much less negative experience, the United States would have been wrestling at least since 1970 with a whole set of factors tending to make third world situations much harder to deal with:

1. Public awareness of a state of strategic nuclear parity. That the United States would suffer devastatingly in any nuclear exchange had been clear to policymakers since the 1950s; only since about 1970 has the American public at large realized this consequence. This alone might have greatly changed the public taste for confrontations or near confrontations, especially in the light of the next factor.

2. Increased Soviet military capabilities. Even if the United States had kept pace, the Soviets would still have had much greater outreach capabilities in this time frame.

3. The quantity and especially the quality of the arms now in the hands of third world governments.

4. Less quantifiable but perhaps even more important, the growing assertiveness of nations and regions and their resentment of outside, and especially superpower, intervention. Clearest in Latin America, this trend is strong elsewhere as well.

5. A loss of control, in the whole community of nations, of intense local conflicts ranging from those of a terrorist character to such devastating wars as those between Iran and Iraq and in Kampuchea. Marked especially by the steady erosion of the role of the United Nations in the security area, this is a worldwide phenomenon. Perhaps it owes something to Vietnam, but there was bound to be a general diffusion of power.

6. A renewed state of cold war, with communication between the superpowers tenuous and a new Soviet leadership, apparently freed of the semiparalysis of several years of a rolling succession and perhaps more ready again to seize and help create third world opportunities.

In short, if the world is in a dangerous overall condition today, Vietnam is only one of the contributing causes. Yet these dangers raise the final and most disturbing question: if recent U.S. policies and attitudes toward the use of force have been less affected by Vietnam than is sometimes supposed—and more in the postwar mainstream—is this good enough?

Activists would answer that it is not, that the times call for a more assertive U.S. policy to meet an increased Soviet threat but in the light of all else as well. Noninterventionists would answer that the United States is and has been too active and should rely overwhelmingly on negotiated approaches and on the nations of the region affected.

I am in the middle. In attempting to deal with multiple threats and potential threats—to its specific interests and to the overall state of world peace that is in the end its most central interest—the United States is, in my view, far too inflexible and limited today in the means at its command. Concern about another Vietnam has too often operated to limit the tools, short of force, that could prevent that outcome. I am less worried about whether the United States will react to some clear challenge than its inability to act flexibly and effectively to head off such a challenge.

The role the United States sought to play in the 1950s and 1960s was in many respects overextended. If it had not come to grief in Vietnam, it might well have done so elsewhere, though hardly as devastatingly. But the United States still has a major stabilizing role, and it has major national interests to protect. Clearly any use of force by a democracy should be subject to the most serious review and the greatest debate possible in the circumstances. But the degree of confusion and division that prevails today—in and out of government, over the use of force and much else — cannot be a sound condition for a great nation.

Many years ago Mark Twain said something that may be a good note on which to close:

> We should be careful to get out of an experience only the wisdom that is in it — and stop there; lest we be like the cat that sits down on a hot stove lid. She will never sit down on a hot stove lid again — and that is well; but also she will never sit down on a cold one anymore.[35]

A lot of important stoves may not be nearly so hot as Vietnam turned out to be.

Notes

1. To take an obvious example, the Soviets routinely use the presence of visiting military personnel (and often civilians as well) in the Soviet Union for indoctrination and training wherever this seems promising; the military who made the April 1978 coup in Afghanistan were the products of such activity. It is deliberately not the U.S. practice in any way other than through the normal exposure to U.S. society and institutions.

2. Richard Nixon, then vice-president, made public statements at the time that appeared to be at least trial balloons for the use of U.S. ground force to hold the line in Vietnam. In his latest book, however, he argues rather that the right course would have been intensive conventional bombing of the concentrated Viet Minh forces around Dien Bien Phu, that the Viet Minh were (in the light of later evidence particularly) near the end of their tether, and that this action alone would have turned the tide. Nixon, *No More Vietnams* (New York: Arbor House, 1985), p. 31. Eisenhower, however, insisted on allied and congressional support for any military action — which was not forthcoming — and, perhaps more decisively, accepted the military judgment of General Ridgway that only ground action on a massive scale could secure the situation in a lasting way. My own hunch, as a back-bench participant at the time, is that the president never intended to act militarily but did see the point of keeping the threat alive to give some bargaining leverage in the Geneva negotiations.

3. Richard M. Saunders, "Military Force in the Foreign Policy of the Eisenhower Presidency," *Political Science Quarterly* (Spring 1985): 97–116.

4. Note also the refusal of the Eisenhower administration to engage in even the most modest show of force in response to Soviet repression of the uprising in East Berlin in 1953 and in Hungary in 1956. Restraint over Soviet behavior toward the satellite nations had even then come to be accepted as inevitable, although the talk of rollback in the 1952 presidential campaign may have led for a short time to different expectations.

5. I can still recall the shudder that went through Pentagon circles when it was made clear, from the White House, that the naval forces deployed, as a precaution and

deterrent, in the offshore islands crisis of 1958 should not assume that they would be free to use their nuclear weapons, even the smallest. There was a frantic rush to provide conventional armament.

6. Saunders, "Military Force," p. 111, says that Eisenhower's advice opposed unilateral U.S. action; allied support (which would not have been forthcoming on all indications) was a necessary condition. The citation, to a memorandum of the meeting by Robert McNamara, is impressive. However, I have permission to note that a different version of the same briefing, by Secretary Rusk, states that the advice was to make a firm stand, "with others if possible, alone if necessary." Interview with Dean Rusk, February 26, 1985.

7. I refer particularly to Harry G. Summers, Jr., *On Strategy: A Critical Analysis of the Vietnam War* (Novato, Calif.: Presidio Press, 1982). Although I agree with much of his analysis, I believe that a strong emphasis on pacification would have been inevitable in any event, and indeed owed more, in its formative phases, to the advice of Sir Robert Thompson, based on British experience in Malaya, than to anything that came out of U.S. counterinsurgency thinking. A separate point on which I query his conclusions concerns the influence on U.S. strategy, even among senior civilians, of systems analysis people in the Pentagon employing the tools of the planning, programming, budgeting system (PPBS). In my experience, whatever their impact on military planning generally, PPBS and its practitioners were very much in the back seat on strategic or even tactical matters.

8. The relative importance of the conventional military balance and the strategic nuclear situation has occasioned a running debate since (even among senior U.S. participants) as to which was the more significant in bringing about the outcome. In the Soviet perception (however one interprets the "never again" statement of Valerian Zorin to John McCloy at the time) the answer was surely "both." Almost certainly the Soviets were already embarked on major buildups of their naval and strategic nuclear capabilities. But the crisis must have intensified both programs markedly.

9. As the action officer in that effort, I do not recall more than formal consultation with the Congress. No specific appropriation was initially sought or needed, with substantial funds available by adjustments in the overall military aid program. That such action was possible and readily accepted must seem startling to those who have had to wrestle with similar possible actions in the 1970s and 1980s.

10. Retrospective views in the Dominican Republic itself are mixed, as reflected in a feature story on the twentieth anniversary of the operation. *New York Times,* May 1, 1985, p. 2.

11. It is necessary to consider briefly the argument, advanced most recently by President Nixon, that the war was really not lost at all—that it had been in effect won by early 1973 and that only the restrictions and cuts imposed by Congress demoralized the South Vietnamese regime, precluded U.S. aid, and thus brought on the debacle of April 1975. Any assessment of this argument involves, first, the impact of Watergate and how far it flowed from Vietnam. Above all it involves the state of U.S. national will in a very narrow time frame (1974–1975) and on the precise issue of Vietnam itself.

The aid cuts clearly hurt. But I wonder if anyone in touch with public opinion at the time believes that U.S. national will could have been maintained at the levels needed to carry out Nixon's secret commitments to Thieu, which clearly implied the return of U.S. air power on a large scale. If that air power was not provided, even with all the U.S. aid conceivable, the South would have had difficulty standing up to the North Vietnamese offensive that was sure to come. This was, it appears, the conclusion of a Special National Intelligence Estimate in the spring of 1974.

The Paris agreements, although probably the best attainable, were loaded with risks and the built-in hazard of the continued presence of the NVA in the South. One need not suppose that a "decent interval" was all that was intended or hoped for, to conclude that the odds were heavily against the viability of South Vietnam under the agreements. At least this particular version of an American "stab in the back" theory deserves the short shrift it has had from most reviewers.

12. William Schneider, "Public Opinion," in Joseph S. Nye, Jr., ed., *The Making of America's Soviet Policy* (New Haven: Yale University Press, for the Council on Foreign Relations, 1984), pp. 11–35, is an excellent short summary on this subject.

13. It can be argued that senior U.S. policymakers less preoccupied with Vietnam might have found a way to head off the 1967 war or the subsequent war of attrition. But this seems to me on the wilder shores of speculation; Vietnam was not that pervasive.

14. That this commitment has never been put in the form of a treaty has been due to a host of factors on both sides, including Israeli reluctance to accept possible accompanying restraints on its freedom of action. But few would question that the U.S. commitment to the survival of a viable Israel is today on a par with, say, the NATO obligation.

15. Such action was proposed, after the event I believe, by a number of neoconservatives, such as Robert W. Tucker, "Oil: The Issue of American Intervention," *Commentary* (January 1975) 21–31, The view that failure to do this was a disastrous signal — in effect permitting "a tiny and militarily powerless nation, Saudi Arabia," to show that it could "blackmail and exact tribute from" the United States — has been reiterated recently by Norman Podhoretz, "The Reagan Road to Detente," *Foreign Affairs* (America and the World 1984): 452. For a concise summary of some of the military and political problems such action would have faced, see International Institute for Strategic Studies, *Strategic Survey* (London: IISS, 1974), pp. 30–32.

16. In this connection it is interesting to note the assessment of U.S. will, and the factors affecting it, at the October 1974 conference of North Vietnam's political and military leaders, which ended with the decision to press forward with a major 1975 offensive. In concluding that the United States would not send troops back to the South, the report referred to "internal contradictions within the U.S. administration and among U.S. political parties. . . . The Watergate scandal had seriously affected the entire United States . . . [which] faced economic recession, mounting inflation, serious unemployment and an oil crisis." Quoted in Summers, *On Strategy,* p. 113.

17. Nixon, *No More Vietnams,* p. 13. Nixon was not, of course, referring only to the use of force; on the contrary, the nearest he comes to specifics in this particular passage is to attack those who opposed, as a "use of American power," "military aid to governments that are not popular in the editorial columns or the salons of the intelligentsia."

18. The high-level Soviet defector, Arkady Shevchenko, for example, writes that as he participated in the preparations for the May 1972 summit in Moscow, he "felt a

clear-cut revival of self-assurance in our leadership." *Breaking with Moscow* (New York: Knopf, 1985), p. 201.

19. The most promising military response (not, so far as I know, considered) might have been some form of quarantine or sea blockade of Cuba itself, an imaginative idea but one immensely hard to justify under existing international law or to sustain public or allied support for, especially with the South Africans supporting the United States. Even this would have affected only the flow of manpower; the supplies came from the Soviet Union, by air and in the latter stages by sea. Trying to block these by in-close barriers would have been a direct confrontation with the Soviet Union on a principle where the U.S. position would have had little international support.

20. The debate is well summarized in Brzezinski's *Power and Principle: Memoirs of the National Security Adviser, 1977–1981* (New York: Farrar Straus Giroux, 1983), pp. 182–186, and in Cyrus Vance, *Hard Choices: Critical Years in America's Foreign Policy* (New York: Simon and Schuster, 1983), pp. 85–88. Brzezinski quotes his contemporary journal, which described his colleagues (Vance, Harold Brown, and General David Jones) as "badly bitten by the Vietnam bug."

At the same time, a linkage between the Ogaden and the SALT II negotiations was debated and in part made by public statements. But even if everything possible had been done to show determination—which, Brzezinski conceded, would have been only "for the record"—his contention that such action "might have avoided the later chain of events which ended with the Soviet invasion of Afghanistan" seems a flight of geopolitical fantasy.

21. Vance, *Hard Choices,* pp. 386–389.

22. In the 1951–1969 period, when I had considerable exposure to contingency plans at various times, I never heard of one involving Afghanistan, at least in local terms. More to the point, every public signal, by word or action, would have indicated that the United States would not use force over Afghanistan.

23. Vance, *Hard Choices;* Brzezinski, *Power and Principle,* pp. 353, 426–427, 432.

24. In Angola the United States was burdened by past association with Portugal, which had sharply limited any U.S. ties with the Angolan rebel groups who contended for power there after the 1974 coup in Lisbon. In Afghanistan, U.S. relationships—despite the existence of aid programs—had always been inhibited, for both parties, by the U.S. treaty relationship with Pakistan, which had an acute running dispute with the Afghans over Pushtoonistan. In Iran the unquestioning and unstinting U.S. support for the shah's policies after 1970, as well as the bloated U.S. presence, were surely factors in the scale of the opposition that undid him. For more detailed argument concerning Iran, see my article, "Who Lost Patagonia? Foreign Policy in the 1980 Campaign," *Foreign Affairs* (Fall 1979): 1–27.

25. For a detailed and thoughtful analysis of the buildup, see Edward N. Luttwak, *The Pentagon and the Art of War: The Question of Military Reform* (New York: Simon and Schuster, 1984), pp. 204–265.

26. Ibid. esp. pp. 258, 264.

27. William Schneider, "Public Opinion," in *Making of Soviet Policy,* pp. 15–16, 20.

28. Alexander M. Haig, Jr., *Caveat: Realism, Reagan and Foreign Policy* (New

York: Macmillan, 1984), pp. 122–123. As to the risks, Haig notes that in conversations with Ambassador Dobrynin, he got the clear impression that the Soviets would not react strongly to pressures on Cuba provided they stopped short of outright attack. Such an attack would have been contrary to the understanding reached after the 1962 missile crisis, that the United States would not invade Cuba. Much is sometimes made of that by those who argue persuasively that subsequent Cuban behavior has given the U.S. ample cause to disavow it. Yet, even if this were done, a Soviet commitment to Cuba would surely remain, so that direct U.S. attack would create an extremely tense situation, with possibilities for Soviet responses in other areas.

29. Although Haig does not note the point, such a program of isolating the local battlefield strongly resembles the Vietnam strategy singled out by Colonel Summers (and originally presented in 1977 by General Bruce Palmer) as the best that could have been followed in Vietnam. This would have been to put a ground force barrier, manned by an estimated six or more divisions, across South Vietnam just south of the seventeenth parallel, extending it into Laos to the Mekong River. Together with a naval blockade, this would have cut off the flow of men and arms from the North and left the Vietcong to be dealt with by the South Vietnamese. Summers, *On Strategy,* pp. 122–124. To my mind, the Palmer program—without the accompanying invasion of the North proposed in some variants—is the most persuasive of the strategy "might have beens," as I argued in an unpublished speech at West Point in April 1983 (actually before reading Colonel Summers's book).

30. Shades again of Vietnam. Although the substance of the decision to commit major forces in July 1965 would have been the same in the absence of domestic policy factors, President Johnson chose to frame that decision in terms that omitted a reserve call-up or major budget increase, largely (I am convinced) because of concern that a great debate at that point would sidetrack much of the authorizing legislation for his Great Society domestic programs. The same was true in early 1966, another excellent occasion for such a debate, when the necessary appropriations for the Great Society might have been adversely affected.

31. Haig, *Caveat,* pp. 127–128.

32. "Look, El Salvador is a tiny country with a few flea-bitten guerrillas. If our country was not traumatized by Vietnam, the whole affair would be concluded very quickly, I assure you." Historian Paul Kennedy responded by asking whether, absent Vietnam, such action would "solve" the problem in El Salvador or in similar third world situations. Edward Luttwak, "What Are the Consequences of Vietnam?" *Harper's* (April 1985): 39.

33. The essential texts of the speeches by Secretary Shultz and Secretary Weinberger are in *Survival* (January–February 1985): 30–35.

34. Quoted in Summers, *On Strategy,* p. 65.

35. Quoted in Edward Friedland, Paul Seabury, and Aaron Wildavsky, *The Great Détente Disaster: Oil and the Decline of American Foreign Policy* (New York: Basic Books, 1975), p. 171.

11
Force Planning and Vietnam

William W. Kaufmann

There is a remarkable continuity in the way the United States has dealt with its postwar defense problems, especially since 1960. Yet during the ensuing decades the United States fought a major war in Vietnam, withdrew from that tormented land in turmoil and confusion, followed that only five years later with the most rapid expansion of its defense budget since World War II, and in 1986—after five years of extraordinary growth—has already reduced appropriations in real terms below the level of fiscal 1985 and is unlikely to increase them by much, if at all, for the rest of the decade. Such a sequence of events hardly leaves the impression of continuity. What, then, is going on? How much change has occurred in the way the United States deals with its defense problems? To what extent can any change be attributed to Vietnam? Are there any lessons to learn from this experience?

The Pullout, 1970–1975

The first years of the 1970s certainly give every appearance of something more than evolution. The United States gradually began and tumultuously completed its military departure from Vietnam. As it did so, the defense budget underwent a substantial decline. In fiscal 1970, defense appropriations had stood at $226 billion (in fiscal 1986 dollars); by fiscal 1975 they had fallen to $177.7 billion (in the same dollars), a decline of 21 percent. Active duty personnel dropped from 3 million to 2.1 million, a reduction of 30 percent. The army lost five divisions, the Navy more than 400 ships (mostly of World War II vintage), and the air force three tactical fighter wings. The all-volunteer force replaced conscription, the bane of the college campuses.

President Nixon, in a number of public statements, seemed to suggest that major changes in defense policy were about to take place. Assured destruction, which gave the president no options, was no longer to be the modus operandi of the strategic nuclear forces. The United States now would plan its conventional forces on the basis of responding to two rather than three more or less simultaneous contingencies. Allies would be expected to bear much more of the burden of containing the Soviet Union. Henceforth the United States would provide troops only to allies prepared to defend themselves.

Within the Pentagon, talk increased of creating an elite professional force with as few as eight army divisions, purged of malcontents, and, as in the 1950s, heavily dependent on nuclear weapons to compensate for their small numbers. Participatory rather then centralized management became the watchword under Secretary of Defense Melvin Laird. He retained the planning-programming-budgeting system (PPBS) established by Robert McNamara in 1962, but the office of systems analysis lost its power to originate force planning recommendations. Instead, the secretary reduced it to drafting budget-constrained and generalized defense guidance and to raising issues about the program objective memoranda (POMs) drafted by the individual services. To all appearances, much of the hated McNamara system had been scuttled; the services were back in charge.

As it turned out, however, there was much less to these changes than met the eye. Defense appropriations continued to shrink in real terms as President Nixon made increasingly large investments in social programs. But they did so in the aftermath of a war in which there remained large balances of budget authority from prior-year funding, a great deal of new equipment left over from the rapid modernization that had been funded during the war years, especially in the army and the air force, and large unused stocks of munitions and other consumables. Although introduction of the all-volunteer force indeed constituted a change, the beginning of pay comparability in the late 1960s already had made military manpower so much more expensive that a reduction in armed forces personnel was probably inevitable, with or without conscription. Even the much-heralded revisions in the major force planning assumptions were more cosmetic than real. The condemnation of assured destruction was essentially an attack on a straw man. The concept itself had served as a convenient if artificial device for containing what had been seen as excessive demands by the air force for intercontinental ballistic missiles and bombers; beneath it the single integrated operational plan (SIOP, the war plan for the strategic nuclear forces) continued to provide the president with a number of attack options. The reduction from three to two in the number of simultaneous conventional attacks to which the United States should be prepared to respond in conjunction with allies may have been thought to be more significant, especially since it seemed to justify lower conventional force levels. In fact, however, the opening to China and a more realistic appraisal of the ability of the Soviet Union to sustain multiple attacks warranted a less demanding assumption. Furthermore, to the initiated, it was not a serious constraint on the demand for forces, as was quickly to become apparent. As for the allies, efforts to get them to reduce their nuclear dependency and do more for themselves had been going on for years.

The gap between rhetoric and reality grew wider once James Schlesinger became secretary of defense in 1973. Although Schlesinger held office for only sixteen months, his list of accomplishments during that short stay proved remarkably long. He succeeded in refocusing attention on the long, steady expansion of Soviet nuclear and conventional forces despite the diversions of Vietnam, arms control, and détente. He made considerable progress in persuading at least the senior officer corps that hand wringing and a retreat into the isolation of military reservations were not the necessary responses to the traumas of the war. He continued the evolution of nuclear targeting and the development of options for theater as well as strategic nuclear forces. He defeated the efforts (exemplified by the Mansfield amendment) to reduce the overseas deployment of U.S. forces and even revived both U.S. and European interest in a full-scale conventional defense of Western Europe. Well before the Arab-Israeli conflict of 1973 and the first of the oil shocks, he began to propose that an attack on the oil states of the Persian Gulf be treated as a major contingency for force planning purposes. Despite the rhetoric from the White House about planning for fewer simultaneous contingencies, he also succeeded in establishing force goals similar to those of the 1960s and in launching the campaign in Congress that was eventually to restore defense appropriations to their prewar level.

Recuperation, 1975–1980

It has become popular to characterize the 1970s as the decade of neglect where defense is concerned. The first five years more accurately fall into the category of rest and recuperation, about the same length of time it has taken the United States to recover from other wars. The next five are best seen as further recuperation and a gradual return to the budgets, programs, and forces of the pre-Vietnam era, with the inevitable modifications brought about by changes in technology and the planning environment.

In fiscal 1960, appropriations for the military functions of the Department of Defense, measured in fiscal 1986 dollars, amounted to $184.1 billion; twenty years later, they stood at $196.9 billion and rising. Modernization of the strategic nuclear triad was well underway with deployment of more powerful warheads on 300 of the Minutemen III ICBMs, development of the MX missile, deployment of the Trident submarine and the C-4 (Trident I) missile, deployment of the air-launched cruise missile, and intensive development of the advanced technology (stealth) bomber. Exploration of various defensive technologies (among them various forms of directed energy) was continuing and being modestly expanded. Although no one had yet solved the puzzle of how to conduct a sustained and nuclear air-land campaign against an enemy similarly armed, modernization of the tactical nuclear forces was going forward, and the Pershing II and the ground-launched cruise missile (GLCM) were being developed at large cost and little military justification as psychological counterweights to the Soviet SS-20 missile and Backfire medium bomber. Yet another concentrated effort to strengthen the conventional defenses of Central Europe and north Norway was proceeding, and following the Soviet invasion of Afghanistan, the Rapid Deployment Joint Task Force came into being. An attempt to deviate from past norms by withdrawing U.S. ground combat forces from South Korea resulted, after much controversy, in the departure of General John Singlaub and one maneuver battalion and the arrival of an additional air force tactical fighter squadron. Strategic mobility was receiving increased support. The number of division sets of equipment prepositioned in Germany was being doubled; ships with military equipment and supplies stored on board were being stationed off Diego Garcia in the Indian Ocean; and eight SL-7 ships had been acquired and were being modified to provide a nucleus of fast sealift for rapid intercontinental deployments. The navy, though decreased in size as a consequence of having retired its large inventory of World War II ships, was undergoing modernization and still retained a powerful capability to protect the main wartime shipping lanes and project power with aircraft carrier battle groups and marine amphibious forces. Indeed, a colonel waking from a deep sleep of twenty years in the Pentagon would have, for the most part, found the plans, programs, and budgets of 1980 quite familiar.

The Feast, 1981–1985

If the 1970s do not represent either a decade of neglect or a radical departure from the planning of the 1960s, can it be said that the first term of the Reagan administration fits the same mold? On the surface, the differences appear to be substantial. The president and the secretary of defense made a great deal more than their predecessors did of the Soviet military buildup, which they described as the greatest in history. They continue to deplore the decade of neglect and insist that the Soviet Union leads the United States in every significant measure of military power, though the White House seems to have closed the window of vulnerability. Yet despite these depressing assessments, the president announces periodically that the United States has come back, stands tall, and presumably weighs heavily on those invisible scales that measure the military balance of power.

The secretary of defense tends to be less sanguine about what the administration has accomplished. But even while expressing greater alarm about supposed U.S. weaknesses and vulnerabilities, he has not hesitated to criticize previous approaches to U.S. security problems as too reactive and defensive and to propose substituting a much more ambitious strategy even before having determined the cost of implementing it. Such a strategy, no doubt updated to include the results of the Strategic Defense Initiative (SDI, or Star Wars), presumably would entail developing leakproof defenses against ballistic missiles, cruise missiles, and bombers, prevailing in a nuclear war (usually not defined), acquiring the capability for worldwide conventional operations of indefinite duration, and deploying the forces to take the offensive (by means of horizontal escalation) against such points of alleged Soviet vulnerability as Murmansk and Vladivostok. It is little wonder that the Joint Chiefs of Staff took these objectives to mean a virtual endorsement of their minimum-risk force—with its 38 army and marine corps divisions, 22 aircraft carrier battle groups, 57 air force tactical fighter wings, and 632 strategic airlift aircraft—and suggested that the bill for it would be substantially higher than the administration was proposing in its first full five-year defense program (FYDP).

The Joint Chiefs may have considered the FYDP plan to request more than $1.6 trillion between fiscal 1983 and fiscal 1987 rather too modest relative to the ambitions of the secretary of defense and the minimum-risk force and may actually have believed that he should have proposed at least $750 billion more. Nonetheless, the difference between what the administration received in budget authority during the first four years and what its predecessors had been granted is dramatic. During the Carter years, budget authority increased by a little more than 13 percent in real terms, and Congress forced some of that on the president. By contrast, budget authority rose by more than 39 percent in real terms between fiscal 1981 and fiscal 1985. Even more impressive, funds for procurement grew in real terms by 61 percent and total investment (procurement; research, development, test, and evaluation; and military construction) by 60 percent. Because of the lag between the appropriation of budget authority and its actual use for the payment of bills, outlays during these same four years rose less than budget authority but still by a substantial 36.2 percent in real terms (compared to 12.4 percent during the four Carter years), which meant an average annual real increase of 8 percent, rather more than the 3 percent a year real growth accepted as a goal by NATO members in 1977 or the 5 percent sought by the Carter administration in its farewell FYDP.

These funding differences permitted the Defense Department to restore the B-1 bomber cancelled by the Carter administration, engage in a Maoist leap forward with the SDI, and make a large down payment on a 600-ship navy featuring 15 aircraft carrier battle groups, 4 surface action groups (centered on battleships), the amphibious lift for 1.5 marine amphibious forces, and 100 nuclear-powered attack submarines. They also enabled the services to reduce rapidly their backlogs of maintenance and repair, put more spare parts in the pipeline, build up war reserve stocks, and accelerate the pace of equipment modernization.

Yet beneath these differences and the rhetoric of change, the strands of continuity remain strong. Whether the strategic nuclear forces are meant to prevail or countervail, their basic task continues to be to survive a Soviet surprise attack in sufficient numbers to penetrate enemy defenses and cover a comprehensive list of targets. The ability to execute such an all-out attack would not, of course, preclude such options as withholding designated forces from attacks on specific sets of targets such as cities.

The ill-assorted theater nuclear capabilities, somewhat modernized by the deployment of Pershing II ballistic missiles, GLCMs, and the submarine-based nuclear Tomahawk (also a cruise missile), still remain excessively vulnerable and lack a reasonable set of military objectives. Meanwhile, the conventional forces—slightly larger in numbers of combat units but increasingly dependent on the reserves for roundout and support services—struggle as before with the problems of forward defense in central Europe, rapid deployment to the Persian Gulf, and the defense of South Korea north of Seoul. Our ancient Pentagon colonel might find some of the newer weapons more difficult to operate and maintain; he probably would wonder how maneuver warfare differs from what he learned to do in World War II and Korea. Otherwise, in spite of the increased funds, he would no doubt feel quite at home. Even the current activity in Central America, with its mercenaries, covert operations, special forces, and efforts to win hearts and minds, hardly would astonish him, no matter how uneasy he might feel about it.

The secretaries of state and defense may debate the conditions under which U.S. combat forces should be committed to action. But whatever the pros and cons, no president will accept enthusiastically the onus of having lost Guatemala, Cuba, Chile, El Salvador, or Nicaragua to communism, whether the Soviet Union has masterminded the local upheaval or has attempted to exploit it. In an attenuated form, the Monroe Doctrine still lives, and President Reagan will attempt to enforce it just as have his predecessors. For better or worse, there is continuity here, too.

Force Planning and Vietnam

George Santayana is probably best known for having written: "Those who cannot remember the past are condemned to repeat it." To emphasize the basic continuity beneath the ebb and flow of U.S. defense policy and force planning may seem to imply the architects of U.S. plans and forces have learned nothing from the last twenty-five years. The implication is not intended. There is, in particular, no escaping Vietnam. However desirable in many ways a return to selective service might be, most planners must know that, barring a dramatic deterioration of international relations or a large and sudden increase in the cost of the all-volunteer force, the war killed conscription and easy access to a large pool of cheap manpower. They must know, too, that despite the much-needed revival of a strong presidency, congressional oversight of foreign military involvement is likely to be more zealous than in the past as a result of Vietnam.

Yet to the extent that the planners remember the past as they rotate in and out of the Pentagon, they also will recognize that the future is always shrouded in uncertainty. Indeed the fog of peace may be even greater than the fog of war. It is true that there should be a close link between foreign and defense policy, that commitments should be tailored to capabilities or vice-versa, that the Defense Department should have a strategy. The fact, however, is that the United States has been and is likely to remain largely a reactive power in matters of defense, responding to the initiatives of others rather than setting clear-cut objectives and determining the forces and strategies needed to reach them with greater or lower risk.

Force planners cannot be certain what kind of contingency might arise, what kind or amount of force might be called for, or even where it might be deployed. True, the United States has a number of treaty commitments and some obligations, as to Israel, Saudi Arabia, and Thailand, that do not take the form of treaties. But there is no way in peacetime (or even in wartime, for that matter) that the nation would support the forces necessary to the simultaneous fulfillment of all those commitments and obligations. Nor is there any significant probability that the Soviet Union and its satellites could challenge all of them at any one time. Force planners, in these circumstances, must use something more restrictive than the standard list of commitments to limit the uncertainty and avoid planning for everything. Vietnam has little to teach about how to do that unless one assumes that a lesson of the war is that the United States can and should return to the tradition of the early Republic and try (perhaps no more successfully than then) to stay out of foreign quarrels. Not many Americans find that kind of isolation an acceptable condition of their security or the appropriate lesson to draw from Vietnam.

Another way to make force planning more manageable in the face of uncertainty is to impose a budget constraint on the Defense Department, and of course that is now done. It would be difficult to argue, however, that there is some number, independently of anything else, that is bound to be right. To recall that the United States spent 36 percent of the gross national product (GNP) on defense at the peak of World War II, as much as 9 percent during peacetime in the 1950s, and more than 8 percent as late as 1963 does not prove that any of these numbers is right or should be adopted. Such numbers simply are reminders that, if necessary, the United States can afford these percentages, as it has done in the past.

It has been argued that because the Soviet Union allocates to defense at least 14 percent of a GNP that is half the size of that of the United States, the latter should set its defense budget at 7 percent of the U.S. GNP. To do that, however, is to ignore the uncertainties about the Soviet numbers, the contributions of allies to the common defense, and the different security problems the two sides think they face. No one, it should be added, really believes the United States should try to duplicate the Soviet military machine, though its size and supposed cost frequently are used as the basis for comparing the relative strengths of the two superpowers and for denigrating U.S. capabilities.

What, then, are the alternatives? The best planners can probably do, considering the uncertainties and the inadequacies of these other methods and measures, is to continue refining the approach they have been using for twenty-five years or more. That approach entails defining specific nuclear and conventional contingencies, relating costs, forces, and performance (as best they can) to objectives, and offering not just a minimum-risk option but a range of possibilities to the secretary of defense and the president.

How much the experience of Vietnam can or should influence this approach is by no means clear. It probably has little or nothing to say about the size and composition of the nuclear forces. Despite the talk about leak-proof defenses, damage limiting, and prevailing, the most the planners are likely to accomplish in this blind alley is high confidence of ensuring that Soviet leaders cannot achieve any meaningful military advantage and leverage with these forces, whatever sets and sequences of targets they might consider attacking. However pedestrian it may sound, the maintenance of the existing stalemate and the relative stability that goes with it constitutes the vital but limited role of nuclear capabilities now and in the future.

Even where the conventional forces are concerned, force plans are likely to be and probably should be shaped by contingencies such as attacks on Central Europe, the oil states of the Persian Gulf, and possibly Korea, since they are the most testing commitments the United States would have to meet. Whether a specific counterinsurgency or special operations case should be included explicitly in force planning is an issue worth more consideration than it has received. In the past, the attitude has tended to be—to paraphrase General Curtis LeMay—that if you can lick the cat, you can lick the kitten. However, where special operations are concerned, there is now a considerable history of these endeavors and of the need for small but highly trained forces dedicated to the mission. It also can be argued, despite the continued insistence on no more Vietnams, that as long as the United States remains heavily involved with the developing countries, it remains prudent to anticipate operations if not on the scale of Vietnam, at least of the magnitude that are being conducted in Central America. However, to plan for such a contingency probably means additional equipment and training for forces acquired for other purposes rather than a large array of units oriented specifically to this purpose.

Whether these particular contingencies should be included in the basis for force planning, it should be evident that the approach itself virtually ensures a considerable degree of continuity in the size and composition of U.S. forces, even in the wake of an event as traumatic as the war in Vietnam. That is probably all to the good, provided that continuity does not simply become routine.

Inefficiencies

Despite the continuity, what remains disturbing is the growing inefficiency with which the planning process has been operating. Short of a prolonged international crisis, it probably would be desirable to have a relatively stable defense budget, one that grows on the average by about 3 percent a year in real terms from, as one example, the fiscal 1982 base. Such a rate of growth, quite similar to the one apparently adopted by the Soviet Union in the first decade of the Brezhnev regime, would preserve the current force structure and permit the upgrading of current weapons, their orderly replacement with more advanced systems, improved reserve forces, adequate strategic mobility, and high readiness and sustainability.

That is not what the United States has been doing. As the trends indicate, it has chosen instead to ride a defense roller coaster during the last fifteen years, with resources falling in real terms well below the prewar baseline, followed by a few years of grudging growth, a dramatic surge in funding during the last four years, and what now is the prospect of stagnation or, worse, a real decline in defense appropriations for the next five. By the end of the 1980s, it still may find itself about where it would have been had it followed a more stable funding policy. Because the process has worked so erratically, however, long-term planning of defense investment has proved extremely difficult. Partly as a consequence, it is highly questionable, especially during the last four years, whether the United States has received a very good return on its investment. Granted the problem of accurately measuring military effectiveness and changes in it, the evidence nonetheless suggests two disheartening conclusions. The first is that once the current cycle of modernization and expansion is completed in the early 1990s, the resulting force will turn out to have only a slightly better performance (admittedly against an improved enemy) from the one that existed in 1981. The second is that a somewhat different pattern of investment, even if instituted as late as fiscal 1986, could lower costs over the next five years by more than $190 billion and provide substantially greater effectiveness against the same enemy.

If these conclusions sound both controversial and presumptuous, a great deal of evidence exists to support them. There now is rather widespread agreement that the Pentagon has a management problem, brought on in part by the generous amounts of budget authority made available during the last four years. Most of the attention and efforts at reform, however, have focused on allegations of excessive overhead charges by contractors, overpriced parts, poor quality control, single-source procurement, and the accumulation of large amounts of unspent budget authority as a result of the decline in inflation and lower-than-anticipated price increases in a variety of defense goods and services. Little thought has been given to the investment choices made by the Defense Department.

It would be difficult to argue against higher standards for defense contractors, less creative accounting practices in the allocation of overhead costs, fewer cost-plus contracts, and more competition within the industry. It would be equally difficult to argue either that major reforms will come about easily and soon or that by themselves they will produce a significant near-term reduction in the cost of defense spending. In some areas, costs may rise as a consequence of instituting and policing these reforms.

This is not to say that the effort should be abandoned. It is to suggest, though, that the current inefficiencies in the acquisition process, however deplorable, are not the main cause of the poor return the United States is getting on its defense investments. Even if most of the waste, fraud, and abuse were suddenly to vanish, the bill would still be extremely high for the increased performance.

The reasons why this is the case are fairly obvious. To begin, the budgets of the last four years were front-end loaded in favor of procurement, in part no doubt to take advantage of what was correctly seen as the temporary openhandedness of the Congress. Because of the rush, choices consisted of running well down the priority lists of the individual services and funding programs that had been rejected in a period of greater scarcity and discrimination. The upshot has been an enormous amount of duplication in and among the three services, the initiation of expensive programs of marginal military utility, and the rejection of other less exciting and glamorous programs with high payoffs in effectiveness.

Nowhere is the kind of inefficiency more evident than in the investments being made in the strategic nuclear forces. To improve the hard-target-kill capability of the strategic offense, the United States currently is pushing ahead with two ICBMs (the vulnerable MX and Midgetman, likely to prove equally vulnerable), the D-5 Trident II submarine-launched ballistic missile (SLBM), advanced versions of the air-launched cruise missile (ALCM), and additional Mark-12A warheads for the Minuteman III ICBM. To penetrate Soviet air defenses once they are upgraded with competent look-down shoot-down capabilities, the United States once again has modernized the B-52H, acquired 100 B-1Bs as a replacement, continued deployment of the ALCM-B, launched the advanced cruise missile (ACM) program, and continued the rapid development of the stealth bomber. Although Congress has rejected large-scale funding of civil defense—still likely to be the most efficient way to save lives in the event of a nuclear exchange—it has embraced rapid increases in less efficient active defenses. The SDI is a special case in point, since it is already evident that the president's objectives for the program are quite unrealistic, considering the large cost advantage the offense has over the defense and that more realistic objectives could be achieved with about a third of the funds being proposed by the Defense Department for the next five years. As might be expected, amid all this high technology and funding opulence, the idea of a straightforward cruise missile carrier with long endurance and a large payload has no visible means of support.

Comparable inefficiencies abound in the conventional forces. The greatest nonnuclear needs are for more reserve training and equipment, additional close air support aircraft, a greatly expanded fleet of fast sealift ships, and close-in protection of at least nine large convoys a month. The army is sensitive to these needs, but it is responding to them by trying to squeeze two more active duty divisions out of a fixed pool of military personnel, buying the Bradley fighting vehicle (which is neither a light tank nor a particularly suitable armored personnel carrier), funding expensive and fragile attack helicopters as a substitute for fixed-wing close air support aircraft, and trying simultaneously to upgrade existing field army air defenses and deploy a new system (Patriot) that, at best, has a checkered history of research, development, test, and evaluation. The air force refuses to buy more of the close air support aircraft so vital to a forward defense during the first days of an attack and concentrates on air superiority and deep interdiction with the F-15 and F-16, although such a campaign would not affect the land battle during its most critical stage. The navy, finally granted its wish for a 600-ship fleet, gives no convincing justification for three more carrier battle groups, four surface action groups, or an additional brigade of amphibious lift—all involving very expensive ships—nor, whatever their purpose, does it demonstrate that they add effectiveness to existing forces at all commensurate with their cost.

Why this extraordinary and indiscriminate proliferation of weapons and equipment has been allowed to occur must remain a question for historians to answer authoritatively. It already seems evident, however, that the centralized planning and discipline that President Eisenhower began to impose with successive amendments to the National Security Act of 1947 has broken down. The secretary of defense and his staff continue to preside, at least formally, over the PPBS. But there is no evidence that they are willing to take initiatives, make hard choices among competing systems, cancel weapons with high costs and poor performance, or demand coordination and complementarity among the programs of the three services. The Joint Chiefs essentially add up the wishes of the services and present them as a minimum-risk force that no one has any intention of buying. Meanwhile, each of the services prepares once again to fight its own war either because it has so little confidence (as in the case of the army) that the other two will buy the capabilities to give it support or because it believes that horizontal escalation or deep air superiority and interdiction are the decisive missions and must therefore be funded to the exclusion of everything else. It is hardly surprising that the portfolio of investments looks considerably less than optimal.

Inefficiencies and Myths

What, if anything, has all of this to do with Vietnam? Perhaps nothing, but a connection does seem to exist. At least two important devil theories have emerged from the war. The first ascribes the U.S. involvement to the usual imperialistic motives and, more interesting, the alleged existence of the capabilities to intervene. It follows from these supposed relationships that the president should be constrained by such means as the War Powers Act and that the forces available to him as commander in chief should be small, poorly equipped, and kept on starvation rations. The second theory is less concerned with the motives for the U.S. involvement in Vietnam than with explaining why it did not "win" the war. One of the main culprits in this theory is the civilian strategists, with their propensity for such petty accounting methods as cost-effectiveness, for attrition instead of strategy (which usually means maneuver warfare and blitzkrieg), and for gradualism and limited war. Accordingly, not only must the military reclaim the bureaucratic turf they lost to the civilians in the battles of the early 1960s, they also must insist on clear-cut objectives and have the freedom to devise the strategies and acquire the weapons necessary to achieve these objectives.

Both theories have had influence. Neither, however, has much foundation in fact. It is not clear whether George Santayana had conspiracy theories and the search for scapegoats in mind when he wrote *The Crime of Galileo*. But he could not have been more contemporary than when he wrote, "The working of great institutions is mainly the result of a vast mass of routine, petty malice, self interest, carelessness, and sheer mistake. Only a residual fraction is thought."

It is understandable, laudable, and desirable to want to tame this process. It remains doubtful that the United States can do so by the means currently in vogue. A democracy, because of its reactive nature, is unlikely ever to define clear-cut objectives before becoming involved in a conflict. Certainly the United States did not do so before lurching into World War II, Korea, and Vietnam. Nor are U.S. policymakers likely to give their military commanders a free hand in the conduct of a future war. The uncertainties of risks created by the existence of nuclear weapons make it highly probable, regardless of those civilian strategists, that relatively cautious and experimental steps will, at least initially, be their strategy.

In the face of these and other uncertainties, it seems equally clear that the United States cannot continue to plan its military posture by a process of consensus in which only lax limits on resources constrain the constituents from going their separate ways. As Congress becomes increasingly skeptical about the return on recent and large investment in defense, resources are going to become increasingly scarce and demands for harder choices and greater complementarity among the services more plentiful. More and more, those demands can be expected to be accompanied not by a revival of unification (the panacea of the 1950s), not by still greater freedom of action for the three services, not by a stronger chairman of the Joint Chiefs of Staff backed by a general staff, but by insistence that the secretary of defense exercise the authority he already has to impose the necessary discipline on the process.

In these circumstances, the lesson of Vietnam is surely that the secretary of defense should be given more disinterested and professional support rather than that he should be resisted, circumvented, and ignored. Ideally, that support should come from a military staff well versed in the knowledge and skills of force planning. However, it is difficult to ask an officer, brought up in a service and obliged to return to it, to divorce himself from the assumed interests of that service and take the responsibility for recommendations that may be sharply at variance with those interests. Inevitably civilians who understand and are sympathetic to the broader interests of the secretary of defense, who are service blind and mission oriented, will be involved in assisting him with the difficult choices he must make.

The services undoubtedly will compete for missions and resources in the future as they have done in the past, and it is almost certainly the case that if they did not, the public would want them to. But in every market, there must be demand as well as supply, together with an ability to minimize the externalities of the competition. The services certainly are entitled to advertise their wares, as all suppliers do; they should not expect to control both sides of the marketplace. The secretary of defense must be able to express the demand, presumably in the form of expanded and more detailed defense guidance. He also must be expected to haggle over the programmatic responses of the services to that guidance. Equally important, he must be free to ignore traditional service boundaries and anticipated treaties about roles and missions in allocating resources and making sure that critical functions such as close air support and strategic mobility are funded adequately.

If there is a lesson from Vietnam about force planning, it is not that the United States should abandon the progress in planning made during the 1960s and renewed during the middle and late 1970s. Certainly it is not that the United States should revert to the anarchy of the 1950s or engage in renewed battles over who owns what turf. Surely it is that centralized planning remains essential and that military and civilian alike must learn to do it better. The need was recognized long ago in the field with the establishment of the unified and specified commands. The case for applying the same principle to the Pentagon is even stronger, if less palatable. But, as Mark Twain said of Wagner's music, it isn't as bad as it sounds.

12
The Legacy of Vietnam
for the U.S. Military

William J. Taylor, Jr.
David H. Petraeus

Vietnam cost the military services dearly. It left military leaders confounded, dismayed, and discouraged. It devastated the armed forces, robbing them of dignity, money, and qualified people for a decade.[1] The army and the marine corps paid particularly high prices. They bore the brunt of what was essentially a ground war and together suffered over 75 percent of the 350,000 U.S. casualties.[2] Although the psychic scars of the war may be deepest among the army and marine corps leadership, the senior leaders of all the services share a similar reaction to Vietnam. There is no desire among any of them to repeat the experience that provided the material for books with such descriptive titles as: *Defeated: Inside America's Military Machine; Self-Destruction: The Disintegration and Decay of the United States Army During the Vietnam Era;* and *Crisis in Command: Mismanagement in the United States Army.*[3] "No More Vietnams" sentiment runs deep in the military, and discussion within the military over when and how to commit U.S. forces abroad has become largely a debate over how to avoid another Vietnam. That sentiment, the legacy of Vietnam for the U.S. military, is the subject of this chapter.[4]

Lessons of Vietnam

In 1968, Samuel Huntington cautioned the participants in a conference on Vietnam, "It is conceivable that our policymakers may best meet future crises and dilemmas if they simply blot out of their minds any recollection of Vietnam."[5] But for a generation or more of U.S. military leaders, especially those in the army and marine corps, that is impossible. The painful experience of Vietnam is indelibly etched in their minds, and from it they have taken three general lessons that influence their advice on the use of force: they have become sensitive to the finite limits of public support for protracted military operations; they have developed a nagging doubt about the efficacy of U.S. military force in solving certain international problems; and they have carried from Vietnam a certain disillusionment with, and greater wariness of, politicians.

Public Support: The Essential Domino

Vietnam showed the military that there are finite limits on how long the public will support a protracted conflict, at least a conflict that is not viewed as a crusade. This was, of course, not a completely new revelation. The Korean War had revealed this scarcely a decade earlier. In fact, it had long been recognized that democracies, the United States in particular, are ill suited for long, drawn-out conflicts. Alexis de Tocqueville observed in the early nineteenth century, for example, that democracies are better suited for "a sudden effort of remarkable vigor, than for the prolonged endurance of the great storms that beset the political existence of nations." A democracy, he wrote,

> can only with great difficulty regulate the details of an important undertaking, persevere in a fixed design, and work out its execution in spite of serious obstacles. It cannot combine its measures with secrecy or await their consequences with patience.[6]

Vietnam validated de Tocqueville's observations in an unprecedented way, and the ability of television to convey the graphic detail of combat to the public gave his cautions even more credence. Leslie Gelb has called public opinion the "essential domino."[7] Vietnam brought home to the military that when it comes to intervention, time and patience are not American virtues in abundant supply. In television, not just the military but all government leaders found a new challenge: how to deal with "a medium that transmits simple surface impressions, while national policy issues are infinitely complex and many-sided."[8]

Post-Vietnam developments have reinforced the recognition of the importance of public support and its limits. The military are keenly aware of the ambiguities of the public's desire for what could be termed cost-free omnipotence. The title of an article by John Reilly in the spring 1979 issue of *Foreign Policy* captured the popular sentiment: "The American Mood: A Foreign Policy of Self-Interest." As Reilly reported, the public favored increased defense spending and more vigorous assertion of U.S. economic and political positions abroad. He noted, however, that a majority of Americans also were "wary of the kind of involvement in the affairs of other countries that characterized U.S. foreign policy in the 1960s."[9] In short, "We should defeat our enemies and impose our will," but "we should not pay any substantial price for it."[10] The eventual impatience with the 1983 marine peacekeeping mission in Lebanon and opinion polls on such hypothetical cases as commitment of troops in Central America remind U.S. military leaders that, as much as the public may miss the prestige and benefits of world preeminence, they remain "reluctant to shoulder the burdens or accept the risks" of U.S. intervention.[11]

The Limits of U.S. Military Power

A second lesson the military have taken from Vietnam is a greater recognition of the limits of U.S. military power in solving certain problems in world affairs. There are lurking suspicions, particularly about the ability of the U.S. military to conduct successful large-scale counterinsurgencies.[12] This should not be overemphasized, however, and should be taken in the context of heightened sensitivity to the limits of public support as well as uncertainty about U.S. politicians.

Quincy Wright once charged the "military mind" with "overconfidence in the military methods as applicable to the solution of all problems."[13] If that overconfidence was ever universal—an arguable assertion—it was certainly shaken by Vietnam. The U.S. experience of having won all the battles but having lost the war, whatever the mitigating circumstances, created among the military a new skepticism about the efficacy of U.S. forces in the third world countries where social, political, and economic factors are the cause of unrest. The feeling has been particularly visible in the public statements of U.S. military leaders about possible introduction of troops into Central America. Shortly before his retirement in 1983, the army chief of staff, General E.C. Meyer, noted that "the problems in Central America are so tied to economic and political conditions, and their solutions are so dependent on local leaders that I wouldn't even know how to design a military solution."[14] General Meyer's sentiments were echoed by General John Vessey, chairman of the Joint Chiefs of Staff, when he stated in 1983: "Neither I, nor any member of the Joint Chiefs of Staff, nor the civilian leaders in the Department of Defense advocate introducing U.S. combat forces to try to implement an American military solution to the problems in Central America."[15]

Of course, many senior officers believe that Vietnam was less an illustration of the limitations of U.S. military power than an example of what happens if that power is limited and not used to best advantage.[16] This feeling springs from a conviction that the U.S. military were so hemmed in by restrictions that they could not accomplish their mission. The lesson for those of this persuasion is that the U.S. military must be given a freer hand in future military operations. Even among them, however, there is a new recognition of the increasing intractability of the rest of the world to U.S. intervention. Even those who remain confident that the United States could win a protracted small war if allowed to acknowledge what General Maxwell Taylor has described as the "great difficulty in rallying this country behind a foreign issue involving the use of armed force, which does not provide an identified enemy posing a clear threat to our homeland or the vital interests of long time friends."[17]

The many seemingly endless struggles around the world reinforce the heightened awareness of the many ambiguities and difficulties associated with so-called low-intensity conflict and serve as reminders of the problems large nations have in fighting small wars.[18] Some of these conflicts, not to mention the marine peacekeeping mission in Lebanon, also illustrate the high costs of operations against guerrillas and terrorists armed with sophisticated weapons. And while watching the Soviet difficulties in Afghanistan with a certain sense of vindication, the U.S. military are at the same time reminded of the difficulties of defeating a determined guerrilla opponent who enjoys sanctuaries in neighboring countries and is fighting in rugged terrain. If a country with relatively few public opinion problems and no moral compunctions about its tactics cannot beat a bunch of ill-equipped Afghan tribesmen, what does that say about the ability of the United States—with its domestic constraints, statutory limitations, and zealous investigative reporters—to carry out a successful action against a guerrilla force?

The Military View of Politicians

The military have traditionally regarded their politicians and political appointees with some apprehension. Vietnam heightened this feeling, leaving senior U.S. military leaders with a more deeply seated suspicion of their civilian leaders. Admittedly this generalization has lost some of its validity in recent years. There appears to be, for example, excellent rapport between the Joint Chiefs of Staff and the current secretary of defense. A poll by *Newsweek* found that 97 percent of U.S. generals and admirals have a "favorable opinion" of President Reagan.[19] Nonetheless, although the military still emphatically accept the constitutional provision for civilian control of the armed forces, there remains from Vietnam a certain doubt about the abilities and motivations of politicians.[20]

Vietnam was a painful reminder for the military that they, not the transient occupants of high office, generally bear the heaviest burden of military conflict. Vietnam gave new impetus to Samuel Huntington's description of what he termed the military's "pacifist attitude": "The military man tends to see himself as the perennial victim of civilian warmongering. It is the people and the politicians, public opinion and governments, who start wars. It is the military who must fight them."[21] As retired General William A. Knowlton reminded the Army War College class of 1985: "Remember one lesson from the Vietnam era: Those who ordered the meal were not there when the waiter brought the check."[22]

Events during the Vietnam era soured civil-military relations.[23] Distrust and animosity developed on both sides. Too many of the military's civilian masters never made a sincere effort to cultivate an effective relationship with the military. Situations were frequently mishandled, with grave repercussions. David Halberstam's report of President Johnson's instructions to Army Chief of Staff General Harold K. Johnson before the latter's important trip to Vietnam in 1965 is revealing:

> General Johnson was sent to Vietnam specifically by Lyndon Johnson, who had given him a real dressing-down. The President had let loose, right in front of members of the general's staff. All he heard from his generals, the President said, was "Bomb, bomb, bomb. That's all you know. Well, I want to know why there's nothing else. You generals have all been educated at the taxpayers' expense, and you're not giving me any ideas and any solutions for this damn little piss-ant country. Now, I don't need ten generals to come in here ten times and tell me to bomb. I want some solutions. I want some answers."[24]

Not surprisingly, President Johnson got some answers. During his visit to Vietnam, General Johnson, according to Halberstam "a man who had many doubts about another land war in Asia," was persuaded by General Westmoreland to recommend the commitment of an army division to Vietnam.[25]

In another instance, President Johnson, never known for his reticence, sent General Westmoreland back to Vietnam in 1966 with a warning unlikely to foster mutual trust and confidence between a president and his senior commander in the field: "General, I have a lot riding on you . . . I hope you don't pull a MacArthur on me."[26] In February 1968, at the height of the Tet offensive, President Johnson extracted from each of the service chiefs a signed statement that the U.S. base at Khe Sanh would not fall to the enemy.[27] Such actions served little more than to poison the relationship between the president and his senior military advisers.

Civil-military relations within the Pentagon during Vietnam were not much better. The military had traditionally viewed military policy and operations as their institutional property. The invasion of their domain in the early 1960s by what many perceived as misguided amateurs and transient meddlers was resisted. As the decade went on, the military became increasingly frustrated by Secretary of Defense McNamara's "obsession with getting control of the defense budget" and by the micro-management of the war effort in general.[28]

The military leadership emerged from the Vietnam era with three general feelings: that their civilian leadership had not understood the conduct of military operations, had lacked the fortitude to see things through, and frequently had different perceptions of what was important (not to imply that the military necessarily had a monopoly on knowledge of what was really important). There was from the beginning of the McNamara era a belief that the civilians in the Pentagon did not understand the complexities and difficulties of military operations. General Thomas White, a former chief of staff of the air force, wrote in 1963: "In common with many other military men, active and retired, I am profoundly apprehensive of the pipe-smoking, tree-full-of-owls type of so-called professional 'defense intellectuals' who have been brought into this nation's capitol."[29]

Many of the military's senior leaders felt they had to fight the war in Vietnam under too many restrictions, in effect, with one hand tied behind their backs. Retired Marine Lieutenant General Victor Krulak recently wrote, for example, "57,900 Americans died in the Vietnam War. A fair case can be made that the number of dead would have been fewer and the result more favorable had we fought the war the way our military leadership wanted."[30]

Two key commanders during the war, General Westmoreland and Admiral U.S.G. Sharp, have repeatedly criticized President Johnson for pursuing a piecemeal, gradualist approach to the war.[31] Westmoreland has also charged that U.S. political leaders failed to understand the nature of the challenge in Vietnam.[32] Retired Rear Admiral Henry Eccles has argued that the civilian micromanagement of the war during the Johnson years minimized the effectiveness of operations and maximized their cost to U.S. troops.[33] Railing at what was perceived as civilian overcontrol, one anonymous general expressed his disgruntlement in the following verse:

> I am not allowed to run the train
> The whistle I can't blow.
> I am not allowed to say how fast
> The railroad trains can go.
> I am not allowed to shoot off steam
> Nor even clang the bell
> But let it jump the goddam tracks
> and see who catches hell![34]

The military also took from the war a certain doubt about whether politicians and appointees could "stick it out" over the long haul in the future. While serving as secretary of state, retired General Alexander Haig "sensed, and understood, a doubt on the part of the military in the political will of the civilians at the top to follow through to the end" of a major military commitment.[35] The failure of the Johnson administration to make the tough decisions and ask Congress for a declaration of war and mobilization has often been criticized by the military.[36] As one retired naval officer put it, "the buck failed to stop at the oval office, . . . no one was willing to take the necessary responsibility"; as a result, "America never really made a commitment on behalf of the Vietnam effort."[37] According to retired Air Force General T.R. Milton, "The U.S. military did not lose that war . . . it might have been won, and won long ago if only there had not been such political inhibition."[38]

That belief is by no means universally held by today's military leaders or even by those who led the services during Vietnam, but it remains, however arguable, a powerful influence on the military's perception of politicians.

In the minds of many military leaders, the strategy of graduated application of air power during Vietnam reflected both the politicians' lack of appreciation for military strategy and a desire to put off tough decisions. "Gradualism," wrote the chairman of the Joint Chiefs, Admiral Thomas Moorer, "forced airpower into an expanded and inconclusive war of attrition."[39] The military judgment of the graduated response policy was summed up by one senior air force officer who said: "We taught the bastards to cope."[40] General Haig later observed:

> If it is easier to escalate step by small step, it is easier for an adversary to respond to each step with a response that is strong enough to compel yet another escalation on our part. . . . If an objective is worth pursuing, then it must be pursued with enough resources to force the issue early.[41]

Finally, Vietnam increased the ever-present tensions between the military and political appointees by leaving each feeling the other was marching to a different drummer. During the war and its aftermath, the military developed a perception that many political appointees were more concerned about their own careers, their own administrations, or their own parties than about the good of the country. The military were increasingly frustrated by the short-term horizon that political appointees of limited tenure seemed to place on many issues. Such frustrations are inevitable and present even in the best of times; Vietnam exacerbated these tensions.[42] "If you happen to work for civilian political appointees," one retired four-star general cautioned a war college audience, "you will probably find that such individuals have different imperatives and a different frame of reference than you."[43] Such feelings also seem to have inspired General E.C. Meyer, then army chief of staff, to remark that the military's "focus must be on a sensible posture over time, as opposed to the 'today' orientation of the politician."[44]

Since Vietnam, the military have become increasingly suspicious of civilian leaders who see military action as a means of finessing a debilitating political situation at home—leaders who exhibit what Miles Kahler has termed the "*Mayaguez* syndrome"—a compulsion to do something to rally the nation's self-image.[45] Beyond that, Kattenburg has observed, the military seem especially concerned over being saddled with another situation where the real objective may be to keep successive presidents from being "tarred domestically with the brush of having lost another round to Communism."[46]

In sum, Vietnam left U.S. military leaders with a new realization of the limits of public support for protracted military operations, doubts about the efficacy of U.S. military power in certain international situations, and more than the usual amount of suspicion of civilian policymakers. The result is a military leadership that is apprehensive about commitment of troops to another unpopular and difficult conflict, being limited in their ability to fight that conflict, and then being left holding the bag long after the politicians have left office.

Effects of the Vietnam Legacy

The lessons today's military leaders took from Vietnam have had a chastening effect on military thinking. A more hardheaded attitude is brought to the analysis of possible future missions. "We've thrown over the old can-do idea," a colonel of Fort Hood, Texas, told Drew Middleton. "Now we want to know exactly what they want us to do and how they think we can accomplish it."[47] The military tend to agree with General Westmoreland, who has continually stressed that henceforth the United States should not engage in war unless it has a clear idea why it is fighting and is prepared to see the war through to a successful conclusion.[48]

The experience of Vietnam has left military leaders more inclined to the all-or-nothing type of advice that characterized the military position during the Eisenhower administration's debate over Dien Bien Phu in 1954 and the Kennedy administration's deliberations over intervention in Laos in 1961.[49] There is a feeling that when it comes to the use of force, the United States should either bite the bullet or duck but not nibble.[50] The U.S. interventions in the Dominican Republic in 1965 and Grenada in 1983 have come to be viewed as model cases. In each, the United States intervened in strength, accomplished its objectives rapidly, and withdrew as soon as conditions allowed.[51] With the public, the military realize, nothing succeeds like success.

Since Vietnam, the military have sought to avoid what General Meyer termed the Vietnam mistake of "putting soldiers out at the end of a string" without the full support of the U.S. people.[52] They have consistently held that force must be committed only when there is "a consensus of understanding among our people that the effort is in our best interests."[53] The public must be made aware of the costs up front. As the army chief of staff, General Frederick Weyand, urged in 1976, "The Army must make the price of involvement clear before we get involved so that America can weigh the probable costs of involvement against the danger of non-involvement."[54] There is also a conviction that "Congress should declare war whenever large numbers of U.S. troops engage in sustained combat" and that the American people must be mobilized because "a nation cannot fight in cold blood."[55] Since time is crucial, sufficient force must be used at the outset—within reason—to ensure that the conflict can be resolved before the public withdraw their support for it. In future wars, cautions Army Chief of Staff General John A. Wickham, Jr., "once we commit force, we must be prepared to back it up and win as opposed to just sending soldiers into operations for limited goals."[56]

The military have also sought to avoid being involved in difficult and ambiguous situations similar to Vietnam. A number of senior military leaders have made known their opposition to committing U.S. forces to Central America "unless the American public supports it and commanders are given a freer hand in waging war than they had in Vietnam."[57]

Finally, there is a conviction that political leaders must define objectives before putting soldiers at risk. In a 1983 speech, General John Vessey, chairman of the Joint Chiefs of Staff, said: "Don't send military forces off to do anything unless you know what it is clearly that you want done. I am absolutely, unalterably opposed to risking American lives for some phony sort of military and political objectives that we don't understand."[58]

In short, the current generation of military leaders has generally been cautious about the use of force. They more nearly conform to the characterization of the military postulated by Samuel Huntington in the 1950s than at any other time in the post–World War II period.[59] "The military man rarely favors war," wrote Huntington:

> He will always argue that the danger of war requires increased armaments; he will seldom argue that increased armaments make war practical or desirable. He always favors preparedness, but he never feels prepared. Accordingly, the professional military man contributes a cautious, conservative, restraining voice to the formulation of state policy.[60]

Military Advice and the Post–Vietnam Use of Force: The Case of Central America

Analyses of military advice in post-Vietnam cases where the use of U.S. military force was considered reveal the chastening effect of the Vietnam legacy. The popular images of U.S. military leaders as "cigar-chomping, balls-to-the-wall warmongers" or as a phalanx of aggressive and activist leaders poised against the country's civilian leadership could not be further from the truth.[61] During incidents in which presidents have considered committing U.S. forces to combat since 1973, the military have rarely been as aggressive as the presidents' principal civilian advisers, and never more aggressive.[62] The military's advice on how to respond to the ongoing problems in Central America in particular illustrates the impact of the Vietnam legacy, as well as some of the difficulties posed by the lessons derived from that legacy.

With few exceptions, the military's feeling about U.S. involvement in Central America can be summed up by the titles of op-ed pieces in the March 11, 1983, *Washington Post,* where Stephen Rosenfield's "El Salvador Isn't Vietnam . . ." was accompanied by Philip Geyelin's ". . . But There Is a Chilling Resemblance."[63]

Since the Reagan administration took office in 1981, there has been disagreement among the president's advisers over U.S. policy toward Central America, particularly with regard to El Salvador and Nicaragua. In the early days of the administration, Secretary of State Haig urged the president to make a stand in Central America. Haig argued that the way to avoid another Vietnam was to pursue U.S. objectives "with enough resources to force the issue early," to avoid the incrementalism of commitment. Haig favored "giving military and economic aid to El Salvador while bringing the overwhelming economic and political influence of the United States, together with the reality of its military power, to bear on Cuba in order to treat the problem at its source."[64]

Arrayed against Haig, although for varying reasons, were the president's key advisers in the White House, Defense Secretary Weinberger, and the military. Haig later wrote about the military:

> The Joint Chiefs of Staff, chastened by Vietnam, in which our troops performed with admirable success but were declared to have been defeated, and by the steady decline of respect for the military—and the decline of military budgets—resisted a major commitment in Central America.[65]

Haig also sensed military doubts about the political will to follow through to the end of such a commitment.

As the gravity of events in Central America increased, the military and Secretary Weinberger reluctantly sent U.S. military trainers to El Salvador and supported administration calls for emergency aid to El Salvador.[66] The military repeatedly affirmed their opposition to the use of U.S. combat troops in Central America.[67] General Vessey and a number of other senior officers stated publicly that they did not advocate trying to implement a U.S. military solution to the problems in Central America.[68]

While seeing danger in any victory for leftist elements in El Salvador or in the expansion of Nicaraguan military power in the region, U.S. military leaders in 1983 did "not see the Central American situation as a peculiarly military one." Rather they stressed that the region's problems were "economic, political, social, and military." In some countries, they saw the military problem as the least important. In others, such as El Salvador, they saw it as "reflecting underlying economic and social strains."[69] As Drew Middleton reported in June 1983, U.S. senior military leaders believed:

> In such situations wholehearted support of the local populations for United States intervention would be questionable. . . . The appearance of even one American brigade in El Salvador would push the peasants toward the leftist insurgents, who would call the arrival of the troops another example of "Yankee imperialism." . . . Any military intervention should be considered only after the Administration has identified the political goals and stated the

military objectives. At the same time, the public must understand the cost to the country in military manpower, money, and time.[70]

By August 1983, the key advocates of a U.S. hard line (defined as increased covert aid and large-scale military exercises in the region) in Central America were Assistant to the President for National Security Affairs (APNSA) William Clark, White House chief of staff James Baker, Under Secretary of Defense Fred Iklé, and the president himself, who was reportedly determined "not to lose El Salvador on his watch."[71] Secretary of State Shultz was emphasizing diplomatic solutions for the problems of the region, and the Pentagon's main concern appeared to be to prevent involvement of U.S. combat troops.[72]

A new military actor appeared about that time, General Paul Gorman, the new commander of the U.S. Southern Command, based in Panama and responsible for all U.S. military activities in Latin America. General Gorman first gained attention when he briefed administration officials on construction of a network of permanent bases in Honduras for use by U.S. forces in an emergency, stressing the long-term potential of such bases.[73] His proposal was supported by the new army chief of staff, General John Wickham, who added, however, that he did not "see the potential for widening involvement of the U.S. military" in Central America.[74]

General Gorman quickly emerged as a major figure in the debates over U.S. policy in Central America, not just in the military but in the political sphere as well. As the *Washington Post's* Leo Jenkins noted: "In a region where the military rules or is likely to be the power behind the presidency, a U.S. general who dispenses arms and commands military advisors often wields authority with governments." Gorman had begun to appear to many as Washington's "virtual proconsul" to the area, "frequently overshadowing senior diplomats and at times overruling them."[75] When Gorman replaced his predecessor, Lieutenant General Wallace Nutting, Jenkins explained, he brought not only an extra general's star to the newly upgraded command but also

increased access to the Administration, and the ear of many of the President's closest advisors, some of whom felt Central American policy was suffering from an excess of political and diplomatic—rather than military —emphasis. . . . Gorman is said . . . to take the military view that force must be met with counterforce if U.S. strategic interests are to be protected in Central America. But like many U.S. military officers who have analyzed the costs and implications of a direct U.S. military intervention in the region, he is said to favor using Central American military force rather than that of the U.S. whenever a counterweight is mustered. Gorman's position is that the way to win in Central America is to upgrade the region's own military through training, military assistance, and increased regional military coordination and cooperation.[76]

Jenkins's observation points out an important distinction in the thinking of the military on Central America. The military are in favor of training and arming the forces of friendly governments in the region (keeping in mind that each country in the region must be addressed individually).[77] They generally favor building bases in countries like Honduras and preparing for any eventuality.[78] At least some feel that the United States should join with the Organization of American States in support of any country overtly invaded by Nicaragua, although if so, "the heart and soul of Nicaragua must be put at risk" and there must be no sanctuaries permitted as in Vietnam.[79] But the military seem to draw the line at any other introduction of U.S. combat forces. There was one report in 1983 that the Joint Chiefs of Staff even "resisted drawing up contingency plans for sending U.S. troops to fight in Central America, partly for fear that civilian leaders in a crisis atmosphere would order the plans implemented before they are assessed adequately."[80] In short, the military seem to want continued U.S. influence in the region without the liabilities of U.S. troops in active fighting.

Thus there is an important distinction between willingness to train and build up the military forces of other countries (or even those of the United States) and willingness to commit U.S. troops to combat. That distinction is sometimes glossed over, as it was in an April 1984 *New York Times* article by Hedrick Smith: "The Pentagon is now in a position to assume a combat role in Central America should President Reagan give the order." Smith described General Gorman as a "hard-charging, vocal anti-Communist" intent on expanding the U.S. military role in Central America.[81] Although there may have been substance to such judgments, the tone of Smith's report resounded with stereotypes of the military. It ignored the military's desire to keep U.S. soldiers out of combat in Latin America. In fact, the three generals he noted as "important advocates of the buildup" had publicly stated what the *Washington Post*'s George Wilson described as "opposition to committing U.S. forces to the region unless the American public supports it and commanders are given a freer hand in waging war than they had in Vietnam."[82]

Testimony by General Gorman in August 1984 before a House subcommittee seemed to indicate that the military's views have not changed. Gorman said he "could foresee no circumstances when it would be useful" to commit U.S. troops to combat in El Salvador. He stated that it would be a mistake for the United States to use combat forces in El Salvador even if the Salvadoran government appeared to be in danger of being overthrown by guerrillas. The arrival of U.S. forces, he said, would likely

> transform the conflict from an indigenous struggle into a very different kind of fighting in which nationalism might cut against the United States. . . . We carry a very historic burden in that region and for the United States to send troops to fight could very well precipitate the kind of events we are trying to foreclose.[83]

General Gorman's views were echoed more recently by General Nutting, Gorman's predecessor in Latin America, shortly before his retirement. Nutting said he is strongly opposed to a U.S. invasion of Nicaragua and described talk about invading Nicaragua as "counterproductive to the long-term coalition we ought to be building in the hemisphere." An invasion of Nicaragua, he said, would jeopardize relations between North America and Latin America; "the less visible we are militarily, the better it will be."[84]

It is difficult to gain the proper perspective on an ongoing internal debate over such a divisive issue as U.S. policy toward Central America. It does seem clear, however, that the military are wary of committing U.S. troops to Central America and that the desire to avoid another Vietnam contributes in some measure to that wariness.

Duration of the Vietnam Legacy

How long the legacy of Vietnam remains an important influence on U.S. military leaders will depend on a number of interrelated factors, among them the general feeling of the public toward the use of military force; the foreign policy goals of presidential administrations; relations between the senior military and civilian policymakers; the world situation; foreign and U.S. experience in the use of military force; selection of senior military leaders; developments in the capabilities of U.S. forces; and the degree to which the Vietnam legacy is institutionalized.

Ultimately, however, the longevity of the Vietnam legacy's influence will depend on the forthcoming generations of military leaders, the lessons they drew from Vietnam, the impact on them of the factors just noted, and their resolution of the ambiguities embodied in the lessons of Vietnam.

It is difficult to determine what the next generation of military leaders holds as the lessons of Vietnam. There seems to be, in fact, a certain amount of intellectual wrestling underway among those officers waiting in the wings for leadership roles over issues raised by Vietnam.

One major topic of debate centers on whether the U.S. military should be used abroad in counterinsurgency operations, and if so, what U.S. forces should do, what tactics they should employ, and how they should be structured.[85] This debate and others seem to be fueling a growing consensus among younger officers that in addition to all the other flaws in the U.S. approach to Vietnam, maybe the military's approach was flawed as well; perhaps U.S. military doctrine, tactics, and personnel practices could have been better. Furthermore, there seems to be a widespread feeling that U.S. military leaders should have been more vigorous in advising the civilian leadership during the war. If political leaders had it so wrong, the question goes, why didn't some generals and admirals quit? Colonel Andrew O'Meara, Jr., expressed these doubts:

The President does not stand alone in bearing the burden of responsibility for past failure. Where were the military advisors who understood the limitations of our conscript Army? Our national defense colleges have taught for years that national purpose is the foundation of national strategy, which in turn sets political objectives, which ultimately shape strategic military plans. Yet we fought a war with a democratic Army, with inadequate popular support, and without clearly defined political objectives. Where were the military advisors to the President? Did they have access to the President? Was their advice offered? Why were the fundamentals cast aside?[86]

The direction the ongoing debates will take is difficult to determine, and, as if that would not be enough to complicate the situation, there will also be considerable importance in how the next generation of military leaders reacts to the ambiguities that reside in the lessons of Vietnam as currently structured. On the basis of the Vietnam experience, most military leaders have concluded that the United States should not intervene in any kind of local war unless there is support at home, clear objectives have been established, success (defined in terms of those objectives) appears achievable within a reasonable amount of time, and U.S. commanders will be allowed to do what is necessary to achieve that success. The difficulty with such guidelines is, as Robert Osgood has pointed out, that "acting upon them presupposes advance knowledge about a complicated interaction of military and political factors that no one can predict or guarantee."[87] The normal response to this kind of uncertainty is, and has been, caution and restraint. That rests uneasily, however, with another lesson of Vietnam: that if the United States plans to intervene, it should do so quickly in order to arrive in force while the "patient" still has strong vital signs. In other words, the country that hesitates may miss the opportune moment for effective action. How the next generation of military leaders approaches that practical dilemma, one that may be impossible to resolve, will be a crucial determinant of their view on the use of force.

In short, many complex interactions will determine how long the Vietnam experience will pervade military thinking. It does seem safe to predict that the legacy of Vietnam will continue to influence the military in the near term, but how much longer it will remain the dominant paradigm in military thinking is difficult to forecast. Major Andrew Bacevich, writing in 1982 about the pacification effort in the Philippines at the turn of the century, noted, "Our . . . penchant for forgetting nasty tropical wars is well known."[88] There is much to his judgment; there have been, for example, few in-depth military analyses of Vietnam.[89] Still, the legacy of Vietnam has informed military thought for over a decade, and one can anticipate that it will continue to lurk in the depths of the military's consciousness throughout the 1980s at least.

Notes

1. These judgments are found in Bruce Palmer, *The 25-Year War* (Lexington: University Press of Kentucky, 1984), p. 204; and Walter Mossberg, "The Army Resists a Salvadoran Vietnam," *Wall Street Journal,* June 24, 1983, p. 22.

2. *Department of the Army Historical Summary* (Washington, D.C.: U.S. Army Center of Military History, 1977), p. 4.

3. Stuart Loory, *Defeated: Inside America's Military Machine* (New York: Random House, 1973); Cincinnatus, *Self-Destruction: The Disintegration and Decay of the United States Army during the Vietnam Era* (New York: W.W. Norton, 1981). Although purportedly a senior field-grade officer assigned to the Pentagon, Cincinnatus turned out to be Cecil B. Currey, a history professor at the University of South Florida and a National Guard chaplain; and Richard A. Gabriel and Paul Savage, *Crisis in Command: Mismanagement in the Army* (New York: Hill and Wang, 1978).

4. We will refrain from offering our opinions on the validity of these lessons; such opinions are irrelevant to the purposes of this chapter. What is important is the Vietnam era experience of today's military leaders, the lessons they took from that experience, and whether the next generation of military officers will be influenced by the legacy of Vietnam when they assume the mantle of leadership.

5. Samuel Huntington, quoted in *No More Vietnams?* ed. Richard M. Pfeffer (New York: Harper & Row, 1968), p. 2.

6. Alexis de Tocqueville, *Democracy in America* (New York: Vintage Books, 1945; Henry Reeve text), pp. 237, 243. See also Amos A. Jordan and William J. Taylor, Jr., *American National Security,* rev. ed. (Baltimore: Johns Hopkins University Press, 1984), pp. 42–57; and Robert E. Osgood, *Ideals and Self-Interest in America's Foreign Relations* (Chicago: University Press of Chicago, 1953), esp. pp. 429–452.

7. Leslie H. Gelb, "The Essential Domino: American Politics and Vietnam," *Foreign Affairs* 50, no. 3 (April 1976): 466.

8. Lloyd N. Cutler, "Foreign Policy on Deadline," *Foreign Policy,* no. 56 (Fall 1984): 113–128.

9. John E. Reilly, "The American Mood: A Foreign Policy of Self Interest," *Foreign Policy,* no. 34 (Spring 1979): 74. For an early post-Vietnam military prediction of the attitude of American society toward the military in 1980, see Richard F. Rosser, "The Descending Spiral of Amilitarism," *Air Force Magazine* 55, no. 6 (June 1972): 64–69.

10. I.M. Destler, Leslie H. Gelb, and Anthony Lake, *Our Own Worst Enemy* (New York: Simon and Schuster, 1984), p. 79.

11. George C. Herring, *America's Longest War* (New York: John Wiley, 1979), p. 267.

12. A superb discussion of the ability of the U.S. Army to cope effectively with future wars of insurgency is contained in Andrew Krepinevich, Jr., "The Army Concept and Vietnam: A Case Study in Organizational Failure" (Ph.D. diss., Harvard University, 1983), esp. pp. 690–709. See also Richard E.K. Brown, "FM 100-5 and Low-Intensity Conflict," *Military Review* 65, no. 3 (March 1985): 72; and Rick Maze, "Military May Lack Ability to Fight Most Probable War, Group Says," *Army Times,* June 10, 1985, p. 28.

13. Quincy Wright, "The Military and Foreign Policy," in *Civil-Military Relationships in American Life* ed. Jerome G. Kerwin (Chicago: University of Chicago Press, 1948), p. 116.

14. General E.C. Meyer, quoted by Walter Mossberg, "The Army Resists a Salvadoran Vietnam," *Wall Street Journal,* June 24, 1983, p. 22. See also Richard Halloran, "General Opposes Nicaragua Attack," *New York Times,* June 30, 1985, p. A-3.

15. "Pentagon Is Opposed to Use of Troops in Central America," *New York Times,* June 5, 1983, p. A-5. This same point has been made by a number of other military leaders. See, for example, Drew Middleton, "U.S. Generals Are Leery of Latin Intervention," *New York Times,* June 21, 1983, p. A-9; George C. Wilson, "Top U.S. Brass Wary on Central America," *Washington Post,* June 24, 1983, p. A-20; Mossberg, "Army Resists a Salvadoran Vietnam"; and Richard Halloran, "General Opposes Nicaragua Attack," *New York Times,* June 30, 1985, p. A-3.

16. Indeed, almost all military officers seem to hold this view to some degree.

17. Maxwell D. Taylor, "Post-Vietnam Role of the Military in Foreign Policy," in *Contemporary American Foreign and Military Policy,* ed. Burton M. Sapin (Glenview, Ill.: Scott Foresman, 1970), pp. 36–43.

18. For a discussion of the concept of low-intensity conflict as used here, see Jordan and Taylor, *American National Security,* pp. 270–293. For an excellent discussion of the problems of large nations in fighting small wars, see Andrew Mack, "Why Big Nations Lose Small Wars: The Politics of Asymmetric Conflict," in *Power, Strategy, and Security,* ed. Klaus Knorr (Princeton: Princeton University Press, 1983), pp. 126–151.

19. The sample for the *Newsweek* poll included more than one out of every four active flag-rank officers stationed in the United States. See "A Newsweek Poll: The Military Mind," *Newsweek,* July 9, 1984, p. 37.

20. Despite these doubts, it is important to recognize that even in the immediate post-Vietnam period, there was always overwhelming support among officers for the principle of civilian control. See, for example, John H. Moellering, "The Army Turns Inward," *Military Review* 53, no. 7 (July 1973): 80; and Franklin D. Margiotta, "A Military Elite in Transition: Air Force Leaders in the 1980s," *Armed Forces and Society* 2, no. 2 (Winter 1976): 173.

21. Samuel P. Huntington, *The Soldier and the State* (Cambridge: Belknap Press of Harvard University Press, 1964), pp. 69–70.

22. William A. Knowlton, "Ethics and Decision Making" (address delivered at the U.S. Army War College, Carlisle Barracks, Pennsylvania, October 22, 1984). Cited with permission.

23. See, for example, Frank A. Burdick, "Vietnam Revisioned: The Military Campaign against Civilian Control," *Democracy* 2, no. 1 (January 1982): 36–52; Stephen P. Rosen, "Vietnam and the American Theory of Limited War," *International Security* 7, no. 2 (Fall 1982): 100–103; and Victor H. Krulak, *Organization for National Security* (Washington, D.C.: U.S. Strategic Institute, 1983), pp. 81–102.

24. David Halberstam, *The Best and the Brightest* (Greenwich, Conn.: Fawcett Crest, 1972), pp. 683–684.

25. Ibid., p. 685. This is not intended to imply that President Johnson was solely responsible for the escalation of U.S. involvement in Vietnam.

26. William C. Westmoreland, *A Soldier Reports* (Garden City, N.Y.: Doubleday, 1976), p. 193.

27. Dave R. Palmer, *Summons of the Trumpet* (San Rafael, Calif.: Presidio Press, 1978), p. 171.

28. Rosen, "Vietnam," p. 101; Henry E. Eccles, *Military Power in a Free Society* (Newport, R.I.: Naval War College Press, 1979), pp. 140–141; Palmer, *25-Year War*, pp. 198–203. It must be said that there were two sides to the relationship. Even before the escalation of U.S. involvement in Vietnam, the civilians of that era felt they had been let down by the Joint Chiefs during the deliberations over the Bay of Pigs invasion, as well as during the Cuban missile crisis. They increasingly came to believe that the military were insensitive to the political realities in which limited wars like Vietnam had to be fought. And, of course, the military made its share of mistakes and misjudgments. While this would be pertinent to a paper on the civilian lessons of Vietnam, however, it is not pertinent here.

29. Thomas D. White, quoted by Bernard Brodie in *War and Politics* (New York: Macmillan, 1973), p. 466, from Thomas D. White, "Strategy and the Defense Intellectuals," *Saturday Evening Post,* May 4, 1963, p. 10.

30. Krulak, *Organization for National Security,* p. 87. See also Wayne P. Hughes, "Vietnam Winnable War?" *U.S. Naval Institute Proceedings* 103, no. 7 (July 1977): 60–65.

31. William C. Westmoreland, "Vietnam in Perspective," *Military Review 59,* no. 1 (January 1979): 34–43; U.S.G. Sharp, *Strategy for Defeat* (San Rafael, Calif.: Presidio Press, 1978), See also the results of Douglas Kinnard's survey in *The War Managers* (Hanover, N.H.: University Press of New England, 1977), pp. 160–163.

32. Westmoreland, "Vietnam in Perspective," pp. 35–39.

33. Eccles, *Military Power in a Free Society,* pp. 140–141. The survey of general officers who served in Vietnam done by Brigadier General Douglas Kinnard also reveals considerable bitterness over civilian interference. See Kinnard's *The War Managers.*

34. Quoted in Richard J. Stillman, "The Pentagon's Whiz Kids," *U.S. Naval Institute Proceedings* 92 (April 1966): 57.

35. Alexander M. Haig, *Caveat* (New York: Macmillan, 1984), p. 128.

36. Palmer, *25-Year War,* p. 190; Harry G. Summers, Jr., "Lessons: A Soldier's View," *Wilson Quarterly* (Summer 1983): 125–135. The failure to mobilize is also a recurrent theme in Summers's *On Strategy: The Vietnam War in Context* (Carlisle Barracks, Penn.: U.S. Army War College, 1981).

37. Roy L. Beavers, "An Absence of Accountability," *U.S. Naval Institute Proceedings* 102, no. 1 (January 1976): 19–23.

38. T.R. Milton, "USAF and the Vietnam Experience," *Air Force* 58, no. 6 (June 1975): 56.

39. Admiral Thomas H. Moorer, quoted by Guenter Lewy, "Some Political-Military Lessons of the Vietnam War," *Parameters* 14, no. 1 (Spring 1984): 2–14.

40. Franklin Margiotta, "A Military Elite in Transition," *Armed Forces and Society* 2, no. 2 (February 1976): 162.

41. Haig, *Caveat,* p. 125.

42. Graham Allison explains these traditional tensions in his *Essence of Decision* (Boston: Little, Brown, 1971), pp. 179–180.

43. Knowlton, "Ethics and Decisionmaking," p. 28. See also Andrew P. O'Meara, "Civil-Military Conflict within the Defense Structure," *Parameters* 8, no. 1 (March 1978): 86.

44. E.C. Meyer, "Toward a More Perfect Union in Civil-Military Relations," *Parameters* 9, no. 2 (June 1979): 83.

45. Miles Kahler, "The Rumors of War: The 1914 Analogy," *Foreign Affairs* 58, no. 2 (Winter 1979–1980): 389.

46. Paul M. Kattenburg, "Reflections on Vietnam: Of Revisionism and Lessons Yet to Be Learned," *Parameters* 14, no. 3 (Autumn 1984): 44.

47. Drew Middleton, "Vietnam and the Military Mind," *New York Times Magazine,* January 10, 1982, p. 90.

48. George Herring describes Westmoreland's views in "American Strategy in Vietnam: The Postwar Debate," *Military Affairs* 41, no. 2 (April 1982): 58.

49. On Dien Bien Phu, see the excellent article by George C. Herring and Richard H. Immerman, "Eisenhower, Dulles, and Dien Bien Phu: 'The Day We Didn't Go to War' Revisited," *Journal of American History* 71, no. 2 (September 1984): 343–363. Arthur M. Schlesinger describes the military position during the deliberations in 1961 over the use of force in Laos in *A Thousand Days* (New York: Fawcett Premier, 1965), p. 227. Roger Hilsman does also and describes the depth of feeling among "members" of the so-called Never Again club against fighting another land war in Asia after Korea in *To Move a Nation* (Garden City, N.Y.: Doubleday, 1967), pp. 127–155. For contemporary views, see George C. Wilson, "Reagan Will Hear Conflicting Advice about Retaliation for Terrorism," *Washington Post,* June 23, p. A-23.

50. Paraphrased from Richard K. Betts, "Misadventure Revisited," *Wilson Quarterly* (Summer 1983): 99.

51. Citations of the Dominican Republic intervention as an example of a good operation include Palmer, *25-Year War,* pp. 190–191; and Lloyd Norman, "The Chiefs: Partisanship Goes Out When 'Purple Suits' Go On," *Army* 20, no. 5 (May 1970): 40.

52. George C. Wilson, "Top U.S. Brass Wary on Central America," *Washington Post,* June 24, 1983, p. A-20; Donn A. Starry, "The Principles of War," *Military Review* 61, no. 9 (September 1981): 20; and George C. Wilson, "War's Lessons Struck Home," *Washington Post,* April 16, 1985, p. A-9.

53. Palmer, *25-Year War,* p. 189.

54. Frederick C. Weyand quoted in Summers, *On Strategy,* p. 25.

55. Wilson, "Top U.S. Brass Wary."

56. Wilson, "Reagan Will Hear Conflicting Advice." See also Richard Halloran, "Reflections on 46 Years of Army Service," *New York Times,* September 3, 1985, p. A-18.

57. Wilson, "Top U.S. Brass Wary."

58. General John W. Vessey, Jr., quoted by Richard Halloran, "A Commanding Voice for the Military," *New York Times Magazine,* July 15, 1984, p. 52.

59. For a study of military influence on the use of force from the end of World War II through the end of the Vietnam War, see Richard K. Betts, *Soldiers, Statesmen, and Cold War Crises* (Cambridge: Harvard University Press, 1979).

60. Huntington, *Soldier and the State,* p. 69.

61. In fact, as Richard Betts's extensive research of crises that took place between 1945 and 1973 revealed, such popular images have never been supported by the evidence. See his *Soldiers, Statesmen, and Cold War Crises.*

62. An analysis of the post-Vietnam cases where the use of force was considered may be found in the forthcoming doctoral dissertation by David H. Petraeus, "Military Influence and the Use of Force in the Post-Vietnam Era" (Princeton University). See also, for example, "Admiral Reported on Line for Head of Military Chiefs," *New York Times,* July 10, 1985, p. A-24.

63. *Washington Post,* March 11, 1983, p. A-17.

64. Haig, *Caveat,* pp. 125, 129.

65. Ibid., pp. 128–129.

66. Isaacson, "Weighing the Proper Role," p. 44; and David Wood, "U.S. Says El Salvador 'Can Be Lost,'" *Los Angeles Times,* February 23, 1983, pp. I-1, I-20.

67. "Pentagon Is Opposed to Use of Troops in Central America," *New York Times,* June 5, 1983, p. A-5.

68. Ibid; Drew Middleton, "U.S. Generals Are Leery of Latin Intervention," *New York Times,* June 21, 1983, p. A-9; George C. Wilson, "Top U.S. Brass Wary on Central America," *Washington Post,* June 24, 1983, p. A-20; and Walter S. Mossberg, "The Army Resists a Salvadoran Vietnam," *Wall Street Journal,* June 24, 1983, p. 22.

69. Middleton, "U.S. Generals," p. A-9.

70. Ibid.

71. Under Secretary Fred Iklé caused a stir in September 1983 when he delivered a speech in Baltimore calling for a military victory in El Salvador and saying negotiations alone could not solve the problem. See Fred Hiatt, "Undersecretary Urges More Salvadoran Aid," *Washington Post,* November 13, 1983, pp. A-1, A-4; Lou Cannon, "The President's Aides Are Losing Their Boss in Translation," *Washington Post,* August 3, 1983, p. A-3; and Lou Cannon, "President's Strong Man Stretches South," *Washington Post,* August 3, 1983, pp. A-1, A-12.

72. Cannon, "President's Strong Man," p. A-22.

73. George C. Wilson, "U.S. Bases Considered for Honduras," *Washington Post,* August 6, 1983, pp. A-1, A-12.

74. Joanne Omang, "New Army Chief Doesn't See Widening Latin Involvement," *Washington Post,* August 9, 1983, p. A-10. As a follow-up, see Jay Finegan, "Buildup in Honduras," *New York Times Magazine,* July 2, 1984, pp. 4–12; and Gordon Mott, "Honduras: Key to U.S. Role in Central America," *New York Times Magazine,* October 14, 1984, p. 84.

75. Leon Jenkins, "U.S. Officer Influential in Latin Region," *Washington Post,* January 3, 1984, p. A-1.

76. Ibid., p. A-13.

77. George C. Wilson, "U.S. Urged to Meet Honduran Requests," *Washington Post,* June 20, 1983, pp. A-1, A-4.

78. Doyle McManus, "U.S. Draws Contingency Plans for Air Strikes in El Salvador, *New York Times,* July 13, 1984, p. A-27; Richard Halloran, "Army Plans for 'What If' Latin War," *New York Times,* May 4, 1985, p. 4; and Bill Keller, "U.S. Military Is Termed Prepared for Any Move against Nicaragua," *New York Times,* June 4, 1985, p. A-1.

79. Wilson, "U.S. Urged to Meet Honduran Requests," p. A-4.

80. Ibid. This resistance was discussed also in Doyle McManus, "U.S. Draws Contingency Plans for Air Strikes in El Salvador," *Washington Post,* July 13, 1984, p. A-27.

81. Hedrick Smith, "U.S. Latin Force in Place If Needed, Officials Report," *New York Times,* April 23, 1984, pp. A-1, A-8.

82. George C. Wilson, "Top U.S. Brass Wary on Central America," *Washington Post,* June 24, 1983, p. A-20.

83. Philip Taubman, "General Doubts G.I. Role in Salvador," *New York Times,* August 2, 1984, p. 3.

84. Richard Halloran, "General Opposes Nicaragua Attacks," *New York Times,* June 30, 1985, p. A-3.

85. See, for example, Andrew F. Krepinevich, Jr., "The Army Concept and Vietnam: A Case Study in Organizational Failure," (Ph.D. diss., Harvard University, 1983); and Peter M. Dawkins, "The United States Army and the 'Other' War in Vietnam" (Ph.D. diss., Princeton University, 1979).

86. Andrew P. O'Meara, Jr., "The Democratic Army and the Nation-State," *Parameters* 8, no. 2 (June 1978): 44. Such feelings, of course, are not entirely new. For an example of an article showing military acceptance that "part of the fault was ours," see Marc B. Powe, "The U.S. Army after the Fall of Vietnam: A Contemporary Dilemma," *Military Review* 61, no. 2 (February 1976): 3–17. In another example, see John R. Galvin, "Cincinnatus Recidivus: A Review Essay," *Parameters* 11, no. 1 (March 1981). On p. 18 Galvin warned that "the American military must stop blaming politicians for inhibiting tactical success in the war and must instead study carefully the . . . lessons that are there to be learned."

87. Robert E. Osgood, *Limited War Revisited* (Boulder, Colo.: Westview Press, 1979), p. 50.

88. Andrew J. Bacevich, "Disagreeable Work: Pacifying the Moros, 1903–1906," *Military Review* 62, no. 6 (June 1982): 50.

89. Exceptions include Summers's *On Strategy,* Palmer's *25-Year War,* Dawkins's *The United States Army and the "Other" War in Vietnam,* and Krepinevich's *The Army Concept and Vietnam.*

13

Past as Prologue: Counterinsurgency and the U.S. Army's Vietnam Experience in Force Structuring and Doctrine

Andrew F. Krepinevich, Jr.

The U.S. Army is enjoying a renaissance of sorts in developing doctrine and forces for special operations. At Fort Leavenworth, Kansas, and Fort Monroe, Virginia, army officers are revising doctrine for terrorism counteraction, unconventional warfare, and foreign internal defense (formerly referred to as counterinsurgency). The army also has increased the forces available to conduct special operations; two of the four Special Forces groups disbanded in the aftermath of Vietnam have been restored, and three Ranger battalions and a Ranger regimental headquarters have been formed. For the first time, the Green Berets and the Rangers have been brought together, along with their associated headquarters and support elements, in the First Special Operations Command (SOCOM). Army Chief of Staff General John A. Wickham has directed the formation of several light infantry divisions, which will be available to augment First SOCOM forces in low-intensity conflict contingencies. Once again, it seems, the army is preparing for counterguerrilla warfare as it was in the early years of the Kennedy administration.

There is one important difference, however, say army officials. The army, they contend, has learned a lesson from its Vietnam experience and will resist being drawn into another low-intensity war unless certain conditions exist that allow for a successful outcome. These conditions, enunciated by Secretary of Defense Weinberger, are that U.S. combat forces should not be committed overseas unless the interests involved are vital to U.S. security, the troops committed are sufficient in number to accomplish the mission, and the U.S. political leadership has "the clear intention of winning." Finally, an atmosphere of popular and congressional support for the war must be present.[1]

These conditions are drawn, in Secretary Weinberger's words, from "lessons we have learned from the past." They are the army's lessons from Vietnam, and they signify the service's determination to ensure that there will be no more Vietnams. And yet, if one examines closely the resurgence of army interest in low-intensity warfare, there exist many disturbing parallels between what transpired between the Korean and Vietnam wars and what happened between the Vietnam War and the present. Indeed, the similarities drive the observer toward the conclusion that if the army has learned any lessons from Vietnam, it has learned the wrong ones. Before engaging in a discussion of these two periods, however, it is important to understand the army's organizational focus as it encountered these unconventional conflicts.

Although the army has a unique role and mission when compared to other large organizations like General Motors or the Department of Health and Human Services, it still shares many basic characteristics with them. Like other organizations, the army has developed certain preferred ways of accomplishing what it perceives to be its tasks and missions. During the first half of this century, the service was consumed by two world wars and a limited conventional war in Korea. Involvement in low-intensity operations was limited to the Philippine insurrection at the turn of the century and isolated instances during World War II. Therefore it should come as no surprise that there emerged in the army a preference, or bias, to approach conflict within an organizational framework, or mind-set, of conventional (or mid-intensity) war. This mind-set has been solidified with the success of conventional operations in these wars.

This conventional war mind-set was supplemented by an acknowledged need to minimize U.S. casualties in limited wars whenever possible for socio-political purposes. The United States, blessed by unsurpassed wealth, was willing to sacrifice great amounts of national treasure to support and preserve its soldiers in combat. This attitude translated into a proclivity on the army's part to expend prodigious amounts of materiel—firepower—to avoid risking its manpower. In army parlance, "It is better to send a bullet [or an artillery barrage, for that matter] than a man" to accomplish the mission. Thus in the Korean War the order went out from U.S. Eighth Army Commanding General James Van Fleet to "expend steel and fire, not men. I want so many artillery holes that a man can step from one to the other."[2] One allied observer of army operations in Korea, Brigadier W.F.K. Thompson of Great Britain, recalled the American use of "prophylactic" firepower, "which means if you do not know where the enemy is, make a big enough bang and you may bring something down."[3]

Aftermath of Korea

When the army experience in Vietnam began in earnest with the end of the Korean War and the collapse of the French at Dien Bien Phu, the service brought its conventional war mind-set and its firepower-oriented tactics along with it. This outlook is not surprising; after all, the mid-intensity environment was one with which the army was doctrinally comfortable. Furthermore, the army had succeeded in previous wars by following the principles and methods prescribed for conventional military operations. Given limited resources and a looming Soviet threat in Europe, this approach must have seemed all the more appropriate to the army leadership.

The army also emerged from the Korean War somewhat disillusioned. After all, it was the first war in over a century the service had failed to "win" (the first ever discounting the War of 1812). The public's waning support for limited war in Korea was attributed to the high cost in casualties and materiel coupled with a "no-win" strategy.[4] A "never again" club of high-ranking officers and their disciples emerged from that war contending, in a manner strikingly similar to Secretary Weinberger, that U.S. troops should be committed only to wars in which the nation was willing to support an all-out effort and set an objective of victory in the tradition of U.S. ("Unconditional Surrender") Grant.[5] Low-intensity conflict was viewed as a mild form of conventional warfare, requiring scaled-down operations along traditional lines. Army Chief of Staff General George Decker remarked, "Any good soldier can handle guerrillas."[6] General Maxwell Taylor, army chief of staff under President Eisenhower and special military assistant to President Kennedy (and later his chairman of the Joint Chiefs of Staff), felt that "any well-trained organization can shift the tempo to that [level of conflict] which may be required." Low-intensity conflict was not an inherently different kind of war, only a "small" war.[7] Forces capable of handling mid-intensity contingencies were presumed capable of dealing with lesser contingencies as well.

Thus, when the army looked at the insurgency in Vietnam between the Viet Minh and the French, it did so through a perceptual lens distorted by a traditional, conventional, organizational mind-set. Even General Ridgway, the army chief of staff at the time of Dien Bien Phu who wisely cautioned against the introduction of U.S. forces to rescue the French, spoke of U.S. involvement in terms of how many divisions it would take to do the job of defeating the Communists.[8] Although the Viet Minh had succeeded in driving the French out of Indochina through a strategy of protracted, insurgent warfare, the chief of the U.S. Military Advisory Assistance Group (MAAG), Lieutenant General "Hanging" Sam Williams, was sent to South Vietnam in 1955 to organize that country's armed forces to ward off a conventional invasion from the Communist North. Even as the insurgency in South Vietnam began to spread in the late 1950s, General Williams remained determined to conduct corps-size maneuvers with the Army of the Republic of Vietnam (ARVN), which he did.[9] In Washington, D.C., the army staff gave "no thought" to the growing threat posed by Vietcong guerrillas.[10] However, when, in December 1960, Radio Hanoi proclaimed the formation of the National Liberation Front (NLF), the political arm of the Vietcong, the U.S.

military could no longer avoid the insurgency problem. But could it adapt itself quickly enough to cope with this new threat operating in what, for the army, was an unfamiliar conflict environment?

Kennedy Counterinsurgency Revolution

In the body of literature devoted to large organizations and their behavior, changes in deeply ingrained organizational methods are considered extremely difficult to effect.[11] Nevertheless, there are four general circumstances under which significant organizational change is likely to occur. One is when an institution or individual overseeing the organization effects a high-level override of preferred organizational practices. This approach was attempted during the Kennedy administration when the president, assisted by the Special Group (Counterinsurgency) (SGCI), attempted to force the army to formulate counterinsurgency doctrine and a compatible force structure to deal with third world national liberation movements.

Kennedy took a direct interest in his push to create a revolution from above in army thinking on counterinsurgency. He personally examined Special Forces equipment and field manuals. Over the objections of the army brass, Kennedy authorized the Special Forces to wear green berets and directed staff sections at the joint and army level be formed to oversee the development of the military's counterinsurgency forces.[12] Kennedy also directed the army to educate its soldiers, particularly its senior officers, on low-intensity warfare, making it clear that a background in the field would be an important, if not a compelling, factor in the selection of future general officers.[13] In a special message to the Congress, the president requested increased funds and troop billets to expand the Special Forces.

President Kennedy, however, could devote but a fraction of his time to reforming the army's view of counterinsurgency. He seemed to realize that, despite his best efforts, the army could slow, if not obstruct entirely, the process of change, so he sought to convince the army in an extraordinary meeting in the Oval Office in late November 1961. To the meeting Kennedy summoned nearly all of the army's major commanders. He appealed to them to adopt his program wholeheartedly and develop the kind of capability that would be needed to defend the national interest in that "long, twilight struggle" against third world Communist insurgents.[14]

Nothing happened. Over the next two months the army leadership submerged its own in-house analysis (the Stilwell Report) of what was necessary to accomplish the president's objectives.[15] The military, however, was only willing to pay lip-service to what several general officers described as a fad foisted on the army by the New Frontier crowd. Studies were done, staff sections were created, and statistics were cranked out "proving" instruction and training in counterinsurgency had increased dramatically. But the army leadership remained distinctly unwilling to divert units of the regular army from their focus on conventional combat operations.[16]

While the president established the SGCI to oversee army progress in detail in a way that he could not, he made the mistake of appointing men to the group who were either novices in the art of insurgency warfare (as in the case of his brother Robert and also Roswell Gilpatric, McGeorge Bundy, and Edward R. Murrow) or men who approached this unconventional topic in a conventional manner (such as Generals Maxwell Taylor and Lyman Lemnitzer). The results, predictably, were unimpressive. At the time of Kennedy's death, army doctrinal guidance on counterinsurgency was categorized by the services' own Combat Developments Command (CDC) as "defective" at the national level, the host country level, and the advisory level.[17] Indeed, the CDC evaluation found that three years after Kennedy initiated the counterinsurgency buildup, "nowhere is there a definitive listing of doctrinal requirements for special warfare."[18] As late as 1967, the Continental Army Command (CONARC) would still note that "there is insufficient doctrine on area [counterinsurgency] warfare."[19]

With a conceptual framework of how to approach the problems of insurgency warfare nowhere to be found, army schools and units involved in training simply fit this new form of warfare into the familiar conventional framework. Infantry battalions practiced closing with and destroying guerrilla forces, presaging the large sweeps and search-and-destroy operations that would become their staple in Vietnam. At the army's Command and General Staff College, officers engaged in a war game of the deployment of a two-division corps to destroy guerrilla bands in a fictitious West African nation.

If President Kennedy could not override the army's conceptual biases concerning low-intensity conflict, he also was unsuccessful in changing the service's priorities through the budget process, a second method of bringing about organizational change. The notion is that large organizations are capable of significant change when faced with major increases or decreases in budgetary authorizations (or, in the case of an organization like Chrysler Corporation, profits). However, deep cuts in the army budget would have witnessed special operations programs among the prime targets for extinction. While the Kennedy administration did provide additional manpower and funds for the army, it was largely unsuccessful in fencing off a large enough portion to make counterinsurgency a profitable enough venture to warrant serious army support. Indeed, the army hoped to use any budget increase to rebuild its conventional forces, weakened by years of attrition at the hands of Eisenhower's massive retaliation strategy. The idea of diverting a large slice of these resources away from its new, heavy ROAD (Reorganization Objectives Army Division) divisions in favor of maintaining units that were even more fragile than the detested pentomic divisions of the 1950s horrified men like Taylor, Lemnitzer, and Decker. Given their view of insurgency warfare as merely a lesser case of mid-intensity conflict, it made sense only to have heavy units that could scale themselves down for a smaller war rather than have light counterinsurgency units attempt to bulk up rapidly for a war in Central Europe.

Furthermore, while increased resources were available under Kennedy's strategy of flexible response, the strategy itself mandated an army ability to conduct simultaneously two major wars (one in Europe, the other in Asia) and one brushfire war. This two-and-a-half war strategy represented a quantum leap in army requirements over the old massive retaliation strategy. Under the latter, army forces were to serve merely as a trip-wire in the event of Soviet aggression in Europe, triggering a massive U.S. nuclear riposte on the Soviet Union and China. Given a considerably expanded menu of contingencies by the Kennedy administration and increased, yet insufficient, resources to prepare for them, it is not surprising that brushfire wars were given short shrift or that the army leadership reinforced its notion that if it could fight a big war, it could certainly fight a little one too.

Although Kennedy failed to promote a revolution from above through either personal involvement or the budgetary process, there were some in the army who sought to change the service's perspective on low-intensity conflict. They were the U.S. senior corps and ARVN division advisers in Vietnam, men who included Colonels Wilbur Wilson, Jasper Wilson, Roland Renwanz, and Daniel Porter and Lieutenant Colonels John Paul Vann and Fred Ladd. They witnessed both the corruption and inefficiency of the ARVN leadership and the impotency of large-scale maneuvers and paper pacification programs in the face of well-organized, well-led insurgent forces. While these advisers, the nerve endings of the army's organizational body, filed numerous reports decrying the sanguinary outlook the MACV had adopted toward the insurgent problem, few filtered back to Washington. When Vann returned to Washington to get a hearing with the Joint Chiefs of Staff, General Taylor, then the chief, had Vann's briefing cancelled.[20] Given their relatively low rank and small numbers and the absence of any high-ranking mentor in the Pentagon, this third method of change, a revolt from below, met with little success.

The final catalyst of change for an organization grown strategically myopic is the shock of a catastrophic performance failure. For the political elite, and for much of the public as well, the army's failure in Vietnam became evident with the Communist Tet offensive of January–February 1968. The attack, which caught the United States, if not its armed forces, by complete surprise (following as it did months of uninterrupted U.S. "victories"), precipitated a full-blown reappraisal of U.S. war strategy. When Generals Wheeler and Westmoreland could only offer newly appointed Secretary of Defense Clark Clifford the prospect of more of the same for an indefinite period, they lost Clifford's confidence, the confidence of President Johnson's distinguished panel of informal advisers (known as the "wise men"), and, finally, the confidence of the president himself. Yet while Vietnamization pulled the plug on army operations in South Vietnam, MACV retained its pre-Tet approach to counterinsurgency operations, as reflected in the continuance of the body count operations mentality, reliance on high volumes of firepower, and the orientation on closing with and destroying the enemy as opposed to securing the population. This operational mind-set is all the more remarkable when one considers that, after Tet, the Communists had, for the most part, regressed to small-unit guerrilla operations. A change in operational orientation finally occurred when large-scale troop withdrawals forced the army to withdraw to its logistical bases on the coast and scale back operations. It was a change dictated by a lack of resources, not a change of view on the army leadership's part.

Army after Vietnam

The army emerged from the Vietnam War far more disillusioned than after the Korean War. There existed considerable bitterness toward the political leadership that had committed the army to the conflict and then, seemingly, abandoned it. There was also bitterness toward the public for lack of support or appreciation for the sacrifices made by those in uniform, who, after all, were only carrying out the policies of the country's leaders, elected by the people themselves. Finally, there was an inner-directed anger at having been pushed into fighting a war on the enemy's terms instead of its own. To discern these feelings, one need only examine the recent writings of army soldier-scholars such as General Bruce Palmer and Colonel Harry Summers.[21] The war, we are told, would have turned out far better had the army not been so preoccupied with counterinsurgency and altered its strategy to fight a more conventional war, maneuvering divisions into a blocking position stretching from the demilitarized zone (DMZ) between the two Vietnams through the Laotian panhandle to the Mekong River, just as called for by the war plans drawn up after the Korean War.[22]

A "no more Vietnams" club has emerged since the war's end, determined not to commit U.S. troops to combat unless, as stated by Secretary Weinberger, the political leadership has the "clear intention of winning."[23] This represents a potential blank check; if the military becomes frustrated in future low-intensity wars, it can escalate the conflict into the more congenial environment of mid-intensity conventional conflict. If it cannot cope with insurgents in El Salvador, it can invade Nicaragua, or (if need be, one would assume) Cuba as well. Along the same lines, the "support of the American people and their elected representatives in Congress" is mandated. This prerequisite is intended to preclude the lack of popular and congressional support that plagued the army during the Vietnam War. Yet from the time President Kennedy dispatched large numbers of combat advisers to South Vietnam in December 1961 to the Tet offensive over six years later, the army did not lack for popular or political support. It is difficult to fault the American people or their elected representatives, when, after that long a period of active engagement, the Joint Chiefs of Staff could offer only more of the same for an indefinite period with no assurance of eventual success.

The prescription of committing U.S. combat forces only to areas of vital interest reflects yet another lesson unlearned from the army's Vietnam experience. Indeed the only two areas that can claim a clear consensus in representing vital U.S. interests—Western Europe and Japan—are sites for future mid- or high-intensity (nuclear) conflict. If the military seeks to define low-intensity conflict contingencies in this manner, it essentially is defining away the need to address this form of warfare.

The problem is that pinning down just what countries represent vital interests to the United States is a subjective exercise. South Korea, not a vital interest in Dean Acheson's speech to the National Press Club in January 1950, became vital literally overnight when invaded in June by forces of the Communist North. South Vietnam, not vital to U.S. interests in 1954 or 1975, was deemed so in 1965.

In sum, it appears the military wants a blank check to fail, and not lose popular support, or to escalate the conflict if it becomes frustrated with the nuances of counterinsurgency warfare as in Vietnam.

Nevertheless, it is easy to sympathize with the army's desire to avoid becoming a victim of the strategic dilletantism that often prevailed in the Kennedy and Johnson administrations during the Vietnam War. Yet attempting to set conditions for the commitment of U.S. combat forces is likely to be as ineffective in the 1980s and 1990s as it was during the years leading up to the Vietnam intervention. At that time, the army held the United States should commit ground forces to the war only if the administration was willing to lift all restrictions on military operations in Southeast Asia and mobilize the reserves.[24] Despite this posturing on the service's part, its forces were committed to the defense of South Vietnam without either condition's being satisfied. The army, in trying to enter the war on its terms, had shortchanged itself on both the doctrine and the force structure it would need to fight successfully in an unfamiliar conflict environment. Thus, in Vietnam the army ended up trying to fight (albeit with certain modifications) the conventional war it had trained for instead of the counterinsurgency war it faced.

If the army is still hoping to set the same kind of conditions for intervention that it did in the decade following the Korean War, it has received (when compared to the effort made during the Kennedy years) little incentive to change its organizational bias against developing forces for low-intensity conflict, counterinsurgency (now foreign internal defense, FID) in particular.[25]

Examining the Reagan administration's push to have the Army develop Special Operations Forces (SOF) gives one a strong sense of déja vu. This time, however, the revolution from above is without the strong presidential personal interest that was evinced by John Kennedy. Nor is there anything resembling the SGCI, which, although flawed, at least provided a sense of high-level concern for low-intensity conflict and a mechanism for linking together the numerous departments and agencies that would have to work together in any future U.S. involvement in foreign internal defense.

The prospects for change through a revolt from below do not appear promising either. There is not even a cadre of high-visibility advisers, as existed in Vietnam, to lead the move toward change. The men running the army today saw their careers boosted in Vietnam when they commanded battalions or served as staff officers in main force units, not in advisory roles. Indeed, once the army completed its pullout from South Vietnam, the service sought to expunge the counterinsurgency experience from its officer corps. The 1973 Arab-Israeli War was seen as a godsend by the Army War College and Command and General Staff College. They used that war to focus attention away from low-intensity conflict and back to the army's preferred modus operandi of mid-intensity conventional conflict. The Vietnam syndrome that engulfed the United States in the mid-1970s found the army right in step as instruction on FID at its service schools literally disappeared.[26]

Since that time, some steps have been taken to reintroduce low-intensity operations into the curricula at the army's branch and service schools. Yet the time devoted to such study remains small compared to the attention given normal (as opposed to special) operations. Recent Army manuals like the Special Forces' *Command, Control and Support of Special Forces Operations* (FM 31-22) and the capstone FM 100-20, *Low Intensity Operations,* place primary emphasis on the kinds of quasi-conventional operations carried out in Vietnam. Thus one finds FM 31-22 emphasizing unconventional operations, with almost no mention of FID.[27] Furthermore, Special Forces units are evaluated and rated almost exclusively on their ability to carry out unconventional warfare operations, as opposed to FID operations.[28] FM 100-20 was reissued most recently in January 1981 (it is being updated). The manual is essentially little more than a restatement of FM 31-16, *Counterguerrilla Operations,* issued in 1967. A perusal of FM 100-20 provides a useful lesson on the contemporary army's difficulty in setting aside conventional doctrine and force structures for low-intensity conflict and on the lessons the service took away from its Vietnam experience. For example, although the manual declares the "organization of counterguerrilla forces is designed around light infantry fighting elements," it goes on to prescribe roles for armored and mechanized infantry units (owing to their greater firepower and mobility).[29] Although the use of firepower is guided by the principle of "minimal essential force," brigade commanders are exhorted to search for main force guerrilla units and bases and, once located, give top priority to their destruction.[30]

Thus the commander's dilemma that existed in Vietnam persists: what has priority, the traditional mission of closing with and destroying the enemy or population safety and security? As in Vietnam, it seems, winning the peoples' hearts and minds finishes a poor second to seeking out main enemy forces and bringing them to battle. Thus, while classical counterinsurgency doctrine calls for placing primary emphasis on pacification, the manual informs brigade commanders that they will "not normally occupy the area for an extended time following an attack."[31] Search-and-destroy operations, reflective of the body count mentality in Vietnam, experience a rebirth in the manual as "strike campaigns."[32] These manuals are, unfortunately, representative of the army's operational concept for FID missions. For instance, in a recent article, "How to Win in El Salvador," the coauthor, a former commander of U.S. military trainers in that country, states that the Salvadoran soldier's first priority should be to "learn the subtle art of locating his enemy's base camps," not securing control of the population.[33]

This mission is consistent with the army's concept of operations for FID, which sees Special Forces involved in operations against insurgent base areas, infiltration routes, and in remote, isolated areas, in that order. This unconventional warfare role, the opposite of counterinsurgency, is viewed as more conducive to the support of conventional operations and is the role the Special Forces played in Vietnam once they reverted from CIA control to MACV.[34] Nowhere is the term *population security* or its equivalent mentioned; rather the document claims that "there is little functional difference between FID and UW [unconventional warfare]."[35]

Similarly, the army's personnel policies do not encourage the development of expertise in low-intensity operations. Soldiers, by and large, are rotated in and out of their units every couple of years, creating considerable turmoil and retarding the development of the language and cultural expertise required of soldiers who may have to interact closely, and over a prolonged period, with the populace of a particular third world nation. For example, officers and NCOs who serve a tour or two in the Special Forces are likely to spend a considerable amount of time in heavy, divisional units over the course of their careers. Those serving in the army's new light infantry divisions (LIDs) face even greater problems, as LIDs have a number of mid-intensity conflict missions that overshadow low-intensity conflict contingencies. It is therefore unlikely that a significant movement will emerge within the service, as in the case of the airborne or airmobile "clubs," to encourage a strong army emphasis on FID.

The political leadership is unlikely to make change any more palatable now in terms of additional resources than was the case under the Kennedy-Johnson administrations. The ends-means disconnect that existed during the two-and-a-half-war strategy days of the early 1960s exists today. Since 1979 the army has witnessed the Carter and Reagan administrations commit it to a major new contingency in the Persian Gulf and a spate of potential low-intensity contingencies in the third world, in addition to the traditional NATO and Northeast Asia scenarios. Yet the army's size has remained essentially unchanged. This ends-means disconnect forces tough choices on the army leadership. Working within manpower limitations that are only partially self-imposed, the service has sought to make some units all things to all contingencies. This approach is not new. It occurred with the army's infantry divisions of the Kennedy era, which were slotted for both European and Asian contingencies and, as part of Special Action forces, against low-intensity brushfire war contingencies as well.[36] The army's LIDs are but the latest attempt to stretch limited resources over seemingly unlimited requirements. Designed to be highly transportable by strategic airlift, LIDs can be moved relatively quickly to the Persian Gulf, Korea, or Central Europe, where they would operate primarily in mountains, forests, or urban areas against enemy forces in mid-intensity conflict environments.[37] Concerns are already being voiced within the service that because of these contingencies, LIDs may need to become heavier. For example, the armor branch has expressed its belief that LIDs should have their own organic tank forces (light tanks).[38] LID military intelligence assets appear to be oriented on conventional conflict intelligence requirements (such as determining the enemy order of battle) as opposed to the more demanding human intelligence functions that play a key role in counterinsurgency operations.[39] As in the Kennedy years, these modifications are motivated by a shortage of manpower resources and a belief that it is a relatively easy proposition to shift gears from conventional war to counterinsurgency.

The final agent of change, a catastrophic organizational failure, is not possible in the absense of conflict. Given the army mind-set, it is unlikely that a disaster would prove any more effective in changing army organizational incentives than Vietnam did nearly twenty years ago.

Conclusions

Low-intensity warfare represents the most likely arena of future conflict for the army. Yet if the service is to be spared another frustrating experience in counterinsurgency warfare, it most likely will be through the wisdom of U.S. third world allies (as in the case of Ramon Magsaysay in the Philippines) or the incompetence of its adversaries (as occurred with the Communists in Greece). The lesson that the army learned in Vietnam is that it does not like counterinsurgency warfare and, it seems, neither does the American public or its representatives in Congress. As in the period following the end of the Korean War, the army is seeking to erect barriers to avoid fighting another Vietnam War just as it sought to avoid another Korea. Thus instead of gaining a better understanding of how to wage counterinsurgency warfare within the unique social, economic, political, and military dimensions comprising that form of conflict, the army is trying through the six tests enunciated by Secretary Weinberger to transform such conflicts into something the service can handle in a more familiar way. Unfortunately, as the army ought to have learned in Vietnam, enemies of the United States are not going to play to its military strong suits; rather, they will exploit its weak points.

The army's current situation is, at least in part, the result of the political leadership's corresponding lack of emphasis on low-intensity conflict. There exists today no persistent, direct high-level emphasis for the development of an interdepartmental approach to the problem of foreign internal defense. Although Kennedy's SGCI was flawed, an interdepartmental group that coordinates the U.S. economic, social, and political responses to insurgency with those of the country targeted by insurgents, as well as with U.S. military power, is an indispensable prerequisite. Such a group (comprising Department of State, Office of the Secretary of Defense, JCS, CIA, USIA, USAID, and NSC staff) would need the power to oversee the development of an integrated capability to carry out U.S. policy in defense of third world states threatened by insurgency and would require the president's personal support and involvement. Emphasis of this type may be the only factor capable of changing the army's perspective on FID.

In the absence of an overarching executive structure to confront insurgencies, there will continue to exist a shortage of resources and incentives motivating the army to overcome its institutional bias toward developing a true capability for FID contingencies. Without a national security structural framework that addresses the interdepartmental obligations associated with FID operations and without the incentives for organizational change within the army, it is difficult to believe the army will develop the capability on its own to carry out successfully U.S. security policy in third world countries threatened by insurgency. Given these limiting factors, perhaps the best the army can do in the short run is to identify the limitations imposed upon it by organizational precedent, resource restrictions, and the political leadership's focus (or lack thereof) on insurgency conflict.

This task is far easier said than done. It requires an understanding of the unique limitations placed on strategy formulation for this type of conflict environment and a recognition that the army, structured and trained as it is, is unlikely to prove itself anything but a very blunt instrument of U.S. policy should it be called upon to intervene in an insurgency war that has moved beyond its formative phases. While this type of self-education would not necessarily improve the army's ability to conduct counterinsurgency warfare, it would at least eliminate the "can-doism" that characterized its Vietnam experience and bring about an awareness of the service's limitations in this kind of conflict. While the political leadership wishes to avoid army generals who might "pull a MacArthur" on them (as President Johnson purportedly fretted over), the army general who can "pull a Ridgway" and clearly state beforehand the costs and limits in committing major army forces to, say, the Philippines or El Salvador, would be doing the nation and its leaders a great service.

In the absence of this kind of recognition by the army, the Vietnam experience takes on a new, more tragic light. In spite of its anguish in Vietnam, the army appears to have learned little of value. Yet at the same time, the nation's policymakers seemingly have reinforced the service's misperceptions derived from the war while contemplating an increased role in low-intensity conflicts. This combination represents a dangerous mixture that may see the army repeating its Vietnam errors instead of learning from them.

Notes

1. Richard Halloran, "U.S. Will Not Drift into Combat Role, Weinberger Says," *New York Times,* November 29, 1984, pp. A1, A4.

2. Colin S. Gray, "National Style and Strategy: The American Example," *International Security* 6 (Fall 1981): 38.

3. Royal United Service Institution, *Lessons from the Vietnam War* (Whitehall, U.K.: Royal United Service Institution, February 12, 1969), p. 7.

4. See John E. Mueller, *War, Presidents, and Public Opinion* (New York: John Wiley, 1973); and Lloyd Norman and John B. Spores, "Big Push in Guerrilla Warfare," *Army* 12 (March 1962): 35.

5. For example, see Richard E. Dupuy, *The Compact History of the United States Army* (New York: Hawthorne Books, 1961), pp. 284–285; Roger Hilsman, *To Move a Nation* (Garden City, N.Y.: Doubleday, 1967), p. 139; and Russell F. Weigley, *History of the United States Army* (New York: Macmillan, 1967), pp. 16–18.

6. Norman and Spores, "Guerrilla War," p. 34.

7. Interview with General Maxwell D. Taylor, June 17, 1982.

8. Senator Gravelle edition, *The Pentagon Papers* (Boston: Beacon Press, 1971), 1: 472.

9. Interview with Major General Ruggles by the U.S. Army Center for Military History (CMH), Washington, D.C., February 27, 1980.

10. Interview with General Taylor.

11. For excellent analyses of the behavior of large organizations, see Graham T. Allison, *The Essence of Decision* (Boston: Little, Brown, 1971); Richard M. Cyert and James G. March, *A Behavioral Theory of the Firm* (Englewood Cliffs, N.J.: Prentice-Hall, 1963); Karl W. Deutsch, *The Nerves of Government* (New York: Free Press, 1966); Herbert Simon, *Models of Man* (New York: John Wiley, 1957); and John D. Steinbruner, *The Cybernetic Theory of Decision* (Princeton: Princeton University Press, 1974).

12. See Thomas W. Scoville, "United States Organization and Management for

Pacification, Advice and Support in Vietnam, 1954–1968: Bureaucratic Politics and Presidential Power" (Ph.D. draft dissertation, [no school given], 1975), p. 50.

13. Norman and Spores, "Guerrilla Warfare," p. 33.

14. Interview with Elvis H. Stahr by Robert H. Farrell, August 18, 1964, CMH, p. 33.

15. Department of the Army (DA), Office of the Secretary of the Army, memorandum for the Secretary of the Army from Brigadier General Stilwell, "Army Activities in Undeveloped Areas Short of Declared War" (Stilwell Report), October 13, 1961. See also DA, Office of the Chief of Staff, memorandum for the Secretary of the Army, "Army Activities in Underdeveloped Areas Short of Declared War," December 8, 1961.

16. For an in-depth analysis, see Andrew F. Krepinevich, Jr., *The Army and Vietnam* (Baltimore: Johns Hopkins University Press, 1986).

17. U.S. Army Combat Developments Command (CDC), "Doctrinal Literature for Special Warfare" (draft), January 1964, CMH, pp. 38–39; and CDC, "USCONARC Comments of the Review and Analysis of the Evaluation of U.S. Army Mechanized and Armor Combat Operations in Vietnam" (MACOV), May 15, 1967, CMH.

18. Ibid.

19. Ibid.

20. Interview with General Barksdale Hamlett, "Senior Officer Debriefing," by Colonel Jack Ridgeway and Lieutenant Colonel Paul Waler, March 11, 1976, U.S. Army Military History Institute (MHI), Carlisle Barracks, Pa., p. 1.

21. Colonel Harry G. Summers, *On Strategy: The Vietnam War in Context* (Carlisle, Pa.: U.S. Army War College); and Bruce Palmer, *The 25-Year War* (Lexington: University Press of Kentucky, 1984).

22. Summers, *On Strategy,* pp. 76–77; Palmer, *25-Year War.*

23. Halloran, "U.S. Will Not Drift into Combat," pp. A1, A4.

24. U.S. Army Pacific Operations Plan (USARPAC, OPLAN 37-64), n.d., CMH.

25. *Foreign internal defense* is but the latest in a long string of army attempts to label what most people refer to as counterinsurgency. Previously employed descriptors are *counterguerrilla warfare, stability operations,* and *internal defense and development.*

26. For example, see Robert A. Doughty and Robert V. Smith, "The Command and General Staff College in Transition, 1946–1976" (Fort Leavenworth, Kans.: Command and General Staff College, 1976), p. 56; Donald B. Vought. "Preparing for the Wrong War," *Military Review* 57 (May 1977): 16–34; and Peter M. Dawkins, "The United States Army and the 'Other' War in Vietnam: A Study of the Complexity of Implementing Organizational Change" (Ph.D. diss., Princeton University, 1979), pp. 437–438.

27. DA, *Command and Support of Special Forces Operations, FM 31-22* (Washington, D.C.: Government Printing Office, December 23, 1981), pp. 9–3, 9–4. See also Robert J. Baretto's excellent article, "Special Forces in the 1980's: A Strategic Reorientation," *Military Review* 63 (March 1983): 2–14.

28. Ibid.

29. DA, *Low Intensity Conflict, FM 100-20* (Washington, D.C.: Government Printing Office, January 1981), p. 211.

30. Ibid., p. 206.

31. Ibid.

32. Ibid., p. 162.

33. Alvin H. Berstein and John H. Waghelstein, "How to Win in El Salvador," *Policy Review* 17 (December 1984): 50–52.

34. DA, Office of the Deputy Chief of Staff for Operations (ODCSOPS), "U.S. Army Operational Concept for Special Operations Forces," n.d., pp. 12–13.

35. Ibid., p. 13.

36. DA, ODCSOPS, letter from Generals Parker and Rosson to CG USCONARC, "Implementation of the U.S. Army Special Warfare Program, FY 1963–68 (U)," October 25, 1962, CMH; DA, ODCSOPS, letter from Generals Parker and Rosson to CG USCONARC, "Implementation of the U.S. Army Special Warfare Program, FY 1963–68," no date; CMH; ODCSOPS, "Special Warfare and Special Forces," April 1, 1965, CMH; and DA, ODCSOPS, Congressional Fact Paper, "Special Warfare Program," April 1, 1965, CMH.

37. DA, Briefing: "The United States Army Light Infantry Division: Improving Strategic and Tactical Flexibility, (1984)."

38. See James R. Hollingsworth, "The Light Division," *Armed Forces Journal International* (October 1983): 84–92; Michael Duffy, "Army's New Light Tank," *Defense Week,* July 16, 1984, pp. 1, 20; and Michael Duffy, "9th Division Gets New Dune Buggy But an Old Tank," *Defense Week,* January 21, 1985, pp. 1–2.

39. See, for example, John M. Oseth, "Intelligence and Low Intensity Conflict," *Naval War College Review* 37 (November–December 1984): 19–36.

IV
The Consequences of Vietnam for U.S. Foreign Policy

14

Whither U.S. Foreign Policy?
The Place of Vietnam in the
Pattern of Containment

Robert E. Osgood

Vietnam as a Catalyst

The destinies of great states and empires seem to be shaped by great forces and factors that have, in retrospect, the semblance of inevitability. When one focuses on the individual features of foreign relations, however, it seems that the careers of great states are determined by personalities and events. My vision of history encompasses both perspectives. This chapter focuses on the larger pattern of U.S. postwar policy and examines the place of the Vietnam War within that pattern. The war—like the Berlin airlift, the Greek-Turkish aid program, the Korean War, Sputnik, and the Cuban missile crisis—was a decisive point in U.S. history.

The Vietnam War was a catalyst, a formative episode that has accelerated and accentuated a basic modification of containment, which continues to be the core of U.S. postwar policy. This modification springs from major developments and trends that were leading in the same direction. It can be characterized as the stabilization and maturing of containment—as the adaptation of global containment to a more complicated and constraining international environment at a steadier level of effort.

One can best comprehend the nature of this catalytic effect by placing the war in the larger pattern of postwar policy, which is formed by three interacting features: the steady geographical expansion of U.S. security interests and commitments, the oscillation between the augmentation and retrenchment of containment efforts, and the growth of domestic and international constraints against the implementation of containment.

The steady expansion of U.S. interests and commitments reflects the largely bipolar structure of international politics and the persistent outward thrust of U.S. and Soviet policies within this structure. Because interests and commitments always have expanded more rapidly than the power to support them if they should be threatened, the United States, like most other great powers or empires, has incurred a chronic power deficit. Periodically wars and crises have revived the intensified fears of the Soviet threat that have prodded the nation to close the gap between interests and power with an augmented containment effort, especially in defense. Yet after each augmentation, these fears subside, and the inveterate national yearning for a return to normal leads to the retrenchment or consolidation of containment. The hyperbolic effects of the presidential political system have amplified this oscillation between augmentation and retrenchment, especially when the shift of mood has coincided with the election of a new president.

The Pattern of Oscillation

Despite these oscillations, U.Y. interests and commitments have expanded consistently. At the same time, however, the changing structure of international politics, especially the diffusion of power and influence among states, and the expansion of U.S. global involvements have imposed, most markedly since the late 1960s, mounting constraints on the exercise of power. These constraints have been accompanied by mounting constraints on Soviet power, which also result from the changing structure of power and the expansion of global involvement. In the long run—let us say at least by the time we have experienced as many years after the Vietnam War as between World War II and Vietnam—these combined constraints may moderate the oscillations of containment as the nation adjusts its conception of security and the Soviet threat, along with its exercise of power. We may be witnessing the beginning of this process, as one of the most prominent oscillations0 which began in the last year of the Carter administration, subsides in the second Reagan administration.

In the context of this pattern of U.S. policy, the Vietnam War precipitated the second postwar period of retrenchment, analogous to, though also quite different from, the period following the Korean War. This retrenchment, in turn, was followed by the third (or Reagan) postwar period of augmentation, analogous to the initial period of the cold war that culminated in the Korean War and to the post-Sputnik years of the Kennedy administration. One of the most significant differences between the Reagan and Kennedy periods of augmentation is the markedly greater constraints on the exercise of power that have emerged since the Kennedy period.

Constraints on Containment

These constraints are by now so well recognized that it is sufficient to list them: the Soviet achievement of parity, or more, in every sector of military strength; the loss of U.S. primacy in trade and monetary relations, concomitant with the emergence of new centers of industrial and technological strength; the squeeze of foreign and defense expenditures imposed by a reduced economic growth rate, increased social expenditures, and a rising deficit; the growing impact of organized antinuclear and other peace groups; the assertion of legislative restrictions on executive power, combined with the fragmentation of congressional power and the growing impact of single-interest groups on foreign affairs; the dependence of major U.S. allies on foreign oil that is subject to political or military disruptions or denial of access; and the rise of nationalism, leftist anti-Americanism, internal instability, and international disorder in the third world. The Vietnam War had nothing to do with most of these constraints, but it did contribute to some of them, and it added its own.

The Legacy of Vietnam

The war contributed to organized nuclear pacifism at home and abroad, to congressional self-assertion, and to the increased impact of single-interest groups on foreign affairs. In this way it affected one of the most immutable elements of containment: the commitment of U.S. nuclear weapons and troops to the protection of Europe in the NATO framework. The popularization and politicization of security issues, stimulated by the organized dissent of the Vietnam War and exported to the publics, media, and educational institutions of democratic allies, accentuated the antinuclear movement that erupted with the intermediate-range nuclear force deployment crisis. This movement aggravated the problem of reassuring European allies that the United States will couple its nuclear forces to the defense of Europe but will not precipitate a nuclear or a conventional war on European soil. Carrying the causal chain a step further, one can reason that the Vietnam experience also contributed to the indispensable role that arms negotiations now play as a mainstay of allied reassurance and as a prerequisite for any major military program.

This interpretation, however, stretches the legacy of Vietnam beyond its most critical direct effects, which have been on the U.S. approach to the third world. Unlike the Korean War, the Vietnam War raised questions about the underlying premises of containment in the third world—about the extent of U.S1 vital interests, the nature and significance of the Soviet or Communist threat, the conditions justifying the direct use of U.S. force, and the utility of military intervention in revolutionary or quasi-revolutionary situations.

For the nation as a whole, these questions fell short of refuting or even clearly challenging the basic premises of containment. Vietnam did not, as the conventional interpretation says, shatter the postwar consensus, which always had left plenty of room for great and lesser debates, especially about the use of U.S. troops outside Europe. It merely showed that there is a limit to the price Americans are willing to pay for a military victory in order to vindicate the consensus in a war for intrinsically less-than-vital stakes that holds little promise of a political victory. Nevertheless, the traumatic experience of losing this war did create a powerful historical legend that impinges on the most troublesome and controversial problem of containment: when and how to use force against non-Soviet Communist countries or forces attempting to attack or subvert friendly countries that are not intrinsically of vital economic or strategic importance to U.S. security. This legend and its lessons, however ambiguous, will lastingly qualify the legend and lessons of Munich and the falling dominoes that ended in World War II, which dominated the formative period of containment.

Consequently containment, even in its most ambitious peacetime revival, is still notably more selective and qualified than before Vietnam. This selectivity is true in spite of the reaction against the Vietnam trauma that subsequent events have wrought. The collapse of the brief U.S.-Soviet détente of the 1970s, due primarily to the continuing Soviet military buildup despite SALT I and the Vladivostok agreement on SALT II and to the surge of Soviet activism in the period from Angola in 1975 through Afghanistan in 1979, did much to overcome the extremities of the Vietnam syndrome. In the perspective of these Soviet actions, the initial Carter effort to subordinate containment and the military instruments of power to human rights, North-South relations, and other items on the global agenda tended to discredit the liberal-idealist alternatives to the familiar thrust of U.S. security policy. As early as 1976, a conservative reaction against détente and the early Carter retrenchment, reflected in the views of some Carter officials as well as in other foreign policy elites, had gained the kind of influence that would give President Reagan his mandate to revitalize containment. Nevertheless, the legacy of Vietnam in U.S. foreign policy is still manifest in the heightened public aversion to using armed forces in gray-area contingencies, in the professional military's reluctance to participate in small wars except under the most favorable conditions for a quick victory for high stakes with assured popular support, and in congressional restraints, legislated and otherwise, on the president's authority to wage war and distribute military and economic assistance.

The full long-term effects of the Vietnam legacy on U.S. foreign policies and actions remain to be seen, since the legacy is only one factor in an equation whose other factors we cannot know. The long-term effects will depend, among other things, on the kinds of threats to containment that occur and on the way the national leadership deals with these threats—whether it tries to defy the legacy of Vietnam and the structural constraints on U.S. power or whether it manages to adapt the rhetorical and operational modalities of containment to these constraints. The first course, defiance, will lead to the repetition of the oscillations of mood and effort that have afflicted containment in the past. The latter course, adaptation, could finally sustain containment on the basis of a steady balance between power and interests. I am betting on the latter course.

Constraints on Soviet Power

One assumption underlying this bet is that the Soviet threat to U.S. security interests will be moderated by constraints on Soviet power that are even more formidable than those on U.S. power. In the high-stake security zones of major U.S. allies, there should be no question about the adequacy of these alliances as deterrents to Soviet aggression, although the problem of reassuring the allies of the credibility and prudence of U.S. protection will continue to be bedeviling. The most troublesome problems of containment will continue to occur in the third world. There the Soviets will continue to avoid direct or even indirect interventions that might bring them into a military encounter with U.S. forces. (Afghanistan was no exception.) But there will be abundant opportunities for forms of intervention short of such encounters and also abundant sources of constraint against the kind of Soviet intervention that would upset the global balance.

Through a variety of military and political means, the Soviets have greatly expanded their influence and presence in the third world, most markedly by exploiting the unique opportunities of the period from Angola through Afghanistan. Their success, however, has gained only a few geostrategic assets while incurring substantial costs and difficulties, including six insurgencies against clients and satellites, costly subsidies to clients, and further demands for subsidies that Moscow feels compelled to reject. Nowhere are the constraints on Moscow's extended empire more marked than in the Middle East. There Moscow's stakes are highest, and the opportunities for exploiting geostrategic positions, indigenous conflicts, and anti-U.S. sentiment seem greatest. Yet the combination of Afghan resistance, Iranian intractability, Syrian independence, the inconclusive Iran-Iraq war, the volatility of Lebanon's disorder, the decline of oil prices and the political weakening of OPEC, coupled with the reaffirmation of U.S. security interests, have so constrained Soviet expansionism as to make the alarms at the time of the Carter doctrine seem oddly excessive.

Moscow will not cease exploiting opportunities to diminish U.S. influence and advance its own, where risks and costs seem minimal. But in the context of other major constraints on its global empire—China's antagonism, Eastern Europe's instability and incipient independence, the costs of military competition with the United States and NATO, and a sluggish domestic economy with a second-rate technological capacity—these Third World constraints engender a sense of overcommitment that seems destined to enforce moderation.

Revised Demands of Containment

For these reasons the classic concept of containment, based on the lessons of the period between the two world wars, seems bound to be qualified by the more complicated realities of the structure and dynamics of contemporary international politics, as well as by the legacy of Vietnam. The independence and instability of many third world regimes; their growing distaste for Soviet intrusion in their affairs; the fluid, pluralistic, unstructured nature of intraregional politics; and the high incidence of national and communal conflicts create countervailing tendencies to one fallen domino leading to another. More clearly than ever, the domino analogy is a misleading simplification of a much more complicated dynamic of regional influence and counterinfluence, which, in fact, increasingly may favor the United States if it skillfully uses the superior means available to it (such as economic aid and preventive diplomacy) to pursue limited, attainable ends, principally preventing the Soviet Union and its allies from turning independent countries into hostile bases for military operations against their neighbors or the United States.

By the same token, it is clearly more unrealistic than ever to think of the third world as a homogeneous area of underdeveloped nationalists, full of vacuums waiting to be filled by a superpower. The third world is more like a disparate aggregation of heterogeneous regions and subregions with more or less stable indigenous balances of power, sustained or upset by regimes with a tremendous diversity of internal and external orientations, all of which the superpowers can influence only marginally for limited ends. This does not mean that the third world will cease to be the most volatile and potentially dangerous arena in the cold war. Quite the contrary. It means that the third world will be full of low-intensity conflicts, small interstate wars, state terrorism, subversion, and insurgency and that the typical kinds of superpower intervention will be ambiguous and indirect, with highly politicized military and economic assistance, covert action, and political-psychological operations predominating. For the United States, this situation means that containment will depend less on waging large-scale conventional or conventional-revolutionary wars than supporting local forces indirectly; conducting raids, rescues, counterterrorist, and peacekeeping or peacemaking operations; and keeping the sea-lanes and air corridors open for the flow of vital resources and for access to land. Even more, containment will depend on all measures short of armed force, which one might classify for lack of a better generic term as micropolitics: military assistance, economic aid, internal political persuasion and pressure, preventive diplomacy, diplomatic mediation, propaganda, and public diplomacy.

The United States nevertheless cannot afford to exclude the possibility of becoming directly engaged in local wars on the scale of the Korean and Vietnam wars, especially if it is not prepared to fight in areas of truly vital interests. But the typical direct engagements probably will be much less intense, though no less messy. If the United States is serious about backing containment with force, it has to be ready to intervene quickly, with little warning. The kind of small war it is likely to face must be fought for less than intrinsically vital interests, defined in limited political objectives. The war itself will be as much a political as a military engagement and therefore will constrain the full application of military capabilities. It probably will lack popular appeal and also may lack positive allied and regional support. Yet the United States cannot afford to make intervention contingent on advance assurance of popular or foreign support. It cannot count on such a war's coming to a rapid resolution, even as defined by limited objectives short of defeating the adversary. The United States cannot expect to win them all. There are likely to be more Lebanons than Grenadas.

Reassessment of Overcommitment

The third world thus poses a challenging environment for the effective application of containment, but this is not the kind of challenge that those who worry most about meeting the military demands of global containment usually have envisioned. Since the Korean War, the proponents of global containment, and particularly the professional military, have worried that the steady expansion of U.S. security interests and commitments into the waning colonial areas, together with the prospect of local Communist aggression supported by the Soviets or Chinese, and more recently, the growing projection capabilities of Soviet forces, would create demands on containment that U.S. resources and political will might be inadequate to meet. The Vietnam War, the Soviet use of Cuban and other proxies to extend its influence in the wake of the collapse of the Portuguese African empire, the collapse of Iran, the Soviet invasion of Afghanistan, and the Nicaraguan revolution have heightened the feeling of overcommitment in the United States. More precisely, the sense of overcommitment arises from the worry that the power of the United States, its allies, and friends may not be adequate to deter or defeat threats to U.S. security interests, that it may not have the resources to protect these interests, and that nobody else will do it for the United States.

As commonly conceived, this situation would seem to pose an insoluble problem. If the United States is not prepared to reduce commitments and its operating conception of vital interests — as few, if any, are explicitly willing to advocate — there would seem to be no way of counteracting overcommitment except periodically to correct it by exploiting Soviet-made crises to augment defense expenditures, which subsequently will languish when the atmosphere of crisis fades. The other ways by which successive administrations have tried to close the interests-power gap are no longer available or have proved deficient.

After the Korean War, the Eisenhower administration proposed to overcome the power deficit of global containment resulting from the fear of future Koreas all around the Sino-Soviet periphery by relying more on nuclear deterrence and on military alliances to reinforce deterrence in the third world (although its greatest successes in military containment were achieved by covert action). After the Vietnam War, the Nixon administration turned to rapprochement with the People's Republic of China (PRC), détente with the Soviet Union, linkage of arms control and grain sales to rules of reciprocal restraint in the third world, and the support of Iran as a security surrogate to close the gap between commitments and power, while the Nixon doctrine implicitly downgraded the scope of third world vital interests. President Carter initially relied on redefining the Soviet threat and building up the infrastructure of world order, only to shift to reviving containment after the Soviet invasion of Afghanistan.

The Reagan administration has sought to close the interests-power gap by augmenting military capabilities. Some high officials, lacking confidence in the adequacy of a military buildup to correct overcommitment without a change in military strategy, have articulated a strategy of horizontal escalation, in accordance with which the United States would counter aggression at one place by extending the war conventionally to another place where the United States presumably would enjoy compensating advantages. Some have sought indirectly to limit the operating conception of U.S. containment interests by defining conditions for the selective use of force. Several private defense analysts would solve the problems of overcommitment by reallocating U.S. conventional military resources from their concentration in Europe to meet more likely contingencies in the third world (particularly in the Persian Gulf area) while counting on increased allied contributions to regional defense to take up the slack.

None of these strategic expedients can solve the problem of overcommitment as it is usually conceived. Some, like substituting nuclear deterrence for local resistance, are obsolete. Others, like horizontal escalation or reallocation of security burdens, if actually implemented, would only aggravate the problem. Efforts to make the military implementation of containment more selective by openly defining the rules of engagement seek a reasonable objective by futile or dangerous means.

But perhaps I exaggerate the danger of overcommitment. Implicit in the common conception of the problem of overcommitment is a view of the Soviet threat that both exaggerates the magnitude of the problem in terms of direct conventional intervention and underestimates the importance of coping with it by blending force with politics in small wars, exploiting the indirect uses of force, and fully using the diversified measures of micropolitics.

Maturing of Containment

The Reagan administration has met the problem of reducing the global power deficit it inherited principally by augmenting military power on the basis of a restored economy but also by using available military power, directly and indirectly, with prudence (as in Central America) and with a willingness to back off from failure (as in Lebanon) as well as a readiness to seize an easy success (as in Grenada). Having restored the perception and much of the reality of military strength and the will to use it, the administration seems destined in its second term to concentrate on moderating the most direct Soviet threat, nuclear military competition, through arms negotiations while trying to preserve the military and economic base of power. It may well succeed. On the one hand, the domestic and external interests of the superpowers, although reflecting radically divergent goals, apparently coincide in seeking some improvement in the climate of relations, and arms negotiations have become the principal vehicle for such improvement. On the other hand, the prospect of actually reaching substantial arms reductions through a comprehensive agreement or of parlaying negotiations into regional accommodations is not so bright as to raise unrealistic expectations or encourage an imprudent relaxation of containment efforts.

Nevertheless, it is sobering to remember that historically Americans have been better at mobilizing to respond to an East-West crisis or an atmosphere of crisis than at husbanding and sustaining the bases of power in periods of relative calm. In periods of crisis, leaders are inclined to exaggerate the threat, but their mobilization of national energies restrains the adversary, restores the confidence of allies, and builds a sound base for moderation. In periods of calm, however, leaders who appeal for moderation and entrenchment are likely to encourage a euphoric retreat from reality toward historic normality, which sets the stage for the next panic. Whether, in the forthcoming period of return to relative calm, containment can be sustained on a steady basis, without the unsettling oscillations of the past, depends on whether it can be adapted to the more complicated, constraining domestic and international environment of foreign affairs. This, in turn, depends on whether the president and the foreign policy elites can infuse containment with patience, realism, and tactical flexibility while maintaining its dynamism.

On this prospect, the pessimists may contend that the successful revitalization of containment rests on fortunate circumstances, which have enabled the nation to feel better about itself without incurring any real military or economic sacrifice. When the full demands of containment in the final years of this century exact their inevitable frustrations and their human and material costs, the pessimists may say the nation will revert to its ingrained habit of trying either to overwhelm the problem in a burst of militancy or trying to escape the problem in a relapse into normalcy.

The optimists, on the other hand, can with equal reason maintain that Americans who care about foreign policy and aspire to influence it—now doubly chastened by the contrasting lessons of the loss of Vietnam and the failure of détente—finally are prepared to sustain containment on a steady basis with an unaccustomed tolerance of things that go wrong in an imperfect world. In this view, the current mood reflects the end of the romantic period of containment, during which either global order would reign or dominoes fall, and the United States would always win in war and peace or else purge the domestic enemy that deprived it of victory. It marks the maturing of containment as the nation learns to act without a guarantee of short-term victory because it knows that if the means of acting effectively are maintained in times of calm as well as crisis, the basic economic, social, and political forces at work in the world favor long-term success.

If the optimists are right, Vietnam will stand, in the perspective of a half-century of containment, not just as the greatest wartime loss of the United States but as the catalyst that helped to revive U.S. peacetime strength on an enduring basis. If the Nixon administration can be said to have rescued containment from Vietnam and the Carter administration to have abandoned and then rediscovered it, the Reagan administration will stand for the revitalization of containment and, one must hope, for the beginning of its stabilization and maturity.

15

Vietnam and the Mellowing of Containment: Implications for U.S. Foreign Policy Attitudes

John E. Mueller

Central to U.S. foreign and defense policy since World War II has been the policy of containment: the notion that the expansion of international communism must be opposed. In general, two arguments, or clusters of arguments, have been used to justify this policy. Using vernacular familiar from the Vietnam era, they can be called the bloodbath argument and the domino argument. The bloodbath argument stresses that communism is evil; people under this system suffer deprivation, are forced to surrender basic human rights, and undergo systematic brutality. The domino argument stresses that communism is a palpable threat: it is aggressive, dynamic, and messianic by nature, and, unless opposed, it will spread cancerously throughout the world step by step, domino by domino, until finally it infects and destroys even the United States either through subversion or outright warfare. The bloodbath argument is basically moral: we must save others from evil. The domino argument is basically practical and self-interested: we must save ourselves from ultimate destruction.

Of the two, the domino argument has been far more potent than the bloodbath argument. Opinion polls during the Korean and Vietnam wars often asked people why the wars should be supported. Compared to self-interested arguments about stopping communism, arguments about defending the attacked and preventing bloodbaths do very badly indeed.[1] Official thinking often reflects a similar view. In a March 1965 memo, Assistant Secretary of Defense John T. McNaughton specifically excluded as a U.S. aim in Vietnam the notion that the involvement was "to 'help a friend.' "[2] A comparison might be made with U.S. opposition to Hitler's Germany. Although the Nazi regime was widely considered to be bad, even monstrous, the United States went into forceful opposition only when the threat became directly pertinent in the form of the Japanese attack on Pearl Harbor and the German declaration of war on the United States. As long as international communism is seen as a genuine threat, support for efforts to oppose it can be mustered. If communism seems merely to be a distant evil infecting faraway lands, support will be comparatively niggling and infirm.

298 • The Consequences of Vietnam for U.S. Foreign Policy

How did containment, and these two arguments, relate to U.S. involvement in Vietnam? Although U.S. participation in the war was largely impelled by domino considerations, the war soon became something of a grim anachronism, and continued U.S. participation became increasingly difficult to justify. This experience in Vietnam contributed to an important change in U.S. foreign policy: a mellowing of the containment worldview, a shift away from the widely held belief that potential dominoes are everywhere. The influence of the Vietnam War on the U.S. conception of containment should not be overdrawn, however; much of this mellowing might well have happened anyway because of other historical changes that were going on in the world at the same time.

A commonly held conclusion in the early 1970s was that Vietnam shattered the U.S. foreign policy consensus, hinging principally on containment. Was this conclusion premature? How did Vietnam affect U.S. foreign policy attitudes? How was public support of U.S. foreign policy changed? Are these changes widely held, or do they reflect only the views of a vocal minority? We are able to examine evidence that deals with these important questions, but first it would be useful to review the dynamics of containment.

Containment Policy after World War II

The policy of containment stresses the lessons drawn from the Munich crisis of 1938: that totalitarian forces are aggressive by nature and that their appetite for more territory grows with the feeding. Thus communism and Communist expansion must be opposed.

Even among those who accepted this basic argument in the immediate postwar years, however, there was debate over how far it should be extended. While there was no great sentiment to push the Soviets out of Eastern Europe, it soon came to be widely agreed that the United States had vital interests in North America, Western Europe, and Japan, and Communist expansion needed to be opposed in those areas. In other regions, the U.S. containment perimeter excluded substantial areas. The Korean War solidly established the conclusion—already manifest in U.S. help for anti-Communist regimes in such noncentral places as China, Iran, Greece, the Philippines, Malaya, and French Indochina—that it was necessary to confront Communist expansion in all sorts of locales, even those not directly tied to vital U.S. interests.[3] Developments in the 1950s and early 1960s reinforced this lesson. Although the most important confrontations of this period were in Western Europe (particularly over Berlin) and in North America (particularly over Cuba), the newly emerging third world became an increasingly significant arena of contest. The United States actively worked in opposition to leftward development in Guatemala, Venezuela, Brazil, Iran, the Congo,

Laos, and South Vietnam. Combat troops were deployed to Lebanon in 1958 and the Dominican Republic in early 1965.

Much of the perceived heightened importance of the third world was due to the challenge and rhetoric of Soviet premier Nikita Khrushchev. Particularly after the successful launch of the Soviet space satellite Sputnik in 1957, Khrushchev confidently proclaimed that his regime was the "wave of the future" and invited the leaders of third world nations to join his team and to link arms with him at the inevitable funeral of the West and capitalism. China, then a Soviet ally, enthusiastically joined in these sentiments: "The east wind prevails," Chinese leaders assured all listeners. This threat of international communism inspired great alarm in Western capitals. There was a frantic scamper to try to catch up with the Soviets in the space race, and efforts were made to counter potential or actual Communist encroachment wherever they appeared on the globe. Potential dominoes were perceived everywhere. Seeking to match his counterpart in Moscow in rhetoric, President John Kennedy grandly declared in his inauguration speech in 1961, "We shall pay any price, bear any burden, meet any hardship, support any friend, oppose any foe, in order to assure the survival and success of liberty."

Vietnam and Containment

The Chinese and the Soviets supported wars of national liberation as a valid and constructive method of pursuing international revolution. Vietnam became an important test case for the policy of containment: a U.S. victory would not only prevent the fall of any immediate dominoes but might well be discouraging to other Communist efforts as well.[4]

By 1965, however, when decisions were made to deploy U.S. combat forces on a large scale into Vietnam, the Communist movement was deeply split. In 1963, after the trauma of the Cuban missile crisis, the Soviet Union began to back away from some of its earlier enthusiasm for revolutionary action. It found itself outclassed militarily, economically, and scientifically by the West, and, still under Khrushchev's leadership, it sought better relations with the United States. In defiance of the highly vocal wishes of its Chinese ally, the Soviet Union signed arms control agreements with the West and, in an admission that it could not even feed itself, purchased large quantities of food from the United States. Thus began a period that was later to be dubbed détente. The Chinese blasted Khrushchev at once for "adventurism" and "capitulationism" on Cuba and, later, for accommodation with the West. China's own foreign policy remained as active as ever; there were even efforts to set up influential Maoist parties in Africa. Most important, the Chinese forged a pseudo-alliance with Indonesia, a country led by the demagogic, anti-American Sukarno, a leader who was backed by the largest Communist party outside the Communist bloc itself. In response to these developments, U.S. opinion shifted: China, not the Soviet Union, was now seen to be the major enemy.[5] If the urgency of containing the Soviet Union waned a bit, the Chinese threat remained substantial.

In this context decisions were made in 1965 to send hundreds of thousands of U.S. troops to Vietnam. South Vietnam seemed on the verge of collapse; preventing such a collapse was deemed essential. C.L. Sulzberger compared the strategic picture to a nutcracker in which the small nations of Indochina were about to be crushed between two hostile pincers: China to the north and Indonesia to the south.[6] Leaders of many of the Southeast Asian nations—potential dominoes—urged the United States to save the situation. Malaysia's prime minister said in 1965, "In our view, it is imperative that the United States does not retire from the scene." Leaders in Australia, New Zealand, Cambodia, Singapore, Thailand, and India agreed.[7] In the United States there was wide agreement with reporter David Halberstam's assessment of Vietnam: "a strategic country in a key area, it is perhaps one of only five or six nations that is truly vital to U.S. interests," or with reporter Neil Sheehan's conclusion: "the fall of Southeast Asia to China or its denial to the West over the next decade because of repercussions of an American defeat in Vietnam would amount to a strategic disaster."[8]

Within two years, such assessments were no longer so widely accepted, not so much because standards changed but because circumstances radically altered. First, toward the end of 1965, there was a political crisis in Indonesia; a Communist coup attempt backfired. In the countercoup, tens of thousands of Communists were killed, and the party was destroyed. Second, China turned inward and became engulfed in its self-destructive Great Proletarian Cultural Revolution.

As a cold war event, then, U.S. intervention in Vietnam lost much of its relevance and resonance; it had become an anachronism. No one appreciated this more than the leaders of the Asian dominoes. When Clark Clifford, soon to become secretary of defense, visited Southeast Asia in late 1967, he was startled by the relaxed attitude in neighboring countries to the war: "It was strikingly apparent to me that the other troop-contributing countries no longer shared our degree of concern about the war. . . . Was it possible that our assessment of the danger to the stability of Southeast Asia and the Western Pacific was exaggerated? . . . Was it possible that we were continuing to be guided by judgments that might once have had validity but were now obsolete?"[9] As McGeorge Bundy observed, although Vietnam seemed vital in 1964 and 1965, "at least from the time of the anti-communist revolution in Indonesia, late in 1965, that adjective was excessive, and so also was our effort."[10] Others increasingly shared Clifford's doubts, and opposition to the war grew both among the public and among the foreign policy elites. The war seemed an endless, costly affair that no longer had a purpose.[11]

In the face of eroding public support, there were arguments other than the domino theory that could be invoked to justify continued U.S. participation in the war. One of these was a version of the bloodbath argument: U.S. withdrawal, it was asserted, would deliver to a merciless enemy the people who had trusted the United States and placed their fate in its hands. Historical examples gave this argument cogency: the brutality of the Communist Viet Minh upon those who opposed them after taking over North Vietnam in 1954, the massacres by the Communists when they briefly held the city of Hue during the Tet offensive of 1968.

As the war continued, however, this bloodbath argument gradually diminished in effectiveness. It is difficult to justify war in order to save lives. The bloodbath argument makes sense only if one can demonstrate the consequences of a Communist victory would be even bloodier than the process used to prevent such a victory. Moreover, it could be argued that after the United States had lost tens of thousands of lives and paid tens of billions of dollars in an effort to save the South Vietnamese from this fate, it was time for the South Vietnamese to take charge of their own destiny.

Other arguments for justifying the continuing U.S. war effort were generally more effective. For example, it was argued that the war must continue because honor and credibility were at stake, because the United States never loses wars, because failure would bring about political chaos in the United States. Most effective of all, in all probability, was the perceived imperative to free the American prisoners still in the hands of the North Vietnamese. Although it may not make a great deal of sense to continue a war costing thousands of lives to gain the return of a few hundred prisoners, it is difficult to exaggerate the potency of this argument. In May 1971, 68 percent of those surveyed in a public opinion poll agreed that U.S. troops should be withdrawn from Vietnam by the end of the year. However, when asked if they would still favor withdrawal if that would mean a "communist takeover of South Vietnam," only 29 percent still agreed. When asked if they approved withdrawal "even if it threatened [not cost] the lives or safety of United States' POWs held by North Vietnam," support for withdrawal dropped to 11 percent.[12]

Containment Outside Vietnam

Meanwhile, as the relevance to U.S. interests of a collapse of South Vietnam became less and less obvious, U.S.-Soviet relations and U.S.-Chinese relations were progressing almost as if the war did not exist. The two major powers concluded several important arms control and trade agreements, and their relations took on a reasonably civil, if not entirely amicable, tone. Negotiations tended to be difficult but productive, quite a contrast from the

1950s where most discussion was carried out at a high-pitched, propagandistic level. In addition both sides avoided confrontation; indeed, since 1962, there had been scarcely a crisis between the two powers worthy of the label. While these developments hardly brought deep friendship between the two sides—both warily continued arms buildups, for example—the arrival and development of détente did help to relax tensions between them. Fears of major crisis and war dwindled.[13] The space race, which had seemed such a vital test just a few years before, was won handily by the United States. These developments caused the Communist threat to seem less urgent and further diminished the impact of the domino argument.

While this mellowing of U.S.-Soviet relations continued, another even more striking change developed as the United States and China moved toward a rapprochement. The Chinese gradually dropped their role as leader and inspirer of revolutionary movements around the globe and began to concentrate on recovering from their own self-inflicted domestic wounds. As a result, perceptions that China was a revolutionary threat were supplanted by desires to integrate China into the world economic and political system.[14] Reinforced by erosion of the political influence of nonruling Communist parties throughout the West, these developments assuaged perceptions of the Communist threat.[15]

Thus the history of containment includes the emergence, over the course of the decade following the large-scale U.S. commitment to the Vietnam War, of a paradox in U.S. policy. Although the war raged between 1965 and 1975 as, supposedly, an ultimate test case between the Communist and non-Communist worlds, relations between the leading powers of these worlds warmed significantly. The United States committed its power and prestige in Vietnam as an instrument of containment; yet containment increasingly seemed less necessary because the threat of global communism was revealed to be more fragmented, less dynamic, and more vulnerable than had been generally conceived in the early 1960s.

This paradox confounds efforts to evaluate the impact of the Vietnam War on U.S. foreign policy. It is often argued that the Vietnam experience made the United States less willing to intervene to prevent the spread of communism; the United States became leery of getting involved in another Vietnam. Such behavior, however, is also consistent with declining concern among many Americans about the threat posed by international communism. Consequently, many of the lessons of Vietnam may be specious; rather, these observations may simply reflect responses to changing global politics. Opinion changes in Western Europe, an area that did not experience the Vietnam War directly, support this alternative conclusion. Many Europeans concluded during this same period that the Soviet Union posed no real threat, and they began to argue that strenuous, costly efforts to contain it had become unnecessary. NATO commander Bernard Rogers observed in exasperation, "The biggest challenge we face in NATO is getting the message across to our people that there is a threat to their freedom down the road."[16] In any case, we must be careful to avoid attributing too much to Vietnam.

Containment after Vietnam

By cold war standards, the immediate post-Vietnam period of the middle and late 1970s marked a banner era for international communism. For the first time since Fidel Castro came to power in Cuba in 1959, significant areas joined the international Communist orbit: Communist regimes won in Cambodia, South Vietnam, and Laos, and pro-Soviet factions took over in Angola, Ethiopia, South Yemen, Afghanistan, Grenada, Nicaragua, and Mozambique.[17] There were sharp leftward lurches in Spain and Portugal that sometimes seemed likely to bring pro-Communist governments to power.

Although these and other developments injected more hostility into U.S.-Soviet relations, several general lessons seem to have been learned from these experiences. These lessons may have contributed to bringing the containment doctrine under question.

First, the domino theory does not work in any direct sense. If one country falls to communism, others will not necessarily collapse or even teeter very much. The topplings of the 1970s did not lead to a cascade of further topplings. Nor did these topplings detract from the credibility of U.S. guarantees to areas of central concern like Japan and Western Europe.[18] To apply the logic of the domino argument—the collapse of a country to communism that triggers instability in other, more important countries—is not of great consequence to U.S. security.

Second, even countries that do succumb to communism do not necessarily stay that way. Unless they are dominated directly by Soviet troops, they may well adapt communism to national circumstances or drift back toward the West. Examples of this fluidity include Mozambique and Portugal and, earlier, Egypt, Sudan, Ghana, Guinea, and Somalia. Communist gains are by no means irreversible. Indeed, the Soviets have been greatly concerned about their inability to foresee, create, and control events within the third world. In fact, "the Soviets have experienced considerable frustration in their attempts to forge a lasting network of reliable client states in the Third World."[19]

Third, countries that continue to accept a form of communism often do not form very attractive models for other countries: Communist gains have often been accompanied by misery.[20] Moreover, having alienated the wealthy West, nascent Communist regimes often find that they are tied to the Soviet Union for whatever niggling support the Soviets can manage. Thus, third world states find they must "continue to rely on the West for trade, investments, and technological assistance, areas in which Moscow cannot compete effectively or advantageously with the West."[21]

Fourth, Soviet gains may have had a sobering impact on the Soviet Union itself. While its new client states were seen initially as a positive gain,[22] the costs to the Soviet Union of sustaining its empire rose considerably during the 1970s and now probably stand at several percent of its GNP.[23] Indeed the Soviet colossus now seems to be in foundering, overextended disarray: involved in an enervating war in Afghanistan, wary of China, overbudgeted in defense, unable either to abandon its empire in Eastern Europe and elsewhere or to make it work, saddled with an economy notable for its creaking lassitude, and plagued within its borders by social and anthropological problems that range from rampant alcoholism to rising Muslim fundamentalism.

Finally, areas that are truly important to the United States—Western Europe and Japan—remain politically stable, while support for Communist parties there is generally on the decline.

Although Soviet-inspired international communism has hardly become tame or benevolent, the movement lacks the effective, infectious dynamism presumed in the domino theory. As Dimitri K. Simes has put it: "The modern Soviet state bears a closer resemblance to a superbly armed Austria-Hungary than to Nazi Germany. . . . Soviet global momentum has declined significantly. . . . The Soviet model of development has lost its appeal for the outside world."[24] Indeed, there is something almost ludicrous about the situation. While Soviet leaders certainly retain a massive military capability, they manage to live in mortal fear of the potential subversive effects on their hold on power of personal computers, videotape recorders, photocopier machines, and telephone books. Their spectacular mishandling, from both a public health and a public relations standpoint, of the Chernobyl nuclear accident highlights the situation.

These lessons and consequences suggest that the fall of distant lands to communism may often be of little real consequence to the United States. From the view of the 1950s that almost everywhere is important, some now argue that almost nowhere is important.[25] Areas that remain vital to U.S. security include North America, Japan, and Western Europe and, probably for reasons more of sentiment than security, South Korea and Israel. The perceived importance of the Persian Gulf area is likely to be tied to the varying need for oil. The rest of the world is, to a considerable degree, beyond the containment pale. Indeed, the Reagan administration has discovered that getting congressional and elite support even for rather inexpensive anti-Communist ventures in Central America, an area close to home, is very difficult. In arguing that Communist gains in the area are undesirable in part because they "will send millions of refugees north," President Reagan was hardly evoking images of the sort of contagion feared by containment theorists.[26]

Implications for U.S. Public Support and Policy

Thus it seems that, for many, the perceived threat of international communism has waned. As a consequence, the containment doctrine's keystone role in U.S. foreign policy has become circumscribed by the perceived reduced validity of its fundamental premise: the domino theory. What are the implications of these changes for U.S. foreign policy attitudes?

It is difficult precisely to assess the impact on public opinion of cold war shifts and of the Vietnam War. It seems likely, however, that neither the Vietnam debacle nor the mellowing of the Communist threat has caused a permanent drop in the public's stated willingness to use military action against encroachment by the forces of communism. People may be less worried by the Communist threat both internally and externally, but now that the experiences of the mid-1970s are absorbed, the public seems about as willing as ever before to confront challenges put forward by the Communists. If support for containment, broadly defined, has mellowed, this decline seems to have occurred among foreign policy elites much more than among the public.

While a decline occurred in the early 1970s in the American public's willingness to fight communism, by the late 1970s there was a significant rebound.[27] Impelled perhaps by the outrage over the Iranian hostage crisis of November 1979–January 1981, support for anti-Communist activism remained at those higher levels in the 1980s. For example, the percentage willing to send U.S. troops to defend Western Europe in the event of a Soviet invasion there rose from 39 in 1974 to 60 in 1980 and registered at 58 in 1985. Support for committing U.S. troops to defend South Korea against an invasion by North Korea rose from 14 percent in 1974, to 20 in 1981, and to 27 in 1983.[28] Some measures, in fact, stand at historical highs. The percentage willing to support U.S. military involvement should the Soviet Union invade Yugoslavia was 15 percent in 1951 and 11 percent in 1974; this rose to 36 percent in 1980 after the hostage taking in Iran.[29]

Elite attitudes, on the other hand, seem to reflect a shift from the global anti-Communism of containment to a more selective and discriminate perspective in weighing interests, threats, and policy responses. Between 1974 and 1978, elite support for sending U.S. troops to defend areas of vital interest like Western Europe rose considerably, while enthusiasm for defending places like Yugoslavia rose only slightly.[30]

Thus, the current of neoisolationism that swept over the United States during Vietnam has largely receded. Public foreign policy attitudes in the 1980s reflect about as much willingness as ever to take actions against Communist expansionism. (However, it should not be assumed that the public was ever gleeful about jumping into anti-Communist combat in faraway places; its unwillingness to see the United States further involved in the Indochina War in 1954, for example, was considerable.) On the other hand, elite attitudes seem changed somewhat: containment is judged valid only in selective application; policy must be proportionate to the importance of interests.

Thus, the combination of the mellowing of containment and the United States experience in Vietnam may have modified the postwar foreign policy elite consensus. Many in this elite wonder why the United States should spend time and effort continuing to worry about the spread of communism in areas that are far from central to U.S. interests. In 1985 Secretary of State George Shultz gave one answer. While he did suggest in passing that the fall of countries to communism usually results in "an increase in Soviet global power and influence," his main reason for actively opposing Communist regimes stressed bloodbaths rather than dominoes. Communism means misery, oppression, and brutality for the countries so controlled, he argued, and the United States should help the people opposing it for those reasons. That is, communism should be opposed because it is bad, not so much because it is a credible and dangerous threat.[31]

This reflects the other lesson of the post-1975 experience. While the domino prediction may not have been realized in the aftermath of debacle in Indochina, the bloodbath prediction did come true to a considerable degree. The catastrophic destruction of Cambodia by the victorious Communists went significantly beyond the imagined horror stories, and the consequences of Communist victory in South Vietnam have been less brutal only in degree. There has been mass imprisonment, extensive bloodshed, severe economic disruption, racial persecution, and a desperate exodus of the disaffected.[32] Communist success in Angola and Afghanistan has meant continued civil warfare along with economic and administrative chaos, and Ethiopia has suffered this plus massive famine.

Another somewhat related reason for opposing international communism might be called Leninism on its head. Because the Soviet Union is saddled with many problems within its borders as well as within its overextended empire, some analysts propose that the United States should seek to exacerbate Soviet troubles through political and economic warfare and by inflicting defeats on its foreign policy. The hope is that by pushing the Soviets' internal contradictions to the point of major crisis, genuine reform will be forced upon that country's ruling circles.[33]

But these approaches are likely to inspire only limited support, particularly from elites. In the past, major anti-Communist efforts were widely accepted because they seemed to counter a perceived threat, not because they were seen to be doing good or because they might help manipulate Soviet policy in a favorable direction. Current anti-Communist ventures in distant areas of the globe are likely to inspire broad support only if the risks and costs remain low. Meddling and tinkering in these areas—support to friendly countries here, aid to anti-communist rebels there—may be accepted. But it seems unlikely that significant intervention will be.

Notes

1. John Mueller, *War, Presidents and Public Opinion* (New York: Wiley, 1973), pp. 44, 48–49, 100–101; and John Mueller, "Some Reflections on the Vietnam Antiwar Movement and on the Curious Calm at the War's End," in *Vietnam as History,* ed. Peter Braestrup (Lanham, Md.: University Press of America, 1984), p. 156.

2. Neil Sheehan et al., *The Pentagon Papers* (New York: Bantam, 1971), p. 432.

3. For excellent discussions of these developments stressing the capping importance of the Korean War, see John Lewis Gaddis, "Was the Truman Doctrine a Real Turning Point?" *Foreign Affairs* 52 (January 1974): 386–401; and Robert Jervis, "The Impact of the Korean War on the Cold War," *Journal of Conflict Resolution* 24 (December 1980): 563–592; and Ernest R. May, "The Cold War," in *The Making of America's Soviet Policy,* ed. Joseph S. Nye, Jr. (New Haven: Yale University Press, 1984), pp. 209–230.

4. In a memo in September 1984, Secretary of Defense Robert McNamara stressed "the impact of a Communist South Vietnam not only in Asia, but in the rest of the world, where the South Vietnam conflict is regarded as a test case of U.S. capacity to help a nation meet a Communist 'war of liberation.' " Sheehan et al., *Pentagon Papers,* p. 278. See also Gunther Lewy, *America in Vietnam* (New York: Oxford University Press, 1978), pp. 424–425. On the issue in the Sino-Soviet debate, see G.F. Hudson et al., *The Sino-Soviet Dispute* (New York: Praeger, 1961), pp. 14, 33–34, 132, 176, 211–214.

5. Between 1961 and 1964, the public was asked four times: "Looking ahead to 1970, which country do you think will be the greater threat to world peace — Russia or Communist China?" The proportion choosing Russia dropped from 49 to 20, and the proportion choosing China rose from 32 to 59. George H. Gallup, *The Gallup Poll: Public Opinion, 1935–1971* (New York: Random House, 1972), pp. 1711, 1811, 1881, 1908–09.

6. C.L. Sulzberger, "Foreign Affairs: The Nutcracker Suite," *New York Times,* April 10, 1966, p. 8E.

7. Lewy, *America,* pp. 421–422; see also Hubert Humphrey, *The Education of a Public Man* (Garden City, N.Y.: Doubleday, 1976), p. 333.

8. David Halberstam, *The Making of a Quagmire* (New York: Random House, 1965), p. 319. Neil Sheehan, "Much Is at Stake in Southeast Asian Struggle," *New York Times,* August 16, 1964, p. 4E.

9. Clark Clifford, "A Vietnam Reappraisal," *Foreign Affairs* 47 (January 1969): 606–607. On these developments, see also John Mueller, "Reassessment of American Foreign Policy, 1965–1968," in *Vietnam Reconsidered,* ed. Harrison E. Salisbury (New York: Harper, 1984), pp. 48–52.

10. McGeorge Bundy, "The Americans and the World," in *A New America?* ed. Stephen R. Graubard (New York: Norton, 1978), p. 293.

11. For a discussion of the rising costs of the war and of the issue of cost tolerance, see John Mueller, "The Search for the 'Breaking Point' in Vietnam," *International Studies Quarterly* 24 (December 1980): 497–519. The Communist side seems to have been virtually unique in the history of warfare over the last 160 years in its

willingness to accept losses (its battle death rate was about twice that of the Japanese in World War II, for example). Those who argue that the communists could have been beaten if the United States had pursued a different strategy in the war need to demonstrate how their proposed strategy would cause the will of this peculiarly fanatical and resourceful enemy to be broken. Consideration of the enemy was notably lacking at the 1985 West Point conference on Vietnam.

12. Opinion Research Corporation release, May 8, 1971. The necessity of getting the prisoners back is supported by Henry Kissinger in his review of the options in the Vietnam negotiations: "unilateral withdrawal . . . would not do the trick; it would leave our prisoners in Hanoi's hands"; and "Vietnamization pursued to the end would not return our prisoners." Henry Kissinger, *White House Years* (Boston: Little, Brown, 1979), pp. 1011, 1039. Apparently the option of ending the war without the return of the prisoners was not even a hypothetical consideration. The emotional attachment to prisoners of war has often been a dominant theme in U.S. history. The issue was central to the lengthy peace talks in the Korean War. Outrage at the fate of American POWs on Bataan probably intensified hatred for the Japanese during World War II almost as much as the attack on Pearl Harbor. Another case in point is the almost total preoccupation by politicans and press with the Iranian hostage crisis of 1979–1981 to the virtual exclusion of issues and events likely to be of far greater importance historically; see John Mueller, "Lessons Learned Five Years after the Hostage Nightmare," *Wall Street Journal,* June 4, 1985, p. 28.

13. For public opinion data on the decline after 1963 in the fear that a world war was imminent, see John Mueller, "Changes in American Public Attitudes toward International Involvement," in *The Limits of Military Intervention,* ed. Ellen P. Stern (Beverly Hills, Calif.: Sage, 1977), pp. 323–344. Also see John Mueller, "Public Expectations of War during the Cold War," *American Journal of Political Science* 23 (May 1979): 301–329.

14. By the 1980s the Chinese announced that they had "only ideological and moral relations" with communist insurgencies in Southeast Asia and expressed their desire to see "stability and prosperity" in the area. Henry Kamm, "China Plays Down Support of Asian Rebels," *New York Times,* February 2, 1981, p. A3.

15. Meanwhile, yet another development was occurring: a considerable decline in the fear of communist subversion at home. Fears of the "concealed enemy," so important an issue in the 1950s, almost completely vanished from the public debate. For example, the number of items under the heading, "Communism–US" in *The Reader's Guide to Periodical Literature* totaled 73 in 1949, 170 in 1954, 37 in 1961, and 6 in the entire decade of the 1970s. See John Mueller, "Trends in Political Tolerance from *1984* to 1984" paper delivered at the 1984 Annual Meeting of the American Political Science Association, Washington, D.C.

16. "How NATO's Top Officer Views the Alliance," *U.S. News and World Report,* October 1, 1984, p. 38.

17. These developments do not seem to have been the result so much of pre-planned Soviet policy as of a cautious assertive opportunism. Stephen T. Hosmer and Thomas W. Wolfe, *Soviet Policy and Practice toward Third World Conflicts* (Lexington, Mass.: Lexington Books, 1983), pp. 66, 135, 168.

18. Moreover, these developments raised amazingly little alarm in the United States: far from engendering the new era of McCarthyism (the original had supposedly been launched by the fall of China in 1949), the collapse of anti-communist regimes in these areas—in the case of Indochina, an utter debacle for U.S. foreign policy—was met largely with shrugging indifference. See Mueller, "Some Reflections," pp. 155–156.

19. Hosmer and Wolfe, *Soviet Policy,* pp. 65–68, 136, 166; see also Ernst Haas, "On Hedging Our Bets: Selective Engagement with the Soviet Union," in *Beyond Containment,* ed. Aaron Wildavsky (San Francisco: Institute for Contemporary Studies, 1983), pp. 93–124; and Elizabeth K. Valkenier, *The Soviet Union and the Third World* (New York: Praeger, 1983).

20. "The flood of Laotian and Cambodian refugees into Thailand was a great help to the government's counterinsurgency efforts, says a Thai General. . . . 'I used to . . . tell the people what Communism would bring. . . . After the refugees came . . . the people would tell *me* about the Communists. They had learned.' " James P. Sterba and Lee Lescaze, "Vietnam's Legacy: Of the Asian Dominoes That Haven't Fallen, Several Are Thriving," *Wall Street Journal,* March 14, 1985, p. 28. Most Grenadans, too, seem to have come to regard their brief brush with Marxist leadership with distaste. See also James P. Sterba, "Bandung Anniversary Spurs Some to Suggest Communism Is Losing Appeal in Third World," *Wall Street Journal,* April 23, 1985, p. 34.

21. Hosmer and Wolfe, *Soviet Policy,* p. 166.

22. Ibid., p. 55.

23. Charles Wolf, Jr., et al., *The Costs of Soviet Empire* (Santa Monica, Calif.: Rand Corporation, 1983); see also Michael T. Kaufman, "Moscow Said to Lose Sway among Africans," *New York Times,* November 22, 1983, pp. A1, 12; and Valkenier, *Soviet Union.*

24. Dimitri K. Simes, "The New Soviet Challenge," *Foreign Policy* 55 (Summer 1984): 113, 118, 122.

25. See, for example, Ernst B. Haas: "Why commit ourselves to maintaining American influence in the Third World? . . . Soviet power in those areas . . . will not pose a military threat to the United States . . . they do not necessarily threaten our way of life. Crudely put, my argument says: who cares what happens to Ethiopia, Laos, or El Salvador?" Haas, "On Hedging," pp. 113–114. Bruce Porter observes: "What the USSR achieved in the Third World between 1973 and 1980 would have been totally unacceptable to the United States only a few years earlier; two decades earlier it might have led to war." Yet, he notes, "The entry of such weak and poorly developed countries as Angola, Ethiopia, Cambodia, and Afghanistan into the Soviet camp does not amount to more than a minor shift in the global balance." *The USSR in Third World Conflicts* (New York: Cambridge University Press, 1984), pp. 242, 238. See also Alan Tonelson, "The Real National Interest," *Foreign Policy* (Winter 1985–86): 49–72.

26. "Excerpts from President's Address," *New York Times,* April 16, 1985, p. A8.

27. See, for example, Mueller, "Changes," p. 335.

28. John E. Reilly, *American Public Opinion and U.S. Foreign Policy 1975* (Chicago: Chicago Council on Foreign Relations, 1975), p. 18; Alvin Richman, "Public

Attitudes on Military Power, 1981," *Public Opinion* 4 (December–January 1982): 44–46; "Opinion Roundup," *Public Opinion* 6 (April–May 1983): 35; and Cathleen Decker, "Most Americans Would Have Quit Vietnam Sooner," *Los Angeles Times,* April 29, 1985, pp. 1, 9.

29. Mueller, "Changes," p. 333; Richman, "Public Attitudes," p. 45.

30. Reilly, *American Public Opinion,* 1975, p. 18; John E. Reilly, *American Public Opinion and U.S. Foreign Policy 1979* (Chicago: Chicago Council on Foreign Relations, 1979), p. 26; William Schneider, "Elite and Public Opinion," *Public Opinion,* February/March 1983, pp. 7–8. For other discussion of elite attitudes, see Ole R. Holsti and James N. Rosenau, *American Leadership in World Affairs: Vietnam and the Breakdown of Consensus* (Boston: Allen and Unwin, 1984).

31. George Schultz, "Challenging the Brezhnev Doctrine," *Wall Street Journal,* February 28, 1985, p. 28.

32. See Nguyen Van Canh, *Vietnam Under Communism, 1975–1982* (Stanford, CA: Hoover Institution, 1983); Jacqueline Desbarats and Karl D. Jackson, "Research Among Vietnam Refugees Reveals a Blood Bath," *Wall Street Journal,* April 22, 1985, p. 29.

33. For versions of this argument, see Richard Pipes, *Survival Is Not Enough* (New York: Simon and Schuster, 1984), and Irving Kristol, "Coping with an 'Evil Empire,' " *Wall Street Journal,* December 17, 1985, p. 32.

16
The Long-Term Significance of the Vietnam Experience

Robert W. Komer

The U.S. Grenada victory reminds us of three important factors that are relevant to a reassessment of the impact of Vietnam: that nothing succeeds like success; the impact of time in healing all but mortal wounds; and the cyclical nature of U.S. foreign policy behavior. I am not alone in suggesting that Vietnam perspectives have altered with the passage of time. One is struck by the different tenor and thrust of most of the chapters in this book compared with essays written in the late 1960s and 1970s. The focus of this book itself is different, in asking "Did Vietnam Make a Difference?" The question mark suggests how much perceptions change over time as the impact of once-traumatic events attenuates and other factors crowd into our consciousness. Most of the chapters in this book suggest that Vietnam has had far less impact on the power position of the United States, on attitudes, and on perceptions than was generally held in the conventional wisdom of the 1970s and early 1980s. Perhaps, in fact, over the longer term, little—or at least less—has changed as a result of the Vietnam experience. Is this true? Or, as is usually the case with the passage of time, are we simply focusing on other larger factors to explain many things that we tended at one point to attribute to Vietnam?

In examining this question, I will advance a series of brief propositions about the longer-term significance of the Vietnam experience. First, Vietnam appears today as much less a watershed in the East-West competition than as an important episode in a long and continuing contest between the superpowers since the end of World War II. Whether the East-West political competition is qualitatively different today than in the 1950s is arguable. Differences, such as they exist, are attributable more to the emergence of U.S.-Soviet strategic nuclear parity than to any watershed effect of Vietnam. Rather, the U.S. Vietnam experience should be viewed as one of a series of factors affecting U.S. willingness to use force in the continuing overall policy of containment.

On the other hand, Vietnam did have a major impact on the East-West military balance. It is hard to overestimate the enormous cost of the Vietnam

War for the U.S. defense posture. In constant 1985 dollars, the direct incremental cost of the Vietnam War was on the order of $330 billion. To this one must add the indirect costs of the Vietnam syndrome—at least $150 billion in defense budget reductions as the United States expiated the war by cutting back on defense budgets.[1] One could also add other costs, such as the higher cost of the volunteer army, a direct consequence of Vietnam. Besides 57,000 lives, the Vietnam War cost the United States on the order of a half-trillion dollars in foregone outlays for defense investment and nondefense programs. (Spending for force structure and operations and maintenance tends to decline much less rapidly than investment when funding is scarce.) Therefore the Vietnam War cost the equivalent of several years of defense investment spending at a time when a steady Soviet defense buildup was still occurring. In addition, U.S. spending for the war triggered massive domestic inflation during the 1970s and the early 1980s. Inflation continually outran budget projections and further eroded real defense output in subsequent years.

The result was a distinct adverse shift in the U.S.-Soviet military balance. There was also an adverse shift in the NATO–Warsaw Pact military balance, despite the modest compensatory increases in European NATO spending during the 1970s. This adverse shift in the balance of power persists today. The defense budget increases of the Reagan and Carter administrations (1978–1985) total less than the half-trillion dollar cost of the Vietnam War and postwar budget cuts. Despite the Reagan reinvestment campaign, the military balance between the United States and the Soviet Union has not improved appreciably, although the balance is no longer deteriorating as it was during the 1970s.

On the other hand, we should be careful not to overstate the importance of a shift in the military balance. Perceptions of reality in international affairs are more important than reality itself. Although the U.S. defense posture was crippled by the diversion of half a trillion dollars on Vietnam while the Soviets were spending heavily on defense, neither Moscow nor U.S. allies seem to believe that the military balance has shifted so much against the United States as to encourage more aggressive Soviet or surrogate behavior. Certainly Moscow does not seem to perceive that the correlation of forces has shifted in its favor sufficiently to justify running greater risks. Quite the contrary, President Reagan seems to be perceived in Moscow and elsewhere abroad as having done much to rebuild U.S. strength and self-confidence—more than has in fact, perhaps, occurred. True, the Reagan administration has tried hard to rebuild military strength. The deficits from the prior decade, caused in particular by the Vietnam War, have not yet been made up, however. The Soviet Union, on the other hand, has had its own problems: a structural economic crisis, the intervention quagmire in Afghanistan, and the post-Brezhnev succession crisis.

The loss of U.S. nuclear superiority may have been hastened somewhat by the Vietnam War. On the other hand, many argue that Soviet determination to achieve a nuclear posture capable of ensuring Soviet victory in a war made the emergence of nuclear parity inevitable. Despite the advent of nuclear parity, however, nuclear deterrence still seems to work, particularly where unambiguous U.S. commitments are concerned, as in Western Europe, Northeast Asia, and the Persian Gulf.

The loss of Indochina failed, in the long run, to undermine the U.S. geostrategic position in the world, even in the Pacific. The really important dominoes—Indonesia, Malaysia, Thailand—did not fall. Indeed, the continuing Sino-U.S rapprochement leaves the United States better off strategically in the Pacific than it was before the Vietnam War. In fact, Americans and their allies have not lost any strategically vital real estate since 1945.

The second proposition concerns the impact of Vietnam on U.S. policy behavior. This impact is at least as significant as that of any shift in the East-West balance of power. What is the political and psychological influence of the war on the apparent turning inward of the United States or, as some have called it, the loss of U.S. nerve? There is little doubt that this turning inward imposed caution on U.S. policy during the 1970s, a caution encouraged by perceptions of circumscribed military capabilities as a result of the Vietnam syndrome. Americans thought for a decade that they were considerably weaker than the rest of the world perceived them to be. This caution persists in the 1980s.

Such caution was reinforced by a series of restrictions imposed by Congress on the freedom of action of the executive branch. Consider, for example, the 1973 War Powers Act, the restrictive amendments on foreign aid and sales, and the congressional prohibition on so-called covert aid to the insurgents in Angola. Here, however, we must distinguish between the short and the long terms. These restrictions may well promote a general shift toward U.S. foreign policy retrenchment. However, this shift does not necessarily signal a fundamental change in containment policy. Rather, these constraints modify the way the United States goes about executing the continuing policy of containment. Short-term impacts tend to be cyclical; they become attenuated over time. After all, "no more Koreas" was the legacy of the Korean War. A dozen years later, the United States intervened with troops in Southeast Asia. "No more Vietnams" may have a similar half-life.

What other significant long-term impacts resulted from the Vietnam experience? Vietnam sharpened perceptions of vital and nonvital interests. The U.S. government and its electorate are more sophisticated about what is and what is not worth fighting for. In hindsight, the loss of Vietnam was not a vital blow to the global U.S. power position. Nor for that matter was the loss of Angola, Ethiopia, South Yemen, even Cuba and Nicaragua. Nor would the loss of El Salvador be vital. It is significant that when the Carter doctrine was proclaimed in January 1980, despite the fact that it far exceeded

U.S. capabilities at the time, there was remarkably little opposition to this bold decision on the part of President Carter to proclaim that the United States would react militarily if the Soviet Union tried to take over Persian Gulf oil. Why was there so little political opposition to what certainly was the most significant extension of U.S. commitments after the Vietnam War? I believe little debate was triggered basically because Persian Gulf oil was perceived at the time to be vital to the West. This mild public reaction to a commitment involving a perceived vital interest was quite different than the post-Vietnam conventional wisdom would have suggested.

Another significant long-term consequence of Vietnam is that it has sharpened distrust of domino theories. The Munich analogy, that we will regret failure to oppose forcibly the takeover of peripheral countries, is generally viewed as imperfect. Although invoked in response to perceptions of successful Soviet intrusion into Africa in the 1970s and Central America in the 1980s, political elites and the public alike remain skeptical of the validity of the assumptions and the force of the logic of domino theories. In both instances, this skepticism prevented mobilization of domestic political support for the U.S. use of force.

Another long-term consequence of Vietnam is that it did sharpen the perception of the limits of power. What Senator Fulbright termed the "arrogance of power" and Stanley Hoffman called "hubris" may have flared up again in Lebanon in 1983, but this arrogance of power certainly did not last very long. A relative decline in U.S. power was occurring in any case and would have continued even without Vietnam. Vietnam, however, certainly sharpened the perception of this decline in U.S. power.

Vietnam also significantly changed the role of Congress in relation to the executive branch. This persistent long-term consequence will make it harder for the executive to send troops to war than it was before 1968. On the other hand, this constraint may well vanish in the next turn of the wheel of executive versus congressional dominance.

Vietnam also gave a much better grasp of how unusable military power is for low-intensity conflicts. It showed how high the cost of political intervention can escalate when military force is involved. Indeed, we are concerned over precisely this problem in Central America today.

Finally, Vietnam has reinforced American popular reluctance to get involved in long wars. Once again this is nothing new. General George Marshall reputedly said in 1941 that the American people were not prepared to fight a seven-years war. If they were not prepared to fight a seven-years war over Europe in World War II, surely we should have taken more into account in the 1960s the essentially ephemeral nature of American enthusiasm for long wars. Vietnam has certainly refurbished this lesson.

There is a final long-term lesson that we have not learned: the principle—clearly violated in Vietnam—that the use of force must be carefully calibrated to the extent of U.S. interests. Two points follow from this proposition. First, vital interests must be clearly differentiated from those that are less vital. The theoretical simplicity of this truism is confounded by the paramount political value of avoiding such distinctions in order to retain strategic flexibility. In addition, the domino theory logic, however discounted it is today, invariably works to inflate perceptions of U.S. interests.

The second point is more subtle and, if violated, can work to undermine the first point. The admonition to keep clear the relative value of U.S. interests leads to use of force policy guidelines such as "employ limited force to serve limited U.S. objectives" and "employ unlimited force to serve unlimited U.S. objectives." One school of defense thinkers argues that, once this clear view of U.S. objectives is attained, force should be employed in order to ensure victory. Whether interests and objectives are clearly defined, this argument is as illogical and dangerous as its subtlety is compelling. To define success in terms of military victory is to stand the logic of ends-means proportionality on its head. The goal of military victory too easily crowds out consideration of the implications of the use of force for other political objectives and interests—vital and secondary. Instead, the military victory goal espoused by this school of analysts suggests a policy of employing unlimited force to serve limited U.S. objectives. In addition to violating ends-means proportionality logic, such a prescription dangerously ignores the distinction between the purpose of battle—military victory—and the purpose of war—to construct peace politically. For example, some argue that the United States should have been willing to employ military force sufficient "to win" in Vietnam. Independent of the clarity with which U.S. objectives were defined, this charge must be condemned for ignoring the implications of pursuing military victory for other U.S. objectives, such as avoiding military conflict with the Soviet Union and the People's Republic of China and avoiding the costs of defeating and (indefinitely) occupying a forcibly united Vietnam.

To summarize these two points, it is not enough to define objectives clearly in terms of their value to vital and nonvital national interests. In addition, decisions to use force must be firmly rooted in consideration of implications for the proportionality of means to clearly conceived ends.

Maybe a democratic society like that of the United States will someday be capable of politically supporting limited interventions for limited purposes. I doubt it. Such efforts are anathema to American political culture. Americans appear to have absorbed all too little from the Vietnam experience about how to cope effectively with low-intensity conflict, particularly in areas of peripheral interest to the United States. Instead of learning from the Vietnam mistakes, Americans have turned their backs on this unconventional war. The military especially have made little effort to learn the tough lessons. Instead the military have reverted to the dogma that the nation should not fight such kinds of war—Vietnam was anomalous; rather, the United States should concentrate on scenarios for Western Europe or Korea. As a former senior Department of Defense offical who forcefully (and successfully) advocated a Europe-first theme in U.S. defense policy, I can attest to the degree to which such thinking reinforced the plausibility of the notion that Vietnam was an aberration and that, as such, the United States should turn away from this experience and get back to first-order basics in Europe. As a consequence of this view, U.S. defense posture was aimed, alternatively, at achieving robust capabilities for either low-intensity conflict or warfare in Europe instead of both. Given the continuing volatility of the third world and Soviet (or Soviet surrogate) willingness to exploit limited-risk situations, limited wars (and especially low-intensity conflicts) are likely to remain a recurrent feature of the international scene. This is evident today in the Middle East and in Latin America. Nonetheless, the United States has not adapted organizationally to the need for flexibility. The army's shift toward light forces seems to be stimulated more by funding and deployability constraints than it is by a perceived need to prepare for low-intensity conflicts.

To sum up, the searing Vietnam experience has left a lasting residue, though these long-term impacts have been attenuated by time and other factors. However, this lasting residue has proved less significant than many previously supposed. We do seem wiser than before about the larger costs of what turn out to be minor conflicts, at least in terms of their strategic significance. We do turn out to be less impressed by domino theories. We do turn out to be more acutely aware of the limitations of U.S. power. Let us hope that this does not prove to be just cyclical. Finally, the poor Vietnam performance does not seem to have left much impact on the military's learning process and on the development of capabilities for fighting in both low-intensity conflicts and in Europe.

Note

1. The way the Pentagon and I calculated this $150 billion was by taking the last pre-Vietnam, (fiscal 1964) defense budget level and, leaving out the Vietnam upsurge, looking at the cumulative shortfalls in military spending from the fiscal 1964 level during the post-Vietnam period from fiscal 1973 to fiscal 1977.

V
Conclusions

17

Did Vietnam Make a Difference? No! Conclusions and Implications

Asa A. Clark IV
Daniel J. Kaufman
George K. Osborn
Douglas E. Lute

"Vietnam, Vietnam. . . . There are no sure answers," lamented veteran correspondent Robert Shaplen in 1970.[1] Writing at the end of the 1970s, George C. Herring quotes Shaplen's lament at the beginning of his history, *America's Longest War, The United States and Vietnam: 1950–1975*, in order to decry the paucity of conclusive answers to the tough questions about U.S. involvement in Vietnam.[2] Why did the United States commit so much to a remote area in which it had previously shown so little interest? What objectives were consciously pursued during this extended commitment? Why did the United States fail to achieve these objectives? What have been the consequences of this humiliating and internally divisive failure?

This book is not a post-mortem of the Vietnam experience of the United States. Rather, this book focuses on Herring's final question: what are the long-term consequences of Vietnam for U.S. national security policy, foreign policy, and politics? Specifically, this book examines two questions: what changes in U.S. national security policy and process are attributable to the Vietnam experience? and what the long-run consequences are of these changes.

Vietnam was a traumatic event. Among the effects can be counted almost 60,000 American dead, some 500,000 American wounded, an unknowable number of Vietnamese dead and wounded, $300-odd billion in U.S. spending (with the associated inflationary pressures and forgone social dividends), and incalculable costs in terms of moral and political capital. Operating over two decades for the United States (over four decades for the Vietnamese), these effects were both extensive and intensive; they resulted in the devastation of Vietnam and the political traumatization of the United States.

At the outset of this book Ernest May defined a great event as a watershed, after which things and people are qualitatively different. What changes were wrought by Vietnam? Change, as viewed by Professor May, can take many forms. For example, foreign policy attitudes might be changed: "No more Vietnams!" Institutions might have changed: the U.S. presidency has been demythologized. The structure of political relationships might have changed: congressional reassertiveness in relation to the executive may illustrate this form of change. Environmental circumstances might have changed: a variety of international factors have combined to catalyze national assertiveness in small nations throughout the world, with the result that superpower hegemony is undermined.

Changes in any of these forms may reflect many causal factors. Changes may reflect cognition as people take lessons learned away from Vietnam. The post-Vietnam syndrome illustrates this source of change. On the other hand, change may be imposed environmentally without regard for cognition or discretion. The emergence of U.S.-Soviet nuclear parity and the spread of nationalism throughout the third world illustrate environmentally imposed change confronting the United States. Finally, changes reflect the inhibiting effects of inertia. For example, although the attitudes of U.S. foreign policy elites appear to have shifted since 1975, public opinion polls indicate the American public continues to hold to certain beliefs about global communism, the domino theory, and the efficacy of the use of U.S. military force to counter these threats.

Is the U.S. national security system qualitatively different because of the Vietnam experience? Was Vietnam a great event? These questions are not trivial, nor do they represent some silly exercise in heuristic labeling. A conclusion that change in U.S. politics or security policy has occurred—Vietnam was a great event—supports the hypothesis that external forces can cause fundamental internal political change. Are the effects of Vietnam as extensive and durable as those of World War II or the U.S. use of nuclear weapons in 1945? What forms do these effects take? Why did these changes occur? Most important, what are the implications of these changes for the U.S. national security system, policy, and politics? On the other hand, a conclusion that Vietnam has made no difference—no lasting, extensive changes in U.S. politics or security policy occurred; Vietnam was not a great event—rejects the external-internal political change hypothesis. Vietnam was traumatic for the United States; why did enduring changes in U.S. politics not occur? What are the implications of this absence of change? In any event, whether U.S. policymaking has changed or not, the world today is different from the 1960s. What conclusions about the Vietnam experience should guide future U.S. policy?

Post-Vietnam effects on U.S. national security process and policy can represent many factors and support many interpretations. For example:

Changes reflect the direct effects of Vietnam.

Changes reflect the effects of a set of complex forces of change; Vietnam, only one of these forces, was a catalyst of change.

Vietnam was spurious; other forces of change (or inertia) were at work. Changes evident after Vietnam would have occurred in any case.

No changes have occurred.

Reasoned judgments about these alternative answers to the first question of this book are difficult. Causality is certainly hard to discern: changes may or may not have been attempted, changes may or may not have occurred, it may be difficult to distinguish the effects of Vietnam from those of other forces of change, lessons may or may not have been learned, "right or appropriate" lessons may or may not have been learned. The absence of change may be as significant as the occurrence of change, in terms of both causes and implications.

Nonetheless, thoughtful answers to these questions about the long-run effects of Vietnam are as valuable as they are difficult to distill. Understanding the effects of Vietnam on the United States is central to U.S. national security policy. At a normative level, understanding the effects of Vietnam on the United States can inform judgments. Did U.S. policy reflect "bad" intentions, "bad" understanding of how these intentions related to circumstances, or "bad" execution? How have the intentions, understandings, and execution of security policy changed since Vietnam? For example, if one believes that the legitimacy of proper U.S. motives was scuttled by deficient implementation and the resulting disastrous outcome, one is interested in evaluating effects and changes in order to succeed in the next instance. Moreover, evidence of changes (for the better) can be viewed as a moral salve for the sunk costs and guilt of the Vietnam quagmire. On the other hand, if one views the U.S. role in Vietnam as fundamentally corrupt morally, one is interested in evaluating effects and changes in order to ensure such instances are not repeated. Finally, assessment of the effects (or noneffects) of Vietnam on U.S. national security is essential for guiding U.S. policy in a dynamic world—a world made different, in part, by the Vietnam War.

Chapters in this book have presented a variety of answers to these questions about the long-run effects of Vietnam. The views of these distinguished authors stand by themselves; they need no editorial commentary, appraisal, or context building. Instead, this final chapter presents the editors' observations and conclusions about the long-run consequences of Vietnam for U.S. national security policy. These remarks are aimed at addressing first-order issues that were central to the Vietnam experience and will continue to shape U.S. security policy in the future.

Did Vietnam Make a Difference?

Was Vietnam a great event, as defined by Professor May, in the context of U.S. national security? Is U.S. national security policy (and policymaking) fundamentally changed as a result of the Vietnam experience? On the one hand, changes are clearly evident: for example, the world is quite different from the 1960s, military conscription ended in 1973 in the United States, and a reassertive U.S. Congress routinely challenges a demythologized presidency. The long-run economic revitalization of the southeastern Pacific stands as one important example of international change brought on by U.S. involvement in Southeast Asia. In addition to buying time and space for the development of ASEAN, U.S. efforts infused the region with capital in the form of direct spending, trade, and investment. Regional economic stability promoted regional political stability. Specific changes in U.S. foreign policy have been characterized in this book; others abound. Some analysts, Earl Ravenal, for example, contend that Vietnam was a great event. In that the Vietnam experience illustrated the limits on the use of force today, Ravenal argues the United States should avoid military intervention anywhere, perhaps even in Europe and Japan.[3] Other observers contend that Vietnam shattered the anti-Communist consensus and destroyed the politically moderating, centrist role of the establishment in U.S. foreign policymaking. There is, as a result, a general "foreign policy breakdown."[4]

On the other hand, caution is in order in weighing an answer to this question. Vietnam was an incendiary and consuming event—too big, too tough, too unfathomable to lend itself to tidy conclusions. As Professor May cautions, it is still too soon to accept solid judgments and conclusions. Nonetheless, the conclusion of the chapter is that the answer is a resounding "no!" Vietnam was not a great event; the U.S. national security system is not fundamentally different after and because of the Vietnam experience. Although the world is different and changes in U.S. politics are evident, three keystones of U.S. security policy remain relatively constant: the containment doctrine and its role as the bedrock of U.S. foreign policy, American political culture, and the fundamental structure of the political system. Vietnam traumatized the United States. Because this trauma did not destroy the political legitimacy of these three keystones, however, the U.S. national security system remains remarkably unchanged; Vietnam did not make a difference.

The containment doctrine has provided the rationale and framework for U.S. foreign policy for four decades. Although President Carter initially attempted to reject the containment doctrine, his policies and rhetoric increasingly reflected the old tenets: for example, his conviction that Soviet-U.S. relations were "the most critical factor in determining whether the world will live in peace or be engulfed in global conflict," the Carter doctrine. [5] This impressive continuity is explained by a number of factors. First, the Soviet Union remains the focal point of U.S. foreign policy. Second, containment as a policy has worked. Whether applied universally (as in the Truman administration) or more selectively (as in the Nixon administration) containment has proved a successful vehicle for U.S. foreign policy for forty years. Third, creation of an alternative foreign policy rationale is inhibited by domestic politics. In trying to distance themselves from their predecessor, incoming administrations are unwilling to devote the time and energy necessary for creating a new strategy. Rather, changes in foreign policy have occurred at the margin in the form of different ways in which the basic containment strategy was to be applied. Moreover, these marginal shifts may have reflected budgetary constraints and presumptions about overall economic policy more than analyses of international interests and threats. Compare, for example, the relationship between Kennedy's flexible response strategy and his liberal economic policies, and Eisenhower's new look strategy and his fiscal conservatism. Both the new look and flexible response were variants of the containment strategy, reflecting a desire for identifiable administration policy and different views of economic scarcity. As Gaddes observes, "Containment has been the product, not so much of what the Russians have done, or of what has happened elsewhere in the world, but of internal forces operating within the United States."[6]

American political culture, a diffuse set of values and attitudes about politics, is by nature resistant to change. Strategic culture refers to those aspects of political culture focusing on foreign affairs. American strategic culture is characterized by Colin Gray as moralistic, ahistorical, legalistic, astrategic, and in terms of exceptionalism and universalism.[7] Characterizations of these cultural traits abound; in any case, American strategic culture is as continuous as it is complex. Political culture is so diffuse, and reflects the aggregate of so many influences, that it is susceptible to change by only the most pervasive and powerful of forces. Vietnam did not make a difference in the sense of reshaping fundamental values and attitudes about the role of the United States in the rest of the world. In addition to the rush of other international events competing for public cognition (such as the 1967 Arab-Israeli War, the adoption of the flexible response doctrine by NATO, détente and Ostpolitik, and strains on the international monetary system), Americans were examining their values in the face of the civil rights movement, the rise of feminism, and a whole range of challenges to traditional authority structures.

The most important keystone of U.S. security policy, the political system—with its myriad of interests and constraints—remains fundamentally unchanged by Vietnam. The foundations of U.S. politics—pluralism, federalism, majority rule, the separation of powers, and others—were not qualitatively changed by the Vietnam experience. These characteristics of

U.S. democracy constitute a thicket of structural inertia that inhibits major change. Alexis de Tocqueville explained these traits of politics in the nineteenth century; his explanation has remained valid over the ensuing fifteen decades. The combination of diffused political power and rapid turnover of public officials creates administrative instability. "Nobody bothers about what was done before his time. No method is adopted; no archives are formed; no documents are brought together. . . . American society seems to live from day to day. . . . It is very difficult for American administrators to learn anything from each other."[8]

In addition, the combination of high legislator turnover and extensive political power vested in the Congress creates legislative instability. "Projects are taken up with great ardor; but as soon as its attention is turned elsewhere, all these efforts cease."[9] Colin Gray explains this instability as a manifestation of the problem-solving ethic in American culture.[10] This short attention span and instability is reflected in the many post-Vietnam changes, including the War Powers Resolution, more stringent congressional oversight of the intelligence community, a more skeptical press. However, these microchanges do not represent major qualitative changes in U.S. politics. In fact, such changes may contribute to the system's ability to continue to work successfully in support of the containment strategy, as it has for four decades. Moreover, this instability prevents purposive and sustained efforts to "coordinate the details of a great undertaking and to fix some plan and carry it through with determination in spite of obstacles."[11]

The fundamental continuity of these three keystones—the containment doctrine as the centerpiece of U.S. foreign policy, American political culture, and the structure of the U.S. political system—accounts for this judgment that Vietnam was not a great event for U.S. security policy. Although the Vietnam experience was traumatic, it fell short of undermining the political legitimacy of politics and national security. The fundamental character of politics and national security remain unchanged; Vietnam did not make a difference. This harsh-sounding judgment raises the question, What can disrupt the legitimacy of the U.S. political system and cause systemic change: a minor event (such as Vietnam)? a series of minor events (such as Vietnam, Grenada, and Beirut)? History points to only a few major events that did cause major qualitative change in policy: the American Civil War, the depression, the industrial revolution, World War II, the introduction of nuclear weapons. These few events changed fundamentally the character of American society and politics. Vietnam did not.

These three keystones of national security have endured and are likely to continue to do so. Short of some major crisis that calls into question the political legitimacy of the political system, the structural inertia of U.S. politics will continue to endure. Lessons will be learned and changes will be made at the margin; however, the fundamental character and structure of the political system will remain.

This conclusion suggests that the Vietnam experience can recur. Are we condemned to repeat that experience? The likelihood that the United States will again use force for similar reasons on behalf of similar interests as in Vietnam is more credible when one considers the long view: the interests and arguments invoked in support of the use of political coercion are strikingly similar for U.S. interventions in South Korea in 1950, Iran in 1951, Guatemala in 1954, Cuba in 1961 and 1962, Vietnam in 1965, the Dominican Republic in 1965, Beirut in 1983, and Grenada in 1983. While these instances represent a range of circumstances, to include a variety of political and moral objectives, these cases are similar in terms of reflecting the effects of the three security policy keystones discussed earlier. Was de Tocqueville correct in observing that "foreign policy does not require the use of any of the good qualities peculiar to democracy but does demand the cultivation of almost all those which it lacks"? Is the United States without those "qualities which, in the long run, make a nation . . . prevail"?[12] For those who were seared by Vietnam, the prospect of "more Vietnams" may elicit disbelief, dismay, and disenchantment.

Vietnam was one event in a period of great international change. Beginning with decolonization in the early 1960s and continuing through the economic upheavals precipitated by exploding oil prices in the late 1970s, the world changed significantly in less than two decades. One can argue whether the United States changed after Vietnam; one can argue whether or not it learned from Vietnam. In any case, the world changed; therefore, the consequences of U.S. policies—enlightened or not by lessons of Vietnam, changed or unchanged—are different. The United States is likely to face similar situations again. What is to be done? What does this likelihood mean? How can we deal with such prospects? How can we be clearheaded, constructive, and thoughtful in serving U.S. interests when confronted by events similar in nature to Vietnam? What lessons and implications are offered by the Vietnam experience that can fruitfully guide future U.S. policy? Before examining these implications, however, it is necessary to remind ourselves of the importance of two precautions about judging long-run effects and their implications: problems with the use of history and the role of blame in distilling lessons from experience.[13]

Problems in Evaluation

Lessons of History

Inspiration for this book reflects Liddel Hart's admonition that "awareness of our limitations should make us chary of condemning those who make mistakes, but we condemn ourselves if we fail to recognize mistakes."[14] As we have argued above, "of all the disasters of Vietnam the worst could be our unwillingness to learn enough."[15] Only through serious reflection on the long-term effects and implications of the Vietnam experience can we understand that traumatic period. Only through such understanding can we hold out prospects for conscious efforts to avoid repeating mistakes—whether first-order or instrumental—and to achieve more enlightened and effective policy outcomes.

If it is difficult to discern the effects of Vietnam; it is even more difficult to judge the value of lessons for the future. First, there is the problem of collective amnesia: people do not want to recall the ugly memories of the traumatic Vietnam era.[16] "There is no profit at this time in hashing over the might-have-beens of the past," Mike Mansfield commented. "Nor is there any value in finger-pointing."[17] In the late 1970s columnist Joseph Harsch observed that "Americans have somehow blocked Vietnam out of their consciousness. They don't talk about it. They don't talk about its consequences."[18] Although this current of subconscious amnesia was overturned in the resurgent activism and foreign policy debates of the early 1980s, too little thoughtful analysis was conducted on the Vietnam case.[19]

A second problem affecting judgments about the effects and consequences of the U.S. experience in Southeast Asia is the notion that Vietnam was unique; therefore, no lessons can be generalized from that experience. "Vietnam was unique," contended McGeorge Bundy. The United States should not "set as the central objective the redesign of our foreign and defense policy so as to avoid another Vietnam."[20] The overriding factor of the conduct and outcome of the Vietnam War was its deeper and uniquely Vietnamese character. At best, U.S. efforts were condemned to fail of their own irrelevance. While Americans viewed the war as necessary to preserve freedom in Asia and to buttress U.S. credibility in an age of deterrence, the Vietnamese were fighting for their lives. What was viewed as a struggle between concepts by one was seen as a total war by the other. In 1962, North Vietnamese premier Pham Van Dong remarked to Bernard Fall that "Americans do not like long inconclusive wars—and this is going to be a long inconclusive war."[21] At worst, U.S. efforts could only exacerbate instability. Under Secretary of State George Ball observed in 1965 that "no one has demonstrated that a white ground force of whatever size can win a guerrilla war—which is at the same time a civil war between Asians—in jungle terrain in the midst of a population that refuses cooperation to the white forces (and the South Vietnamese)."[22]

If the Vietnamese character was the pivotal factor in the war, how can valid lessons be generalized to other circumstances? In these remarks, Samuel P. Huntington summarizes the conclusion of this uniqueness argument:

> If we remember the past we are condemned to misread it. . . . The right lesson, in short, may be the unlesson. . . . The Vietnam problem was a legacy of Western colonial rule. . . . Vietnam was, in addition, the one European

colony in which . . . Communist groups established an early ascendancy in the nationalist movement. The struggle for independence led to a divided country, a sequence of events which seems unlikely to be duplicated in the future. Finally, the American involvement came at the end of a cycle of active American concern with foreign affairs which seems unlikely to be repeated for some time in the future. Every historical event or confluence of events obviously is unique.[23]

The third obstacle to the use of history for drawing prescriptive conclusions is the difficult problem of human interpretation of history. "One of the few unequivocally sound lessons of history is that the lessons we should learn are usually learned imperfectly if at all."[24] In his book *Perception and Misperception in International Politics,* Robert Jervis examines in detail the effects among experience, perceptions, and learning that can confound the best efforts to explain the past and prescribe behaviors for the future.[25] For example, people perceive selectively in order to reinforce their preconceptions. "Men use the past to prop up their own prejudices," observes historian A.J.P. Taylor.[26] People tend to learn from first-hand experiences. Because they tend to be more concerned with what occurs rather than why it occurs, however, learning is superficial. People want to avoid past failures and emulate past successes. As a result, so-called lessons learned are overgeneralized and overapplied. Insufficient regard is given for subtle, but perhaps critical, differences across cases; instead, continuity across cases and similarity between cases are exaggerated. Faulty generalizations are compounded by the fact that different past personal experiences develop different perceptual predispositions in people, which may lead to learning of different lessons by those who experience the same event. Finally, people are too uncritical of their lessons learned. Important questions are ignored. Is this event representative of the class of phenomena about which I want to generalize? Why is this event a good model for deriving lessons for future behavior? What characteristics are critical to these lessons and peculiar to this event? Will the absence of these characteristics in other cases invalidate application of these lessons? To the degree these questions are ignored and lessons are treated as prescriptive wisdoms to be applied (indiscriminately) across cases, the use of history can be dangerous. The lessons may be wrong or, at a minimum, too blunt. Based on personal observations from narrow experiences and confirmed only anecdotally, these lessons too often have not been distilled sufficiently through exposure to tough, critical questioning to stand as generalizable lessons.

Professor Jervis describes a particularly subtle but common malady that affects all rational decision makers: people tend to justify their own behavior. In doing so, they tend to exaggerate the value of their achievements and devalue the worth of their failures. This tendency can work to reinforce policy inertia and incrementalism, apart from any conscious or substantive decision to do so.[27]

Albert Wohlstetter summarizes the faulty generalization obstacle:

> Of all the disasters of Vietnam, the worst may be the "lessons" that we'll draw from it. . . . Lessons from such complex events require much more reflection to be of more than negative worth. But reactions to Vietnam . . . tend to be visceral rather than reflective.[28]

It is enough to be aware of these difficulties; we can afford neither a conclusion that Vietnam offers no lessons for today nor an overreaction to failures there in the form of a conclusion that the United States must not intervene again. Both views are simplistic, if not wrong. Although Vietnam was unique, there are aspects of that experience—both first-order and instrumental—that have and will recur. As Frizzell and Thompson remark, "If there will be 'no more Vietnams,' there certainly will be many more guerrilla wars, counterinsurgency efforts, urban battles, problems of 'costing' weapon systems, and problems of unity of command in some theater of action."[29]

Who Is to Blame?

Whether explicit or implicit, presumptions about the locus of blame affect how lessons are learned. In the case of successes, lessons endorse measures to exploit success. In the case of failures, lessons reflect indictment of those to blame and advocate corrective measures. Obviously, all the problems of human interpretations of history—preconceptions, misperceptions, and overgeneralization, for example—described earlier are at work in these judgments. Thus the question of who is responsible—more commonly, who is to blame—is nontrivial in the extreme. The quality of lessons learned, and agreement over the validity of these lessons, depends on the quality of the process of fixing responsibility and agreement over these decisions.

How does this concern relate to the assessment of the long-term effects and consequences of Vietnam? Although the politics of passion that was omnipresent during Vietnam has receded with time, the quality of evaluations of U.S. policy, in particular of who was responsible for U.S. policy in Vietnam, remains uneven. Similarly, disagreement over these judgments continues. Why did U.S. policies in Southeast Asia take such paths? Why did U.S. policies result in such outcomes? Explanations abound. One answer points to the uniqueness and subtleties of Vietnamese society: the United States had few area experts who understood these crucial local circumstances. Another reason hinges on the asymmetrical commitment of the protagonists: the North Vietnamese were resolute in their commitment to a total struggle, in contrast to both the South Vietnamese and Americans. The

United States underestimated the North Vietnamese. The United States employed a strategy of flexible response, based on notions of signaling American resolve through controlled escalation of force, that was totally inappropriate to the stakes perceived by North Vietnam. Another explanation focuses on the fact that bureaucratic repertoires of the principal U.S. agencies—the armed services, for example—were followed without regard to local conditions. Fueled by the arrogance of power, American idealism, or imperialism, were the prime motives. The combination of domestic U.S. politics—no elected official could afford to be viewed as having "lost Vietnam"—and the "slippery slope" of successive increases in commitment were at fault. Or, American anticommunism, shaped by the containment doctrine, led the United States into situations from which there was no easy retreat.[30] There is ample room for disagreement over who is to blame across these diverse explanations of the Vietnam experience.

One way to examine the consequences of disagreement over responsibility is to look at how judgments focus on actors, in particular, the military. In assessing the role and responsibilities of the military in Vietnam, it is necessary to identify the level of analysis on which judgments are to be made. For example, on one level—that of technical military proficiency, or tactical operations, strategic and tactical logistics operations—it can be argued that the military performed with distinction and "won" the battle. Crucial to this view is the assumption that Vietnam was a war between two countries, South and North Vietnam. The United States intervened in support of one party to this war in order to promote a variety of its own policy objectives. However, when viewed on another level—one that emphasizes the paramount importance of social, cultural, and political Vietnamese factors—the military's performance failed. The military's technical prowess was as irrelevant as it was impressive. In this view, Vietnam was a single civil war between Vietnamese; U.S. intervention was doomed to fail of its own irrelevance. To paraphrase the poignant remark of a North Vietnamese colonel, "the fact that you Americans won the military battle was irrelevant to our victory in the [political] war."

These different interpretations are important for the quality of the lessons learned and the degree of support they attract. Was the United States defeated militarily? No, many argue. Neither, however, did the United States achieve any form of military victory. Did the United States lose the war and hence fail to win the peace? Yes. It is far less clear, however, to what degree the military should be held ultimately responsible for this defeat. After all, few policymakers, in any agency, at any level, understood the deeper and uniquely Vietnamese character of the war, a character that paid little respect to American notions of incrementalism and gradual escalation, a character that heeded instead the absolute of Vietnamese total war. With the advantages of hindsight, it is too easy to forget how complex the forces at work in

Vietnam were and how ill suited and ill prepared Americans were for understanding these complexities. Vietnam was about nuances, including, for example, notions of superpower global and regional political equilibria, the confluence of a Vietnamese civil war and the expansionist designs of the North Vietnamese in relation to Indochina, and the burden of sustaining domestic political support for a limited war in a faroff place of arguable strategic value.

To expect the military, trained to serve as an efficient and effective instrumentality of policy, to be more sophisticated in political ends-means analysis and to prove more sensitive to the nuances of Vietnam than civilian policymakers is unrealistic. If the military were guilty of strategic incompetence, so were the civilian leadership, the Congress, and the American people (at least until 1970). Thus, the military can hardly be indicted for a lack of courage in its efforts to achieve U.S. objectives in Vietnam; for the most part, the military did not understand. This is the great tragedy: the military must be indicted for strategic incompetence—and so should everyone else.

What are we to make of these debates? These different interpretations are directly consequential for the lessons derived and prescriptions for the future. For example, Colonel Harry Summers (and Secretary of Defense Caspar Weinberger, among others) maintains that the key to Vietnam and future Vietnams lies in clearly defining objectives and then employing military force decisively to win.[31] While this is hard to fault in the abstract, it is never easy to define interests and objectives clearly in Vietnam-type situations. Moreover, it is critical to lock definitions and judgments about victory firmly into a context of broader political interests and objectives. In arguing the United States should have fought decisively to achieve victory against North Vietnam, Summers ignores the importance of avoiding escalation to superpower military conflict in Asia. As Clausewitz reminds us, the purpose of battle is victory; the purpose of war is peace. Objectives must be clearly defined relative to interests; force must be used only in proportion to those objectives and interests.

A second theme runs through some of the revisionist literature: a stab in the back theme.[32] If only the political leadership had allowed the military to prosecute fully the war to win, the United States could have achieved victory over the North Vietnamese. In addition, the argument continues, the military was left holding the smoking gun when the crime was exposed. Where were the civilian leaders who gave the orders and imposed the constraints? This theme is both wrong and insidious. First, it fails to appreciate the nature of the Vietnam War and the fact that no form or degree of U.S. force could have achieved any reasonable definition of victory (short of militarily defeating and occupying Vietnam indefinitely). Second, it insidiously deflects responsibility for the defeat onto the civilian leadership. This scapegoatism undermines the quality of civil-military relations inherent in civilian control of the military. In so doing, this theme has the effect of absolving the military from the imperative for intellectual introspection in order to understand better the complexities of low-intensity conflict in the future.

In addition to focusing on particular actors, analysis of policy ends and means is a second way to appreciate the consequences of differing judgments about responsibility for U.S. policies in Vietnam. Different interpretations of the roles of ends and means lead to different conclusions about prescriptive lessons for the future. The view that achievement of legitimate U.S. objectives in Vietnam was derailed by inappropriate means leads to lessons about proper means for such ends. An example of this instrumentalist school is General William Westmoreland's indictment of incrementalism and gradual response. Had the United States employed military force decisively, argues Westmoreland, the war could have been won without provoking domestic political opposition.[33] In rebutting the "slippery slope" arguments of those who charge that the United States never clarified its goals or understood the difficulties of achieving them, Robert Komer, former director of the Civilian Operations and Revolutionary Development Support agency in Vietnam, provides another version of the intrumentalist perspective. Komer contends that officials knew all along how tough it was to achieve explicitly defined objectives; there was no ends-policy gap. Rather, the complete inappropriateness of the organizational repertoires of the major U.S. agencies (such as the armed services) for these objectives denied any prospects for success. The goals of pacification and nation building were both legitimate and appropriate to the Vietnam situation, contends Komer. However, tasking the armed services to implement these policies inevitably led to a policy-performance gap. Valid goals were corrupted by programs attuned to what the services could do well—large-scale, combat-oriented operations—rather than to what was appropriate for these goals.[34] In addition, turning to the armed services to carry the burden of U.S. policy in Vietnam resulted in a substantial Americanization of the war. Almost nothing could be more inappropriate to the goal of nation building. Komer concludes that a counterinsurgency agency should be created for the explicit purpose of conducting programs in support of the same tasks he advocated in Vietnam.[35]

The other view is that no form of means could succeed; the ends of U.S. policy in Vietnam were inappropriate or impossible to achieve. George Ball argues that the simple factors of race and nationalism were decisive in Vietnam; the United States could not play any large-scale constructive role in developing political stability in Vietnamese society. This assertion forces the conclusion that the United States must be extremely discriminating in its evaluation of insurgencies. Decisions to intervene must be guided by sensitivity to factors peculiar to the particular country, the importance of limits on the form and extent of intervention, and the value of maintaining low political visibility of U.S. programs and presence.

Thus, in assessing the long-run effects and consequences of Vietnam, we must remain sensitive to the importance of presumptions about intentions, policies, outcomes, consequences, causes, and responsibilities in judgments about the quality and generalizability of lessons for the future. Self-consciousness and thoughtful debate are the keys to understanding long-run effects and their consequences. We violate these precautions at our own risk. For example, lessons based on indictments of one particular actor are too simplistic. Similarly, it is dangerous to derive lessons from analysis of ends or means exclusively. No matter how thoroughly done, such reasoning is incomplete. For example, those who argue that U.S. goals in Vietnam were wrong espouse lessons about criteria for intervention in the first place. They may fail, however, to assess critically the merits of the means employed and conclude that the technical programs used in Vietnam are right. The key is to know where to use these means of intervention. The other side of this concern is that the instructive lessons revolve around means for intervention; the presumption that the United States can intervene constructively may go unchallenged. In this case, the issue is how to intervene. Neither view is wise.

If wiser policy is the goal, we must remain cautious about using historically based lessons, conclusions, and prescriptions. This admonition carries two postulates about generalizing effects of the Vietnam experience. First, we must continually challenge presumptions about who and what caused particular effects in the case of Vietnam. What elements does this explanation leave out? Who and what other factors should be included in explanations that form the basis for lessons or wisdoms derived from this experience? How do these lessons or wisdoms change when these other factors are integrated? Second, how similar is the case of Vietnam to other cases to which we would generalize? Is the Vietnam experience representative of the class of events in which we are interested? How applicable are generalizations from Vietnam to other cases? With these caveats in mind, we can turn to the implications of the Vietnam experience for U.S. security policy.

Lessons

Two themes are examined here: the effects of presumptions, explicit in the containment doctrine, about the indivisibility of U.S. interests in the world, and the role of U.S. foreign policy consensus. These themes lead to lessons about the American worldview: how policymakers and the public perceive the world and what role conceptions follow for the United States.

U.S. Interests: Divisible or Indivisible?

Drafted in 1950, NSC-68 was the first comprehensive postwar statement of U.S. strategy. One key presumption highlighted the importance of the balance of power and its sensitivity to disruption as a result of intimidation or the loss of credibility (as well by direct military or economic actions):

> Since everything that gives us or others respect for our institutions is a suitable object for attack, it also fits the Kremlin's design that where, with impunity, we can be insulted and made to suffer indignity the opportunity shall not be missed. . . . The Soviet Union is out to demonstrate to the free world that force and the will to use it are on the side of the Kremlin and that those who lack it are decadent and doomed. [36]

This perspective underlined the importance of perceptions of political will as both influences on and measures of the balance of power. Ever concerned about piecemeal aggression (so-called salami tactics of the domino theory), NSC-68 reflected the assumption that U.S. interests are indivisible. Failure to respond to threats could lead to "a descending spiral of too little and too late, of doubt and recrimination, of ever narrower and more desperate alternatives . . . and gradual withdrawals until we discover one day that we have sacrificed positions of vital interest."[37]

This logic led, perversely, to a credibility trap, aptly characterized by journalist William Whitworth: "We have the balance in order to deal with the problem, and we have to deal with the problem in order to preserve the balance. The theory is eating its own tail."[38] President Johnson defended his decisions to escalate U.S. military involvement in Vietnam: "We must say in Southeast Asia—as we did in Europe—. . . . 'Hitherto shalt thou come, but no further.'"[39] Months later, President Johnson echoed this theme: "To leave Vietnam to its fate would shake . . . confidence . . . in the value of an American commitment and in the value of America's word."[40] However, the more the United States committed its influence to Vietnam in order to preserve its national credibility, the more U.S. credibility became dependent on the success of U.S. policies in Vietnam. To paraphrase Whitworth, means were eating their own ends.

What were the consequences of the assumption, explicit in the containment doctrine as formalized by NSC-68, that U.S. foreign policy interests are indivisible? Inherent in containment were the seeds of a dangerous trap. The doctrine's absolute logic—contain Communist (particularly Soviet) expansionism—impelled the view that all expansionism must be contained. Expansionism in any form must be countered lest the credibility of the United States to stand by its interests become suspect. Such a view obscured discrimination of critical distinctions (for example, the Sino-Soviet split went unacknowledged by U.S. leaders for years) and inflated the perceived importance of marginal events (such as American perceptions of the stakes in Vietnam).

A number of perverse effects may follow from this trap. As an event is perceived as increasingly important, marginal interests are inflated and seen as increasingly vital. In turn, this inflation of interests (and accompanying rhetoric) reinforces perceptions of national efficacy. Perceptions of increased importance of events lead to perceptions of increased capabilities to influence these events. (The alternative, recognition of a growing ends-means gap, is unpalatable psychologically, institutionally, and politically.) These forces feed an ends-means dynamic in which stakes grow but the choice remains constant: mobilize the resources necessary to fulfill the commitment at stake, or renege on the commitment to these so-called vital interests.

How should these two unaccountable outcomes be balanced? Paying the bill to fulfill the commitment is infeasible in domestic political terms. Reneging on a commitment, on the other hand, is undesirable in foreign policy terms. Because this choice refocuses the issue onto one of the national credibility of official commitments, the effective importance of the original issue may recede, paradoxically, as its importance in official rhetoric as a symbol of national credibility continues to increase.

Such trends exacerbate ends-means disproportionality and further constrain political flexibility. The United States found itself trapped in a number of dilemmas in Vietnam. First, proportionality of ends was violated if officials conceded that only limited interests were at stake in Vietnam; the costs of large-scale military intervention would not be balanced by achievement of vitally important objectives. Moreover, such an admission would, in effect, condemn the United States to defeat, given the total commitment of the North Vietnamese. If, on the other hand, vital interests were at stake because U.S. global credibility was seen as on trial, the United States faced a no-win choice: escalate in order to win (at the risk of failing or triggering a wider conflict involving the Soviets or PRC) or deescalate and retract the U.S. commitment. In either case, the United States faced circumstances in which its credibility—one of the motivating concerns of containment—would be at least partially jeopardized. A second dilemma lay in the notion that involvement in Vietnam was designed to symbolize U.S. resolve to many audiences: the North and South Vietnamese, the PRC, the Soviets, U.S. allies, and the American public. Given the variety of these audiences and their disparate perceptions of the interests at stake in Vietnam, how effectively could military intervention signal U.S. resolve and credibility?

This was poor strategy: ends were weakly conceived and reflected the simplistic presumption of the indivisibility of international politics; means employed were disproportionate to ends. Historian John Gaddes indicts this ends-means disproportionality of U.S. strategy during Vietnam as

> the expansion of means to honor a commitment made as a substitute for means; the justification of that commitment in terms of a balance of power made shaky by its very existence; the defense, in the interest of credibility, of policies destructive of that credibility; the search, ultimately, for domestic consensus by means that destroyed that consensus.[41]

The Role of Consensus?

This pattern was by no means automatic. Foreign policy doctrine and doc-trinal consensus serve useful roles: in promoting policy focus and coherence, in providing a framework within which routine actions can be handled by the foreign policy bureaucracy, in facilitating implementation of policies in ac-cordance with directives agreed upon in the policy formulation stage, in moderating debate and reinforcing policy continuity, and in articulating foreign policy goals and objectives that serve national interests. However, as Ian Smart cautions, "consensus is not some sort of absolute good. Consensus is essentially a means to good or . . . evil ends."[42]

Many qualifiers must be weighed in considering the value of a foreign policy consensus: on what scope of policy? on ends or means? among whom? by what means? for what motives? at what political price? These final two questions are crucial for, as Smart reminds us, "there is no free consensus."[43] There is little value in consensus per se, although the creation and mainte-nance of consensus always entails political costs. Just as consensus in support of bad policy is clearly harmful, consensus that transforms legitimate ideas into dogma precludes discrimination, priorities, and choice. Doctrinal con-sensus can be beneficial if the above questions are resolved selectively; for ex-ample, issues, ends, and means are chosen selectively. Most important, the motives of consensus are carefully sorted and selected: consensus on what ends to what consequences? Only if selectively focused can policy consensus serve to complement and facilitate policy measures that effectively serve political goals. Only in this way can policy consensus avoid becoming a substitute for clearheaded political analysis, leadership, and action.

As Richard Betts and Leslie Gelb argue, the foreign policy consensus sup-porting the containment doctrine led to political paranoia and intellectual rigidity.[44] The worldview defined by the containment doctrine fostered beliefs in the legitimacy of global U.S. interests, the global threat of mono-lithic communism to these interests, and the appropriateness of military responses to this threat. Consensus over these beliefs promoted a political milieu of doctrinal righteousness in which these beliefs went generally unquestioned and were ultimately reified. In such a climate, analysis of and debate over the substantive validity of these beliefs was difficult, to say the least. Consensus had the effect of reinforcing the blunt application of a blunt and doctrinaire doctrine in which prime value was accorded to consistency. Thus the requisites posited by Ian Smart for the conservative role of consen-sus—selectivity and discrimination—were ignored, and the flexibility and discretion so necessary for strategy to support foreign policy and national political interests were absent. Betts and Gelb conclude that U.S. intervention in Vietnam was inevitable under these circumstances.

In conclusion, the doctrinal flaws of containment—the presumption that interests are indivisible, most of all—were compounded in their consequences by the U.S. foreign policy consensus. The consequences of bad strategy were exacerbated by the American consensus. The results of this dysfunctional combination included reliance on unexamined but overgeneralized slogans, strained allied relations, insensitivity to national and local circumstances, disrupted relations with the Soviet Union and the PRC, and, ironically, weakened credibility.

The lesson that emerges from this assessment is the danger of the allure—ethical, political, conceptual—of comprehensive worldviews or perspectives that assume too much and strain to prescribe too much. Particularly when supported by a domestic political consensus, a comprehensive worldview risks imputing homogeneity to a world that is, if anything, diverse and becoming increasingly heterogeneous. This danger is especially keen for the United States because of the undercurrents of legalism, moralism, exceptionalism, and chauvinism that characterize American strategic culture.[45] The price of such a framework, so tantalizingly useful for guiding coherent interpretations of the world, is increasing incongruence with the world. This danger—that consensus may impel overgeneralization of foreign policy doctrine—applies as well to any other major power in world politics. Irving Kristol observes that "consensus is what sustains an ideological foreign policy, and no great power—not the United States, not Russia, not China—can have a foreign policy that fits neatly into an ideological *Weltanschauung.* "[46]

Fixes

Continuity, reflecting the effects of the three keystones, characterizes U.S. foreign policy. Therefore, the United States will have more Vietnams. This prospect is more likely to the degree the streak of universalism in American political culture prevails and the containment strategy is applied strictly and broadly. This prospect is even more likely in an ideologically charged political atmosphere in which the merits of a U.S. foreign policy consensus are extolled or a consensus operates. How are we to deal with the prospect of more Vietnams?

Ends

One approach is to revise the ends of U.S. foreign policy. This approach might take many forms—for example, neoisolationism or more precise delineations between vital and secondary interests. Explicit identification of the U.S. interests involved is one of the criteria espoused by Secretary of Defense Caspar Weinberger for considering the use of military force. Alternatively, ends might be refined by stripping out the moral pretentiousness that Americans often attach to U.S. national interests. George Kennan suggests U.S. intervention should be considered only in cases that are directly "injurious to our interests, rather than just our sensibilities."[47] Continuing, Kennan argues the United States should "restrict our undertakings to the limits established by our own traditions and resources. It would see virtue in our minding our own business wherever there is not some overwhelming reason for minding the business of others."[48] Although these admonitions have appeal conceptually, they offer little hope in practice: national interests are both invariant and ambiguous; the politics of policymaking is intrinsically the stuff of value conflicts in interests and morals.

Means

Another approach is to refine the means of U.S. foreign policy. For example, improvements in intelligence collection and analysis can fine-tune the resolution power of U.S. security policy. Similarly, efforts by U.S. intelligence and diplomatic agencies to develop relations with so-called third force political movements in developing countries represent a constructive middle course between concession of a left-leaning country to the second world and the strident rollback approach of the extreme advocates of the Reagan doctrine. Organizational remedies are always attractive; restructuring of agencies and procedures is relatively easy and provides visible evidence of constructive reform. Some organizational fixes are more important than others. Four decades of reform proposals, punctuated by recent policy failures in Vietnam, Desert One, Lebanon, and Grenada, have accumulated sufficient political momentum to compel reform of the Joint Chiefs of Staff system. Finally, changes in U.S. military force posture are aimed at achieving more flexible, sustainable, and lethal military forces for all conceivable contingency operations: AWACS aircraft, light infantry divisions, battleship-centered surface action groups, and military assistance programs, for example. Other changes in foreign policy means have been discussed in this book.

Although these changes are certainly constructive, their impact on U.S. national security remains at the margin because of the enduring nature of the three keystones of the national security system: the containment doctrine, American political culture, and the structure of U.S. politics. The system will work: means-oriented changes are absorbed into the system in service of these three keystones.

Strategy

The containment doctrine has served as the guiding principle of U.S. foreign policy since World War II. As such, containment has provided the overarching rationale for U.S. strategy for four decades. Strategy has many meanings, however. It links national political ends (interests, goals, intentions, objectives) and policy means (programs, capabilities, instruments, resources). Strategy may be viewed as a coherent, intellectual framework that describes, interprets, and explains world politics and prescribes appropriate policy responses. Alternatively, strategy may be viewed as a rational process for guiding policy through ends-means analysis. Finally, strategy may be viewed as a dynamic stream of ad hoc, politically expedient policy adjustments. All three characterizations are accurate, particularly the last. In any case, the purpose of strategy is the effective employment of force (or threatened employment of force) in support of national goals.

Effectiveness reflects the degree of proportionality maintained between these national goals and the capabilities mobilized. As a simple illustration, consider the case in which limited means are employed in support of unlimited (vital) ends. Assuming symmetrical stakes and influence between the protagonists, the initiating state loses: it fails to achieve objectives that serve its vital national interests. In the other case, in which the initiating state employs unlimited means for limited (nonvital) interests, the initiator may also lose if second-order effects such as unintended escalation or unnecessarily expended resources exceed the intrinsic value of the limited interests originally at issue. Assessment of these ends-means costs and benefits is made more difficult by the necessity of weighing short- and long-run effects. Strategy is more a continuous stream of ends-means linkages than a finite solution to a discrete problem. Nonetheless, effective strategy guides the continuous process of weighing the value of interests relevant to a particular issue and employing force-oriented policy instruments in proportion to the value of those interests.

Should strategy consist of a coherent, tautly crafted conceptual framework for guiding policy? Alternatively, should strategy be comprised of a set of questions about how force should be used in a particular situation and a set of generalizable, loosely prescriptive answers to those questions? What is the appropriate trade-off between consistency and flexibility in strategy? What is the value of strategy as a coherent framework? How dependent on a domestic political consensus should strategy be? What are the implications of this degree of dependence?

Strategy that purports to provide a taut conceptual framework for policy is fatally flawed by its emphasis on comprehensibility and generalizability. International political influence, whatever the degree of cooperation or coerciveness involved, is situational, reciprocal, perceptual, dynamic, and relational. International influence depends on the relative value and commitment accorded to an issue by the actors in a particular situation and the skill and credibility with which these actors employ means of influence against one another. Strategy, the application of force for the purpose of influencing others in order to support national interests, is subsumed in the general context—if at the more coercive end of the continuum—of international influence. Strategy, as Clausewitz observes, guides war, which is an "act of force to compel our enemy to do our will."[49] Similarly, in order to be effective—by maintaining proportionality between ends and means—strategy must be appropriate to the particular circumstances of each situation. Therefore, attempts to generalize comprehensive forms of strategy are condemned to fail by their bluntness. Selectivity and discrimination are crucial to avoiding the dangers of blunt strategy as well as those of an overgeneralized foreign policy consensus.

This conclusion is easily illustrated. How many wars was the United States fighting simultaneously in Vietnam? One might argue U.S. combat forces were engaged in at least three wars: the air war in the North, the air war in Laos, and the war in South Vietnam. One might also argue that the war in South Vietnam reflected four distinct wars (in the corps tactical zones), or even sixty-odd wars (in the individual provinces). Some analysts also differentiate between the war involving primarily U.S. combat forces and the war involving primarily Vietnamese forces. In any case, although there was a variety of wars being fought simultaneously by the U.S. in Southeast Asia, only one strategy (controlled escalation) guided these disparate efforts. U.S. strategy was thus twice flawed: the doctrine of controlled escalation was inappropriate against the totally committed North Vietnamese, and the diverse military measures employed in each of these operational campaigns were neither mutually supporting nor did they clearly support controlled escalation.

This illustration of the dangers of any comprehensive strategy is instructive. How, for example, should the United States plan and prepare for the next Vietnam? Can we conceive of any comprehensive, generic strategy for maintaining ends-means proportionality in a future Vietnam-type situation? No. Or even for Vietnam replicated? No. This conclusion casts grave doubts on the value of efforts to develop a strategy for low-intensity conflict, for example.

On the other hand, consider the merits of strategy as a set of questions. Limited in content to analytical questions that should guide consideration of the use of force, this approach emphasizes flexibility. Such strategy places a premium on adaptability and the sharpened quality of analysis achieved through tough debate. These advantages may be outweighed by the costs: strategy and policy may be perceived as expedient and inconsistent, and political support for any particular policy, let alone for a broad-based consensus, may be achievable only at high political cost. In each instance, the administration must invest political capital in order to build support for policy tailored to the particular circumstances. However, credibility is less at risk because maintenance of a broad and consistent consensus is less important. Policy consistency is sacrificed at the margin in order to sharpen policy selectivity. This trade-off seems justified: policy consistency has less intrinsic value than does ends-means proportionality. In the case where a specific policy may be wrong and its supporting consensus unfounded, the ad hoc character of building this consensus preserves choice, self-consciousness, and flexibility by avoiding reification of the specific policy into a universal context. On the whole, then, this approach to strategy appears more desirable: implementation costs are more than compensated for by the sharpened quality of policy analysis and the preservation of selectivity.

This conclusion supports a conception of strategy based on incisive evaluative criteria for weighing the use of force rather than some overarching prescriptive framework. Such a conclusion is only as compelling, however, as the potency of the specific criteria. What questions might serve such an important purpose? The following set of questions, drawn from international relations scholars, is suggested for guiding policies regarding the use of force:

Ends

Proportionality of ends: What interests are at stake? How vital are these interests relative to one another and to other, tangentially related interests?

Mutual needs: Who is more dependent on whom for achievement of their objectives? Are mutual needs symmetrical or asymmetrical?

Degree of commitment: Who is more strongly committed to their interests at stake?

Responsiveness: What is the pattern of relations between these countries? Are relations between them typically cooperative or conflictual? How will the inertia of these relations affect their behavior?

Means

Capabilities: What capabilities are available for conducting what appropriate functions?

Credibility: Are these capabilities credible? (Are there precedents? How consistent and congruent have declaratory and action policy been? Are these capabilities proportionate to the interests at stake?)

Proportionality of means.

Cost Calculus

Moral costs: How well are just cause criteria satisfied? What are the purposes of the use of force: for example, self-defense, humanitarian, to stop genocide? to counter foreign intervention against a national regime, or on the side of a regime that oppresses deep-seated insurgency? self-determination? to aid a regime confronted by a nationalist political rebellion or civil war? (All but the last purpose meet the *jus ad bellum*.) How do the just conduct criteria of discrimination and proportionality constrain the use of force?

Escalation costs: What is the likelihood that the use of force will trigger escalation (of means, of ends, of protagonists, for example)?

Withdrawal costs: What are the costs of withholding or withdrawing the use of force and renouncing the stakes (for example, for national prestige, for alliances)?[50]

These evaluative criteria can help guide assessment of the circumstances particular to each situation. By comparing the costs of using force in order to influence protagonists with the costs of not doing so, we can rigorously judge the merits — the ends-means proportionality — of security policy. In this way, use of force decisions can be made on the basis of more discriminating analysis.

Conclusions

In 1985, former Secretary of Defense James Schlesinger worried over the incongruities and dilemmas of international politics confronting the United States in the 1980s. These discontinuities produce policy-consensus gaps for U.S. foreign policy. In North-South relations, where there is no ends-means (or commitments-power) gap, there is no consensus over strategy. In East-West relations, where there is an ends-means gap, there is consensus on strategy. Is the existence of policy-consensus gaps inevitable? wonders Schlesinger.[51] What implications follow? Perhaps none. Such unevenness is the norm in contemporary international politics; impulses to interpret these different gaps in any singular fashion must be resisted. Concerns that power, policy, and consensus should be viewed as homogeneous or that they should be evenly distributed across regions must be discounted. Little credence should be granted to suggestions that U.S. policy should strain to achieve some international balance in power, policy, and consensus. One cannot even be certain what such a suggestion means. Such concerns are dangerous in the sense they impel aggregate (global or regional) rather than more discriminating (national, ethnic) perspectives of foreign affairs.

In thinking through U.S. national security policy, we should be wary of trusting interpretative or doctrinal schemes whose grandness transcends notions of crude geopolitical priorities such as two-and-a-half wars, Europe first, or continental versus maritime strategies. While the heuristic power and dazzling coherence of grand conceptual models is useful in more scholarly endeavors, reliance on such constructs for strategy runs severe risks: hidden assumptions, unexamined prescriptions, camouflaged normative biases, comprehensiveness purchased at the expense of discrimination, and the dangers of reification, overgeneralization, and misapplication.

The solution to the lessons and changes derived from the Vietnam experience — the crucial importance of the prevalence of diversity and local circumstance over homogeneity and uniformity in international politics, the imperative of conceiving an appropriately high-resolution and flexible strategy, the danger of consensus — lies in development of a sense of moderation and limits in conceptions of the U.S. role in world affairs, development of a sense of otherliness to offset American cultural and political self-absorption, sharpening the selectivity and discrimination of American perceptions of world affairs, and ensuring continuous, critical examination of U.S. strategy and foreign policy.

Robert Jervis suggests a number of ways to minimize misperception and reinforce selectivity: force policymakers to make their assumptions and forecasts explicit; encourage routine representation of alternative views, disagreement, and debate in decision making; and develop awareness of the dangers of perceptual errors and overgeneralization.[52] Obviously, decision-making agencies must have available the advice of national and regional experts. In addition, experts from a variety of disciplines and institutional perspectives should be available to provide collective counsel. This is a genuine problem in the U.S. government: although an ambassador has available the advice of his country team, the availability of such diversified and expert counsel is not replicated again until the interdepartmental group level. Especially decisions taken at intermediate policy levels are likely to be contaminated by institutional perspectives.

Are these recommendations anything more than strawmen? After all, admonitions to "be smart!" are as old as they are lacking in operational content. Moreover, it may be politically infeasible to exercise flexibility and discrimination in U.S. foreign policy. Previous failures include those of George Kennan — whose conceptual architecture of containment was premised on the value of regional diversity and independent regional power centers — and President Jimmy Carter — who attempted to redirect the thrust of U.S. foreign policy from a focus on East-West security affairs to a more flexible concern for human rights conditions.

The most important catalyst for effectively dealing with prospects of more Vietnams lies in the most important of the keystones of U.S. security policy: U.S. politics. If consensus or centralized political authority promotes groupthink and unexamined policy assumptions, turning the political environment on its head should yield the opposite result. Measures, such as those mentioned above, should be taken to ensure policy processes are exposed to the full force of open political debate.

One effect of the Vietnam experience, the splintering of the postwar foreign policy consensus on containment, provides the United States with a critical advantage in this regard in the 1980s. A schism in foreign policy attitudes has emerged after Vietnam: although the public continues, remarkably, to perceive foreign affairs in almost unchanged terms of the containment worldview, foreign policy elites are significantly more skeptical than the public (and elites during the cold war) of the efficacy of military force in Vietnam-type situations.

This schism in foreign policy attitudes has important consequences. First, as a wedge in foreign policy debate, the schism obstructs consensus. In the absence of agreement on an overarching framework within which foreign policy can be crafted, foreign policymaking is more intensely politicized. This absence of agreement affects the policy process by raising the political costs of conceiving and executing foreign policy. In turn, this schism affects policy outcomes as muddling through, ad hoc-ism, and inconsistency become more commonplace.

Although this schism reflects different notions about the scope and nature of the U.S. global role, both the public and elites agree, for example, that the use of force is legitimate in situations involving vital U.S. interests. The schism reflects differences in the degree of discrimination that must be exercised in contemplating the use of force, not acceptance or rejection of the use of force altogether. Debate over foreign policy has been deradicalized by the psychic trauma of the fiercely ideological clashes in politics during the Vietnam war. Extreme leftist ("the enemy is us") and extreme rightist ("the enemy is the Russians") perspectives have been generally discredited. In this sense, we can speak of a moderating effect of the Vietnam war debates; self-righteous dogmatism has been supplanted by respect for debate within mainstream values and a current of pragmatism. Americans have become more sophisticated in their understanding of foreign policy issues; simplistic, ideologically prescribed policies are viewed with distrust by the public today.

These two countervailing trends intersect to shape U.S. foreign policy attitudes. The schism gives impetus to disagreement and debate; deradicalization acts to depolarize disagreement and debate. One hopes that the result is the best of both worlds: sufficient debate to avoid singlemindedness; sufficient agreement to avoid policy paralysis.

The longer-term consequences of schism and deradicalization in U.S. foreign policy attitudes are unclear. One conceivable result is that a credibility gap could emerge from a combination of policy immobilism, caused by excessive politicization, and highly charged rhetoric in public debate. Another possibility is that the elite versus public schism could itself became intensely politicized, creating shocks throughout U.S. politics. In general, however, the mellowing of containment should be seen as a healthy influence. Reinvigorated and responsible public debate has a leavening effect on the quality of the content of U.S. foreign policy. Singlemindedness, wrong-headedness, dogmatism, and oversimplification are the casualties of vigorous policy debate. On the other hand, the price of vigorous debate is unified domestic political support (or, at least, the appearance of unified support). Such debate, so healthy for the quality of conception of foreign policy, perversely erodes its credibility and therefore may undermine the quality of the execution of foreign policy.

No matter how dissatisfying this state of affairs may be in the abstract, it is the price of the political system. The price of rejecting this dilemma on normative grounds is willingness to accept the reverse dilemma: highly unified policy formulation and execution. U.S. policy toward the PRC during the cold war represents the quality of policy resulting from that state of affairs. Thus we are left with a hope—that U.S. foreign policy will be wise in serving U.S. interests well—and a prospect—that the mellowing of containment, caused in part by the Vietnam experience, has created a mixed set of responsible U.S. foreign policy attitudes that are certain to provoke and sustain a fairly robust level and quality of public debate. As long as policy is born of vigorous debate, domestic political support will not be mobilized by resort to slogans, symbols, or doctrines. Rather, political support will coalesce around foreign policies to the degree they hold out prospects for serving U.S. interests. If this conclusion is right, we should not lament the passing of global containment and its attendant golden age of consensus; rather, we should treasure the emergence of discriminating containment and its attendant brass age of dissensus.

This point is illustrated in the 1986 case of U.S. aid to the contras fighting against the Sandinista regime in Nicaragua. In appealing to the public and the Congress for support for his request of $100 million in aid to the Nicaraguan contras, President Reagan invoked rhetoric highly reminiscent of the domino theory and containment from the cold war: Nicaragua is a "cancer" in the Western Hemisphere, a potential Soviet "beachhead" in North America, a haven for dope smugglers and terrorists, "an outlaw regime" of Marxists-Leninists. Nicaragua will become "a second Cuba . . . a second Libya, right on the doorstep of the United States." In response, House Speaker O'Neill worried that "I see us becoming engaged, step by step, in a military situation that brings our boys directly into the fighting."[53] Both views echo the rhetoric of past debates; both views reflect reactions to a blunt form of containment strategy.

Yet only one week earlier, President Reagan spoke of aid to Nicaragua in terms of the democratic revolution sweeping the world: "the cases are more different than people realize, that we have to use different instruments in different ways in dealing with each. . . . The drive for national freedom and popular rule takes different forms in different countries, for each nation is the authentic product of a unique history and culture."[54] These remarks reflect appreciation for local circumstances and a sense of limits. Nonetheless, critics of the president indict his overly singular worldview and the likemindedness of the advisers close to him. Where are the devils' advocates to challenge first-order assumptions and to debate alternatives to the use of force? these critics ask.

The extensive congressional debate over the president's request reflected public skepticism on many points. What were ultimate U.S. aims in Nicaragua? Why? How would this aid request move relations toward those aims? What follow-up measures were likely in the event aid failed to have the desired effects? Although Congress ultimately approved the aid request, the president faced serious political opposition. Inflated foreign policy rhetoric, evoking themes of the containment doctrine and the zero-sum game stakes at risk in Nicaragua, undermined the credibility of a presidential campaign to win approval of such a minor response to the threats invoked. In short, in the absense of a clear expression of ends-means proportionality, the U.S. political system was unwilling to ratify automatically the president's aid request.

The extensive public debate illustrated the absence of consensus on the validity of containment for Nicaragua. The schism in U.S. foreign policy attitudes was confirmed. More important, the vigorous debate illustrated the vibrancy of politics that is the best hope for avoiding the dangers discussed in this chapter. This outcome illustrates the advantage of U.S. policymaking, unconstrained by strategic consensus and doctrinal righteousness. The absence of these fetters helps tie policy to the political goals related to a particular situation. Moreover, the policy debate triggered by a set of first-order questions is absolutely compatible with the open politics of the U.S. political system.

U.S. foreign policy and national security policy are dependent on effective strategy. Strategy is effective to the degree proportionality is maintained between ends and means, issue by issue, and, in a loose sense, in the aggregate. To be effective, strategy must achieve selectivity, flexibility, and pragmatism. This is the lesson of America's experience in Vietnam. Implementing this lesson is no easy task. As Leslie Gelb and Richard Betts conclude in their book on Vietnam, Americans "always talk about 'the changing world' but too rarely of the related need to change policies. It is to this end—to think of policy-making as an act of adjustment as well as an act of creativity and leadership—that the system must work."[55]

This conclusion poses a paradox. On the one hand, the durability of the three national security keystones means that Vietnam did not make a difference for U.S. policy over the longrun. Because the U.S. national security system remains fundamentally unchanged by the Vietnam experience, the United States is confronted by the prospect of more Vietnams. On the other hand, the lesson of the Vietnam experience—U.S. foreign policy must rest on respect for diversity and otherliness, reflect rejection of universalism and comprehensive policy frameworks, and be guided by strategy as an open-minded, adaptable set of sensibilities—orients on the value of pragmatism, flexibility, and the need to change policies.

How are these two implications of the fact that the Vietnam experience did not make a difference to be reconciled? This paradox can be reconciled to the degree that pluralism, the bedrock of the U.S. political system, is free to operate unfettered by self-righteous doctrines and calls for foreign policy consensus. Changes in the world, to include the Vietnam experience, splintered the postwar foreign policy consensus. As a result, contentiousness, disagreement, and debate have increasingly characterized U.S. foreign policymaking.

Is this politicization of foreign policy new, or does it represent a return to the norm that prevailed before the foreign policy consensus of the last four decades? In the context of U.S. history, which is the norm: foreign policy based on national consensus or foreign policy based on disagreement and debate? The answer is the latter, particularly in this century. Just as de Tocqueville observed in the 1830s, pluralism and political disagreement have traditionally characterized U.S. foreign policymaking. More recently, it is fair to say that political debate about first-order foreign policy questions effectively ended in June 1950 when, in response to the outbreak of the Korean War, NSC-68 established the framework that dominated U.S. foreign policy until the latter stages of the Vietnam war. The foreign policy consensus that prevailed during this period, viewed generally as the norm in American politics, was anomalous. The "mellowing of containment" and the splintering of the foreign policy consensus represent a return to traditional politics.

The fact that these characteristics of U.S. foreign policymaking in the 1980s—contentiousness, disagreement, and debate—are both constructive for the quality of U.S. foreign policy and compatible with American pluralism is cause for optimism. Although Vietnam did not change fundamentally the U.S. security system, the experience with Vietnam unfettered the intrinsic nature of U.S. politics in the context of foreign policy. This restored tradition—of foreign policy shaped by the free-wheeling debate and conflict endemic to American politics—holds out hopes that the United States will be "clearheaded, constructive, and thoughtful in serving U.S. interests when confronted by events similar in nature to Vietnam."

Notes

1. Robert Shaplen, *The Road from War: Vietnam, 1965–1970* (New York, 1970), p. 283.

2. George C. Herring, *America's Longest War, The United States and Vietnam: 1950–1975* (New York: John Wiley, 1979).

3. Earl C. Ravenal, "The Strategic Lessons of Vietnam," in Anthony Lake, ed., *The Vietnam Legacy: The War, American Society, and the Future of American Foreign Policy* (New York: New York University Press, 1976), p. 272.

4. See I.M. Destler, Leslie H. Gelb, and Anthony Lake, *Our Own Worst Enemy: The Unmaking of American Foreign Policy* (New York: Simon and Schuster, 1984).

5. John L. Gaddis, *Strategies of Containment* (Oxford: Oxford University Press, 1982), p. 345.

6. Ibid., p. 357.

7. Colin S. Gray, "National Style in Strategy: The American Example," *International Security* 6 (Fall 1981).

8. Alexis de Tocqueville, *Democracy in America,* ed. J.P. Mayer and Max Lerner (New York: Harper & Row, 1966), p. 192.

9. Ibid., p. 230.

10. Colin S. Gray, "American Strategic Culture and Military Performance," in *Defense Technology,* ed. Asa A. Clark, John F. Lilley, and Douglas E. Lute (Lexington, Mass.: Lexington Books, 1987).

11. de Tocqueville, *Democracy,* p. 211.

12. Ibid.

13. For an excellent discussion of problems with lessons of history in general, and with respect to Vietnam in particular, see David Petraeus, "Lessons of History and the Lessons of Vietnam" (unpublished paper, U.S. Military Academy, 1986).

14. Quoted in W. Scott Thompson and Donaldson D. Frizzell, ed., *The Lessons of Vietnam* (New York: Crane, Russak, 1977), p. iii.

15. Quoted in Richard M. Pfeffer, ed., *No More Vietnams?* (New York: Harper & Row, 1968), p. 6.

16. For further development of this theme, see Herring, *America's Longest War,* pp. 264–265.

17. Quoted in Joseph Siracusa, "Lessons of Vietnam and the Future of American Foreign Policy," *Australian Outlook* 30 (August 1976): 236.

18. Joseph C. Harsch, "Do You Recall Vietnam—and What about the Dominoes?" *Louisville Courier-Journal,* October 2, 1975.

19. See John Lovell's insightful remarks in chapter 7 about the problem of collective amnesia in the U.S. Army during the 1970s.

20. Quoted in Siracusa, "Lessons of Vietnam," p. 233.

21. John P. Roche, "Can a Free Society Fight a Limited War?" *New Leader,* October 21, 1968, p. 5.

22. Under Secretary of State George W. Ball to President Johnson, "A Compromise Solution in South Vietnam," memo, July 1, 1965, in *The Pentagon Papers* (New York: Bantam Books: 1971), p. 449.

23. Samuel P. Huntington, *Military Intervention, Political Involvement and the Unlessons of Vietnam* (Chicago: Adlai Stevenson Institute of International Affairs), pp. 1–2.

24. Bernard Brodie, quoted in Ole R. Holsti and James N. Rosenau, *American Leadership in World Affairs* (Boston: Allen and Unwin, 1984), p. 25.

25. Robert Jervis, *Perception and Misperception in International Politics* (Princeton: Princeton University Press, 1976).

26. A.J.P. Taylor, *From Napoleon to Lenin* (New York: Harper & Row, 1966), p. 64.

27. Jervis, *Perception and Misperception,* p. 406.

28. Quoted in Pfeffer, "No More Vietnams?" p. 4.

29. Thompson and Frizzell, *Lessons of Vietnam,* p. vi.

30. For a concise summary of the variety of causes of U.S. policy in Vietnam, see Leslie H. Gelb and Richard K. Betts, *The Irony of Vietnam: The System Worked* (Washington, D.C.: Brookings Institution, 1979), pp. 14–23.

31. Harry Summers, *On Strategy: A Critical Analysis of the Vietnam War* (New York: Dell Publishing Co., 1982).

32. For example, see ibid. Also see William Westmoreland, *A Soldier Reports* (Garden City, N.Y.: Doubleday, 1976). Also see the view argued by former Secretary of Defense James Schlesinger in Earl C. Ravenal, *Never Again: Learning from America's Foreign Policy Failures* (Philadelphia: Temple University Press, 1978), p. 71.

33. Westmoreland, *A Soldier Reports,* p. 410.

34. Robert Komer in Thompson and Frizzell, *Lessons of Vietnam,* p. 223.

35. Robert Komer, *Bureaucracy at War: U.S. Performance in the Vietnam Conflict* (Boulder, Colo.: Westview Press, 1986).

36. Nitze memorandum, "Recent Soviet Moves," February 8, 1950, p. 142, quoted in John L. Gaddis, *Strategies of Containment* (Oxford: Oxford University Press, 1982), p. 92.

37. NSC-68, April 14, 1950, in *Foreign Relations of the United States: 1950,* I (Washington, D.C.: U.S. Government Printing Office), 264.

38. William Whitworth, *Naive Questions about War and Peace* (New York: Norton, 1970), pp. 105–106.

39. Lyndon B. Johnson, address at Johns Hopkins University, April 7, 1965, in *Johnson Public Papers: 1965* (Washington, D.C.: U.S. Government Printing Office), p. 395.

40. Ibid.

41. Gaddis, *Strategies of Containment,* p. 243.

42. Ian Smart, "Banquet Address to the Student Conference on United States Affairs," U.S. Military Academy, November 18, 1985.

43. Ibid.

44. Gelb and Betts, *Irony of Vietnam,* pp. 363–369.

45. Quoted in Destler, Gelb, and Lake, *Our Own Worst Enemy,* p. 272.

46. Paraphrased from *Time,* March 31, 1986, pp. 14–15.

47. George F. Kennan, "Morality and Foreign Policy," *Foreign Affairs* (Winter–Spring 1985–1986): 209.

48. Ibid., pp. 217–218.

49. Carl von Clausewitz, *On War,* ed. and trans. Michael Howard and Peter Paret (Princeton: Princeton University Press, 1984), p. 75.

50. These criteria are drawn principally from K.J. Holsti, *International Politics: A Framework for Analysis* (Englewood Cliffs, N.J.: Prentice-Hall, 1983), pp. 144–159. Also see Roland A. Paul, "Toward a Theory of Intervention," *Orbis* (1972).

51. James Schlesinger, quoted in *New York Times,* February 7, 1985.

52. Jervis, *Perception,* p. 423.

53. Quoted in *New York Times,* March 14, 1986, p. A7.
54. Ibid.
55. Gelb and Betts, *System Worked,* p. 369.

Index

About the Contributors

William P. Bundy has served in several policymaking positions, including assistant secretary of defense for international security affairs and assistant secretary of state for East Asian and Pacific affairs. Most recently he served as editor of *Foreign Affairs.*

Vincent Davis is Patterson Chair Professor of International Studies and the director of the Patterson School of Diplomacy and International Commerce, University of Kentucky. His many publications include *The Admirals Lobby* and *The Post-Imperial Presidency.*

Norman A. Graebner, a historian, is professor of public affairs at the University of Virginia. He has authored and edited numerous books on U.S. foreign policy and the cold war period.

William W. Kaufmann, a long-time consultant on defense issues throughout the executive branch, is a lecturer at the Kennedy School of Government, Harvard University. His many publications include *The McNamara Strategy* and *The 1986 Defense Budget.*

Louis W. Koenig recently retired as professor of government at New York University. He is the author of *The Invisible Presidency, Congress and the President,* and *The Chief Executive.*

Robert W. Komer, under secretary of defense for policy from 1979 to 1981, is teaching, lecturing, and consulting on American defense issues. During the Vietnam War he was the chief architect of and adviser for the South Vietnamese government's pacification program. He has written numerous articles on defense matters and recently authored *Bureaucracy at War: U.S. Performance in the Vietnam Conflict.*

Andrew F. Krepinevich, Jr., a major of air defense artillery in the U.S. Army, is assigned to the executive secretariat, Office of the Secretary of Defense. He formerly was an assistant professor of political science at the U.S. Military Academy, West Point. He is the author of *The Army and Vietnam*.

John P. Lovell is professor of political science at Indiana University. Among his numerous publications are *Neither Athens nor Sparta? The American Military Academies in Transition* and *The Challenge of American Foreign Policy*.

Ernest R. May is professor of history at Harvard University. His many publications include *Lessons of the Past: The Use and Misuse of History in American Foreign Policy*.

Charles Mohr served as a foreign correspondent for fifteen years for the *New York Times* and *Time* magazine, including four and one-half years in Vietnam. He is a reporter in the Washington, D.C., bureau of the *New York Times*.

John E. Mueller is a professor of political science at the University of Rochester. He is the author of *War, Presidents, and Public Opinion,* an analysis of public opinion during the Vietnam War, and he has written articles on Vietnam for numerous journals.

John M. Oseth, a lieutenant colonel in the U.S. Army, is an intelligence officer assigned as special assistant to the chairman of the Joint Chiefs of Staff. He is a former assistant professor at the U.S. Military Academy, West Point. He is the author of *Regulating U.S. Intelligence Operations*.

Robert S. Osgood was professor of U.S. foreign policy at the School of Advanced International Studies, the Johns Hopkins University. He recently served as a member of the secretary of state's policy planning council. Among his many publications are *Limited War: The Challenge to American Strategy* and *Limited War Revisited*.

David H. Petraeus, a major of infantry in the U.S. Army, is assistant professor of international security studies at the U.S. Military Academy, West Point. He is the author of several articles on the impact of Vietnam on the U.S. military.

William J. Taylor, Jr., a retired colonel in the U.S. Army, is the chief operating officer and director of political-military studies at the Center for Strategic and International Studies, Georgetown University. He has written numerous books and articles on national security affairs.

Richard H. Ullman is a professor at the Woodrow Wilson School of Public and International Affairs, Princeton University. He has served in the Department of Defense and on the staff of the National Security Council. He has published extensively on American foreign policy.

Wallace Earl Walker, a lieutenant colonel in the U.S. Army, is an associate professor of political science at the U.S. Military Academy at West Point. He is author of *Changing Organizational Culture: Strategy, Structure, and Professionalism in the U.S. General Accounting Office.*

Philip D. Zelikow is a foreign service officer assigned to the Mutual and Balanced Force Reduction delegation in Vienna. He previously taught national security affairs at the Naval Postgraduate School, Monterey, California.

About the Editors

Asa A. Clark IV, a lieutenant colonel of infantry in the U.S. Army, is associate professor of international relations at the U.S. Military Academy at West Point. He is a coeditor of and contributing author to *The Defense Reform Debate*.

Daniel J. Kaufman, a lieutenant colonel of armor in the U.S. Army, is associate professor of national security studies at the U.S. Military Academy at West Point. He is a coeditor of and contributing author to *U.S. National Security Policy: A Framework for Analysis*.

Douglas E. Lute, a major of armor in the U.S. Army, was formerly assistant professor of international relations at the U.S. Military Academy at West Point.

George K. Osborn, a colonel in the U.S. Army, is professor of social sciences at the U.S. Military Academy, West Point. His career has focused on U.S. national security issues, especially in Asia.